18824

DATE DUE

EB 2 5 97					
EB 1 6 98					
GAYLORD					PRINTED IN U.S.A.

D1159680

THE TRUMAN PRESIDENCY

The
Truman Presidency

◈

THE HISTORY OF A
TRIUMPHANT SUCCESSION

◈

Cabell Phillips

THE MACMILLAN COMPANY
COLLIER-MACMILLAN LIMITED, LONDON

Library of Congress Catalog Card Number: 66-16709

Fourth Printing 1969

The Macmillan Company
Collier-Macmillan Canada Ltd., Toronto, Ontario

Printed in the United States of America

For Michael and Suzanne
in lieu of a portfolio

CONTENTS

◈◈◈◈◈◈◈◈◈◈◈◈◈◈◈◈◈◈◈◈◈◈◈◈◈

Preface

HARRY S. TRUMAN was a quite ordinary man. He was also a quite extraordinary President. It was this seeming paradox in values, this dichotomy in the image of a living figure of history, that led me, in part at least, to write this book.

No man is "made" for the Presidency. But all of the strong and uncommon Presidents have come to the task with some conspicuous capacities, either innate or acquired, for excelling in the role. This is true of the strong Presidents who come most easily to mind—Jefferson, Jackson, Lincoln, the two Roosevelts, Wilson, and Lyndon B. Johnson. Truman entered the Presidency with no more promise of greatness than a Millard Fillmore or a Calvin Coolidge. His tenure, moreover, was the least tranquil, the most bedeviled by partisan strife, of any President since Andrew Johnson. Yet, when he left office seven and three-quarter years later he had put an indelible imprint of greatness on both the Presidency and the history of his time.

How could so ordinary a man adapt so well to the most exacting political office in the world? That was what I wanted to find out.

Another reason for writing this book was that nowhere, I felt, had the story of this significant and dramatic chapter in the American Presidency been told in the proportioned and coherent sort of way it deserved. Mr. Truman's memoirs in two volumes, exhaustive and enlightening though they are, suffer from the common deficiency of most such works: a lack of objectivity. Other writers, by and large, have focused on particular phases of the era but ignored the background into which they fit.

As a newspaperman in Washington I had lived in fairly close professional proximity to the Truman administration from its beginning to its end. I knew most of its principal figures; I knew its friends and I knew its enemies. So when Peter Ritner of the Macmillan Company raised the question of filling this literary vacuum and asked insistently, "Why not you?" I was persuaded in time to say, "Well, why the hell *not* me?" And so the book was begun, and now, a little more than three years later, it is finished.

This is not a definitive history of the Truman administration. Rather, it is the story of the Truman Presidency done in journalistic perspective. Nor is it an "approved" work; indeed, it has been done with minimal assistance from Mr. Truman. (See "A Word About Presidential Libraries" in the Notes on Sources.) The focus of the book is on the significant highlights of Mr. Truman's career in the White House. Its aim is to show what kind of person he was as man and President, the nature of the problems he faced, his style and strategy in coping with those problems, and finally the impact of his tenure on the institution of the Presidency. The result, I hope, will at least partially fill the vacuum that Peter Ritner and I talked about early in 1962.

A great many people have helped me with this book and I have acknowledged my debt to most of them in the text and in the Notes on Sources. There are a few, however, whose encouragement and assistance were literally indispensable and to whom I want to pay a special measure of gratitude.

Clark M. Clifford, who was the White House Special Counsel from 1946 to 1950, was the most effective and the most heavily relied upon member of President Truman's personal staff. With great patience and generosity Clark gave me many hours of his time and a virtually free rein in the voluminous personal files he brought away from the White House.

Dean G. Acheson, who was either Under Secretary or Secretary of State throughout most of the Truman years, was not only the chief architect of the foreign policy that evolved in that period but a principal adviser to President Truman on affairs of state generally. Moreover, he had a deep personal attachment to Mr. Truman, which gave him, among all the official family, a unique understanding of the President's personality and aspirations. He, too, was most generous to me with his time and his files.

Others to whom I am especially indebted are Averell Harriman, who served in a variety of critical diplomatic and domestic posts under President Truman; Leon H. Keyserling, who was a member and later Chairman of the Council of Economic Advisers; the late David D. Lloyd, who was a Special Assistant on the White House staff; Paul A. Porter, who served in a number of confidential roles both administrative and political during the administration; and Stephen A. Mitchell, who was Chairman of the Democratic National Committee in 1952. Among my fellow members of the Washington press corps, Arthur Krock, James Reston, and Felix Belair, Jr., of the New York *Times*, and Edward T. Folliard of the Washington *Post*, drew freely on their well-stocked memories and their store of anecdotes to help me out. The library staff of the *Times* Washington Bureau, with the very best of grace, performed many times for me as an unpaid research corps.

This book was Peter Ritner's idea, and I am grateful for his persistence with it, for his excellent editorial counsel, and for his humane (which is to say, atypical) attitude about deadlines. Such merits of syntax and grammar as it contains are due in large measure to the wizardry of Mrs. Adele Garrett. Michael O'Keefe of the New York *Times* Sunday Department searched acres of photo files to produce the pictures used for illustrations.

A wife who can coexist with a husband who spends three years writing a book should be rewarded with mink and diamonds. This is the due of my wife Syble, who in addition gave me valuable critical judgments on the manuscript, did much of the typing, returned overdue books to the library, and kept my spirits up.

CABELL PHILLIPS

Washington, D.C.
September, 1965

For each President, we must remember, is
the President not only of all who live,
but, in a very real sense, of all who have
yet to live. His responsibility is not
only to those who elected him, but also to
those who will elect his successors for
decades to come.

                              —John Fitzgerald Kennedy

THE TRUMAN PRESIDENCY

CHATER 1

Prologue

"Good god," we said, "Truman will be President!"

There were fifteen or twenty of us reporters crowded on hard wood benches under a stuffy canvas canopy at Fort Myers, across the Potomac River from Washington. It was late on the afternoon of Thursday, April 12, 1945. We had been invited over by the Army for the unveiling of a new weapon that had lately been introduced into the Pacific theater. It was, as I recall, some kind of recoilless rifle, and it had been cutting the Japanese to ribbons. A Major was explaining its details to us. As he talked, another officer, grim-faced and ashen, strode into the tent and without preliminaries interrupted him.

"Gentlemen," he said, "there's been an awful tragedy. President Roosevelt died at Warm Springs an hour ago."

We sat for a moment—perhaps only for an instant—stunned and paralyzed. Most of us knew that Roosevelt was ailing. We had seen him at his fourth inaugural in January, standing gaunt, gray, and hollow-eyed on the south portico of the White House, supported by his son James, taking the oath of office. We had seen him again, only ten days ago, in his wheelchair on the floor of the House of Representatives delivering his report on the Yalta Conference. He had seemed even more wasted, more weary then. There was talk that he had cancer or a brain tumor or had suffered a heart attack. We knew he was a sick man, but no one, even those few among us who had grown fed up with FDR, had quite contemplated the unspeakable event of his dying. The thought was like the pillars of the temple coming down, and no one could bring himself to dwell upon it. Even less had we looked beyond the unthinkable event to its palpable consequence.

But now, in this moment of shock, we did think of the consequence. Some one said it, softly, dazedly, almost as if he were thinking aloud: "Good God, Truman will be President." We turned and looked at him and nodded our heads, and we repeated the phrase, aloud or silently to ourselves. That thought seemed to be the only one that struck with clarity through the tumult of images and fragmentary memories that churned through our heads, and it seemed mordantly to underscore what already was disaster enough.

The same thought and phrase ran through millions of minds in offices and bars and living rooms all across the nation that evening as the news of Roosevelt's death flashed along the radio channels. The King was dead, yes, but who would be King? The image was blurred, indistinct, and, to all but a handful, discouraging in varying degrees. To the majority of Americans, Truman was a cardboard figure, a brash midwestern politician whom FDR had picked almost capriciously as Vice President, as the least aggravating compromise between Jimmy Byrnes and Henry Wallace—or between the Southern conservatives and the radicals of the Political Action Committee of the Congress of Industrial Organizations.

Truman? Yes, as a Senator, he had done some good work with that war investigating committee. And come to think of it, he was supposed to be a "clean" politician. He'd never gotten personally mixed up in the scandals of the Pendergast machine out in Kansas City, where he had come from. People had seen something of him fleetingly in the last campaign, had heard his flat Missouri diction, his earthy and unpretentious rhetoric, and it had sounded like a muffled gong—whether you liked Roosevelt or hated his guts—against the majestic sonorities to which the public ear had become attuned in the past twelve years. Was the fate of the nation and the world, still locked in history's greatest war, to pass from the hands of a titan to this anonymous and undistinguished yeoman?

It was and it did. And history has rarely witnessed a more heartening triumph of the simple virtues of unpretentiousness, honesty, and courage. Harry Truman was, and remains, an ordinary man; not an *average* man, as he so often has been depicted, but an ordinary man who must make do without any special endowments of genius, intellect, or charm. His strength lay in his ability to do the best he could with what he had and not to despair over what he did not have. That is wisdom denied the average man. But ordinary men are palpable and plentiful, and a few reach greatness because they know, and make the best of, what they are. Harry Truman never suffered the illusion that he was another Roosevelt or Churchill, neither did he agonize over whether he was their inferior. Destiny linked his life to theirs in an apocalyptic enterprise, and each rode it out to greatness according to his own fashion. Truman, "right on all the big things, wrong on most of the little ones,"* was a great President.

Men do not make history. They are borne by it like autumn leaves on a rushing stream—to oblivion, to disaster, or to glory. Survival depends on navigational skill—and a good measure of luck. That stream was in full flood when Harry Truman was caught up in its center current. The world in his lifetime had been convulsed by cosmic upheavals of population, technology, and social unrest. Political vacuums had been created through the waverings of the world balance of power. Vast forces had been unleashed from the British Empire, Western Europe, the Soviet Union, the Far East, and the Western Hemisphere, rushing to fill those voids in the hurricane that was World War II. And beyond its predestined outcome, almost but not quite obscured at the horizon by the smoke of battle, were the Age of the Atom and the Age of the Cold War, two ominous shadows that were to lengthen suddenly and change the course of history.

These were not man-made forces. Neither Hitler nor Stalin nor Roosevelt nor Fermi had set them in motion, nor could they stop them. They were the inevitable product of many events from times past, flowing together like trickles of water down the mountainside to converge in a mighty torrent in the valley. That was the implacable stream of history on which Harry Truman—"the little haberdasher from Kansas City"—rode as President of the United States.

Our Major spoke to us. "I guess you fellows will want to get back to your offices. Your transportation is waiting outside."

We drove back in silence, our minds variously preoccupied with the challenge of how to handle this biggest of stories for our papers,

* This appraisal is commonly attributed to the late Speaker Sam Rayburn, one of Truman's oldest and stanchest friends.

and how to convey in cold type the sense of tragedy and national peril that overwhelmed us. The rolling slopes of Arlington Cemetery, white-dotted with the infinite marble markers of dead heroes, passed on our right. We turned onto Memorial Bridge and swept around the Lincoln Memorial—another reminder of greatness and sadness, and now bathed in the soft light of a gathering dusk—and on up Seventeenth Street to Pennsylvania Avenue and the White House, where most of us stopped off. Already, across the street, a scattering of people stood singly or in little clusters at the edge of Lafayette Square, staring in reverent silence at the great white mausoleum, its windows faintly illuminated through the drawn curtains. In the lobby of the Executive Wing, a hundred reporters milled restlessly about, talking in subdued tones or lounging disconsolately in the big leather chairs. Steve Early, the Press Secretary, his face flabby and ashen, passed through from time to time with scraps of information on what was going on in the main residence. Jonathan Daniels, his eyes red-rimmed, Bill Simmons, and other White House functionaries came and went. Edward Stettinius, the Secretary of State, his handsome face streaked with candid tears, strode through wordlessly and down a corridor leading to the Cabinet room. A little before 8 o'clock, Early emerged from his office and read in a strained, gravelly voice the first public utterance of the thirty-second President of the United States: "For the time being I prefer not to hold a press conference. It will be my effort to carry on as I believe the President [sic] would have done, and to that end I have asked the Cabinet to stay with me."

We phoned this bulletin to our papers, but most of us continued to hang around because we did not know what else to do. When finally I left about midnight, a thousand or more people were strung out along the edge of Lafayette Square. I crossed the street and walked among them. They seemed rooted where they stood, and there was scarcely a sound save for muted bits of conversation and occasionally a lonely sob. Some kept their vigil through the night.

Vice President Harry S. Truman, natty as always in a double-breasted gray suit, white shirt, and blue polka-dot tie, sat in the big leather chair on the dais as the presiding officer of the United States Senate. A dozen Senators nodded in their chairs or fiddled with papers on their desks while E. R. Moore, of Oklahoma, droned through a seemingly interminable speech about a pending water treaty with Mexico. Neither was the Vice President paying much attention. Instead, he was writing a dutiful and chatty letter to his mother and sister back home.

Dear Mamma and Mary—I am trying to write you a letter from the desk of the President of the Senate while a windy Senator is making a speech on a subject with which he is in no way familiar. . . . Hope you are having a nice spell of weather. . . . Turn on your radio tomorrow night at 9:30 your time, and you'll hear Harry make a Jefferson Day address to the nation. I think I'll be on all the networks. It will be followed by the President, whom I'll introduce. . . . Hope you are both well and stay that way. Love to you both. Write when you can. Harry.

As he finished, he looked at the big clock on the facing wall—it was getting on toward five—caught the eye of Majority Leader Alben Barkley with a knowing glance, and signaled the adjournment of business for the day. In the ornate, chandeliered lobby behind the chamber, he chatted briefly with a couple of Senators, handed the letter to his administrative assistant to be mailed, and set off at a brisk pace across the Capitol, through the fading light of the rotunda, and down a narrow, winding corridor on the House side to the secret retreat of his good companion Speaker Sam Rayburn. There he would find a bracing draught of bourbon and branch water and the cheery fellowship of Mr. Sam's "Board of Education."

This was pretty much the pattern of his days. There was no sweat in being Vice President for Harry Truman; he had never had it so good.

As he pushed through the big mahogany door, the Speaker said to him:

"Harry, Steve Early called you just a minute ago. He wants you to telephone him at the White House right away."

The call was put through. Early's voice was oddly strained. "Please come right over, Harry," he said, "and come to the residence, through the main Pennsylvania Avenue entrance."

Truman's face hardened as he put down the phone. "I have to go to the White House at once, and as quietly as possible," he said. He had no knowledge of what this summons was about, but he sensed its urgency. He left without another word, located his chauffeur, and was driven off.

"I reached the White House at 5:25 P.M.," Mr. Truman has recalled, "and was immediately taken in the elevator to the second floor and ushered into Mrs. Roosevelt's study. Mrs. Roosevelt herself, together with Colonel John and Mrs. Anna Roosevelt Boettiger and Mr. Early were in the room as I entered, and I knew at once that something unusual had taken place. Mrs. Roosevelt seemed calm in her characteristic, graceful dignity. She stepped forward and placed her arm gently about my shoulder.

" 'Harry,' she said quietly, 'the President is dead.'

"For a moment I could not bring myself to speak.

"The last news we had had from Warm Springs was that Mr. Roosevelt was recuperating nicely. In fact, he was apparently doing so well that no member of his immediate family, and not even his personal physician, was with him. All this flashed through my mind before I found my voice.

" 'Is there anything I can do for you?' I asked at last.

"I shall never forget her deeply understanding reply.

" 'Is there anything *we* can do for *you?*' she asked. 'For you are the one in trouble now.' "

Now that the Vice President had been notified, Steve Early got representatives of the three press associations on a simultaneous telephone hookup and made the first official announcement of Roosevelt's death. It spread instantly by wire and radio to every part of the nation and the world. Mr. Truman called Mrs. Truman at their Connecticut Avenue apartment, told her the news, and asked her to come with their daughter, Margaret, to the White House immediately. He then called Chief Justice Harlan F. Stone and asked that he come as soon as possible to conduct the swearing in of the new President. Early and Daniels, meanwhile, summoned members of the Cabinet and the congressional leaders. Some others, who had heard the first bulletins on the radio, rushed to the White House of their own accord. The center of activity was now the large Cabinet room, uncomfortably crowded with officials and with scores of reporters and White House staff members standing in the adjacent corridors and doorways. There was a low murmur of voices as some tried desperately to find something to say to relieve the almost unbearable tension, and here and there a Cabinet secretary or a White House clerk gave way quietly to tears.

At a few minutes after seven Justice Stone arrived. He and Mr. Truman took their places at one end of the room under a portrait of Woodrow Wilson. Mrs. Truman stood at her husband's left, dabbing repeatedly at her eyes with a wet handkerchief. As the clock's hands showed 7:09, Harry Truman, standing erect and grim-faced, his eyes unnaturally magnified behind the thick lenses of his glasses, repeated the simple oath, ". . . and will to the best of my ability, preserve, protect and defend the Constitution of the United States. So help me God." As he completed the words, the thirty-second President of the United States took the Bible in both hands and reverently put it to his lips.

CHAPTER 2

<<<<<<<<<<<<<<<<<<<<<<<<<<<<<<<<<<<<<<<<<<<<

It's a Long Way to the Top

Son of the Middle Border

"WHO THE HELL is Harry Truman?"

People began asking that question when he first ran for public office in Jackson County, Missouri, in 1922. They asked it when he ran for the Senate in 1934, and again when he was nominated for the Vice Presidency in 1944. Many, in honest perplexity, were still asking it when he had been sworn in as President of the United States.

There has always been an insistent quality of plainness about the man that, but for the accident of the Presidency, would make him forever indistinguishable in almost any crowd. His "projection," as Madison Avenue might say, is at least neutral, at most negative. Neither in manner, speech, nor appearance does he present any of the outward attributes of forcefulness or dignity or command out of which the popular image of leadership is compounded. He had none of the romantic aura of destiny that clung to Franklin Roosevelt throughout his life; none of the aristocratic worldliness of Winston Churchill; nor the stony arrogance of Stalin; nor the self-assured mysticism of de Gaulle. Even in the Senate, a hospitable stage for exhibitionists, he was, for most of his ten years there, largely lost among the anonymous backbenchers. And the reason clearly was that Truman himself never sought to fit himself into the grand pattern. He considered himself no more than an ordinary man, and the world took him at his own value.

And ordinary indeed were his roots, deeply embedded in the rustic, egalitarian society of the middle western frontier. His grandparents on both sides had emigrated from Virginia and Kentucky to the Missouri country early in the decade of the 1840's. John Anderson Truman, Harry's father, was born in Jackson County in December 1851 and pursued variously the life of a farmer and livestock trader. He was known locally as "Peanuts" because of his short stature; he had the quick temper and lively humor that often go with a compact frame. In 1881 he married Martha Ellen Young, the 29-year-old daughter of Soloman Young, a neighbor of the Trumans' in the farming community of Hickman's Mill, in Jackson County. She, too, was small and vivacious, but where John Truman had a streak of the gambler and speculator in his makeup, Martha Ellen had the iron will and sense of duty that went with her Baptist faith. The young couple set up housekeeping in a small white cottage in the village of Lamar, some distance south of Jackson County, where John pursued his vocation of farmer and horse trader and his avocation of Democratic politics.

The year 1884 proved to be a banner one for the Trumans. John collected a $75 bet from a leading Republican in Lamar on the election of Cleveland over Blaine (almost as long a shot as betting on a Democratic victory in 1948), and his first child was born on the afternoon of May 8. They named the boy Harry and gave him a middle initial, S., but never agreed on what the letter stood for.

Both by necessity and instinct, John Truman found it hard to stay put anywhere for very long. A few years after Harry's birth, the family moved in with the Youngs on their large farm near Grandview, in Jackson County. Later they moved to Independence; briefly to the village of Belton; for a short time into the bustling new metropolis of Kansas City; and then back to Independence again. Ultimately, though, Independence became "home," and Harry and his brother and two sisters grew up there. In his memoirs, President Truman recalled this home:

My father bought a big house on South Chrisler Street with several acres of land, a wonderful strawberry bed and a fine garden. At the same time, he was operating a farm southeast of town and went into buying and selling cattle, hogs and sheep.

With our barns, chicken house and a grand yard in which to play, all the boys and girls in the neighborhood for blocks around congregated at our house. We always had ponies and horses to ride, goats to hitch to our little wagon, which was made like a big one. An old harness maker in

Independence made Vivian [his younger brother] a set of double harness just like the big set. We would harness two red goats to the little wagon and drive it everywhere around the place. Years later this good old harness man defeated me for Eastern judge of the Jackson County Court.

We made a number of new acquaintances, and I became interested in one in particular. She had golden curls and has, to this day, the most beautiful blue eyes. We went to Sunday school, public school from the fifth grade through high school, graduated in the same class, and marched down life's road together. For me she still has the blue eyes and golden hair of yesteryear.[1]

A long bout with diphtheria when he was ten left young Harry with permanently impaired eyesight, for which he has had to wear glasses ever since. This eliminated him from most of the rough-and-tumble of schoolboy athletics. He turned to books, and found in them the vicarious experiences he, himself, was denied. History fascinated him particularly, and he began to devour everything available in the little town's public library, getting to know the heroes of Plutarch and Carlyle as intimately as those of the Civil War. "My debt to history is one which cannot be calculated," he has said. "Reading history, to me, was far more than a romantic adventure. It was solid instruction and wise teaching which I somehow felt that I wanted and needed. Its lessons were to stand me in good stead years later."

Music, too, became an absorbing preoccupation for him. Martha Ellen Truman had attended a "female academy" near Lexington, Missouri, as a young lady and had picked up a modest taste not only for books but for the piano as well. She taught its rudiments to young Harry, and at the age of 13 he began to take regular music lessons from a teacher in Independence. He became proficient enough to make him think seriously, for a brief time during his high school years, of following music as a profession.

The influence of his mother on Harry Truman's character was profound. She had in her makeup the tough-fibered, resolute qualities of the women of the frontier, from whom she was immediately descended. Duty was sacred and its performance inescapable. Waste and sloth were not only wicked but repugnant as well. Truth was less an adornment of the soul than an imperative of one's daily conduct. One said what was in one's mind without devious evasions. One lived by the eternal verities as set forth in the Bible about damnation and salvation, good and evil, heaven and hell, and went regularly to church because it was a natural part of life. But one need not be a bluenose about these things; righteousness was not a cross to be borne in pain. Martha Ellen described herself as a "light-foot Baptist," which meant that she did not regard dancing and other worldly diversions with the pious horror that was prevalent among many of that faith. Gaiety and discipline, duty and fun, thus blended harmoniously in the household in which Harry Truman grew to young manhood. And on this experience the kernel of his character was formed: to do what has to be done the best one can and without remorse or self-pity.

"I never take a problem to bed with me at night," he once said after becoming President. "When I've made a decision, I know it's the best decision I can make under the circumstances and I stop worrying about it."

Harry Truman graduated from the Independence high school without special honors but well up in his class. He hoped briefly for an appointment to Annapolis, but his poor eyesight ruled him out. Charley Ross, Elmer Twyman, and some of his other classmates went off to college, but a stroke of bad luck in the grain market had wiped out the Truman family's liquid assets, and young Harry began to look for a job. Like any youngster with no career in view, he held a variety of jobs, including that of timekeeper on a railroad construction project, and in time wound up as a clerk in a bank in Kansas City. His family had moved there in 1902 after their financial crisis. Three years later all but Harry returned to the Young farm at Grandview. Then, in 1906, he decided to join them there. Grandfather Young was dead, John Truman was getting on in years and unequal to running the place alone, and young Harry came to the conclusion that he would rather be a farmer than a banker.

It was a good decision, for this was a decade of great prosperity for American agriculture. The years from 1909 to 1914 were, in fact, to be signalized during Harry Truman's first years in the Senate as the standard of "parity" against which farm relief payments were to be measured. In good years the Grandview acres yielded as much as $15,000 income. This enabled John Truman to pay off his debts and his son to splurge by buying one of the first automobiles to be seen in that part of Jackson County—a four-cylinder Stafford with a straight-up-and-down windshield and brass Prestolite headlights as big as a locomotive's. With so much mobility and status, he was able to step up his attentions to that blue-eyed blonde in Independence, Bess Wallace, whom he had been courting since high school days; to go regularly to the meetings of the Masonic lodge, which he had joined in nearby Belton; and to keep up with the weekly drills of the National Guard Company in Kansas City of which he had become a member.

By 1916, as Europe's war clouds cast their shadow westward, 32-year-old Harry Truman, full of beans and ambition, had just about everything he wanted out of life except that girl. Whatever progress he was making in that direction was, however, interrupted when his National Guard outfit was mustered into service and rechristened the 129th Field Artillery of the 35th Division. In the process he was designated a First Lieutenant, and in September 1917 he was ordered to Fort Sill, Oklahoma, for training. His division shipped out for France in March of the following year. He saw New York for the first time during a 24-hour leave just prior to embarkation. In that same crowded day he did two other important things: he bought himself three extra pairs of glasses, and he placed urgent farewell telephone calls to his mother, in Grandview, and his girl, in Independence.

The 35th Division, including Battery D of the 129th Field Artillery, Captain Truman commanding, saw almost as much action under fire as any outfit in the American Expeditionary Force. They fired their first barrage on the night of September 6 on a sector in the Vosges Mountains. From then until the armistice on November 11 they were almost continually engaged in combat at Saint-Mihiel, on the Meuse-Argonne front, before Verdun and finally at Metz. Battery D was a tight, hard-working outfit, not especially heroic but dependable in the clutches. It panicked once under fire; groused extravagantly about the mud, the cooties, and the chow, and occasionally "liberated" too much French wine. But it threw a lot of steel at the Germans, and some of the men were cited for bravery. Battery D had a reputation for undisciplined rowdiness when it landed in France. When Captain Truman replaced its former commander on July 11, he set out to correct that in characteristic blunt, straightforward fashion.

"When I first took command of the battery," he said to Jonathan Daniels years later,[2] "I called all the sergeants and corporals together. I told them I knew they had been making trouble for the previous commanders. I said, 'I didn't come over here to get along with you. You've got to get along with me. And if there are any of you who can't, speak up and I'll bust you right back.' We got along."

Truman's war experience made two important contributions to his character. It obliterated forever the gnawing sense of physical inadequacy that he had carried over from childhood, and it gave him a sense of command. A certain cockiness of manner he had acquired now had a solid underpinning of self-confidence.

"My whole political career," he was to say many years later, "is based upon my war service and war associates."

Harry Truman had not only won his part of the war. He also won the girl of his dreams. He was discharged from the Army on May 6, 1919, and on June 28 he and Elizabeth Virginia Wallace were married in Trinity Episcopal Church, at Independence. After a short honeymoon they settled down in the spacious white clapboard Wallace house at 219 North Delaware Street, which has been home to them ever since, the White House notwithstanding. Their only child, Margaret, was born there February 17, 1924.

Politician by Chance

Harry Truman was 35 years old when he came home from the wars, acquired a wife, and began to cast around for a suitable niche in the civilian world. He had been a tolerably good farmer and a tolerably good bank clerk, but neither of these occupations appealed to him now. But he could afford to be a bit choosy; he estimated his net worth in cash and farmlands at about $15,000, with no strings attached. Undoubtedly, he was caught up in the same euphoria that then afflicted most Americans in the immediate wake of the war. There was (or seemed to be) a booming prosperity, with factories working overtime to supply the pent-up demand for goods and gadgets, and with workers getting higher wages than they had ever received before. President Wilson was having his troubles with the Versailles Treaty and the League of Nations Covenant. His desperate efforts met a wall of hostility in Congress, and in much of the press as well. There was an almost impenetrable public apathy to most of the political problems of the day as middle-class America turned its back on the troublesome abstractions of war and peace and the state of mankind. Nor did it perceive, as the decade of the twenties arrived, that Warren Harding's utopian "normalcy" was to be bought at the price of a disastrous inflation and unemployment and a 40 percent drop in farm income. This was the age of "boosterism" in the best of all possible worlds, and the dour critiques of

H. L. Mencken and Sinclair Lewis were scarcely audible in Independence or Kansas City, Missouri.

The evil portents of the time were no more visible to Harry Truman than to the Moguls of Wall Street. He chose to go into the haberdashery business with a wartime buddy, Eddie Jacobson, with whom he had run a profitable company canteen during the war. They pledged to the venture everything they owned and all they could borrow. It was a time of high hope—and of sudden disaster.

In the fall of 1919 Truman and Jacobson opened for business in a choice Kansas City location, across the street from the then new Muehlebach Hotel. The partners had pooled their resources, signed a long-term lease on their store, and laid in a $35,000 stock of men's furnishings. The first year they did well: The depression had not begun to bite, and the nearby Kansas and Missouri farmers were getting $2.15 to $2.25 a bushel for their wheat. There was a brisk trade in such luxury items as silk shirts at $16 each, and what was almost equally satisfying to the neophyte merchants was that their store was becoming a popular hangout for scores of their wartime buddies as well as newer friends. But by the beginning of 1922 the slide was on. Wheat hit a low of $1.44 a bushel that winter; scores of nearby farms had been sold under foreclosure; and jobless men were walking the streets. The proprietors of Truman & Jacobson saw an inventory that had cost them better than $30,000 suddenly reduced in value to about $10,000. Meanwhile, their creditors and bankers began to put on pressure for settlement of accounts due.

In the summer of that year they went under. The two partners made every effort to pay their debts, and that effort left a lasting shine on their reputations in Kansas City. Jacobson ultimately was forced into bankruptcy in 1925. Truman managed to avoid this dread expedient, although when he came to the Senate in 1934 there was still an unsatisfied judgment of $8,944 outstanding against him in favor of the Security State Bank of Kansas City. In time, however, every claim against the firm of Truman & Jacobson was settled.

There was, however, one significant dividend from the haberdashery episode. One day in the spring of 1922, just before the firm was to go out of business, a big black Locomobile drove up to the curb in front of the store. Out of it stepped the commanding figure of Michael J. Pendergast, brother of Tom, the heavy-handed Democratic boss of Kansas City and environs. Truman knew the Pendergast clan only at a distance, although Mike's son, Jim, had been a fellow officer in the 129th Field Artillery. Truman had never been active in local politics, and his Democratic loyalty was largely a matter of inheritance from his father. In that very year, as a matter of fact, he had voted for a Republican for the first time in his life— for Major John L. Miles as Marshal of Jackson County.

The visitor leaned a heavy elbow on the showcase and looked his man in the eye.

"How'd you like to be county judge," he said. (The position in Missouri is not a judicial one, but administrative.)

"I don't know," the startled Truman responded.

"Think it over," said Mike. "If you want it you can have it." And he turned and walked out.

As Harry Truman's formal entry into politics has been reconstructed by local observers, the consensus is that the Pendergasts needed him a good deal more than he needed them. Truman at that time—the summer of 1922—badly needed a job, it is true, but there were other avenues open to him besides the public payroll. On the other hand, Boss Pendergast badly needed a presentable and winning candidate for the Eastern District of Jackson County. He was at war with another factional Democratic boss, Joe Shannon; and still a third, Miles Bulger, was nipping at his heels. At stake in the 1922 election was not only control of the patronage-rich county government, but control of the Democratic organization as well. The Pendergasts were not then openly involved in the criminal activities that cut them down later, but they were a rough, tough lot and the target of much suspicion. In the circumstances, it was obvious that no ordinary hack wearing the Pendergast colors would stand a chance against the relatively respectable candidates whom the Shannon and Bulger factions had put into the field.

It is Mr. Truman's belief that Jim Pendergast was responsible for putting his name on the table for consideration by the party leaders. In any event, the argument was made that Truman was a Baptist and a Mason (the "Goats," as the Pendergast organization was known in distinction from the Shannon "Rabbits," was top-heavy with Irish Catholics); that he was a war veteran and an ex-officer who was popular with his men; that he had good family connections all over the county; and that his political record was virginally blank. From Truman's viewpoint, the job offered a comfortable income and a certain status, and he felt that he might enjoy a political career. In a few days he accepted Mike Pendergast's offer.

Mr. Truman gives the following account of the election:

Even with Mike Pendergast's backing it was far from certain that I could win the nomination. The primary campaign was a very bitter fight. There were five candidates: a banker named Emmett Montgomery who had the support of the "Rabbit" faction; a road overseer by the name of Tom Parent, who had the support of the Bulger faction; James Compton who had been judge once by appointment and had been trying to be elected ever since; George Shaw, a road contractor who was honest (very unusual in Jackson County at that time), and myself, who had the support of the "Goats" or Pendergast faction.

I had an old Dodge roadster which was a very rough rider. I kept two bags of cement in the back of it so it would not throw me through the windshield while driving over our terrible county roads. I went into every township—there were seven of them—and into every precinct in the Eastern District. Luckily, I had relatives all over the county, and through my wife I was related to many more.

When the votes were counted [in the primary], I had a plurality of nearly three hundred. Mr. Shannon said the voters preferred a busted merchant to a prosperous banker. Most people were broke, and they sympathized with a man in politics who admitted his financial condition.

The election that followed was a walkaway. All the Democrats on the ticket won, although we three judges of the county court promptly began a factional fight among ourselves. The presiding judge was a member of the Shannon faction—the "Rabbits." The other district judge and I were "Goats," and we promptly took all the jobs. We ran the county, but we ran it carefully and on an economy basis.[3]

The weight of the evidence is that Harry Truman made a good judge; that he was industrious and conscientious in looking after the county's affairs; and that he was scrupulously honest in the handling of contract awards and other expenditures. Out of his modest salary he continued to make regular payments on the obligations left over from his haberdashery venture. He was defeated for reelection in 1924—the only such defeat he has ever suffered—and for the next two years he scraped a livelihood out of selling membership in an automobile association. But two years later, and again with the firm backing of the Pendergasts, he ran for chief judge and was elected by a whopping majority of 16,000 votes. He was to remain thereafter a permanent feature of the political landscape.

The Senator from Pendergast

"Harry S. Truman is accustomed to having political offices he didn't seek thrust upon him, and Tom Pendergast has been given perhaps more credit than he deserves for bringing up a future President of the United States," according to William M. Reddig, an on-the-spot observer of Mr. Truman's early years. Continuing, he says:

Mr. Truman was Uncle Tom's second or third choice for the job of United States Senator in 1934, and he wore the boss' collar more lightly than any important figure ever identified with the machine. The collar didn't chafe very often for the two good reasons that the Independence man had a strong mind of his own together with a highly developed sense of party regularity, and Tom Pendergast was able to see and appreciate the rare quality of this combination.

The result was that Truman made his faithfulness to Pendergast a political legend, and the Boss exercised his control in such a way that Truman was able to say in 1939, after the Pendergast crash: "Tom Pendergast never asked me to do a dishonest deed. He knew I wouldn't do it if he asked me. He was always my friend. He was always honest with me, and when he made a promise he kept it."[4]

One of the most fascinating anomalies of Harry Truman's career is that he, a man of such impeccable personal honesty and political integrity, could have maintained so close a relationship and dependence upon the Pendergast machine without being corrupted by it. For the machine was, beyond question, one of the most brazen and corrupt in the whole glittering history of American bossism. But Truman's political enemies, as well as more objective students, have combed through the records time after time and not found one substantial clue of Truman's complicity in any of its myriad misdeeds.

Thomas J. Pendergast, a big, lethargic man with the gruffly benign manner and the granitic features of an aged Indian chief, was the leader of a family dynasty in 1934 that had ruled Kansas City, and occasionally the State House at Jefferson City, for half a century. Until the last years of his life, Big Tom, himself, seems to have been reasonably honest in his personal dealings. He was a family man and a churchgoer, and the master of various business enterprises that fattened, but not immoderately, upon the favor of public officials. But if he did nothing directly to promote the rackets and the vote-stealing that made Kansas City a civic cesspool, he lent his enormously protective shadow to those who did. Johnny Lazia, for example, who gradually extended his control of prostitution, gambling, and the bootleg liquor trade from the city's teeming North Side to much of surrounding Jackson County, was one of "Tom's boys." So was Henry F. McElroy, the despotic City Manager who controlled the city's purchases and its police department like a private fiefdom. And when municipal and state elections came around, Big Tom Pendergast picked the candidates for office with the solitary deliberation of a chess player—and in most instances elected them with the same unerring finesse. "Ghost voters" in some wards and precincts, the Kansas City *Star* found after one particularly odorous election, outnumbered those legitimately registered. Roving bands of hoodlums systematically beat up election officials and poll watchers, smashed ballot boxes, and even resorted to kidnapping and murder to maintain the dominance of the Pendergast machine in Kansas City throughout much of the nineteen twenties and thirties.

It was not long after he had sent his new Senator to Washington in 1934 that Big Tom fell from his perch above the tumult, his hold weakened by a psychopathic mania for betting on the horses. Individual wagers of five and ten thousand dollars were common for him, and his obsession reached the point where he regularly shut himself up in his private office each afternoon and sat with headphones on, connecting him directly with whatever tracks around the country had attracted his patronage for that day. As his losses mounted (Federal agents were to estimate them at $600,000 for 1935 alone), his need for instant cash rose proportionally. The answer came in January 1935. An emissary from a group of insurance companies offered him a bribe of $750,000 to get a favorable ruling out of the Missouri insurance commission on relinquishing a $9,000,000 fund which had accumulated in escrow, pending adjudication of a contest over rate increases. Since the state insurance commissioner was Pendergast's own man, the "fix" was a relatively easy one. Tom got his payoff—in installments of one or two hundred thousand dollars at a time, in cash, during 1935 and 1936—delivered to him in a brown Gladstone bag by a courier who flew down from the insurance group's headquarters in Chicago for the purpose.

The gambling mania and his resort to theft had undermined Big Tom's health and his grip on the sordid empire he controlled. The authorities at last began to peel away the clumsy disguises that for so long had concealed and rendered immune the rackets and the vote frauds on which the Pendergast machine had flourished. Finally, in 1939, the whole insurance scandal was exposed when Federal tax agents traced the path of the bribe money from Chicago to Big Tom's personal cash box. He was convicted of evading more than $800,000 in income taxes and sentenced to pay a fine and serve fifteen months in prison.

"I am sorry this has happened," Senator Truman said in Washington, "but I am not going to desert a ship that is in distress." Six years later—in January 1945—old Tom Pendergast, broke, dispirited, an exile in the city he once ruled, died alone in his twenty-room mansion. Vice President Truman, a man to whom loyalty was always the supreme virtue, flew out from Washington in an Army bomber to pay a final debt of gratitude to the man who had been his friend and mentor.

Moralists will find it difficult to exculpate Harry Truman while condemning the machine of which he was a part. To Truman himself there was no paradox in his relationship with the Pendergasts. He understood the nature of organization politics and the code of loyalty by which it survives. "United we stand, divided we fall" applies equally to the Third Ward as to the Union of States. A political organization is not an uplift society; it is a blunt instrument for seizing and using power. As a realist, Truman knew he could have no political life in Kansas City—or the nation—without the aid of Pendergast, but as a man of honor he knew he could keep his private life intact from that of the machine. It is trite but true that politics makes strange bedfellows, and no stranger pair ever climbed under the sheets together than Harry Truman and Tom Pendergast. Until 1934 County Judge Truman was too small a cog in the Pendergast machine to affect its course one way or the other, even if he tried. So he did what many another smart political comer has done: He rode the machine as far as it would take him but kept his hands clean along the way. That is a pragmatic rather than a moralistic philosophy, but under the rules of our political system it is what pays off.

"I controlled the Democratic party in eastern Jackson County when I was County Judge," Truman told Jonathan Daniels. "Mike [Pendergast] turned it over to me. In any election I could deliver eleven thousand votes and not steal a one. It was not necessary. I looked out for the people and they understood my leadership. The vote-stealing in Kansas City was silly."

Harry Truman carried his belief in organization politics right into the White House, which accounted in no small measure for his success as President.

Harry Truman was fifty years old in 1934 when he got the call from Big Tom that was to alter forever the course of his life and of history. He had by now gone as far up the political ladder as he could go as a $6,000-a-year County Judge, with a good record of efficiency and independence from boss rule. He thought longingly of running for Governor. Then, when the state was redistricted in 1933, he thought of running for the new congressional seat that had been created in Jackson County. But Pendergast had other men in mind for those posts, and Truman swallowed his disappointment. He gave virtually no thought to trying for the Senate seat of Republican Roscoe C. Patterson, which was up that year, for he assumed The Boss had worked out his plans for that also. However, Pendergast had run into unexpected difficulties about the Senatorship that threatened his control of the Democratic organization in the state.

By tradition, one Senator had always come from the western half of the state, around Kansas City, and was therefore a Pendergast man, and the other from the eastern half, based on St. Louis, the limited preserve (in 1934) of Mayor Bernard L. Dickmann. Pendergast's man had lost out to Republican Patterson in 1928. The "eastern" Senator was Democrat Bennett C. Clark, who had been elected in 1932. Now Clark was backing the candidacy of another "easterner," Jacob L. "Tuck" Milligan, for the Democratic nomination to oppose Senator Patterson in the general election. If Milligan should win, Clark (son of the famous Champ) would thus be in a position to challenge Pendergast's claim to being boss of the Democratic Party in all of Missouri, an intolerable thought to Big Tom. An added complication was that Pendergast, as a staunch anti-Roosevelt man, had been getting short shrift on the favors and patronage of the New Deal, while Senator Clark, who was only slightly less adamant in his opposition to FDR, was being sedulously courted by the powers in Washington. Big Tom thus needed his own man in Washington—first, to preserve his balance of power in Missouri, and second, to direct into the proper Missouri channels the flood of jobs and relief money flowing from the Federal cornucopia.

He turned first to ex-Senator Jim Reed, an old reactionary from the days of the Wilson administration; then to Joe Shannon, his factional rival within the Kansas City organization, whom Pendergast had sent to Congress some years earlier just to get him out of the way; and then to James P. Aylward, for many years the Democratic chairman of Jackson County. All, for one reason or another, declined the honor of running for the Senate.

Again, as it had been in 1922, it was Jim Pendergast who proposed to his uncle that he consider the attributes of Judge Truman for political advancement. He had the best public image of any member of the organization in Kansas City, Jim argued; he was a veteran, a Baptist, and a high dignitary in the Masonic Order; he was widely known around the state; and, what was even more important, he had put himself squarely on the side of the New Deal. As distasteful as this fact might be the son argued, to the old man, it would be a highly potent factor in contrast to the pallid New Dealism of Clark's man, Milligan. Jim sensed, if Big Tom did not, that the New Deal had introduced another kind of ball game into the political stadiums and that Harry Truman was the only man in the Pendergast dugout equipped by reputation and instinct to make a showing at the plate. Tom knew only that he had been backed into a corner by Clark and by the refusal of his first three choices to make the race. Grudgingly, he gave his imperial nod.

Mr. Truman has given the impression that he had to be induced to run for the Senate, that Jim Pendergast and Jim Aylward spent the better part of a night in his hotel room at Sedalia (where he had gone to make a speech), urging his consent. The fact seems to be that he was stunned and delighted at the offer and that his hesitancy that night was a stratagem born of the realization that the organization now needed him as badly as he had needed the organization. Considering his political ambition and his previous disappointment at being passed over for Governor and for Congressman, it is inconceivable that he should not have leaped, inwardly at least, at being offered an even greater prize—a candidacy for the United States Senate. In any event, after the meeting in his hotel room broke up early on the morning of May 14, he wrote a note to himself that said:

It is 4 a.m. I am to make the most momentous announcement of my life. I have come to the place where all men strive to be at my age. In reading the lives of great men [here some reflections on moral integrity and self-discipline]. . . . And now I am a candidate for the United States Senate. If the Almighty God decides that I go there I am going to pray as King Solomon did, for wisdom to do the job.[5]

At all events, he lost no time filing for the primary, and he plunged at once into his first statewide campaign. It had become a three-way contest with the entry of Representative John J. Cochran, also of St. Louis, under the colors of that city's current Democratic boss, Bill Igoe. The Pendergast organization poured its full strength into the campaign in the Kansas City and Jefferson City areas, and Truman took to the road to cover the rest of the state in an unrelenting, 15-hours-a-day barnstorming tour. As a leading member of the County Judges Association he had at least one friend and dependable political contact in every county in the state. He hammered at the theme of being "heart and soul for Roosevelt" and chided his opponents for their lukewarmness.

The Clark-Milligan and Cochran forces concentrated, naturally enough, on Truman's identification with the Pendergast machine. The Union Station Massacre of the previous summer, when mobster Frank Nash and three Federal agents escorting him to Leavenworth Penitentiary were mowed down in the heart of the city by machine-gun bullets, had put Kansas City in the criminal Big League along with Chicago and New York. The municipal elections in the spring of 1934, with the machine fighting a determined reform movement, had been one of the most outrageously fraudulent on record. And in July of that year—right in the middle of the primary campaign— Johnny Lazia, boss of the rackets in Kansas City and Big Tom's chief enforcer, was killed by a shotgun blast as he got out of his car in front of the Park Central Hotel, where he lived.

Crime and corruption in the Pendergast domain seemed, indeed, to be reaching a peak that summer as Judge Truman—indisputably a Pendergast man—pounded doggedly but buoyantly over the highways and backroads of outstate Missouri. To the folks in the ball parks and courthouse squares, this cheerful, plain-spoken, unpretentious fellow with his thick eyeglasses and neat double-breasted suit, just didn't seem to fit into the background of big-city wickedness that his enemies were painting for him. Tuck Milligan reviled him as "Pendergast's office boy," and Cochran called him "the Munchausen of politics." Truman met these jibes in good humor, reminding his audiences that he was a farmer by trade, that he had a clean record as County Judge, and that as a citizen of Independence he had never voted in Kansas City in his life. Sure, he would say, he had the support of the Democratic organization of Jackson County (a permissible euphemism for the Pendergast machine) but so had Bennett Clark when he ran for the Senate in 1932. "Clark came begging for it with his hat in his hand, and he was damned glad to get it, too," he told every audience, and they would laugh and cheer delightedly.

His big pitch continued to be his all-out support of the New Deal and its dramatic efforts to rescue the farmer, the little businessman, and the hordes of jobless workers from the stranglehold of the depression. In this he had his opposition over a barrel, for Clark, Milligan, and Cochran were of the old, left-behind school of conservative Democrats who were still telling their disbelieving constituents that "that man in the White House" was leading the country to ruin. Most people felt themselves pretty well ruined already. The New Deal looked like a way out of their troubles, and Truman seemed to know the way. They gave him their votes—a plurality of 40,000 over Cochran, the second man.

Predictably, Jackson County went overwhelmingly for Truman, giving him a 13-to-1 margin over the combined vote for his two opponents. St. Louis gave Cochran an almost equally lopsided margin. But, significantly, Truman built up enough support statewide so that, had the two big city totals been eliminated, he still would have won the nomination. In this he had achieved for Big Tom what the old man needed most—the undisputed title of Democratic boss of all Missouri. He had achieved something still more important to his own career—stature as a politician and vote-getter in his own right. This fact was lost on most of the nation's press, for the result seemed to confirm their assumption that Boss Pendergast had "done it again." The violently anti-Pendergast Kansas City *Star*, however, was considerably more perceptive. It said in a postelection editorial: "Jackson County has found him a capable and honest public official . . . a man of unimpeachable character and integrity. . . . With Judge Truman in the Senate, Missouri can expect that its interests will be safeguarded and advanced from a national standpoint."

The general election in November was anticlimax. Truman was elected Senator over the Republican incumbent, Patterson, by a landslide majority of 265,000 votes.

Harry Truman was sworn into the Senate on January 3, 1935. He was a member of one of the largest classes of new Senators ever to be inducted into office at one time—thirteen of them, all Democrats. Normally, he would have shared during the opening ceremonies the anonymity of his brother freshmen. But many on the floor and in the galleries sought him out with their eye. He was a bit special, a curiosity, something of a freak—"the Senator from Pendergast" a columnist had called him.

"I was under a cloud when I got to Washington," he said later.

And indeed he was, but a part of it was of his own making and not due to the Pendergast shipping label which it was assumed he wore. He was also under a cloud of self-doubt, of insecurity at finding himself one of the exalted company of the United States Senate. His history reading had drenched this chamber in heroic grandeur for him, and now at close range he recognized the faces of Titans of his own day—the leonine Borah of Idaho, the supercilious and acid-tongued George Norris of Nebraska, squinch-faced old Cactus Jack Garner, Vice President of the United States, high up on the President's dais. And all about him were men who had been governors or congressmen or college presidents or great lawyers and industrialists, and they made the little ex-County Judge from Missouri uneasy about his right to mingle among them. He resolved to take night courses at a local law school in his spare time to make up for his deficiencies. He never got around to it, of course.

"There is hardly a record or a memory of that time," Jonathan Daniels has written, "which does not reflect a humility which went beyond modesty almost to apology."

The new Senator paid a hat-in-hand courtesy call at the bureau of the Kansas City *Journal-Post*, the only important paper in Missouri that had supported him, and confessed to the correspondents there that he was "green as grass and ignorant as a fool about practically everything worth knowing." He eagerly sought advice about almost everything from senior members of the Senate. He was as pleased as a schoolboy one day when red-bearded Jim Ham Lewis, of Illinois, stopped by his back-row desk to tell him: "For the first six months you'll wonder how you got here. After that you'll wonder how the rest of us got here." He rented a modest, two-bedroom apartment on Connecticut Avenue for his family, which now included, in addition to Bess and ten-year-old Margaret, his mother-in-law, Mrs. Wallace. He found it so difficult to live in Washington on his $10,000 Senate salary that he put Mrs. Truman on his office payroll at $4,500.

If he was "Pendergast's messenger boy" in those early months in Washington, it apparently was a role that Truman assumed, and in moderation, rather than one which was imposed upon him. His normal responsibilities as a Senator required him to look after the interests of his constituents. And some things he did not need to be told to do—for example, improving the relations between the Democratic organization in Kansas City and the central bureaucracy in Washington.

Tom Pendergast's stubborn refusal to take his place among the

Roosevelt rooters had created a chasm which the freshman Senator hoped to bridge. One of the few friendships he made among the high-level New Dealers was with Harry Hopkins, the boss of the Works Progress Administration. Truman persuaded Hopkins to name a Pendergast man, Matthew S. Murray, WPA Administrator for the state, an appointment that was to go sour a few years later when Murray was jailed for tax evasion. Truman also did missionary work for his state at the Reconstruction Finance Corporation, the Farm Security Administration, and other outlets for New Deal largesse, but he found that most of the favors and patronage were reserved for his senior colleague, Bennett Clark.

He sought to have an interview with the President on this score—and to appease his own ego as well—but he received only a courteous brush-off from the White House staff. He would be in Washington five months before he would get an audience with Roosevelt, and a pretty cursory one at that. At the Department of Justice, Attorney General Homer Cummings held the Missouri freshman an affable arm's length away; his FBI sleuths were already poking into the reeking cesspool of Kansas City's rackets and politics, and Cummings was not disposed to share confidences with a Pendergast henchman, which he assumed Truman to be.

Truman told the Kansas City *Star* in June that he frequently received telegrams from Pendergast asking him to vote one way or another on legislation. But, he said, "I don't follow his advice on legislation. I vote the way I believe Missourians as a whole want me to vote." This drew some sneers from the cynics, but Truman underlined his point emphatically a few weeks later when he voted for the Public Utility Holding Company Act, which Big Tom was known to oppose. The following year he defied Pendergast more pointedly when he voted for Pat Harrison instead of Alben Barkley to be Senate Majority Leader. Truman said later that this was the only time The Boss had called him on the telephone about a vote, and he did it this time, Pendergast told him, at the behest of the White House and the Democratic party chief, Jim Farley.

Truman was hopping mad, not at Big Tom but at Roosevelt and Farley, who had scarcely recognized his existence up to that time.

"I'm tired of being pushed around and having the President treat me like an office boy," he told a reporter as he stalked angrily off the Senate floor that day. "They better learn downtown right now that no Tom Pendergast or anybody else tells Senator Truman how to vote." And to be sure the message got home, he went straight to a telephone and told the same thing to Steve Early, the White House press secretary.

For all his brashness and his self-doubts, Truman was an industrious and conscientious Senator. He was lucky in his major committee assignments, being named to Appropriations and Interstate and Foreign Commerce, two of the most important committees of the Senate. He rarely missed a session of these groups, faithfully read and digested the vast number of documents that came before him, and soon established a modest reputation for knowing what he was talking about on the infrequent occasions when he spoke up. His tutelage on the Appropriations Committee was particularly valuable; no President ever entered the White House with a better understanding of government finance and the mystique of the appropriating process than he. His experience on Interstate and Foreign Commerce at the knee of that accomplished dragon slayer, Chairman Burton K. Wheeler of Montana, underpinned with names, dates, and places the folklore Truman had brought from the Middle West about the evils of Wall Street and the great monopolists of steel, rails, and oil. The liberal Wheeler, who had run on the Progressive ticket with "Fighting Bob" LaFollette in 1924, had a profound influence on Truman, maturing and crystallizing the Missourian's instinctive but somewhat fuzzy liberalism.

Throughout his early years in the Senate, Truman was a faithful and consistent follower of the New Deal line. He voted for all of Roosevelt's major bills, such as the Wagner Labor Relations Act, Social Security, adherence to the World Court, strengthening of the Tennessee Valley Authority, even for the so-called court-packing plan. He was chairman of the subcommittee that brought out the Civil Aeronautics Act of 1937, designed precisely according to Roosevelt's wishes, and he defended it against Republican assaults on the floor. He was a convivial fellow off the floor and made a number of friends, being taken into Garner's intimate circle of bourbon-drinking cronies who assembled in the Vice President's rooms after adjournment each day for philosophical discourse. He remained, however, pretty much of a cipher in the Senate hierarchy, an amiable but undistinguished backbencher who rarely made a speech and who was likely to make a botch of it when he did. The prospect of such an exercise always terrified him.

But he was beginning at last to emerge out of the demeaning shadow of "the Senator from Pendergast." His colleagues were be-

ginning to accept him for what he was, and the White House began
to pass a few small favors his way.

He suffered a setback in 1938—an event stemming from his stubborn sense of personal loyalty and political regularity. Two years
earlier, in November 1936, the Pendergast organization had outdone
itself iṇ rigging a statewide election. In Kansas City alone more than
50,000 fradulent votes had been cast to sweep the Democratic ticket
to victory. This time the reform forces would not be stopped, and
they invoked the Federal power in their behalf. A grand jury was
convened, and the U.S. District Attorney in Kansas City, Maurice
Milligan, brother of "Tuck" and protégé of Senator Clark, brought
in a squad of FBI agents to dig out the evidence of corruption.
Behind Milligan stood two Federal judges of stern Republican recti-
tude, Albert L. Reeves and Merrill E. Otis. Scores of Pendergast
henchmen were summoned and quizzed behind the grand jury's
doors—mostly the small fry from the precinct clubs and the City
Hall payroll, but now and then a figure of more imposing stature
would make the pilgrimage too. Plainly, the heat was on in earnest
this time, and indictments began to flutter down like autumn leaves.
Would it reach the top, to Big Tom and Mike and McElroy and the
others? Kansas City and St. Louis were on edge, and the rest of the
nation watched the story unfold in breath-holding suspense.

Early in 1938, and almost at the height of the drama, District
Attorney Milligan's term ran out and his nomination for reappoint-
ment was sent to the Senate by President Roosevelt. Truman was
not consulted and he was furious. In the first place he thought, na-
ïvely, that Milligan's crusade was just another chapter in the continuing warfare between the "ins" and the "outs" in Kansas City.
Truman was not about to reward a Democratic official who was
harassing the regular Democratic organization. He did not know
that the Federal men had already picked up a trail of hundred-
dollar bills leading from the insurance brokers' offices in Chicago in
the direction of Tom Pendergast's little office on Main Street in
Kansas City. He was to learn nothing of this until much later.

Secondly, he considered the nomination a personal rebuff and a
violation of his Senatorial prerogatives. (Milligan came from his
part of the state, not Clark's.) He had protested the appointment
to the Attorney General. It was almost unheard of for a Senator's
wishes in such an appointment to be so rudely ignored, particularly
when the Senator had gone down the line for the administration on
practically every issue as Truman had done.

Normally a Senator has the sympathy and the votes of his colleagues on an issue such as this. But on the day Harry Truman rose to oppose the confirmation of Maurice Milligan, he stood virtually alone, surrounded by hostile and cynical faces. Again, he was "the Senator from Pendergast," defending a corrupt machine and its Boss. No one was impressed when he said his opposition to Milligan antedated the vote-fraud investigations. While the prosecutor had turned up some genuine culprits, Truman said, at the same time "there are people being railroaded in these wholesale convictions who are no more guilty than the members of this body." He did not object, he went on, to Milligan remaining as a special prosecutor to complete his investigation, but the duly appointed District Attorney should be one "who is acceptable to the Democrats in that community." But "the Democrats in that community" seemed clearly to his listeners that day to mean the Pendergast machine. When the vote on confirmation was taken, only Senator Truman voted "No." Not one member of the Senate walked over to his desk to commend him for gallantry in a lost cause or to console him in defeat. He had never looked worse, and he would not look worse even on the day a year later when Big Tom Pendergast pleaded guilty in Federal Court to Milligan's charge that he had failed to pay income tax on the $430,000 bribe he had taken from the insurance men.

Harry Truman was a badly dispirited man and financially strapped as 1940 and the end of his first term approached. He thought seriously of going back to Independence and the simpler life there instead of running for a second term. His best friends told him his chances of reelection were bleak. The Pendergast organization, which had boosted him easily to victory six years earlier, now lay in ruins. The center of political gravity in the state had shifted to St. Louis, which had long been enemy territory. He had absolutely no money of his own to finance a campaign—or even to block the foreclosure of the mortgage on his mother's farm at Grandview a prospect that made him particularly bitter. If he ran he probably would be beaten; if he dropped out he would be a quitter. His dilemma in 1940 was almost the prototype of one he would face in 1948—and so was his solution. He would be anything before he would be a quitter.

Two events early in 1940 stiffened his pride and his determination. First, Governor Lloyd Stark, whom Truman despised as a renegade for having turned against the Pendergasts, announced his candidacy for Truman's seat. Second, President Roosevelt, who was known to favor Stark, attempted in rather heavy-handed fashion to buy Truman off by offering him an appointment to the Interstate Commerce Commission. These kicks to his vanity were all the persuading Truman needed.

"I sent the President word," he said afterward, "that I would run if I got only one vote—mine."

It was not easy, but he found a dozen friends who were willing to stand with him and help him run his campaign. Among them were Roger Sermon, the grocer-Mayor of Independence; John Snyder and Harry Vaughan, two buddies from his National Guard outfit, who would figure prominently in Truman's life later; Jim Vardaman, from St. Louis; Roy Harper, Philip J. Welch, and a handful of other minor politicians from around the state; and finally, his competent and knowledgeable administrative assistant in the Senate, Victor Messall. Jim Pendergast, presiding over what remained of his uncle's shattered empire in Kansas City, promised whatever help he could give, "even if it's only two votes, mine and my wife's."

It was a ramshackle campaign which this team mounted late in the spring of that year, starved for money, support, and even hope. They scrounged contributions wherever they could find them, a few dollars at a time, and Truman stretched his own bank credit to the limit with a loan of $1,000. They could not hope to match the opulence of Stark's outlay, as the governor was personally wealthy. Truman bounced around the state in his old Chrysler coupe, sometimes with a friend driving and sometimes alone. There were few big rallies, since they cost money, so Truman went to see the people instead of bringing the people to see him. Ten to fifteen hours a day through the broiling summer he popped unheralded into countless farmers' barns and feed lots, into village stores and restaurants and banks, into county courthouses and city halls, shaking hands by the hundreds, swapping small talk, asking for votes.

"I just wanted to come down and show you folks that I don't have horns and a tail just because I am from Jackson County," he would say, flashing his warm, disarming grin. The people were cordial to their Senator when he turned up and found him an engaging, straightforward sort of fellow who talked their language and didn't put on airs. Gradually things began to look up in the threadbare Truman camp.

Maurice Milligan had thrown his hat into the ring to make it a three-cornered race for the Democratic Senate nomination. Also, there was now a two-man race for the Democratic nomination for Governor. Hence, the Democratic organization in the state was split in several directions, and the climate was ripe for some quiet, behind-the-scene horse trading. The most coveted prize to the Truman forces was the backing of Democratic leader Robert E. Hannegan of St. Louis. This could be had, it developed, if Truman would get behind Hannegan's choice for Governor, Lawrence Mc-Daniel. This was a tricky maneuver all around because Hannegan's power rested in considerable degree on his good relations with the New Deal bosses in Washington, and Washington's Senate choice was Stark first, and Milligan second. But neither Stark nor Milligan would turn a hand for McDaniel, whereas Truman presumably could deliver whatever vote potential still resided in the old Pendergast machine in the Kansas City area. So the deal was made for Hannegan to dramatically throw his support to Truman, but with action delayed until the last critical days of the campaign.

Another factor was also slowly improving Truman's outlook. Some of his Senate colleagues, such as Lewis Schwellenbach of Washington, Sherman Minton of Indiana, Alben Barkley of Kentucky, and, most importantly, Burt Wheeler of Montana, had agreed to come into Missouri and make a few speeches for him. This gave a tone to the campaign that had been lacking before; it helped to identify the struggling candidate with figures of national stature and to dissipate some of the Pendergast tarnish.

But there was an even greater dividend. Truman had worked closely with Wheeler on railroad legislation that had won the gratitude of the powerful railroad brotherhoods. Wheeler, after his visit to the state, passed the word to the labor leaders that a good friend of theirs was in trouble in Missouri and that they had better do something for him. They did, in one of the greatest saturation efforts of the kind up to that time. "Truman Clubs" sprang up almost overnight at every railroad terminal and roundhouse in the state, and the infection spread quickly to the union halls of the AFL and other labor organizations. Money began to come into the Truman headquarters, and the whole campaign began to show new muscle and drive. Then, ten days before the primary election, more than half a million copies of a special "Truman Edition" of *Labor*, the brotherhoods' weekly newspaper, flooded into Missouri, reaching not only every union man in the state but thousands of Rural Free Delivery boxholders as well.

Even so, the primary election on August 6 was a photo finish. Truman won renomination but by a statewide plurality of only 7,476 votes. The winning margin came from the St. Louis precincts, where Hannegan's prearranged last-minute switch away from Stark gave Truman an edge in the city of 8,311 votes. The Senator carried his own Jackson County (including Kansas City) by 20,000, but this was a far cry from the more than 100,000 margin he had piled up in 1934 when Big Tom Pendergast was calling the plays. In the general election that followed, Truman beat his Republican opponent handily by almost 50,000 votes. But his coattails, which had carried Hannegan's friend McDaniel safely through the primary, were not sturdy enough to put McDaniel into the governership. This went by a hairline margin to Republican Forrest Donnell.

The 1940 campaign was Truman's toughest, and in many ways his most valuable, campaign. First, it established him beyond question as a Senator who had won election in his own right. He was nobody's man but his own, and when he got back to Washington he was to have a new measure of admiration and respect from the New Deal hierarchy. Second, it was a seasoning experience which gave a hard new sophistication to his political craftsmanship. Now he understood at first hand, as he never had before, the nature and employment of partisan political power, the secrets and subtle nuances of the public mind, the "art of the possible" through compromise and accommodation to surmount political obstacles. And, on a more practical level, he had forged a political bond with organized labor that would serve him through many vicissitudes to come.

Years later, after he had entered the White House, the one-time "Senator from Pendergast" wrote out in longhand this brief reflection on that troubled phase of his career:

In his [Pendergast's] prime he was a clear thinker and understood political situations and how to handle them. His word was better than the contracts of most businessmen. His physical breakdown in 1936 got him into serious trouble.

I never deserted him when he needed friends. Many for whom he's done much more than he ever did for me ran out on him when the going was rough. I didn't do that—and I am President of the United States in my own right.

Because Pendergast was convicted of income tax fraud and went to Federal prison at Leavenworth, he has been used by people opposed to me in an effort to discredit me. But nobody has ever been able to hurt me politically by slander and abuse. Nobody ever can.

Politics force men into contacts with all manner of people, but men of principles need never surrender them in order to gain or to hold public office.[6]

There is no surer path to fame for a member of Congress than the chairmanship of a headline-producing investigating committee. Getting such a committee going is no small feat. First, the member of the House or Senate must find a target for inquiry that is both valid and dramatic. Second, he must sell the idea to the leadership, making sure that some prejudiced elder does not spike his guns in advance or preempt the chairmanship for himself. And finally, he must manage committee affairs with a proper mixture of administrative skill and showmanship, being ever mindful of which toes he steps on. It is a challenging exercise in political finesse with rewards for the successful and punishment for the bungler.*

Harry Truman's second term in the Senate was dominated by his chairmanship of the Special Committee to Investigate the National Defense Program. It was a good performance that lifted him out of the obscurity of "just another middle western Senator" and set him up for the Vice Presidency.

The idea came to him through his work on the Appropriations Committee, where, during the buildup period prior to Pearl Harbor, hundreds of millions of dollars for new Army camps, airplanes, shipbuilding, and munitions were being force-fed into the defense pipelines. What came out at the other end seemed often to be a trickle or, even worse, a chaotic, slapdash spray, while a lot of contractors, manufacturers, and union bosses were getting inordinately rich. His suspicions were sharpened by what he saw with his own eyes at Camp Leonard Wood and other military installations in Missouri as he barnstormed the state during his reelection campaign. Suspicion turned to conviction a few months later when he made a quiet inspection tour on his own through a dozen states from Maryland to Florida to Texas. Everywhere he ran into the same sort of thing: cantonments slapped together with green lumber and shoddy plumbing at extravagant costs; hordes of unnecessary workmen idling on the job and enriching union treasuries through the purchase of work permits; huge orders for planes, trucks, steel, and other war supplies let on cost-

---

* Estes Kefauver almost certainly did himself out of the Democratic Presidential nomination in 1952 because his Senate crime investigation splashed suspicion on a number of important party functionaries in cities like Jersey City, Chicago, and Los Angeles. The massive grass-roots support he piled up in the primaries was set at naught at the convention because the big city bosses (and President Truman as well) wanted nothing to do with him.

plus contracts with exorbitant profits; small suppliers and manufacturers being pushed to the wall as orders and scarce-material priorities pyramided in the hands of big business; lobbyists and influence
peddlers enriching themselves with fat and unearned commissions.
Presiding over and contributing to this chaos was, he found, a tangle
of government agencies which often competed among themselves
and whose duties overlapped.

Truman saw these things through the trained and cynical eyes of
the County Judge who, a decade earlier, had gone to the mat with
sleazy road builders, fly-by-night contractors, and crooked or in-
competent politicians in Jackson County. To his pragmatic mind
one cleans up a mess of this kind in the same way, whether it is on
a county or a national scale: You get honest men to dig out the
facts and then call the culprits to account. And you do it while the
deed is fresh, so others won't be tempted to follow their example.
"We were interested in doing a surgeon's job to cure," he said later,
"not in performing an autopsy to find out why the patient died."

Truman proposed to a listless Senate in February 1941 (there
were only sixteen members on the floor as he finished his speech)
that a special committee be set up to investigate fraud, incompe-
tence, and bureaucratic mismanagement in the defense program.
With little debate, the resolution was approved and a seven-man
committee was named with the Missourian as its chairman. His
request for an initial appropriation of $25,000 (on the same day, the
Senate voted to increase the national debt limit to an unprecedented
$65 billion) was whittled down to $15,000, not so much out of
penury as out of caution against the investigation "getting out of
hand"—that is, becoming embarrassing to the administration.
Chairman Truman hired a first-class lawyer from the Justice Department, Hugh Fulton, as counsel, and a sharp-witted young
Boston Irishman, Matthew Connelly, as chief investigator, and set
to work.

For the next three and a half years the Truman Committee, as it
came to be known, was a model of probity, thoroughness, and conscientious fact-finding. It soon gained a full measure of respect, in
Congress and downtown, and the Senate gave it all the money it
needed, $100,000 at a time. It did not seek headlines, but it made
them by virtue of its startling disclosures and its thoughtful, constructive recommendations for legislative or administrative remedies, many of which were put into effect. In particular, the committee avoided the temptation of trying to tell the President and the
generals how to run the war. At the outset Truman had borrowed

from the Library of Congress its only copy of the hearings of the Civil War Committee on the Conduct of the War. He studied its yellow pages closely and resolved that his committee would not visit upon Roosevelt the humiliation, the obstacles, and the presumptuous meddling that a Republican Congress had imposed upon Lincoln from 1863 to 1865 with nearly disastrous results. He remembered from his own reading of history what Lee had said of that committee: that it was worth two divisions to the Confederate cause. The Truman Committee stuck strictly to the issue of how the business of supporting the war effort was being conducted; how contracts were awarded and fulfilled; how the economic and manpower resources of the nation were being utilized; and how the bureaucracy responsible for this effort (it mushroomed enormously after the attack on Pearl Harbor) was discharging its responsibility.

"The committee was directed to examine every phase of the entire war program," Mr. Truman recalled later. "It was not organized to tell the war agencies what to do or how to do it. It was not to substitute its judgment for their judgment. The idea of the committee was to conduct an investigation of the defense effort in order that mistakes could be remedied before irretrievable damage was done.

"I was determined that the committee was not going to be used for either a whitewash or a smear in any matter before it but was to be used to obtain facts and suggest remedies where necessary."[7]

In many instances the committee was able to move in and break bottlenecks where regular agencies of government were powerless. One of the first problems it tackled, in April 1941, was a coal strike that threatened the railroads and many industries. The issue was a new wage contract in which the Southern mine operators insisted upon the retention of a wage differential that gave them an advantage over the Northern mines. This was objected to by both the miners' union and the Northern operators, but the Southerners dug in for a long fight. The committee called before it spokesmen for the miners and the operators for a preliminary hearing on April 28. When it was over, Chairman Truman handed the recalcitrant Southern mine owners an ultimatum: If coal wasn't being dug within twenty-four hours, he would summon each of them to come before the committee and explain in person why his quarrel over wages should be allowed to endanger the national welfare. The dispute was settled the next day, and coal began to move.

Many times the committee spotlighted serious roadblocks in a

vital area of production the facts of which were known only in closed
industry circles. Coincident with the tremendous stepping up of
airplane production in the first year of the war, it became apparent
that the country faced a critical shortage of aluminum. Production
of this relatively new metal was a virtual monopoly of less than half
a dozen companies, all existing under the shadow of the giant
Aluminum Corporation of America. Prospective new manufacturers
were discouraged from entering the field because of protected processes and priorities on the available supplies of ore—bauxite—held
by the established manufacturers. After a spirited series of public
hearings before the Truman Committee, the Defense Plants Corporation and the Office of Production Management, key units in the
defense bureaucracy, unlocked the doors to more competition and
greater production in the aluminum industry.

The Office of Production Management (OPM) soon became a
particular target of the committee. This was the government's principal agency for channeling the nation's productive energies, machines as well as manpower, into the war effort. In a peculiarly
Rooseveltian compromise to satisfy the demands of both labor and
management for protection of their interests in the war boom, OPM
was given two heads instead of one. Its "codirectors" were William
S. Knudsen, an amiable, slow-moving engineering vice president of
General Motors, and Sidney Hillman, the volatile, politically-
conscious president of the Amalgamated Clothing Workers of America. In this polarized atmosphere the OPM stumbled and fumbled
its way through innumerable conflicts and crises, often unable to
give clear-cut decisions or to issue firm directives. On the one hand,
OPM was loaded down with WOC's (business executives serving
the government Without Compensation), who often gave the impression of being the special ambassadors within the bureaucracy of
DuPont, General Motors, and United States Steel rather than disinterested public servants. At one point, the Truman Committee revealed, sixty-six of the biggest United States corporations with
WOC's serving the government had received $3 billion worth of
government contracts within a year, while hundreds of their smaller
competitors either starved or subsisted on crumbs. Balancing the
industry representatives on the other hand were scores of union
officials and labor lawyers, some of them also serving WOC, whose
principal mission seemed to be to see that any grant of favor or
relief to an industry group was matched by a corresponding grant to
its workers. Hillman was accused on occasion of countermanding

contract awards to antiunion employers, and Knudsen was sometimes charged with favoring nonunion areas for the location of new
defense plants. OPM was a house divided and in perpetual conflict
with itself.

The committee blasted OPM in a special report in October 1941,
which Chairman Truman followed up with a bitter speech in the
Senate. He said that both Hillman and Knudsen had to go and that a
unified agency had to be devised to take the place of the hydra-
headed OPM. Results were not long in coming. An Executive Order
from the White House abolished OPM and set up the War Production Board in its place under the unitary command of Donald M.
Nelson, a Sears Roebuck executive with a knack for getting along
with both labor and management without favoring either.

The Truman Committee was a potent force for efficiency and
honesty in the defense program. It put the finger on scores of
crooked contractors and influence peddlers, and it worked notable
reforms in government contract procedures and in the administration of wartime economic controls. Often by the simple act of exposure it broke stubborn production bottlenecks (as in synthetic
rubber and steel production capacity) and thus for clarity materially
advanced the nation's preparedness for war. By the summer of 1944
it had issued forty-four studies and reports and, according to its
chairman, saved the government $15 billion.

For Harry Truman it brought a flattering measure of national
recognition, the uniform admiration of his colleagues in the Senate,
and a new respect among the downtown bureaucrats, beginning
with the White House. No longer "the Senator from Pendergast," he
had the weight to put his man from St. Louis, Bob Hannegan, into
the chairmanship of the Democratic National Committee. And
when, in the spring of 1944, Hannegan tossed Truman's name on the
table for FDR's consideration as a running mate, the President
rubbed his chin reflectively and said, "Yes . . . yes . . . I put him in
charge of that war investigating committee, didn't I?"

The Cream of the Jest

The story of how Harry Truman got the Democratic nomination
for Vice President in 1944 is an almost unbelievable melodrama, set
variously in the White House and the smoke-filled rooms of a Chi-

cago hotel and laced through with intrigue, reward and punishment, suspense, and a surprise ending.

The story evolves out of the simple fact that President Roosevelt would not take a commanding hand in the matter of selecting his running mate. He was tired, his physical afflictions were beginning to take their toll, and he was heavily preoccupied in the conduct of the war and in the grand designs for the peace that was to follow. His preference was to let Henry Wallace remain in office as Vice President. That was the line of least resistance; moreover, he liked Wallace. Beyond that, he cared less about who was chosen for the office than about who was hurt by not being chosen. Throughout the early months of 1944 he stubbornly resisted the efforts of his aides and political advisers to draw him into serious discussion of the question.

Wallace, as the incumbent, had the inside track. He had Roosevelt's confidence, and the President had sided with him in the flaming dispute that year between Wallace and Jesse Jones, the conservative Texas patriarch who ran the Reconstruction Finance Corporation, over industrial mobilization for the war. But Wallace's liberalism was politically a great deal less negotiable in wartime than in peace. He was distrusted by most of the politicians; he was feared by the business community; and he was thoroughly hated throughout most of the South. Moreover, there were many thoughtful people in that year who foresaw that FDR, sixty-two years old and beginning to show the strain of three terms in office, might not survive four additional years in the White House. The man elected Vice President in 1944 might well become President before 1948. The prospect that the moody, erratic, and unpredictable Wallace, the man with a penchant for occult philosophies and applied altruism, might one day sit in the President's chair was an intolerable specter to many.

In the late spring, with convention time drawing near, some of the big wheels in the Democratic organization began to chip away at the President's confidence in Wallace as a running mate. At Roosevelt's request Edward Flynn, the New York City Democratic boss, made a swing through some of the more sensitive political centers of the country to sound out local sentiment. He reported back that Henry Wallace probably would cost the ticket more support than almost any other occupant of the No. 2 spot. Roosevelt's devotion to Wallace began to weaken, but it did not fasten visibly on any of the other possible entries in the field.

Another who had an inside track—or at least convinced many that he did—was James F. Byrnes, former Senator from South Carolina, former Supreme Court Justice, and now Director of War Mobilization. Sharp-minded, aggressive, and ambitious, Jimmy Byrnes had been one of Roosevelt's first, though unannounced, choices for Vice President four years earlier. He was quietly dropped when Archbishop Spellman of New York suggested to the President that because Byrnes had renounced his Catholic faith millions of Catholics would refuse to vote for him.*

Whether or not Byrnes knew of this at the time, he did not let it stand in his way when talk of his availability for 1944 began to be heard. Byrnes has recalled that his first intimation that Roosevelt would like to have him on the ticket came in December 1943, in a conversation with Harry Hopkins. Later, he has written, Roosevelt himself dropped many suggestions in his hearing that Byrnes would make an excellent candidate and should go after the nomination. Similar intimations came to him from others close to the President, including, according to his account, Hannegan and Frank Walker, the Postmaster General. Byrnes says that up until the early summer he turned all such overtures aside because he did not want to run.[8]

It does not appear that Roosevelt ever gave Byrnes an unequivocal endorsement. However, as evidence of the President's purported interest in his candidacy continued to mount, and as Henry Wallace's prospects in the weeks immediately before the convention began to fade, Byrnes recalls that "I found myself beginning to think about it seriously." He thought about it seriously enough to make his candidacy known on Friday, July 14, only a few days before the convention was to open. That same day he called Senator Truman in Independence, said the President had given him the "Go" sign on the Vice Presidency, and asked Truman to put his name in nomination.

At the time of Brynes' call, Truman was packing his wife, Bess, and daughter, Margaret, into the family Chrysler to drive to Chicago. As chairman of the Missouri delegation and its member on the Resolutions Committee, he had to be on hand several days before the convention's formal opening on Wednesday, July 19. He was somewhat surprised by the news from Byrnes but told his caller:

* Jonathan Daniels recorded this verbatim view of Roosevelt's in his diary on June 27, 1944. It had been made to him and two other White House aides in an informal conversation with the President that day. Mr. Byrnes, in 1950, asked Cardinal Spellman (he had been elevated from Archbishop) if the incident was true. Spellman replied: "No such opinion was ever conveyed by me to the President."

"Why sure, Jimmy, if that's what the President wants I'll not only nominate you but I'll work for you."

He had scarcely gotten back to his packing when the telephone rang again. This time it was Senator Alben Barkley, also calling from Washington. Barkley said that since the Vice Presidential race seemed to be opening up he had decided to get into it, and he would like Truman to make the nominating speech for him. Truman, a bit overwhelmed, told his good friend from Kentucky that he had just committed himself to Byrnes, who, he understood, had been given the Presidential green light.

"I went to Chicago fully committed to Byrnes and determined to do all I could to see that he won the nomination," Mr. Truman later recalled.

Truman was fully aware that there was some agitation in his behalf for the nomination, particularly by Democratic Chairman Bob Hannegan and Edwin Pauley, the party treasurer. But he did not take it seriously and thought, moreover, that he had succeeded in squelching it. Only the day before Byrnes' call, in fact, he had issued a statement to the press in Kansas City saying that he did not want the nomination and had no intention of seeking it. This was a reiteration of what he had said several times previously, beginning in the spring, and he meant it. His reasons were several.

First, he knew the job could not be had without Roosevelt's endorsement, and this he was certain would be denied him. While his status in Washington had risen markedly in the last few years, he was still an outsider at the White House. Moreover, he had ruffled the administration's feathers more than once through the disclosures of his defense program investigating committee, and only a few months earlier he had spoken out resoundingly in favor of Senator Barkley, who had resigned his Senate Majority Leadership in an angry dispute with President Roosevelt. For such reasons Truman regarded his own chances of winning a Presidential nod as decidedly inferior to those of such favorites as Wallace and Byrnes and the three or four others whose names had begun to crop up.

Second, he was sitting pretty where he was, so why monkey with a good thing? He had won fame and friendships in the Senate beyond his fondest imaginings of a few years ago, and he was top dog in the Democratic hierarchy of Missouri. This was a long stride for a busted haberdasher and for the timid neophyte who had stumbled onto the national stage ten years earlier under the scornful obloquy of "the Senator from Pendergast." Truman the pragmatist knew a good thing when he saw it, and another term or two in the Senate was what he wanted.

Finally, he, too, sensed the potentially morbid destiny of the man who would be elected Vice President under Roosevelt this year. It was not a thought on which he dwelt long or often, but when he did the implications appalled him. The mantle of Washington, Jefferson, Lincoln, and Roosevelt would not fit the narrow shoulders of Harry Truman. What was more, the White House would be a hell of a place to bring up a young girl like his Margie. The Presidency was not for him.

When Truman told the reporters who greeted him as he checked into the Blackstone Hotel in Chicago that Friday afternoon that he was not a candidate himself, that he was working for Jimmy Byrnes, he was telling the truth. But he did not know all the facts in the case.

Two weeks earlier a quartet of kingmakers back in Washington had, by a process of elimination, settled on Harry Truman as the running mate who would do the least injury to Franklin Roosevelt's prospects of winning an unprecedented fourth term as President. They were Bob Hannegan, the Democratic chairman; Ed Pauley, the California oil mogul and Democratic treasurer; Ed Flynn, the Democratic boss of New York; and Sidney Hillman, the chief of the burgeoning and powerful Political Action Committee of the Congress of Industrial Organizations (PAC). They were bound more by a consensus than by a conspirators' oath, but they were to conspire aplenty. Hillman's commitment was conditional: He would go for Truman only in the event that Henry Wallace's case became hopeless, which it seemed to be doing. Hannegan, Flynn, and Pauley argued that Wallace would drag the ticket down to defeat in the South and the Middle West. All agreed that Byrnes would cost the Democrats vital Negro support in the North and Catholic support everywhere. As for the other names that had been tossed up—Supreme Court Justice William O. Douglas, Ambassador John G. Winant, Senator Barkley, shipbuilder Henry Kaiser, and a handful of favorite-son governors—all presented insurmountable handicaps of one kind or another.

The man with the fewest handicaps and with some tangible advantages was Harry Truman. He had a good record as a war investigator, he stood well with labor, he had voted with the New Deal, he came from a border state, and Roosevelt really had nothing very much against him. Hannegan, the "pol" from the sweaty precincts

of St. Louis, whom Truman had brought to his present eminence,
was the principal champion of his benefactor. Truman was his man,
and Hannegan set out to put him across, with or without consent.

As convention week approached, the kingmakers needed either a
deliberate assist for their design from Roosevelt or an assurance that
he would not cut them down. In his typical way, FDR was continuing to "play it cozy." In rambling discourse about the convention
and the campaign, he conceded that Wallace might be a burden-
some weight on the ticket, but he would not disavow Wallace nor
would he do more than to muse inconclusively about Byrnes, Douglas, Truman, and the other possibilities. The suspense for Hannegan
and the other practical party men who had a convention and a
campaign to prepare for was becoming intolerable. They dared not
try to force the President's hand nor to go behind the back of so
ruthless a political executioner. To have done so by leaks to the
newspapers or by floating trial balloons could spell disaster for
Truman's prospects. Wallace had powerful men in his corner, and
Byrnes was backed by such titans as Frank Walker and Mayor Ed
Kelly of Chicago. There was nothing for Hannegan and his men to
do but sweat it out.

Finally, the time came to make a last try to smoke the President
out on his choice. A dinner meeting was arranged with him at the
White House on the evening of Tuesday, July 11, only eight days
before the convention would open. Those in attendance were Hannegan, Walker, Mayor Kelly, Flynn, Pauley, George Allen, and John
Boettiger, Roosevelt's son-in-law. Thus, all three of the leading
contenders—Wallace, Byrnes, and Truman—were represented
around the Presidential table by deputies. Just what went on at that
meeting is clouded by the varying recollections of the participants.
This much, however, seems to be clear: On the strong insistence of
Flynn and Hannegan, Roosevelt finally agreed that Wallace would
be an impossible drag on the ticket. The President said, however,
that he could not publicly drop Wallace, for whom he had a great
fondness, but that he would give only a weak and equivocal endorsement to be read at the convention, leaving the field open to
other contenders.° Thereafter he discoursed aimlessly with his usual

° His letter, dated July 14, was addressed to Senator Samuel D. Jackson of Indiana,
permanent chairman of the convention. In three short paragraphs it bespoke the
President's respect and friendship for Wallace, and added: "For these reasons I
personally would vote for his renomination if I were a delegate. At the same time I
do not wish to appear in any way as dictating to the convention. Obviously, the
convention must do the deciding. . . ." The letter was intended to be read at the
opening session of the convention.

charm and verve on politics and politicians without touching once on what his guests most wanted to hear—whom he *did* want on the ticket with him at Chicago the next week.

Such, at least, is the reconstruction by one of the few living persons in 1965 who is in a position to know what went on at that dinner table discussion twenty-one years ago. That is Paul A. Porter, today a prominent Washington attorney, who in 1944 was publicity director for the Democratic National Committee and a right-hand man to Chairman Bob Hannegan, now deceased. Flynn, also deceased, recorded in his memoirs that the *tone* of the President's comments about Truman made it clear that the Missourian was his preference and that he, Flynn, managed to terminate the discussion in time to forestall a contradiction. Byrnes says he was told by Walker that while both Truman and Douglas were mentioned, the President said nothing to diminish his partiality for Byrnes. Porter's recollection, based on conversations with Hannegan in the days immediately following the meeting, is this:

> From what Bob told me, the President didn't put the finger on anybody after expressing his doubts about Wallace. They all fenced around trying to get him to speak up, but the Old Man just wasn't going to play it that way. He had his own reasons, whatever they were, for being cagey, and he wasn't going to give them the satisfaction they were after.
>
> But when the evening broke up and they were all outside getting their coats, the President called Bob back into the room. He reached over and took Bob by the wrist and said something like this: "Okay, Bob, we'll make it Truman."
>
> This was in great confidence, and I don't think Hannegan told it to anybody except me and maybe Ed Pauley—up to the time of the convention, anyway. Maybe the President put him under wraps at the time; I don't know.
>
> But somewhere along the way—it must have been within the next couple of days, because Hannegan was in Chicago by Friday—the President gave him a "Dear Bob" letter which said, in effect, he would be happy to have either Bill Douglas or Truman on the ticket with him.
>
> That letter was postdated to the opening day of the convention, July 19. But I know for a fact that Hannegan had it in his pocket when he got to Chicago. He liked to be a real mystery man about it: He'd whisper around that he had it cold in writing that the President wanted Truman but that he couldn't reveal the letter—not yet anyhow.[9]

As the vanguard of the conventioneers converged on Chicago over the weekend, the talk in the lobbies and the bars was all about Wallace and Byrnes. The Vice Presidency was, of course, the most important thing the convention had to decide, and it was the chief topic of speculation. The word that Wallace was sinking had already sent Byrnes' stock soaring. On Sunday he opened headquarters in an elaborate suite on the top floor of the Stevens Hotel, where he held open house for the delegates. He was bouncing with confidence.

This early momentum of the Byrnes drive so alarmed Hannegan when he reached Chicago on Friday that he put in a distress call to the President at his home in Hyde Park. Roosevelt was preparing to leave early the next day for the West Coast. At Hannegan's urging he agreed to pause briefly for a conference as his train passed through Chicago. Saturday afternoon Hannegan and Pauley made a secret pilgrimage to a siding at the LaSalle Street Station and boarded the Presidential special. They pleaded for an outright endorsement of Truman as the only way of avoiding a head-on collision between Wallace and Byrnes, which Wallace might conceivably win. The President was unmoved: He had promised Wallace that he would not give a stronger endorsement to anyone else than he had given him.

"Well, at least, Mr. President," Hannegan said in desperation, "let's change the order of names in that letter you gave me in Washington. Make it 'Truman or Douglas' instead of 'Douglas or Truman.'"

The President consented at last to this, and he called in his secretary and had the letter retyped then and there.* It read:

July 19, 1944

Dear Bob:

You have written me about Harry Truman and Bill Douglas. I should, of course, be very glad to run with either of them and believe that either one of them would bring real strength to the ticket.

Always sincerely,
F D R

Honorable Robert E . Hannegan
Blackstone Hotel
Chicago, Illinois

---

* Mr. Truman as well as some other chroniclers of this event believe that the President previously had given Hannegan a handwritten note on a scrap of paper saying, "Bob: It's Truman. FDR." No such note has ever been found, and Porter and Mr. Hannegan's widow are certain that it never existed. The original of the "Truman-Douglas" letter quoted here was given to the Truman Library by Mrs. Hannegan after her husband's death.

Now Hannegan began to put pressure on Truman directly and also through the devious convolutions of the political grapevine. Truman, meanwhile, was talking up Byrnes. Sunday morning he taxied uptown to the Ambassador East to have breakfast with Sidney Hillman to try to promote Byrnes' cause with the PAC.

"No," Hillman told him. "We are for Wallace. But we would have two choices after Wallace. The second of those would be Douglas. I'm looking at our first choice now."

Truman protested he was not a candidate. He intended to do everything he could, he said, to put Byrnes across.

That afternoon Hannegan came to Truman's hotel room and told him that he had to run because the President now definitely wanted him on the ticket. "Tell him to go to hell," Truman snorted. "I'm for Jimmy Byrnes."

The next morning (Monday) Truman had breakfast with two labor leaders: Phil Murray of the CIO and A. F. Whitney of the railway trainmen. They, too, told him that if Wallace washed out they would center their support on him. Later that day the Missouri delegation caucused and voted, over Chairman Truman's pleading protest, to put his name in nomination. Governor Herbert O'Connor of Maryland let it be known that the Free State would be for Truman on the first ballot if he were nominated. On Tuesday morning the St. Louis *Post-Dispatch,* which had rarely found much that was good to say about their Junior Senator, carried a lead story from Chicago, saying, "Truman is now the talk of the convention." And in the same edition its syndicated columnist Marquis Childs wrote exultantly: "Senator Truman has greater eligibility than any of the other contenders for the Vice Presidency."

Mystified, flattered, and also troubled, Truman went up to Byrnes' suite on Monday afternoon to report what was happening. The spry South Carolinian was in good spirits and told his visitor not to worry, that the President would straighten things out in due time.

According to his own account in his published memoirs, Byrnes, too, had been getting reassuring reports on his status from Hannegan, Frank Walker, Mayor Kelly, Mayor Frank Hague of Jersey City, and even some labor bosses such as Al Whitney of the trainmen. He figured his first-ballot strength at an impressive 700 votes. Byrnes was aware throughout, he has written, of the violent opposition of Flynn and Hillman. But he was secure in the belief that, once Wallace had been torpedoed by release of the President's am-

biguous letter, Roosevelt's known preference for Byrnes would
cancel out all objections to his nomination.

However, a series of events in the next forty-eight hours punc-
tured Byrnes' confidence. He attended a strategy conference with
Hannegan and a small group of labor leaders on Monday night and
was told bluntly that the labor bloc would oppose him. Through
emissaries he learned of a reported telephone conversation sometime Tuesday between the President, on the West Coast, and Flynn,
Hannegan, Pauley, and other pro-Truman leaders. The President
was supposed to have told them that, in view of the labor opposition, he was willing to drop Byrnes entirely and to back Truman.
When Byrnes tried to telephone the President at San Diego that
night to check out this report, Roosevelt could not be reached. Finally, on Wednesday, Hannegan released the Truman-Douglas letter to the press. Jimmy Byrnes was done for. He had nothing whatever bearing the magic signature of FDR to confirm his claim of
preferment. Bitterly disillusioned, he announced his withdrawal
from the race, "in deference to the wishes of the President," and
went home to South Carolina.*

This rapid sequence of events spinning wildly beyond his reach
left Harry Truman bewildered, embarrassed, and hotly resentful.
He did not like being a pawn in even so big a game as Vice Presidential politics, and the job was no more attractive to him after all
the tugging and hauling he had witnessed than it had been before.
He told Bob Hannegan angrily that night as the convention's first
session adjourned that he still was not a candidate and didn't intend
to be one.

That was still his position the next afternoon when Hannegan
telephoned him and asked him to come to a meeting of party leaders

---

* There is an unbridgeable gap between the recollections of the two chief pro-
tagonists in this drama, differences as to both detail and intent.

Mr. Byrnes, in his memoir, *All in One Lifetime,* depicts himself as the victim of a
conspiracy in which Roosevelt and Hannegan were the principal actors. He feels that
they deceived him and used him as a bellwether to undermine Wallace and to create
an opening for Truman, whom they secretly favored all along. He ascribes to Roosevelt
the famous phrase, "Clear it with Sidney," meaning that the President set this manifestly unattainable condition of Hillman's consent as the price of his own outright
endorsement of Byrnes. No one else directly involved recalls such an injunction by
the President, but the phrase became a popular Republican slogan in the election
campaign.

Mr. Truman, in his *Memoirs,* tells a wholly different story, some details of which are
unsupported elsewhere, of how and by whom support for his candidacy built up during the convention week. He, too, suspects a conspiracy, directed against him by
Byrnes, for he has written: "I believe, therefore, that Byrnes knew that the President had named me at the time he called me in Independence and asked me to nominate him at the convention."

in Hannegan's suite. When Truman walked into the room he faced the toughest masters of Democratic politics—Flynn, Kelly, Hague, Pauley, Walker, and, of course, Hannegan. With one accord they told him he had to run, that he owed it to the party, to the President, to the country. As they argued, the telephone rang. Hannegan, seated on the bed, answered it. As if by a prearranged signal the room suddenly became quiet. The voice on the other end of the wire was audible to those standing near, and particularly to Truman, seated on the bed next to Hannegan. It was Roosevelt.

"Bob," the President said, "have you got that fellow lined up yet?"

"No, Mr. President," Hannegan replied. "He is the contrariest Missouri mule I've ever dealt with."

"Well, you tell him that if he wants to break up the Democratic party in the middle of a war, that's his responsibility."

Hannegan hung up the phone and turned to Truman. "Now what do you say?"

"My God," Truman mumbled.

Friday, the last day of the convention, was a nightmare of noise, confusion, and the razzle-dazzle peculiar to these aberrant festivals. The Wallace forces, angry but undaunted by the effort of the bosses to undermine their man, stormed the old Chicago Coliseum in force and even infiltrated the main floor reserved for the delegates. Wallace, his long arms swinging and his eyes aglow, had come to Chicago on Wednesday, too late to check the Truman tide but now trying desperately not to be engulfed by it. He cashed all his commitments on the first ballot: he got 420½ votes to 319½ for Truman, with the rest scattered among a host of favorite sons. On the second ballot he was demolished before a dozen states had been polled, as one favorite son after another stepped down in favor of the Senator from Missouri. Wallace salvaged only 105 votes out of that second ballot to 1,031 for Truman.

Truman's nomination, James A. Hagerty wrote in the New York *Times* the next day, "was a triumph of the big city bosses." It was that, all right, but it was something more, and Jonathan Daniels said it in these words:

As time passed, it became increasingly clear that this was not only an important convention in American history but one which qualifies as almost the cream of the American political jest. Truman was nominated by men speculating beyond the death of Roosevelt who knew what they wanted but did not know what they were getting.[10]

CHAPTER 3

◇◇◇◇◇◇◇◇◇◇◇◇◇◇◇◇◇◇◇◇◇◇◇◇

A Dubious Millennium

The Atom Bomb

THE DECISION was now irrevocable. Only a lesser disaster could avert the larger disaster that was about to blast mankind into a new and excruciating epoch of life on earth. The responsiblity reached back with chilling finality to "the little man from Missouri" who now sat uneasily in the White House.

It was 2:45 o'clock on the dark but starlit morning of August 6, 1945. On parallel runways of the Army Air Force Base on Tinian Island, a dot of coral in the Pacific Ocean 1,500 miles southeast of Japan, three monstrous B-29's glowed dully in the dark, their revved-up engines intruding hoarsely upon the silence like growling dragons. At a command from the control tower, Colonel Paul W. Tibbets, Jr., at the controls of the *Enola Gay* on the center runway, eased his throttles forward cautiously. The dangerously overloaded ship shuddered sluggishly into motion. Slowly, agonizingly she picked up speed, and, just as the end of the two-mile-long ribbon of concrete whipped under her nose, her great wings lifted her uncertainly into the air. Behind her, the other two ships in the flight were halfway down the runway when the *Enola Gay* became airborne. In loose, triangular formation they bored northward into the trackless night.

When cruising altitude had been reached, a "deadhead" with the *Enola Gay*'s six-man crew, Navy Captain William S. Parsons, with a

weird kit of tools under his arm, descended into the cavernous bomb
bay. There, in its special cradle, lay a black metallic monster of the
approximate size and shape of a baby whale. It was known variously
to the chosen few who had ever laid eyes on it as "Thin Boy," or
"The Thing." It was wholly dormant and innocuous as Captain Parsons clambered down into its nest. Only the night before, four B-29's
in succession had crashed trying to take off from Tinian. If the
Enola Gay, with its special cargo, had suffered a like fate, a properly
activated "Thin Boy" probably would have blown a good part of
Tinian Island off the map. So Captain Parsons, one of the few men
around who had been trained at Alamogordo, volunteered at the last
minute to fuse the world's first airborne atomic bomb while in flight.
He hoped reverently to God that he knew how, and that he could do
it in time. He was far from certain.

Four alternative targets in the Japanese homeland were circled on
the chart that Colonel Tibbets carried on his lap. An hour ahead of
him were three reconnaissance planes to scout the weather over
each target. Clear visibility from 30,000 feet was a requisite for this
greatest of all air strikes. As daylight crept up out of the eastern
horizon and spread across the sky, the *Enola Gay's* navigator, Captain Theodore Van Kirk, was advised by radio code that conditions
over Target One, the city of Hiroshima, were ideal. He and Colonel
Tibbets set their course accordingly, and the bombardier, Major
Thomas W. Ferebee, got into position behind his bombsight. "Zero
instant" had been calculated for 9:15 o'clock. At 8:50 the shoreline
of Honshu, the main Japanese island, swept past in brilliant sunlight
far beneath them. At 9:11, with the two accompanying observation
planes deployed a mile away, one on each side, the *Enola Gay*
reached her "initial point" for a straight run directly over her target.

What premonitory emotions and anxieties gripped the men
aboard is not recorded—whether they shouted "Bombs Away!"
"There she goes!" "Take this, you bastards!" or anything at all.
William L. Laurence, on special military leave from the New York
Times as press officer for the Manhattan Engineer District, was the
only reporter with a next-to-eyewitness proximity to this awesome
venture. From his privileged listening post in the main communications center at Tinian, he followed the minute-by-minute progress of
the flight and interviewed the crew when they returned that afternoon. He captured some of the drama in these words:

The *Enola Gay* had a four-minute run on a perfectly open target. Maj.
Ferebee manipulated the cross hairs on his bomb sight until the target

was at the intersection between his course line and his rate line. The great moment had come. He synchronized on Hiroshima and let go. . . .

Those inside the *Enola Gay* first saw a little pinpoint of light, purplish-red. In an instant the pinpoint grew into a giant ball of purple fire, a half mile in diameter. The great fireball suddenly exploded into a huge mass of swirling flames and purple clouds. Out of it came giant concentric white rings of fog, as though the earth itself were blowing mighty smoke rings.

Suddenly out of the swirling purple cloud came a huge column of smoke. . . . Then came another phase. The ten-thousand-foot column suddenly grew into a giant mushroom, with tremendous clouds of dust swirling about its base for a distance of three miles. . . .

At exactly 9:15 this morning Hiroshima stood out under the clear blue sky. One tenth of a millionth of a second later, a time imperceptible by any clock, it had been swallowed by a cloud of swirling fire as though it had never existed. The best watches made by man still registered 9:15.[1]

Halfway around the world, the United States destroyer *Augusta* was a day out of Norfolk, bringing the almost-brand-new thirty-second President of the United States home from his first international conference, at Potsdam. As he sat at lunch on August 6 with the ship's crew, an officer handed him a radiogram that had just been received. It read:

To The President
From the Secretary of War
   Big bomb dropped on Hiroshima August 5 at 7:15 P.M. Washington time.[*] First reports indicate complete success which was even more conspicuous than earlier test.

In later years, the President recalled:

When I read this I signalled to the crew in the mess hall that I wished to say something. I then told them of the dropping of a powerful new bomb which used an explosive twenty thousand times as powerful as a ton of TNT. . . . I could not keep back my expectation that the Pacific war might now be brought to a speedy end.[2]

The decision to atomize Hiroshima not only brought the war in the Pacific to a speedy end but did much, much more.

Joseph Stalin probably knew more about America's atomic-bomb project than Harry Truman did when he became President. In fact,

_____

[*] August 5 in the Western Hemisphere is August 6 in the Eastern.

Truman did not even know it existed on the evening when he was sworn in, and it was almost two weeks later before he was to get his first full-dress briefing on the mysterious operations of the Manhattan Engineer District (the administrative euphemism behind which this greatest of wartime gambles was concealed) from the Secretary of War, Henry L. Stimson. Yet, in less than three months he would be called upon to make the most awesome decision any President had ever been asked to make—whether to loose this most terrifying weapon ever devised by man upon human targets.

No man has ever walked with less preparation into a greater tangle of problems than did Truman when he stepped across that anomalous Constitutional threshold that separates the figurehead Vice Presidency from the towering and lonely responsibility of the Presidency. Since his inauguration in January, he had seen President Roosevelt privately only three times, and each occasion was brief and inconsequential. In his established role as presiding officer of the Senate he was almost totally isolated from the flow of issues and decisions in the executive branch of government, save as they directly concerned legislation. What he knew of the grand strategies of war and peace, then approaching an apocalyptic climax, he picked up largely from the papers and the gossip of the Senatorial cloakrooms.

"The President," Woodrow Wilson wrote nearly half a century ago, "is at liberty both in law and in conscience to be as big a man as he can."

But a Vice President can be only as big a man as his President wants, or permits, him to be. FDR groomed no one to be his successor, and if he ever regarded Harry Truman as anything more than a congenial makeweight on the Democratic ticket in 1944, the fact is lost to history. Nor is there much evidence that the Vice President himself contemplated or tried to prepare for the historic crisis that enveloped him on that April evening in 1945. At a later time he said:

I felt that I had lived five lifetimes in my first five days as President. I was beginning to realize how little the Founding Fathers had been able to anticipate the preparations necessary for a man to become President so suddenly. It is a mighty leap from the Vice Presidency to the Presidency when one is forced to make it without warning. Under the present system a Vice President cannot equip himself to become President merely by virtue of being second in rank.[3]

Of all the vast complexities that leaped out at Truman when he was thrust into the White House, none was more formidable and demanding than the A-bomb. The conduct of the war was, in a relative sense, in the hands of the generals and the admirals; there was no question but that the formative work on the United Nations should go forward; and domestic affairs could, if need be, continue to operate under their own momentum, for a time at least. But the discovery and harnessing of atomic energy involved uniquely personal responsibilities for the President. Only a handful of men, out of tens of thousands engaged on the atomic program, knew all its dimensions or were able to guess at its limitless implications. But each major step in this two-billion-dollar fantasy required the President's personal consent. And he alone, in all the world, must say Yes or No to that awesome, ultimate question, "Shall we drop the bomb on a living target?"

Among the few people in the world who did know, however imperfectly, what was going on at Oak Ridge, Tennessee, and Los Alamos, New Mexico, and at Hanford, Washington, were Premier Stalin and his top associates in the Kremlin. They had enjoyed for more than a year fairly accurate and up-to-date intelligence supplied them through the espionage network served by the German physicist Klaus Fuchs, who was attached to the Manhattan Engineering District (MED) in a highly responsible and confidential role. (This desolate fact was not known to American authorities until several years later, when Fuchs was caught at his spying by the British.) Senator Truman almost blundered into the select company of the informed in mid-1944. As Chairman of the Senate War Investigating Committee, he decided to send his investigators down to see what was happening to the hundreds of millions of dollars of appropriated funds being swallowed up by that hush-hush operation in Eastern Tennessee. He was dissuaded just in time by the personal plea of Secretary Stimson, who came in great agitation to his office and told him: "Senator, I can't tell you what it is, but it is the greatest project in the history of the world. It is most top secret. Many of the people who are actually engaged in the work have no idea what it is, and we who do would appreciate your not going into those plants."

Almost a year later—the date was April 25, 1945—Stimson was relieved to be able to go to the White House and tell the new President in detail what the state of progress on the A-bomb was and to speculate about its enormous implications. Almost at the outset of the MED program in 1941, Stimson had been designated by President Roosevelt to be his chief civilian liaison with the scientists and military men carrying on the work. On this visit to the White House, he brought with him Major General Leslie R. Groves, the chief administrative officer of the project, who explored the main technical aspects of the work for the new President.

The substance of Groves' report was that, as the culmination of five years of totally unparalleled scientific effort, a workable atomic bomb was now almost a certainty. The remaining doubts, he said, would be resolved sometime after the middle of July when an actual test explosion would be attempted in the New Mexico desert. If it succeeded at all, this explosion would yield an equivalent force of about 500 tons of TNT. Thereafter, he went on, the first "operational" bomb would be ready for use around the first of August. And—in what turned out to be a historic understatement—this one should have twice the killing force of its prototype, or the equivalent of 1,000 to 1,200 tons of TNT. It was a 20,000-ton bomb that hit Hiroshima, and "Thin Boy" was already obsolete before it was dropped.

(Not every one shared General Groves' optimism. Admiral William D. Leahy, the crusty old sea rover who had stayed on briefly as White House Military Adviser after FDR's death, also sat in on the briefing for Truman that morning. When Stimson and Groves had departed, he warned the President: "The damn thing will never go off, and I say that as an expert on explosives." Some of the scientific people of the MED were equally, if less picturesquely, skeptical.)

For his part of the discussion that morning, Secretary Stimson dwelt less on the weaponry aspects of atomic energy than on the larger questions of its place in broad military and political strategy and the moral implications of America's monopoly of it.[4] (The British and Canadians were junior partners in the enterprise, but the essential techniques had been developed by the United States.) There was first, he said, the issue of whether such a terrifying weapon should be used at all. Beyond this was the question of our obligation to humanity as the custodians of this secret cosmic force, and how that custodianship was to be exercised in a postwar world full of jealousies and tensions. He urged the President to look beyond the immediate prospect of the first man-made atomic blast to the tremendous long-range ramifications that would begin immediately to ensue. At Stimson's suggestion, Mr. Truman agreed to the prompt creation of a special committee of distinguished civilians to study, and to advise him on, the whole range of moral and political issues presented by the emergence of atomic energy as a totally new aspect of civilization.

Rarely has there been a government committee of higher caliber than the so-called Interim Committee which resulted from this talk. Stimson, whose record of public service went back to the Taft administration, was its chairman, and on its roster were such names as James M. Byrnes, former Supreme Court Justice and War Mobilizer and soon to become Secretary of State; Ralph A. Bard, Assistant Secretary of the Navy; Vannevar Bush, director of the Office of Scientific Research and Development, and James B. Conant, who left the presidency of Harvard to become chairman of the National Defense Research Committee. Serving in an advisory capacity were several of the brightest luminaries from the new science of nuclear physics—such as J. Robert Oppenheimer, Enrico Fermi, and Arthur H. Compton, each of whom had had a commanding role in the capture of atomic energy.

The minutes and final report of this group are still classified and beyond common reach, but Herbert Feis[5] has done a thorough job of piecing together the proceedings from many competent sources. There were, he says, two basic items on the agenda: (1) how this new source of energy (characterized by Stimson as having "more effect on human affairs than the theory of Copernicus and the law of gravity") was to be controlled internationally, particularly with respect to Russia; and (2) how the bomb was to be used in the war against Japan (Germany now being on the brink of defeat).

On the first proposition, the committee was unable to arrive at a clear-cut consensus. Opinions varied all the way from the argument that it should be jealously hoarded as an exclusive American secret, with this country assuming the Messianic role of enforcer of the world's peace, to the opposite extreme where we would immediately take the Russians into our confidence and, with them, deliver the secret into the hands of an international commission under the control of the United Nations.

As one reviews the rationale of these arguments that took place in such tense secrecy two decades ago (to me, there is an antic parallel here to the opening witch scene of *Macbeth*), one is ruefully reminded of how much of its time mankind spends going nowhere on a treadmill. The arguments have not changed, and the dilemma is the same in 1965 as it was in 1945: How shall we control atomic energy? How shall we blunt its power for evil and sharpen its poten-

tial for good? How, indeed, can we save ourselves from immolation
on an atomic pyre that we have built and fueled with our own
hands? These awesome questions have not been answered through
countless hours of international wrangling, bullying, and negotiation, nor through prayer, nor through "peace strikes," nor through
the scientists' blind search for a damper or counterforce against the
atomic holocaust. On this, as on so many stubborn cold war issues,
that evolved in the late 1940's, we are still pumping that treadmill.

On the second proposition, raised by the Interim Committee, a
sharper consensus *did* emerge: that the bomb should be used as soon
as possible against a major military target to force Japan promptly to
her knees. There were both pros and cons to this, of course. Most
importantly, a group of scientists at the atomic project in Chicago,
headed by Leo Szilard, protested vehemently against the debase-
ment of their efforts by turning it to the lethal purposes of warfare.
They also argued strongly against the doctrine of an atomic monopoly, pointing out that the principles of atomic fission were already
known to scientists in many parts of the world. Any effort by this
country to hoard its knowledge of atomic energy, they said, would
only feed the envious and probably warlike determination of other
nations to develop the bomb for themselves.*

Another viewpoint commanding attention was that the bomb
should be employed against Japan, but only by means of a nonlethal
demonstration in the ocean or on a deserted island. There was general revulsion within the committee, according to Secretary Stimson's recollections, against the idea of the mass slaughter that would
result from bombing a populated center. But weighing against this
was the prospect that the conventional ground, sea, and air attack
then being waged against the fanatical Japanese would take at least
another year and possibly as many as one million American and
British casualties before victory could be achieved. One or maybe
two well-placed atomic bombs should, on the other hand, end the
war in a matter of days.

As for the alternative of a harmless demonstration, there were
sound arguments against that, too. To make it effective, the event
would have to be widely billed in advance so that the enemy could
see the awesome blast, or at least know about it and be properly
intimidated. But in the then current state of atomic science, there

---

* Atomic "proliferation" is a greater concern to Washington as this is being written
(1965) than the imminence of atomic war. Besides the United States, Great Britain,
Russia, France, and Communist China now possess atomic weapons.

was no absolute assurance that this primitive device would go off as planned, or that the delivering plane and its crew would not be demolished in the process. Such an eventuality, it was reasoned, would be a mortal blow to the image of Allied invincibility and probably would encourage Japan to fight on more determinedly than ever. It could also, it was believed, cause the Russians, who had promised at the Yalta Conference to get into the war against Japan three months after Hitler was disposed of, to drag their feet.

There was, after all, in that baleful, tortured summer of 1945, just one overriding objective to American world policy: to whip Japan and end the war in the shortest time with the least possible cost in men and money. The debate in the Interim Committee therefore resolved itself in forwarding to the President the following historic conclusion on what to do about the atomic bomb: *"We can propose no technical demonstration likely to bring an end to the war. We can see no acceptable alternative to direct military use."*[6]

The controversy over the moral rightness of this conclusion has never ceased. But it seemed not greatly to trouble President Truman, to whom it was clear and logical that bombs to be used in the war against the Axis had always been the end purpose of this whole gigantic effort.

Thus reinforced, he embarked aboard the *Augusta* on July 7 for his first meeting with Prime Minister Churchill and Premier Stalin at Potsdam. Their basic purpose was to correlate plans for a peaceful Europe (V-E Day had occurred on May 8) and for finishing the war in the Pacific. On the evening of the 16th, Stimson, who had followed the President over by air, handed him, at the "Little White House," in Potsdam a message just received from General Groves in Alamogordo, New Mexico. In strictly homemade code, it read as follows: "Operated on this morning. Diagnosis not yet complete but results seem satisfactory and already exceed expectations." To Prime Minister Churchill's headquarters, the Secretary sent this meaningful paraphrase: "Babies satisfactorily born." Both meant the same thing: The static test in the New Mexico desert had handsomely succeeded. The atom bomb was a reality at last.

Now only three important steps had to be taken before the doomsday bell would be tolled.

On the 24th, President Truman at Potsdam OK'd what amounted to the final orders for the *Enola Gay's* historic flight. Directed to General Carl A. Spaatz, Commanding General, U.S. Army Strategic

Air Forces, and signed by General Thomas C. Handy, Acting Chief
of Staff, the orders read in part:

The 509th Composite Group, 20th Air Force [the atomic strike force]
will deliver its first special bomb as soon as weather will permit visual
bombing after about 3 August, 1945, on one of the targets: Hiroshima,
Kokura, Niigata and Nagasaki. . . . Additional bombs will be delivered on
the above targets as soon as made ready by the project staff. . . . Dissemi-
nation of any and all information concerning the use of the weapon
against Japan is reserved to the Secretary of War and the President of the
United States.[7]

Next was the problem of what and how to tell Stalin, now that the
secret of the bomb was about to unfold itself. Truman and
Churchill conferred anxiously about this. Their dilemma was to
convey to the smilingly treacherous old dictator just enough to head
off his complaints that his allies had bypassed him, but not enough
to reveal the true nature of the weapon. (They put off to an uncertain tomorrow facing up to the ultimate political realities raised by
the bomb.) So, at the conclusion of their formal Big Three session
on the 24th, Truman strolled nonchalantly around the table to
where the Russian leader was chatting with some of his aides.

"I casually mentioned to Stalin," the President has recalled, "that
we had a new weapon of unusual destructive force. The Russian
Premier showed no particular interest. All he said was that he was
glad to hear it and hoped we would make 'good use of it against the
Japanese.'"

Truman and Churchill chortled smugly over their coup as they
left the conference together, blissfully ignorant that the enigmatic
Russian Premier had scored a point in one-upmanship against them.
What he could have said, but didn't, was: "So? I've known about it
all along."

Finally, there was the question of whether the Japanese could be
induced to surrender before the A-bomb was used against them. The
country had already been hammered into near helplessness. Tokyo
and dozens of Japan's other major cities had been turned into
charred shells by the massive fire raids of the B-29's. Its navy and its
air force had been reduced by the summer of 1945 to virtual impo-
tency. Only its army remained strong, and it was known that the
fanatical Japanese soldiery could make an invasion of the Japanese
homeland a costly and long-drawn-out butchery. While there had
been some tentative and ambiguous peace feelers from Tokyo by
way of Moscow, the Allies insisted on "unconditional surrender" as

the sole price of peace. (Churchill demurred over this rigidity, but since the United States was carrying the main burden of the Pacific fighting, he let the President have his way.)

The text of a proposed ultimatum to the Japanese rulers had been drawn in Washington several weeks earlier. Truman gained Churchill's assent to it on the scene at Potsdam; and the assent of Chiang Kai-shek, the Nationalist Chinese leader, by radio. The text contained no hint of an atomic bombing, but sternly promised utter destruction of the Japanese homeland, just as Germany had been destroyed, unless the terms of unconditional surrender were immediately met. The ultimatum (later known as the Potsdam Declaration) was issued on the evening of July 26, and its content was beamed to Japan repeatedly for the next twenty-four hours by the powerful radio transmitters of the Office of War Information on Saipan. Two nights later, millions of leaflets were dropped over Japan from Flying Fortresses. They repeated the substance of the Declaration, but with an ominous new note added. Eleven cities were listed, of which at least four would shortly be picked for total destruction from the air. "Attention Japanese People," the leaflets read, "Read this carefully as it may save your life or the life of a relative or a friend."

It is now known that there was a violent split within the Japanese governing hierarchy at this time in late July over whether to continue the unequal struggle or to give up. The fate of the Emperor and his sacred status, which the Allies had failed to clarify in their surrender terms, seems to have weighed powerfully in behalf of those who counseled a fight to the death. At all events, it was this side that prevailed. Premier Suzuki disclosed the government's official position when he told Japanese reporters on the afternoon of July 29: "I believe the joint proclamation of the three countries is nothing but a rehash of the Cairo Declaration. As for the government, it does not find any important value in it, and there is no other recourse but to ignore it entire!y and resolutely fight for the successful conclusion of this war."

His defiant words, broadcast to the world, stamped "Go" on the flight orders of the *Enola Gay*.

The bomb that exploded a thousand feet above Hiroshima killed upwards of 78,000 people, most of them instantly, which was nearly twice as great as the number who survived with injuries. It demolished practically every house within a three-mile radius of the target zero, or about 99 percent of the city's buildings. The second

bomb, dropped on Nagasaki two days later, was even more powerful. The war with Japan was over before a third bomb could be
made ready.

The precise day and hour on which President Truman said the
fateful "Yes" that launched this millennial weapon cannot be determined with accuracy. It is nowhere recorded in writing, and memories now are faulty. It could have been when the Interim Committee's unanimous report was laid before him on June 1. His consent
then would have had to be relatively tentative, on a "when and if"
basis, for the success of the experiment still had to be proved at
Alamogordo. More likely, the decisive moment was when he assented to the order to General Spaatz on July 24, for at that instant
the point of no return was reached. It must be remembered that
there never was much question in anybody's mind as to what the
goal of the MED was: It was to produce an atom bomb, and a bomb
has only one use. Mr. Truman boarded this awesome train of events
just as it was approaching the terminal, and he showed no disposition to alter its course or schedule. On the other hand, he was as
cognizant as anyone of the bomb's terrifying potency, and Mr. Stimson had done his best to acquaint him with its staggering implications. The President could not have approached that moment of
ultimate decision on July 24—the explicit order to the Air Force to
drop the bomb—totally indifferent to the easier alternative of
procrastinating for a few days. But whatever he may have felt at
the moment, he did not procrastinate, and in retrospect he has no
regrets for his decisiveness. "The final decision of where and when
to use the bomb was up to me," he has said. "Let there be no
mistake about it. I regarded the bomb as a military weapon and
never had any doubt that it should be used."

In support of this decision, Henry Stimson wrote some years
later:

Had we continued [without using the A-bomb] until the projected
invasion on November 1, additional fire raids of B-29s would have been
more destructive of life and property than the very limited number of
atomic raids which we could have executed in the same period. . . .

The face of war is the face of death; death is an inevitable part of every
order a wartime leader gives. The decision to use the atomic bomb was a
decision that brought death to 100,000 Japanese. No explanation can
change that fact and I do not wish to gloss it over. But this deliberate,
premeditated destruction was our least abhorrent choice. The destruction
of Hiroshima and Nagasaki put an end to the Japanese war.[8]

Two decades later, with that special acuity of 20-20 hindsight, it is possible to disagree with that conclusion. It is fully evident now that in July 1945 Japan already was a beaten foe and that the will to resist had about run out. Her peace feelers during that month and earlier were sincere even if ambiguous. Toward the end, they were almost frantic, as intercepts by U.S. Navy Intelligence of code communications between Tokyo and the Japanese Ambassador in Moscow have shown. On the very day that Premier Suzuki publicly scorned the terms of the Potsdam Declaration, the Supreme War Council on which he sat was split down the middle on the question of surrendering. If the Allied ultimatum had suggested a face-saving status for the Emperor, such as was accorded him a few days later in the actual document of surrender, the Council almost certainly would have voted then to capitulate. Sakoh Tanemura, deputy chief of staff for the Japanese Army during World War II, has since said: "The Americans blundered in not guaranteeing the safety and status of the Emperor. Otherwise the war would have been over before A-bombs were used."[9]

This very question was debated at Potsdam by President Truman and his advisers—Mr. Byrnes, the Secretary of State, and General George Marshall, the Chief of Staff, among others. The decision to leave the point about the Emperor vague was a deliberate one, but the reason therefor remains obscure. Had the decision been otherwise, it might never have been necessary to fire an atomic bomb after the one at Alamogordo, even in practice.

Perhaps the atomic millennium had to be born out of the agony of death in any event. Had it not been at Hiroshima, it *might* have been at Washington or Moscow a few years later. But Harry Truman cannot be blamed for having lacked the prescience of hindsight. He made this great decision, as he did so many in his career, forthrightly on the basis of the best information available to him at the time, and cleared his conscience of any remorse. Moralists will debate the rightness of that decision for generations to come, but for the man who made the decision the debate ended when the decision was made.[*]

[*] Historian Samuel Eliot Morison, writing in the perspective of almost two decades, says: "It is evident that the atomic bomb was the keystone of a very fragile arch. Certainly the war would have gone on, and God knows for how long, if the bomb had not been dropped. . . . It simply is not true that Japan had no military capability left in mid-August. . . . If the Emperor had told them to fight to the last man, they would have fought to the last man.—*The Two-Ocean War* (Little, Brown, 1963), p. 572.

End of the War

Being a President, Harry Truman has said, "is like riding a tiger. You have to keep on riding him or be swallowed."

His first few days in office were a time of uncertainty and confusion as he tried to measure his job and as the nation tried to measure him and the catastrophe that had put him where he was. During that initial weekend, in fact, the living President was almost overlooked as a grief-stricken nation paid its last homage to the one who had just died. Harry Truman seemed lost in the crowd on that sun-drenched morning of Sunday, April 15, standing next to the tall, black-draped figure of Eleanor Roosevelt, as FDR was buried in the rose garden of his ancestral Hyde Park home. On the preceding Friday, his first full day in office, Truman had fled almost in desperation to the Capitol for an emotional leave-taking from his old haunts and companions in the Senate. Leaving a luncheon in the office of Senate Secretary Leslie Biffle, he solemnly told a group of waiting reporters: "If you fellows ever pray, pray for me now." On Monday, he addressed a joint session of Congress, promising to continue the policies of his predecessor and imploring the legislators and the American people for patience and understanding. There was a moment of throat-tightening pathos for millions who tuned in their radios on the Capitol that day when, just as the new President began to speak, they heard a hoarse whisper from Speaker Sam Rayburn: "Wait, Harry, until I introduce you."

This was the first full-length view most of the public had had of the man who had caught the scepter of leadership as it fell from Roosevelt's hands. By and large, they were compassionate, indulgent, sympathetic, but hardly reassured. Nor did the one man who seemed best equipped to evaluate the new leader offer much encouragement. Roy Roberts, editor of the Republican Kansas City *Star*, who had watched Truman's career for more than a decade with a measure of professional detachment, wrote that first week in a widely republished article:

What may the nation expect from its new President? For the time being, simply carrying on. The nation may take confidence on that score.

Harry Truman is no man to rock the boat. He is not as cautious as Calvin Coolidge, who took office under somewhat similar circumstances two decades ago. But he has the innate, instinctive conservatism in action of the Missouri-bred countryman. They want to know where they are going before they leap. And they are not fond of leaping just for the pleasure of headlines. . . .

The real significance will be the shift from personal government back to what is called, for lack of any better term, constitutional government. . . . The sheer fact he is [the] average man is probably Truman's greatest asset as he undertakes these new overpowering responsibilities.[10]

Like many conservatives, long and bitterly disenchanted with FDR, Roberts saw in Truman a more pliable sort of fellow with whom the conservative community could do business. The estimate was not entirely based on wishful thinking, for Truman's political profile had not become clearly etched at the time. But the day would come when Roberts would have to take back his bland encomium.

The Truman family moved into Blair House, the Government's guest residence diagonally across Pennsylvania Avenue from the White House, on Saturday, April 14, allowing the Roosevelt family time to gather and remove its belongings. When the President was ready to leave the office that evening, he was startled to find a squad of Secret Service men standing by to escort him on the perilous, one-hundred-yard journey, and not a little bemused to discover that the traffic lights at the intersection turned red in all directions at his approach in order to facilitate his crossing.

His confusion was subtly compounded in the next few days as he struggled, on the one hand, to grasp the issues of the Presidency, and on the other, its managerial reins. There were frequent, long-drawn-out seminars with Secretary of State Edward R. Stettinius, Jr., who seemed to float ineffectually on the tide of great events; with Treasury Secretary Henry A. Morgenthau, Jr., happily pregnant with his scheme for a pastoralized Germany; with the scholarly, avuncular Secretary of War, Henry L. Stimson, and his opposite number in the Navy, the tense and troubled James V. Forrestal. To understand the state of the war, the new Commander in Chief spent long hours in the White House "map room" with two experts whom he revered almost without limit—the Army Chief of Staff, General George C. Marshall, and the White House military adviser, Admiral William D. Leahy. Truman's extraordinary ability to grasp and retain facts, and his willingness to submit to the drudgery of seriously studying long, complex reports, was soon to make a most favorable impression on these aides.

At the outset he had asked the Roosevelt Cabinet and White

House staff to stay with him, but early in that first week he brought in half a dozen familiar helpers who had been with him on Capitol Hill. Among them were Rose Conway, the gentle and efficient spinster who serves him even today as personal secretary; a raucous, back-slapping, wartime buddy from Missouri named Harry Vaughan to be a sort of general factotum and cheerer-upper; and a brashly competent young Irishman, Matt Connelly, who was set up as appointments secretary to stem the tide of fortune-seekers and well-wishers who converged upon the White House, eager to help, to be helped, or just to "say hello to good old Harry."

Jonathan Daniels, a White House aide of that period has recalled:

He seemed all things to all men, and all men including New Dealers and anti-New Dealers, Roosevelt friends and Roosevelt enemies, old friends and new ones, members of the 129th Field Artillery, old-time Pendergast politicians, Truman Committee members, the eager and the ambitious, seemed to expect that he would be all things to them. His insistent modesty at that moment seemed almost designed to help the thinking of those who hoped to be bigger than he was, underestimating the stubborn Middle Border strength behind the modesty.[11]

He held his first press conference on April 17. Around his desk in the oval office, 348 reporters, the largest number on record to that time, crowded shoulder to shoulder. In an unprecedented gesture of good will, they applauded him at the end of the conference. And he addressed by radio the millions of American soldiers and sailors pinned down at battle stations all around the globe, reassuring them that the leadership on the home front was in safe hands. Also in that hectic week of April 16 he signed his first bill (extending the life of the Lend-Lease Act); received his first foreign dignitary, Anthony Eden, the British Foreign Secretary; issued his first Executive Order, seizing the strike-bound plant of the Cities Service Corporation at Lake Charles, Louisiana; met for the first time with his Cabinet; received a delegation of Republican leaders headed by Senator Robert A. Taft, who pledged him their bipartisan support; issued his first veto (of a private bill for the relief of one Ben Grunstein); bought a poppy from 5-year-old Margaret Ann Forde to open the annual fund-raising drive of the Veterans of Foreign Wars; agreed with his legislative leaders to press for an extension of price control and wage stabilization laws; learned that the U.S. 9th Army had been hurled back from one of its two bridgeheads on the Elbe River, and that Russian armies meanwhile had pressed to within 24 miles of Berlin; appointed his boyhood friend, Washington correspondent

Charles G. Ross, to be White House Press Secretary (together, they phoned Miss Tillie Brown, in Independence, who had been their English teacher in high school, to appraise her of the event. "You and Harry have both made good, and I am very proud of you," Miss Tillie told them); and made an impromptu lunchtime visit to his bank at Fourteenth and G Streets, creating thereby one of the worst brief traffic snarls in Washington history (he learned then that the President doesn't go to the bank; the bank comes to the President). Finally, late on Friday night, sitting alone in the drawing room at Blair House, he faithfully wrote his weekly letter home:

Dear Mamma and Mary: Well, the Washington Post had your pictures yesterday morning and the finest kind of statements from both you and Vivian. My press staff said that the smartest press agent in the world could not have written any better ones. I told them that my family all told the truth all the time and that they did not need a press agent.

I have had a most strenuous time for the last six days. I was sworn in at 7:09 p.m. Eastern War Time Apr. 12 and it is now 9 p.m. April 18th. Six days President of the United States! It is hardly believable.

. . . Had to spend all (yesterday) afternoon and evening preparing a five minute speech for the radio for the fighting men and women. It was after one o'clock when I turned in. This day has been a dinger, too. I'm about to go to bed, but I thought I had better write you a note.

. . . Soon as we get settled in the White House you'll both be here to visit us. Lots of love from your very much worried son and bro.

Harry

But the overriding preoccupation in Washington, as in most of the rest of the world, was the war in Europe, now obviously drawing to a climax. The German Reich of Adolf Hitler had been reduced to an ever-narrowing battlefield, blasted day and night by tons of Allied bombs. In the ten months since the Normandy landings, the *Wehrmacht* had been driven back more than 700 miles from its anchor positions on the Atlantic and was now facing overwhelming American and British superiority on its home territory. Germany's greatest industrial resources in the west and her transportation system had been smashed; her civilian population was demoralized and in panic; and her retreating armies were being reduced to guerrilla tactics. On the eastern front, the Red armies in the same period had driven the *Wehrmacht* back nearly 600 miles from its farthest advance into White Russia and now stood within 30 miles of Berlin itself. Vienna was occupied on the south, and the mountains of Czechoslovakia were being sealed off as a possible escape route.

On the day Roosevelt died, Russian and American armies met at the Elbe River, signifying that Germany finally had been cut in two and that her doom was sealed. On April 25, word reached Washington and London that Heinrich Himmler had offered through Sweden's Count Bernadotte to surrender along the whole Western Front, but not those armies facing the Russians in the east. Churchill and Truman promptly rejected the offer and reiterated the Allied demand for unconditional surrender on all German fronts simultaneously. The Russians were not engaged in Italy, so that, after long secret negotiations, the million-man Nazi army there offered on the 29th to lay down its arms, its surrender was accepted by the American and British commanders. On May 2, the world learned that Hitler had killed himself on April 30 in his underground bunker in Berlin. Three days later, emissaries of the crumbling Reich sought permission to come to General Eisenhower's headquarters in Rheims. There they again sought to divide the Allies by surrendering their western forces only. It was obvious that what they feared more than military defeat was occupation of their beaten country by the Red Army and its political commissars.

And here was an instant on which the course of postwar history pivoted. For had the Germans been enabled to concentrate their remaining strength against the Russian advance from the east, the pattern of Communist power in central and western Europe *might* have been vastly different today from what it is. But this very eventuality had been considered by Roosevelt, Churchill, and Stalin at Teheran and at Yalta at a time when the fast disintegration of Nazi capabilities could not be foreseen, and when the war in the Pacific was still going heavily against the Allies. So the proposition was rejected. Now, at Supreme Headquarters American Expeditionary Forces in Rheims, on May 5, 1945, General Eisenhower curtly told his visitors that their conditions were unacceptable. Early on the morning of the 7th—in the presence of representatives of the United States, Great Britain, France, and the Soviet Union—General Alfred Jodl, in behalf of the German High Command, signed his name to the articles of surrender. "I can see no alternative; signature or chaos," he muttered.

V-E Day, proclaimed on May 8, came as something of an anticlimax to the American public, for its advent had been seen and felt for days. It was formally signalized at 9 o'clock that morning, when

President Truman, still less than a month in office, went on a nation-wide radio hook-up to announce:

This is a solemn but glorious hour. General Eisenhower informs me that the forces of Germany have surrendered to the United Nations [this was a calculated overstatement; the UN had not yet been officially born]. The flags of freedom fly all over Europe. For this victory we join in offering our thanks to the Providence which has guided and sustained us through the dark days of adversity. . . . We can repay the debt we owe to our God, to our dead, and to our children only by work, by ceaseless devotion to the responsibilities which lie ahead of us. If I could give you a single watchword for the coming months, that word is work—work and more work. We must work to finish the war. Our victory is only half won.

V-E Day and V-J Day were three months and a world apart. Even before the collapse of Hitler in May, Allied men and weapons were being diverted from the European to the Pacific theater of operations in one of the greatest military-naval concentrations in history. Joint command of the final assault against Japan was vested in General Douglas MacArthur and Fleet Admiral Chester W. Nimitz. It included British naval forces under Lord Louis Mountbatten. As recently as March, the Combined Chiefs of Staff in Washington had estimated that as much as a year to a year and a half would be required to bring the Japanese empire to heel, particularly if, as seemed evident to them, the job would have to be done in a mile-by-mile invasion of the home islands. (The A-bomb was still a scientific uncertainty, and it could not be included in strategic planning.) The cost of such an operation, from beachhead to the heart of Tokyo, was reckoned at a million American casualties and perhaps half as many British.

Allied forces had come a long way back since the humiliating retreat from Bataan in the winter of 1941. In the spring and early summer of 1945 they were safely reestablished in the Philippines, and the scarred and blood-soaked beaches of Okinawa and Iwo Jima were theirs. Guam fell in June after an 82-day siege that had cost 45,000 American and 94,000 Japanese casualties. From air bases in these outlying islands, American war planes by the hundreds flew around-the-clock missions against targets in the homeland, deluging them with incendiaries and explosives with virtually no opposition except from generally ineffective antiaircraft fire. "We are sending Japan back to the Stone Age," said General Curtis LeMay, the Air Corps Commander.

American and British naval vessels shelled the coasts almost at will, and mined the sea approaches so thoroughly as to create a virtually impenetrable blockade. Japan's great cities and once-powerful industrial complexes had been ruined or crippled; the production of weapons had fallen to a trickle; fuel and raw materials supplies had dwindled almost to the vanishing point; 8,000,000 of her people were homeless; and the daily ration of rice and other essential foods had been reduced to 1,500 calories. The offensive power of her navy and air force, which up to only a year before had made her the sovereign-by-conquest of almost half a billion Asians in an arc stretching some 5,000 miles east, south, and west from the main home island of Honshu, had been all but extinguished.

But the Japanese Army was still relatively intact, relatively well fed, and relatively well armed, with some 3,000,000 men in Japan proper and another 1,500,000 to 2,000,000 in Manchuria and the China mainland. It was being held in reserve to meet the expected invasion, and upon it rested the hopes and the stubborn defiance of those in the Emperor's war council who scorned surrender and demanded resistance to the bitter, suicidal end.

The principal belligerents in the war against Japan were the United States, Great Britain, and China. But China was proving an ever more ineffectual ally. By early 1945 the Nationalist forces of Generalissimo Chiang Kai-shek were spending a good deal more time and effort fighting (or dug in against) the Communist armies of Mao Tse-tung than fighting the Japanese, who held all of Manchuria, Korea, Formosa, and a large portion of North China. Thus, to effect the defeat of Japan, the Allied Powers counted heavily on Russia's intervention—that is, on Russia's moving across her Asian border to attack the Japanese from the rear in Manchuria. A binding agreement to this end was made with Stalin at Yalta in February 1945.

Mr. Truman wrote later:

The Chiefs of Staff were grim in their estimate of the cost in casualties we would have to pay to invade the Japanese mainland. As our forces in the Pacific were pushing ahead, paying a heavy toll in lives, the urgency of getting Russia into the war became more compelling. Russia's entry into the war would mean the saving of hundreds of thousands of American casualties.[12]

By the summer of 1945, of course, that sense of urgency was considerably diminished. The promise of the A-bomb all but eliminated the necessity for getting the Russians into the war against

Japan. But by the time the Allied leaders met at Potsdam in July, Russia had already abrogated her treaty of friendship with Japan and had begun secretly to mass an invading army along the Manchurian border. In any event, the whole plan had generated so much momentum by this time that nothing short of a miracle of statesmanship could have altered it. On the day the second A-bomb fell— on Nagasaki, August 7—Russia declared war on Japan and sent her armies swarming into Manchuria. On the 10th, the Japanese sued for peace, and at 7 o'clock on the evening of August 14, in the cataclysmic year of 1945, President Truman soberly announced to the world that history's greatest and costliest war had ended.

Washington erupted with joy. Hundreds, later thousands, massed on Pennsylvania Avenue across from the White House. When the President and Mrs. Truman appeared on the North Portico to acknowledge their cheers, the mob broke through the barriers which, throughout the war, had kept pedestrians to the north sidewalk, and stormed up to the high iron fence. The President, to the dismay and anxiety of his Secret Service detail, walked gaily along the inside of the fence, grasping one congratulatory hand after another. Then he returned to his office, where he called, first his mother, in Grandview, and then Mrs. Roosevelt. "I told her," he said later, "that in this hour of triumph I wished that it had been President Roosevelt, and not I, who had given the message to our people."

As the fruits of victory of World War II were harvested, the seeds of the cold war were already sprouting in the stubble. The hot war had been the biggest, bloodiest, costliest, and most devastating that civilized man had ever contrived. It had lasted five years, 11 months, and 14 days. Fifty-six nations had been engaged—forty-nine of them on the side of the Allies, and seven on the side of the Axis. A total of 85,000,000 men had been brought under arms, and 14,000,000 had been killed or had died, 251,000 of them Americans. This total was more than all the combat deaths in all the wars fought since 1793.[13]

Never had there been so many problems left in war's wake. President Truman had come on the scene just as the shape of these problems was beginning to be discerned. They involved in every major instance the failure of the Allied political and military leadership to properly assess the true nature of the dynamic Communist strategy of world conquest.

Among the legacies that Truman received from Roosevelt was a determination that a *modus vivendi* between the West and the So-

viet Union could be found in patience and tolerance. The argument
ran as follows: Allay Russian fears that her borders were menaced,
or that the democracies were hostile to her form of government, or
that she would be left behind in the postwar march toward economic plenty, and Russia would cast her lot on the side of peace and
freedom. To this end, the Allies at the Teheran and Yalta conferences had gone far in acceding to Russia's concern about having
friendly powers on her border in the postwar European arrangement,
and had eagerly sought Russia's participation in the war against
Japan once Germany was defeated. It was Roosevelt's view that all
these agreements must be strictly adhered to, even when our faith
was provoked by a Russian finesse or by an outright violation. The
attitude was something like that which anxious parents, steeped in
modern child psychology, extend toward a fractious offspring: Be
indulgent about his tantrums, and they will go away.

Truman felt obligated to carry out this policy of Roosevelt's, but
almost from the outset he was assailed by misgivings. Within his
own official family there was a strong element (but numerically in
the minority) that regarded Russia's good intentions with deep
skepticism. Among them was Ambassador Averell Harriman, who
had reported from his post in Moscow during April:

> We now have ample proof that the Soviet government views all matters
> from the standpoint of their own selfish interests. They have publicized
> to their own political advantage the difficult food situation in areas
> liberated by our troops such as Italy, Belgium and France. . . . The
> communist party or its associates everywhere are using economic diffi-
> culties in areas under our responsibility to undermine the influence of the
> western allies and to promote Soviet concepts and policies. . . . The
> Soviet Union and the minority governments that the Soviets are forcing
> on the people of Eastern Europe have an entirely different objective. We
> must clearly recognize that the Soviet program is the establishment of
> totalitarianism, ending personal liberty and democracy as we know and
> respect it.[14]

Churchill shared this skepticism. In many communications, with
both Roosevelt and Truman, he admonished them to take a deeper
concern for the political realities of a postwar world in which Russia
would wield a power comparable to that of the Western Allies.
Later, he was to write in his memoirs:

> As a war waged by a coalition draws to its end, political aspects have a
> mounting importance. In Washington, especially, longer and wider views
> should have prevailed. It is true that American thought is at least disin-

terested in matters which seem to relate to territorial acquisitions, but when wolves are about, the shepherd must guard his flock, even if he does not himself care for mutton. At this time [spring and summer of 1945] the points at issue did not seem to the United States Chiefs of Staff to be of capital importance. . . . Nevertheless, as will not now be disputed, they played a dominating part in the destiny of Europe, and may well have denied us all the lasting peace for which we had fought so long and hard.

We can now see the deadly hiatus which existed between the fading of President Roosevelt's strength and the growth of President Truman's grip of the vast world problem. In this melancholy void one President could not act and the other could not know. Neither the military chiefs nor the State Department received the guidance they required. The former confined themselves to their professional sphere; the latter did not comprehend the issues involved. The indispensable political direction was lacking at the moment when it was most needed. The United States stood on the scene of victory, master of world fortunes, but without a true and coherent design.[15]

It is reasonable to conjecture that Truman did perceive these trends; that even in these early weeks in office his intuition led him to distrust Russian sincerity. It would have taken a good deal more sophistication than he possessed at the time to look beyond the palpable instances of Soviet intransigence that appeared daily before his eyes, to that impalpable tomorrow when, through patient application of the golden rule, the Russian leaders would be cleansed of suspicion and greed. But he mistrusted his own judgment, and the men who might have backed him up, such as Churchill and Harriman, were figures whom he knew but slightly or not at all. On the other hand, the men whom he did know and on whom he was forced to rely daily—Stimson, Leahy, Marshall, and, to a lesser extent, his European commander, General Eisenhower—were obsessed with the military rather than the political implications of the war. They concurred in the Roosevelt doctrine of getting along with the Russians at all costs. Smash Germany and Japan, they argued, and the postwar world will take care of itself. In addition, of course, Truman labored under a sense of obligation to continue in the steps of his predecessor.

For all these reasons, then, and contrary to a lifetime habit, he did not play his hunch. Thereby he lost one of the great opportunities of history. For if ever there was a time when the cold war might have been averted—when the pattern of Communist conquest in Europe and Asia might have been ruptured—it was in those critical three months from May to September, 1945.

The strategy for the conquest of Germany had been laid out in broad generalities at Teheran and Yalta. American and British armor, moving from west to east, would meet Russian forces moving from east to west somewhere in the approximate center of Germany. Their union would cement the destruction of the Reich as a military power. The occupation of Germany was planned in equally broad generalities by the European Advisory Commission sitting in London in 1944. It defined three broad areas of American, British, and Russian control (later a fourth area was carved out for France), with the capital city of Berlin, physically within the Russian sector, to be administered jointly. The arrangement was predicated on military, not political, considerations. Its purpose was more to facilitate the surrender of Germany than to establish a pattern for postwar administration.

But even by the late months of 1944, Russia's political aims in Europe were beginning to show through her military aims. In the wake of her conquering armies in Poland, Czechoslovakia, and Hungary came her political commissars. Now, in April and May of 1945, the Allied pincers was closing on Germany faster than had been anticipated. To Churchill, this held an ominous portent for the future. He foresaw that wherever Russian military power penetrated into Germany and Central Europe, Russian political power could not thereafter be dislodged. In repeated appeals to Roosevelt, and then to Truman, he urged that "we join hands with the Russians as far to the east as possible." By this he meant that the enormous momentum of the Americans and the British on the Western Front should not be slowed down to accommodate the slower pace of the Soviets on the Eastern Front. Even should the Western armies drive deeply into the prearranged Soviet zones of operation, he argued, we should hold these positions for their bargaining value in the post-surrender negotiations with the Russians. In particular, he pleaded that the Western partners press on to Berlin, which late in April appeared as easily within their grasp as in the grasp of the Russians.

But strategy had now become a matter for day-to-day decision by Eisenhower. He halted General Bradley's advance at the Elbe River and then turned all of his energies southward. Berlin, in his view, had become a secondary target, and he left it to the Russians. And as General Patton's forces roared into Czechoslovakia, Eisenhower acceded to Russian requests that the capture of Prague be left to the Red Army. It was clearly Eisenhower's intention to scrupulously respect Russian rights in her zones of occupation as far as the immediate military necessities would permit. To the British, this seemed appallingly unrealistic,* but the American General was firmly upheld by his Commander in Chief. "I could see no valid reason," Mr. Truman said later, "for questioning an agreement in which we were so clearly committed, nor could I see any useful purpose in interfering with successful military operations. The only practical thing to do was to stick carefully to our agreement and to try our best to make the Russians carry out their agreements."

With this quixotic decision, the stamp of inevitability was placed on the cold war. It began with "the German problem," and "the German problem" remained the hard, stubborn core of the cold war for many years to come.

* For a highly revealing, almost poignant, explanation of this viewpoint read Chapter 17 of Churchill's *Triumph and Tragedy*.

CHAPTER 4

◇◇◇◇◇◇◇◇◇◇◇◇◇◇◇◇◇◇◇◇◇◇◇◇◇◇◇

Peace in the World

"Members of the Human Community"

J ANUARY 20, 1945, was a cold, bleak and memorable day. At noon,
several thousand chilled dignitaries and ordinary citizens
were gathered on the White House lawn below the South Portico.
Above them a gray, aging man who would soon die gripped the
lectern tightly and in a voice that was weary but yet vibrant and
inspiring, addressed them in these words:

We have learned that we cannot live alone, at peace; that our own well-
being is dependent on the well-being of other nations far away. We have
learned that we must live as men, and not as ostriches, nor as dogs in the
manger. We have learned to be citizens of the world, members of the
human community.

Franklin D. Roosevelt, in his fourth inaugural address, thus defined the legacy he would pass on in just eighty-three days to Harry
Truman. Roosevelt had not only carried the nation through history's
greatest war; he had also charted a grand design for perpetual
peace, but it would be up to his successor to carry it out. And this
was to prove an infinitely more complex and long-drawn-out task
than bringing the Axis to its knees. For the welding of a "human
community" composed of "citizens of the world"—a world society
founded on Western ideas of human dignity and political freedom—
presupposed the acceptance of certain concepts which some partic-

ipants in that community simply were not prepared to accept. Worldly sophisticate that he was, Roosevelt had not been faced with the profound alteration in the distribution of world power which the war had wrought—a distribution in which Britain and its old European alliance would give way to the counterbalancing force of the United States on one end of the beam and the Soviet Union on the other. A common military foe, Nazi Germany, was the only cement that bound Communist Russia into a wartime alliance with the West. But beyond the military objective was a political objective, and no common ground was to be found there between the Communist East and the democratic West. Even as the hot war for military supremacy was reaching its end, the cold war for political supremacy was gathering headway. Its two major antagonists were to be the United States and the Soviet Union. And Harry Truman, looking not at all like a world statesman as he took his Vice Presidential oath of office on that January 20, was, in less than three months, to become America's Commander in Chief in this new and highly charged conflict.

The keystone of Roosevelt's design for peace was the United Nations, an international "town meeting" which would outlaw war and to which men of every race and nation could look for justice and protection. Its premise was in The League of Nations. Its preliminary outlines were first sketched by Roosevelt and Churchill in the Atlantic Charter, in 1941. It was further defined, with Stalin's participation, in the Moscow Declaration of 1943. It was blueprinted at the Bretton Woods and Dumbarton Oaks conferences of 1944. Concrete plans for its implementation were adopted at Yalta in February 1945. One of Truman's first official acts as President, on the evening of April 12, 1945, was to announce that the organizational meeting to write the UN's charter, scheduled for San Francisco in only ten days, would proceed without interruption.

"I wanted to make it clear," he has since recalled, "that I attached the greatest importance to the establishment of international machinery for the prevention of war and the maintenance of peace. . . . I knew that in a world without such machinery we would be forever doomed to the fear of destruction."

The conference opened in San Francisco's handsome Opera House with solemn and impressive ceremonies on Wednesday, April 28. Representatives of forty-six nations were in attendance—all those who had joined in the war against the Axis. A number of Latin-

American governments had barely managed to get in under the wire; they had withheld their declarations of war until as late as March, and formally joined the conflict then only because it appeared to be the only direct channel to membership in the new international club.

President Truman, in a short address piped in by telephone, set the tone of the meeting by appealing to the world representatives to "rise above personal interests" and create a security organization that would "redeem the terrible sacrifices of the last six years." Anne O'Hare McCormick, writing in the New York *Times,* gave her impressions of that opening day's session in these words:

From the press balcony, these representatives of countries in all parts of the earth looked oddly alike. Less than a dozen women's hats, the turbans of the Indian delegates and the white Kaffiyehs of the sons of Ibn Saud were the only notes of color. There was no buzz of talk, no hum of excitement. . . .

The mood of the assembly was so like the mood of the war—a war without parades, without slogans, without songs. Yet, the drama was there. It was there in the absence of Franklin D. Roosevelt, in the absence of Poland. It was there in the calm clear tones of the new President coming over the air. . . . The fact that the opening act was simple, grave and under-stated added to its impressiveness.

But around the conference table on that opening day there were a few significantly empty seats, the most conspicuous being those of Argentina and Poland. Argentina had been excluded, largely on Russia's insistence, because of her flagrant collaboration with Germany during the war. The absence of Poland was due to more complex and stubborn causes.

A provisional government for Poland composed of representatives of "all democratic elements" in the country had been agreed upon as far back as Teheran and restated at Yalta, to take over until free and open elections could be held after the close of the war. A Polish Government-in-exile, which had been organized by General Sikorski and later was headed by Stanislaw Mikolajczyk, had been set up in London at the time of the fall of Warsaw. Britain and the United States had insisted that this group should have an important role in the provisional government. But it was the Red Army which had liberated Poland from the Nazis, and now it occupied all of the country and the eastern provinces of Germany up to the Oder River. It had set up its own puppet government in Warsaw, and now contended that this regime satisfied the conditions laid down at

Teheran and at Yalta for a provisional government representing "all democratic elements" in Poland. Britain and the United States would have none of this as long as the London Poles were excluded, and so refused to agree to the seating of the Warsaw government at San Francisco. Stalin seemed disposed to pull out of the conference altogether, or at least to cripple it by stalling, unless he could have his way. Thus a nasty stalemate threatened the proceedings even before the first gavel fell.

Of all the thorny diplomatic nettles thrust into Harry Truman's hands when he became President, the Polish question was by far the worst. In it was the very essence of the ideological and political split between Communist Russia and the non-Communist West. It contained the germinal seed of the cold war. The Western Powers depended upon the Yalta agreements as the definition of Poland's status. So, ostensibly, did the Russians, but with the inflexible determination that they would interpret, observe, or ignore such agreements in whatever manner was necessary to reach their goals. Churchill had long sensed this, and it filled him with foreboding. Roosevelt had become reluctantly aware of it shortly before he died. But the Chiefs of Staff, ever fearful of Russia's staying power as a military ally, warned strongly against any political gesture that threatened to disturb the delicate *status quo*. And many of the others around the President continued to insist that the only way to ensure that the Russians would be "good partners in peace" was to be indulgent and tolerant toward their whims.

One who never shared that simple faith was Averell Harriman. Scion of one of America's "sixty families," he had come into public service with his good friend Franklin Roosevelt in 1933, and stayed on to become one of the nation's most capable diplomats and international troubleshooters—a role he has continued to fill intermittently ever since. From his vantage point as America's wartime Ambassador to Moscow, he saw with chilling clarity the cynical, single-purposed direction of Soviet postwar policy. In many reports and cables to Washington, beginning in the latter part of 1944, he had stated his convictions as emphatically and as dramatically as he knew how. But had his views got through to the top policy makers? How ready was the "win the war" clique at the White House to persuade the new President to buckle at this critical showdown over the UN in order to ensure Russia's future participation in the war against Japan?

Upon Roosevelt's death, Harriman felt that it was desperately important for him to get back to Washington as soon as possible in order to put his views about Russia's intentions before Truman. He scarcely knew the man—the extent of his acquaintanceship was having shaken hands with Truman as Vice President a couple of times —and what he did know was not wholly reassuring. So it was with some misgivings that he walked into the oval office at the White House on the morning of April 21 to lay the most complex current problem in foreign relations before a President who had been in office only a little more than a week.

His misgivings were soon dispelled. Harriman himself later recalled:

I had talked with Mr. Truman for only a few minutes when I began to realize that the man had a real grasp of the situation. What a surprise and a relief this was! He had read all the cables and reports that had passed between me and the State Department, going back for months. He knew the facts and the sequence of events, and he had a keen understanding of what they meant.

Before I left Moscow, I had arranged for Mr. Molotov, the foreign minister who was to be Russia's chief delegate to the UN conference, to stop in Washington on his way to San Francisco for a conference with the President. I wanted him—Molotov—to learn from the very highest source that we would not stand for any pushing around on the Polish question. And I hoped the President would back me up.

When I left that first conference with him that day, I knew the President's mind didn't need any making up from me on that point.[1]

Harriman brought Molotov, along with Soviet Ambassador Gromyko, to the White House late on the afternoon of Monday, April 23. Also sitting in on the conference were Secretary Stettinius; Charles E. ("Chip") Bohlen, one of the State Department's leading Russian experts; and Admiral Leahy. When the amenities were disposed of, the President steered the conversation directly onto the subject of the sanctity of agreements among nations. Britain and this country had scrupulously observed every agreement made at Yalta and elsewhere, he said, but did not consider agreement to be a one-way street.

Molotov, with a note of truculence, said that his government had been just as scrupulous.

Well, they hadn't been as far as the Polish issue was concerned, the President said bluntly, and he meant to inform the Foreign Minister here and now that this country would not assent to a seat at the UN table for the Polish government as then constituted. He hoped

Mr. Molotov would convey precisely that message to Premier Stalin.

Bristling, Molotov said: "I have never been talked to in my life like this."

"Carry out your agreements and you won't get talked to like this," the President shot back.

It was on this sharp note that Mr. Truman's first confrontation with a top Soviet official ended. "He got quite rough with Molotov," Harriman has recalled, "so much so, in fact, that I was becoming a little concerned. But I must say I was quite proud of the new President."

It was a brave gesture, but only partly successful. Russia made a pretense of consulting the London group headed by Stanislaw Mikolajczyk on the provisional government for Poland. Russia went as far as to bring twenty of the London exiles to Moscow for talks early in May—and promptly put sixteen of them under arrest for having plotted against the Soviet regime during the occupation. Posts in the new government were given to the other four, with Mikolajczyk sharing the Vice Premiership with a then-unknown Communist Party functionary, Wladyslaw Gomulka.

This less-than-half-a loaf compromise pleased no one—least of all the non-Communist Poles in and outside Poland. But it seemed to be the best deal obtainable at the time, and when the Russians sweetened it by agreeing to drop their opposition to Argentina (for whose admission the U.S. was under mounting pressure from other Latin-American governments), Washington and London capitulated. On June 23, one day before the historic signing ceremony by which the United Nations would be transformed from hope to reality, Poland was admitted into the family of "peace loving states."

Was this the "great sellout" that it is so often alleged to have been? The probability is that it was not—not consciously and callously in any event. The papers that would finally clarify the question are not available to the researcher; they are under lock and key either in the State Department or in Mr. Truman's private possession. What seems to have been the case was that American and British negotiators were under increasing pressure to get some sort of settlement on the Polish controversy before it wrecked the UN. So when the Russians made a token gesture toward accepting some of the London Poles into the Warsaw government—and agreed to give up their opposition to seating Argentina as well—it was concluded that this was better than no bargain at all, and it was accepted. At the least, it could be claimed that democratic elements had gained a foot in the door at Warsaw, which was more than they had had, and with luck they might in time be able to force it a little wider. It is a fact of history, of course, that they did not.

The conference at San Francisco was one of the most historic of modern times. It succeeded, where all previous efforts had failed, to create a viable international political forum and an instrumentality for enforcing peace. That it has not, in two decades, fully lived up to its glittering promises is a good deal less surprising than that it has endured at all, and in relatively good health and repute. In the act of being born, it survived the same stresses and abrasions that have inhibited its growth and effectiveness in maturity—the hostile in-compatability of the Communist and non-Communist worlds.

The conference ran for sixty-three days. There were moments when it appeared that it must certainly fall apart over some stub-born contretemps between the delegates from East and West. At the very outset, Comrade Molotov churlishly objected to the designa-tion of Secretary Stettinius, chief delegate of the host nation, as conference chairman. Having made his symbolic gambit of ill will, he thereupon withdrew it. He made a pointless but calculatedly embarrassing issue of colonialism out of the discussion on the future of the mandated territories. For weeks he refused to yield on the question of voting procedures in the Security Council, insisting against the massed pressures of the major as well as the smaller nations on the right of the Security Council to dictate the agenda for the General Assembly. In all, however, the delegates resolved some twenty-three proposed amendments to the provisional charter. And at noon on June 26, they assembled for the last time in an outward show of satisfaction and good will to attest the completion of their joint effort.

The climactic scene was the auditorium of the Veterans Building. The backdrop to the stage was formed by the brilliant array of the flags of the fifty nations present, draped from gilded flagpoles. For-ward, a large circular table covered with green baize dominated the stage. On the table were two large books bound in gleaming, hand-tooled blue leather. One was the Charter of the United Nations, the other the Statute for the Court of International Justice, the text of each reproduced in the five official languages of the conference—English, French, Russian, Spanish, and Chinese. At the stroke of noon the Chinese delegate, representing the first victim of Axis ag-gression, led the procession of signers to the stage in a rite that most of the world confidently believed would exorcise aggressive warfare forever.

President Truman had flown out to San Francisco for the historic ceremony. When the last name had been affixed—Yugoslavia's—he stepped forward to the microphone. There was a note of unconcealed triumph and faith as he addressed the assembly in his flat, midwestern accent.

The Charter of the United Nations which you have just signed is a solid structure upon which we can build a better world. History will honor you for it. Between the victory in Europe and the final victory in Japan, in this most destructive of all wars, you have won a victory against war itself. . . .

What you have accomplished in San Francisco shows how well the lessons of military and economic cooperation have been learned. You have created a great instrument for peace and security and human progress in the world.

The world must now use it.

If we fail to use it, we shall betray all those who have died in order that we might meet here in freedom and safety to create it.

If we seek to use it selfishly—to the advantage of any one nation or any small group of nations—we shall be equally guilty of that betrayal. . . .

Let us not fail to grasp this supreme chance to establish a world-wide rule of reason—to create an enduring peace under the guidance of God.

The voice was the voice of Harry Truman, but the words were the words of Franklin Roosevelt, distilled through the facile pen of Sam Rosenman. But in this seeming incongruity there was an extra measure of vitality and hope. This was Truman's first address to the world community, and in it the world found reassurance that the completion of Roosevelt's grand design was in the hands of a true believer.

If he was to be the leader of the world community, Truman needed a pilot of his own choice.

Three days after the Charter-signing ceremony in San Francisco, Mr. Truman announced that Edward R. Stettinius, Jr., was being moved upstairs to the post of permanent Ambassador to the UN and that his place as Secretary of State was being taken by James F. Byrnes, an old Senate colleague and sometime political competitor of the President. The departure of Mr. Stettinius from the State Department was generally expected and not widely mourned. His performance in office, and at the UN conference in particular, had impressed many people as lacking in experience and grasp for so exacting a job. The choice of Mr. Byrnes as his successor produced no surprise. There was only puzzlement about the relationship between him and the President. It was an unstable and unhappy relationship, as time was to show.

Jimmy Byrnes, a man of volatile temperament and caustic tongue, was embittered by his rejection for the Vice Presidency at the 1944 Democratic convention. He is reported to have asked Roosevelt thereafter for the State Department portfolio in place of the job he was holding as economic stabilizer. He was turned down on this, too, but as consolation the President unexpectedly asked him to come along to the meeting with Churchill and Stalin at Yalta. Mr. Byrnes had no major role in those deliberations, but he put the shorthand he had learned many years before as a court reporter to good use by making verbatim transcripts of the sessions he attended. Then, some weeks after his return to Washington, convinced at last that there was no future for him in foreign affairs, he stepped reluctantly down from the Washington stage and went home to South Carolina to brood. Two days after Roosevelt died, he was back in Washington and was among the dignitaries who rode the official funeral train to Hyde Park and return.

It was on the ride back to Washington that Truman first suggested to Byrnes the possibility of his appointment as Secretary of State, once the UN conference was out of the way. "He almost jumped down my throat taking me up on it," the President said later.[2]

There were varying motivations for this proposal. First, the new President was ignorant and apprehensive as to all the commitments, secret as well as open, his predecessor may have made at Yalta. Byrnes had been there, he reasoned, and Byrnes should be able to tell him all about it. Second, Truman as a Senator had always stood slightly in awe of the quick-witted, sharp-tongued South Carolinian. He had been genuinely flattered when Byrnes, the summer before, had asked him to put his (Byrnes') name in nomination for the Vice Presidency before the Democratic convention. When the erratic dice of political fortune came up, "Truman" instead of "Byrnes" for that prize, Byrnes was crushed and resentful, and not a little suspicious that Truman himself had secretly conspired against him. Truman sensed this and, as allergic as any man alive to an accusation of disloyalty, felt a compulsion to propitiate Jimmy Byrnes' hurt feelings as well as his own unreasoningly troubled conscience.

That he had, at the same time, some presentiment that the two of them might not be able to pull together in close harness—as, indeed, they could not—was illustrated a few days before Byrnes' appointment was announced on June 30. The President called Olin Johnston, a South Carolina Senator who had long suffered Byrnes' contempt, and apprised him of his plans. He said:

"I'm doing it, Olin, because I think it's the only way I can be sure of knowing what went on at Yalta. But I don't expect him to be around for very long."

That was a poor guess. For a year and a half Jimmy Byrnes remained this nation's foreign minister, spending more time out of Washington than in it. As the President's alter ego at countless international conferences, he supplied the main thrust for Truman's foreign policy. He might have succeeded better than he did had it not been for his tendency to try to reverse his and the President's roles.

An Iron Curtain in the Making: Potsdam

In the emerging pattern of the cold war, few events were more instructive to the new President than the Potsdam Conference. Here at first hand, and not through the eyes of others, he saw an Iron Curtain in the making.

In his first weeks in office, Truman had read, and been deeply troubled by, a long and eloquent letter that Churchill had written to Stalin on April 29, 1945. It had been inspired by a rancorous exchange between the two leaders over the manner in which Soviet occupying forces in Poland, Austria, Hungary, and Bulgaria were imposing Communist regimes on the liberated peoples, and arbitrarily refusing access into those areas to representatives of the other Allies. In the most conciliatory terms, Churchill pleaded for a more forthright and candid attitude by the Russians toward the grand design of a postwar world of peace and mutual understanding. He wrote:

There is not much comfort in looking into a future where you and the countries you dominate . . . are all drawn up on one side, and those who rally to the English-speaking nations and their associates are on the other. It is quite obvious that their quarrel would tear the whole world to pieces and that all of us leading men on either side who had anything to do with that would be shamed before history. Even embarking on a long period of suspicions, of abuse and counter-abuse, and of opposing policies would be a disaster hampering the great developments of world prosperity for the masses which are attainable only by our trinity. I hope there is no word or phrase in this outpouring of my heart to you which unwittingly gives offense. If so, let me know. But do not, I beg you, my friend Stalin, underrate the divergencies which are opening about matters which you may think are small to us but which are symbolic of the way the English-speaking democracies look at life.[3]

The great goals so hopefully defined at Yalta, and brought so nearly within reach by the swift pace of military success in Europe and the Pacific, were being eroded by nationalistic hostility between the conquering powers. The fruits of victory were being shaken from the tree just as they were ripening. It took no great prescience on Harry Truman's part to realize that if those fruits were to be harvested before they spoiled, fate had thrust the responsibility upon him.

It obviously was important for him to get to know Churchill and Stalin face to face. The war on both the European and Pacific fronts was rolling toward a climax. There was a need to assure a coordinated effort for the final victory, and for dealing with the immediate postwar problems of the conquered nations.

Shortly after the surrender of Germany on May 7, Truman called Harry Hopkins, Roosevelt's most trusted confidential emissary, and asked him to go back to Moscow with Ambassador Harriman to see Stalin.

There was a concealed as well as an open strategy in calling on Hopkins. The gangling former social worker, with his blunt and unpretentious manner and his acute political perception, had, over the years, won not only Stalin's affection but his respect as Roosevelt's personal deputy. To have him turn up in Moscow now in a similar role for Truman should convince the suspicious Russian dictator that, though Roosevelt was gone, there was to be no break in the continuity of American policy and objectives. The more obvious part of Hopkins' mission was, first, to go over the stubborn Molotov's head to break the deadlock over UN voting procedures which he had precipitated at San Francisco, and second, to feel out Stalin on the subject of another heads-of-state conference. From Hopkins' mission there emerged the plan for a three-power meeting in Potsdam in mid-July, a proposal to which Churchill had already assented.

The essential purpose of Potsdam was to put in motion the plans made at the Yalta Conference in February. That historic meeting in the Crimea probably had seen the high-water mark of allied unity, optimism, and idealism. As the three most powerful leaders of the world toasted one another at their final banquet on the Black Sea, Roosevelt likened the atmosphere of the future to that of a family; Stalin said that the tests of peace would be no less strenuous than those of war, but that their alliance would be equal to the challenge; and Churchill averred that "the fire of war has burned up the misunderstandings of the past." There is good reason to think that Churchill was speaking from brandy and good fellowship that night. He was not really deluded by the outlook for the future, with Russia's military might already thrusting deep into Eastern and Central Europe. As a world politician of the old school, he leaned toward a reconstituted system of spheres of influence to preserve a postwar balance of power, an idea that was incompatible with Roosevelt's One World concept. But in order not to be a spoilsport he joined in the amenities.

What actually was done at Yalta was this:

Poland's eastern border was to be approximately at the old Curzon line established after the First World War, but she was to get some new territory in the west from Germany in the final peace settlement. A provisional government representing the main democratic forces in Poland was to be installed and to hold power until "free" elections under Allied supervision could be held.

Yugoslavia, where the Communist partisans under Tito had already secured the upper hand, was to have a supervised political settlement approximating that devised for Poland.

Germany's occupation zones were expanded to include France as a fourth power. But how a conquered Germany was to be administered between the time of her defeat and the conclusion of a peace treaty was, after much inconclusive debate, set aside for settlement at some future date.

The *other Axis satellites in Europe* were awarded a vague promise of democracy and free elections.

Russia promised to enter the war against *Japan* three months after the defeat of Hitler. For this, she was promised some substantial concessions in China, about which it was thought best to keep Chiang Kai-shek in the dark for the time being, principally to prevent a leak to the Japanese.

The constituent assembly for the *United Nations* was set for April

25, and membership was extended to the Ukrainian and Byelorus-
sian Soviet Socialist Republics as a partial counterbalance to the
weight of the British dominions and the U.S.–oriented Latin-American nations.

In retrospect, it can be seen that what was wrong with Yalta was
not what was given away to the Russians in secret agreements but
what was not nailed down in open agreements. In the place of commitments there were vague mutual undertakings, stated in hopeful
generalities. What destroyed the mortar in this flimsy structure was
not so much a misplaced faith in Russian integrity as a misreading
of Russia's concept of her manifest destiny. At all events, Yalta's
loose ends and smoldering fuses had to be gathered up and somehow
dealt with. Potsdam was the logical and inevitable sequel.

President Truman boarded the destroyer *Augusta* at Newport
News, Virginia, early on the morning of Saturday, July 7. She put to
sea almost immediately, with the *Philadelphia* as her sole escort. In
his party of fifty-two were Secretary of State Byrnes, Admiral
Leahy, Press Secretary Charley Ross, and a group of specialists from
the State Department and the military services. Twenty unhappy
newspaper correspondents were quartered on the *Philadelphia*, and
subsisted on daily briefings supplied by Ross via radiotelephone.

The President enjoyed his trip thoroughly; it was his first ocean
voyage since he had come home from Europe on a troop ship in
1918. He strode briskly about the deck in a gay sports shirt and
white sailor's cap; ate frequently in the junior officers' and crews'
mess from an aluminum tray; scampered up and down ladders to
examine the ship from propeller shaft to crow's nest; discovered a
distant cousin among the crew; and wrote about it all in breezy
informality to Mamma and Mary.

The party disembarked at Antwerp on the 15th and were welcomed ashore by General Eisenhower, who took the President on a
brief automobile tour and then flew him to Berlin in a C-54. The
"Little White House" was a handsome yellow stucco villa facing a
small lake in the community of Babelsberg, about halfway between
Berlin and Potsdam. The British and Russian delegations were similarly quartered in the same community.

Truman was eager to meet his two opposite numbers, and he was
also a little awed by the prospect. He had planned to call first on
Stalin to allay the Generalissimo's suspicions that he and Churchill
might have been cooking up something behind his back. (This defer-

ence to Stalin's presumed sensitivity, incidentally, was to color much of what happened subsequently.) Stalin, however, was a day late arriving in Potsdam; it developed that he had suffered a mild heart attack. The following day, Churchill took the initiative and came to pay his respects to the President.

Mr. Truman later recalled:

I did not feel I was meeting a stranger. I had seen him on several occasions when he had been in Washington, although I had not talked to him then. We had had a number of telephone conversations since I had become President, and in that way a personal contact had already been made.

I had an instant liking for this man. There was something very open and genuine about the way he greeted me. I liked to listen to him talk.[4]

For his part, Churchill recorded that he was impressed on this first exposure by the new President's

gay, precise, sparkling manner and obvious power of decision.

. . . He invited personal friendship and comradeship, and used many expressions at intervals in our discussion which I could not easily hear unmoved. I felt here was a man of exceptional character and ability, with . . . simple and direct methods of speech, and a great deal of self-confidence and resolution.[5]

Stalin put in an appearance at the "Little White House" the following day. He was so much unlike the image that Truman had carried in his mind—comparatively small of stature, reticent in speech, and with an avuncular kindliness of manner—that the President was somewhat overcome with pleasure and insisted that his visitor stay for lunch. When, back at home months later, he made the offhand remark, "I like Joe Stalin," it was the honest Missourian speaking. But he was never deluded about the yawning difference in viewpoint between them.

The Russians were technical hosts at the conference, since Potsdam and all this part of Germany was in their zone of occupation. They had scrounged the finer homes throughout the area for the best furniture, linens, and tableware available, and had appropriated Cecilienhof Palace, once the estate of former Crown Prince Wilhelm, as the site of the conference.

The opening session was held at 5 o'clock on the afternoon of Monday, July 17, and Stalin, presiding, moved that Truman be named the permanent chairman of the conference. A hundred yards away, behind well-guarded barricades, several scores of reporters representing the international press raged futilely against their exclusion from the palace grounds and also over the fact that they were to be denied even dry, perfunctory daily briefings about what was going on. The wall of secrecy at Potsdam was to remain impenetrable, even to judicious and self-serving leaks.

The Polish dilemma overhung the Potsdam meeting like a black thunderhead which never erupts but stubbornly refuses to go away and let one get on with the plowing. Churchill and Truman were at a disadvantage, and they knew it. Stalin held the trump cards with his Red Army firmly planted in Poland and with a handful of obedient Polish Communists fronting as a "free" provisional government. Moreover, he knew precisely what he wanted for Poland, and the others did not know what they wanted. The extent of their design was somehow to prevent its becoming a captive Communist State, but to avoid in the process an open rupture with Stalin. The issue came up on the first day's agenda. Stalin proposed that all recognition be finally withdrawn from the Polish government-in-exile and that all its assets—some 20,000,000 pounds sterling frozen in British and Canadian banks—and the manpower and equipment of the 150,000-man Polish Army operating under British command, be transferred to the Warsaw regime. Churchill said he was reluctant to "cast adrift" the Polish patriots who had fought so valiantly against the Axis, and Truman said all such steps should be postponed until genuinely free elections had been held.

The debate, frequently interrupted by other pressing issues, dragged on for many days and was tossed back and forth between the heads of state and their committee of foreign ministers.

Where was Poland's western border to be? The language at Yalta had been vague: "The three heads of Government . . . recognize that Poland must receive substantial accessions of territory in the north and west." From the discussions, Roosevelt and Churchill had assumed that the Oder River had been accepted as the western limit of Poland's gain. But the Poles and the Red Army had, by the spring of 1945, already pushed far across the old German frontier, and the Russians said the new lines should rest on the western reaches of the Neisse River. The British argued that this would drive millions of Germans from their traditional homes. The Americans pointed out that ceding almost one-fourth of Germany's most productive agricultural region to Poland would rob the rest of Germany, already faced with famine, of an important source of food.

Who will feed the four or five million Germans whom you will force into other occupation zones by this move? Truman wanted to know.

Let them buy from the Polish farmers, Stalin said blandly.

Using American relief money for the purpose? the President demanded angrily. Not on your life!

The days of wrangling exhausted everyone's patience. The Poles, backed by the Russians, obviously could not now be forcibly deprived of their squatter's rights in Germany. Nor could the sovereignty of their *ad hoc* government be contested as long as they promised eventual free elections, which they unblushingly did. Stalin sat tight in the snug knowledge that he had presented his Western partners with a *fait accompli* which they could not undo.

Secretary Byrnes at last devised a wobbly formula for getting off the hook: The conference would accept the *status quo* as a temporary reality and pass the final solution of the major issue, Poland's western borders, along to the framers of a German peace treaty. Twenty years later, that treaty is still to be framed.

The acrimony and distrust generated in the dispute over Poland carried over into the deliberations about the future of the former Axis satellites, Rumania, Hungary, and Bulgaria. One of the products of the Yalta Conference had been a "Declaration on Liberated Europe." This committed the three Allies to work together to help these States achieve internal stability and democratic governments of their own choosing through free elections. Here, again, an earnest but vague statement of principles was taken by the Western leaders to provide a blueprint for action, and by the Russians to afford a field for maneuver.

As the Nazi forces were driven out of these territories, the Red Army gained a virtually free hand in the initial take-over: They were Russia's neighbors and Russia had suffered most heavily at their hands during the fighting. But in the provisional governments that followed the Nazi evacuation, democratic leaders were jostled about as ruthlessly as were the Fascists and monarchists. Only Communists landed in positions of control. British and American members of the Allied Control Commissions, which were supposed to administer these countries jointly during the transition, were literally frozen out or isolated. When Churchill protested that "an iron fence" had come down around the British mission in Bucharest, Stalin angrily dismissed his complaints as being "all fairy tales."

Much the same pattern had emerged in Austria. Russia had acquired a zone of occupation there that encircled the city of Vienna. But it had been agreed at the same time (at Yalta) that all three Allies would share administration of the capital city, with the precise sectors of occupation to be devised later. Nazi resistance in Austria collapsed in the spring of 1945, and the Red Army moved in. When the British and Americans announced that they were prepared to send representatives into the city, the Russians refused them entry. While the Western leaders fumed and protested futilely over this rebuff (Churchill's previously quoted letter to Stalin was inspired by the Austrian impasse), the Soviets installed a "people's democracy" of their own unique design. They resurrected a 77-year-old former Chancellor of the Austrian Republic, Karl Renner, to head a provisional government heavily weighted with Communists, and promptly extended it recognition. Only then, early in June, did they grant permission to their Allies to send representatives into Vienna. (Actually, Renner succeeded later in putting together a more representative government than did the other Soviet puppets, and Austria's postwar history has reflected this fact.)

Truman went to Potsdam in the belief that the conference would set the terms and start the machinery for writing peace treaties with the former Axis satellites as well as with Germany. In his view, Italy, a principal Axis partner in Europe, was already entitled to be dealt with as a sovereign power. It had switched sides late in the war, it had held elections, and it had set up a reasonably acceptable and representative government under the Presidency of Ferruccio Parri, whose leadership of the anti-Fascist underground stretched back into the prewar years. It remained only, in Mr. Truman's hopeful view, to persuade the Russians to permit a similar resurgence of political free will in the other satellite nations to set the machinery of peace in motion. But the Russians were not to be so easily persuaded to give up the empire they were creating. Italy was to get no special consideration that was not accorded to Rumania, Bulgaria, and Hungary. If Italy was ready for the writing of a peace treaty, Stalin insisted, the other three were ready for full diplomatic recognition.

Truman and Byrnes bashed their heads against this wall repeatedly, with only token support from their British colleagues. Churchill and Eden, with longer memories than the Americans, could not readily forget Italy's "stab in the back" by casting its lot with Hitler. British soldiers had been sacrificed by the thousands in the long march north from Sicily. Nor did the two British conferees share the Americans' faith that democratic institutions could be imposed on the people of the Balkans, where freedom had scarcely ever been known, simply by the device of a diplomatic formula. Moreover, Churchill was bound by an understanding he had reached with Stalin in 1944 (Truman was probably unaware of it at the time) that the Russians would keep hands off Greece if the British kept hands off Rumania and Bulgaria. The Americans' efforts to find a path through all these tangled skeins of strategy and intrigue led Benjamin V. Cohen, a staff member of the U.S. delegation, to note: "Unfortunately, we find that when we agree with the Soviets, the British disagree, and when we agree with the British, the Soviets disagree."

In the end, Potsdam left the future status of the Axis satellites papered over with ambiguities. Italy and Austria would, in time, hack their way through to varying degrees of sovereignty, but Rumania, Bulgaria, and Hungary were left exposed to the inexorable, and possibly inevitable, westward course of Communist empire.

Germany was the principal magnet that had drawn the leaders to Potsdam. The Nazi dragon had been subdued and chained. Now came the problem of how to draw its fangs, purge its malevolent spirit, and domesticate its still great potential energies. Earlier plans to break Germany up into smaller, semiautonomous states or of reducing it to a pastoral backwater, had been abandoned. But from this bridgehead of common agreement, the paths of the three Allied leaders led in different directions. Stalin, understandably, wanted a Germany forever neutralized as a military threat to Russia. But he also wanted, just as avidly, a Germany that would be a powerful forward bastion of Communism in the heart of Europe. Churchill also wanted to crush Germany's war-making potential, but with his long political view he wanted a Germany viable enough to resume its historic function as a counterpoise to Russia's expansionist ambitions westward. Truman, conditioned at the time to think more of Russia as an ally against Japan than as a threat to the peace of Europe, wanted primarily a Germany reconstituted along democratic lines that would not remain indefinitely a dependent on American charity.

Because the Americans and the British were not agreed on their strategy, the Russians sat down at the poker table with the best cards in their hand. In retrospect it is now clear that the American command decision—shared by Truman, Marshall, and Eisenhower —to halt the surging western advance across Germany in the closing weeks of the war so that the Russians might catch up with them from the east, froze the evolution of postwar Germany into its present tortured mold. Had the Western Allies pushed on beyond the Elbe River, had they taken Berlin and advanced as far as they could into Czechoslovakia and Austria, they would, at the least, have had powerful leverage on their side with which to confront the Russians in countless later bargaining sessions.* This was the strategy that Churchill had repeatedly implored the Americans to follow, and as his words are reread today they have a poignantly prophetic quality.

This unfolding peril he had described in a long communication to his foreign secretary, Anthony Eden, on May 4, in which he wrote:

I fear terrible things have happened during the Russian advance through Germany to the Elbe. The proposed withdrawal of the United States Army to the occupation lines which were arranged with the Russians and the Americans in Quebec . . . would mean the tide of Russian domination sweeping forward 120 miles on a front of 300 or 400 miles. This would be an event which, if it occurred, would be one of the most melancholy in history. After it was over and the territory occupied by the Russians, Poland would be completely engulfed. . . . The Russian frontier would run from the North Cape in Norway . . . along the frontier between Bavaria and Czechoslovakia . . . (across Austria) to the Isonzo River, behind which Tito and Russia will claim everything to the east. Thus, the territories under Russian control would include the Baltic provinces, all of Germany to the occupational line, all of Czechoslovakia, a large part of Austria, the whole of Yugoslavia, Hungary, Rumania, Bulgaria until Greece in her present tottering condition is reached. . . .

This constitutes an event in the history of Europe to which there has been no parallel, and which has not been faced by the Allies in their long and hazardous struggle. . . . The Allies ought not to retreat from their present positions to the occupational line until we are satisfied about Poland, and also about the temporary character of the Russian occupation of Germany, and the conditions to be established in the Russianized or Russian-controlled countries in the Danube valley. . . . All these matters can only be settled before the United States armies in Europe are weakened.[6]

* Benjamin V. Cohen, on reading this chapter, comments: "How could we really expect to keep Russia, a major Ally, out of Germany? And what would have been the effect of repudiating the zonal arrangement which we had insisted upon? It must be remembered that three-quarters of Germany's population and resources wound up in the Western zones of control."

There were severe military handicaps to the fulfillment of Churchill's strategy, it is true, and the pros and cons about it would, in the words of historian Herbert Feis, "lead into a book-long thicket." But it is a fact that American planners, from the Presidents (both Roosevelt and Truman) down, remained far more preoccupied with the immediate task of winning the war than with the consequences of victory. Truman, at this early stage and throughout the sessions at Potsdam, was inevitably dependent upon the judgments of the advisers he inherited along with the Presidency. Many of these were skeptical of Churchill's judgment and not a little apprehensive about his probable influence on the new President. Mr. Truman, with perhaps a touch of hindsight, has written:

I could feel with Churchill and fully share his views on the problem that lay ahead. But I could not go along with him on method . . . we were still in the midst of a major war in the Pacific. Furthermore, there was public clamor at home for the return of our troops not going to the Pacific.

I had already indicated to Churchill my intention to live up to the commitments we had entered into with respect to the zones of occupation, and we had no intention of extending ourselves beyond these zones. I took this position after consulting with our military chiefs. Russian tactics and aims were, of course, of much concern to us. . . . But I could not agree to going back on our commitments. Apart from that, there were powerful military considerations which we could not and should not disregard.[7]

It was against this tangled background of ideals and objectives that the Potsdam conferees tackled the problem of Germany. It broke down into three main parts: political control, economic reconstruction, and the payment of reparations.

The political issue was disposed of with relative ease, mainly because it was only sketched out in broad strokes and a minimum of detail. Administration of Germany was to be in the hands of a four-power (including France) Allied Control Council, with each of the occupying powers carrying out the Council's policies within its respective zone of occupation. These policies were to provide for the reformation of the German State through the gradual resumption of local self-government "on democratic principles"; the extinction of National Socialism as a party and as an ideal; political freedom for all non-Nazi groups; and the suppression of all military activity. These agreements had the virtues of reasonableness and flexibility— so much so, in fact, that before the summer was out the Russians, without seeming overtly to be violating the letter of the agreement, had established a Communist regime in their sector and suppressed all other political activity. Today, two decades after Potsdam, the goal of a politically united Germany is more distant than ever.

President Truman offered the conference a broad formula for getting the German economic machine going again. It provided in general for ignoring zonal lines and treating the country as an economic unit; for breaking up the old cartels and concentrations of economic power; and for imposing priorities on production to assure adequate supplies for the occupation forces and to maintain a minimal standard of living for the German people. All these suggestions were subjected to long discussion and compromise. For example: While the Truman formula stipulated that commodities and manufactured goods should flow without hindrance across occupational lines according to the usual patterns of commerce, the Russians, mindful of the great assets they had inherited in the coal mines of Silesia and the vast farmlands of the northeastern provinces, objected. In the end, the proviso was stricken and the problem left up to the Control Council. The eventual result was, of course, that the food and fuel resources of eastern Germany were drained off to Poland and the Soviet Union and thus denied to the rest of Germany.

The question of reparations inevitably became enmeshed with the question of Germany's economic rehabilitation. Which was to have priority? And were reparations to be levied against the total of Germany's plant and productive capacity, or against what was left after supplying the German populace? The Russians were for reparations first, and civilian needs some other time. Stalin, at Yalta, had advanced a figure of ten billion dollars as representing his country's probable war claims against Germany. Now, at Potsdam, he asserted that bargaining should start with, not end with, this figure. Without waiting upon the niceties of any agreement, his troops had already begun dismantling and shipping home to Mother Russia entire factories and other vast stocks of war booty from Hungary, Rumania, Bulgaria, and parts of Germany. Churchill complained particularly that the Russians were confiscating oil refineries in Rumania which were owned entirely by British interests. Stalin said this might have happened in a few instances, since Russia's oil industry had been virtually wiped out by the Germans. But this, he said, was a "trifling matter" over which the conference hardly needed to bother itself.

Later, Mr. Truman observed:

The reason Stalin said this was a "trifling matter" was that he had already obtained possession of the equipment.

It was funny to watch him. Every time there was something like this, where the Russians had stolen the coffin and disposed of the body, he was always very careful to insist that it be settled through diplomatic channels. But where it was a matter of Franco Spain or Yugoslavia, he was very anxious that the matter be put on the table and settled. I saw what was going on.

The argument over reparations seems to have been conducted in a maze of semantics, with no meaningful beginning or end. Britain and the United States did block Russia's demand for the right to use forced German labor and for a flat ten-billion-dollar reparations due-bill, substituting for it a somewhat more rational percentage of existing and future resources. They, themselves, were making no claims for reparations. But they also had to abandon their cardinal idea of treating Germany as an economic whole. There obviously was no way of preventing the Russians from lifting out whatever they wanted in their own zone of occupation, formula or no formula. So it was agreed, in substance, that each power would satisfy its reparations claims from its own zone exclusively, an unhappy compromise that went far toward cementing the ultimate partition of Germany into the mold that exists today.

That most vexing of conflicts between Russia and the West—the question of the right of access to Berlin by the occupying powers—received only glancing attention at Potsdam. It was not then envisioned as an issue in anything like the proportions to which it since has grown.

President Truman seems to have harbored genuine fears when he arrived at Potsdam that the Russians might welsh on their agreement to take part in the war against Japan. This had been covered in what was to be judged, years later, the most notorious of the secret agreements at Yalta.

In exchange for her agreement to enter the Japanese war within three months after the end of the war in Europe, Russia was promised redress of most of the losses she had suffered in the Russo-Japanese war of 1904. This meant the return of the ports of Darien and Port Arthur in Manchuria, control of the Chinese Eastern Railroad, some small territorial gains in the Japanese islands, and a free hand politicially in Outer Mongolia. These commitments, so vitally affecting the future of China, were to be concealed from Generalissimo Chiang Kai-shek until the trap was ready to be sprung on the Japanese. But, in the summer of 1945, Mr. Truman had his doubts about Russia's intention to go through with her bargain. In later years he wrote:

There were many reasons for my going to Potsdam, but the most urgent to my mind was to get from Stalin a personal reaffirmation of Russia's entry into the war against Japan, a matter our military chiefs were most anxious to clinch.

Mr. Truman's military chiefs were, indeed, pressing him hard on this during that summer, even in the face of the growing likelihood that the atom bomb would prove a reality. But he was getting some contrary advice, too. Ambassador Harriman, in numerous personal and written communications to the President, said it would be a lot harder, at this stage of things, to keep the Russians out of the Japanese war than to get them in. Japan clearly was being beaten into submission by the growing ferocity of American air attacks. The Russians knew this, he argued, and had every intention of getting in on the kill and having a hand in postwar settlements in the Far East with a minimum risk to themselves. Navy Secretary Forrestal furnished the President, shortly after the latter's arrival at Potsdam, with copies of intercepted Japanese code messages to Ambassador Saito in Moscow, indicating that Tokyo was ready to accept almost any surrender terms that would preserve some shred of the Emperor's divine integrity. (As in the case of Germany, the United States was insisting upon "unconditional surrender" for Japan.) General Eisenhower added his note of warning against bringing the Russians into the Pacific war, and so did Prime Minister Churchill.

But Mr. Truman had brought his Chiefs of Staff along to Potsdam, and they went promptly to work with their opposite numbers in the Russian military delegation to work out detailed plans for getting a Russian army into Japanese-held Manchuria. These talks went more smoothly than any others at Potsdam. Meanwhile, Stalin and Molotov, in their talks with the President and Secretary Byrnes, raised no problems with respect to political settlements in the Far East that had not already been agreed upon at Yalta. They did, however, offer new assurances of their willingness to cooperate with the United States and Chiang Kai-shek in securing, for the Nationalist Government, political control throughout postwar China.

Mr. Truman thus concluded that any political disadvantages

which might ensue from having the Russians as an ally against Japan
(the Harriman-Churchill thesis) were outweighed by the military
risk of excluding them (the Marshall—Harry Hopkins thesis). The
A-bomb news from Alamogordo, which reached the President on his
first day at Potsdam, precipitously lowered the military advantage
of Russia's intervention to approximately zero. But his decision was
only momentarily shaken by this development. His Baptist morality
would not let him then seek some devious way out of the commitment that Roosevelt and Stalin had agreed upon at Yalta. Moreover,
the machinery to implement the agreement had begun to roll, and
there was no graceful way to halt it.

He and Stalin came to an understanding on the matter during the
first few days at Potsdam, with Churchill's grumbling acquiescence.
"We were at war," Truman has since written, "and all military arrangements had to be kept secret. For this reason mention of it was
omitted from the official communiqué at the end of the conference.
This was the only secret agreement made at Potsdam."

It was on this basis, then, that the ultimatum to Japan was put in
final form, and U.S. Ambassador Patrick J. Hurley, in Chungking,
was directed to get the approval of Generalissimo Chiang Kai-shek
not only to the ultimatum, which was in effect a veiled warning of
the A-bomb, but to the Yalta agreements concerning Russia's entry
into the war. This was accomplished promptly and without undue
difficulty. The proclamation calling on Japan to surrender was issued from Potsdam on the night of July 26. Russia was not a signatory to it, because her intention to declare war on Japan was still
a secret. The swift and momentous sequence of events which followed are already known.

A brief and largely irrelevant footnote to Potsdam is in order
here.

Early in his visit, Truman found it fascinating to examine the war
damage in and about Berlin and to visit with the American and
British troops. His guide on these expeditions was General Eisenhower.

On one of these occasions, when General Bradley was also along,
the history-minded former Artillery Captain began to ruminate
about the place in history of great military leaders. These had been
his heroes, from Hannibal to Pershing, and he knew their careers
and characters intimately since boyhood. And now he had another
to add to this celebrated hierarchy. Impulsively he turned to Ike

and said: "General, there is nothing you may want that I won't try
to help you get. That definitely and specifically includes the Presidency in 1948."

Mr. Truman omitted this incident from his memoirs, but the General did not. He has written:

I doubt that any soldier of our country was so suddenly struck in his
emotional vitals by a President with such a sincere and certainly astound-
ing proposition as this. . . . To have the President so suddenly throw this
broadside into me left me no recourse but to treat it as a very splendid
joke, which I hoped it was. I laughed heartily and said: "Mr. President, I
don't know who your opponent will be for the Presidency, but it will not
be I." There was no doubt about *my* seriousness.[8]

This little tableau was to haunt the President's political life later.
His more enthusiastic partisans tried often to belittle the incident or
even to deny that it happened. Mr. Truman has never denied it, but
he has often admitted to a substantial change of heart since. His
contempt for Eisenhower, the political leader, is as profound as his
admiration for Eisenhower, the soldier.

The conference at Potsdam adjourned at 3 o'clock on the morning
of August 2. It had run for seventeen days. Toward its end, the
British electoral process, reflecting the unrest and impatience
sweeping the world as the tensions of war relaxed, unseated
Winston Churchill as Prime Minister and put Clement Attlee, the
scholarly but ineffectual Socialist, in his place. It was thus that
Attlee's then unfamiliar name was attached to the final communiqué
and protocols of Potsdam, along with the names of Truman and
Stalin.

What came out of Potsdam? The substantive yield was not great,
and the Western leaders knew it, although they could not publicly
confess it. A Council of Foreign Ministers had been formed to carry
on the unfinished work of the consortium, most particularly the
actual drawing of peace treaties for the conquered nations. Poland
remained an ugly gash in the edifice of peace, and the effort to
paper it over with the ambiguous language of compromise was not
successful. The same was largely true with respect to Rumania,
Bulgaria, Hungary, and Yugoslavia, although the prospect of creating truly democratic regimes in those countries was never a wholly
realistic one. But Austria and Italy, where American and British
forces were in firmer control when the war ended, gained reassurance from Potsdam of a non-Communist future. The design for a

German control program worked out by the conferees might have sufficed had its spirit been observed, but the Russians had no such intention, as was clear before the conference adjourned. There was nothing that the Western partners, committed to the rule of good faith, could do except hope for the best. The reparations formula was less than ideal, but it had at least the virtue of preserving most of the important productive facilities in the Western zones of occupation. Russia did come into the Japanese war on schedule. But whether her future role in Asia would have been any different had she not come in is debatable.

A significant consequence of the Potsdam meeting was a hardening of attitudes between East and West that made inevitable the ultimate ringing down of the Iron Curtain. The Americans and the British came away from Potsdam reluctantly convinced that a new menace threatened the peace of the world—namely, that Russian Communism would dominate all of Europe. The Russians, confirmed in their Slavic philosophy that all who are not with you are against you, came away convinced that the West was intent upon depriving her of the fruits of victory. These concepts have not altered in twenty years.

For Harry Truman, only three months a President, Potsdam had been a priceless and a depressing experience. He has written:

As I left for home, I felt that we had achieved several important agreements. But more important were some of the conclusions I had reached in my own mind and a realization of what I had to do in shaping future foreign policy. . . .

Force is the only thing the Russians understand. And while I was hopeful that Russia might some day be persuaded to work in cooperation for peace . . . [he knew that] the Russians were planning world conquest.

I was glad to be on my way home.[9]

CHAPTER 5

◇◇◇◇◇◇◇◇◇◇◇◇◇◇◇◇◇◇◇◇◇◇◇◇◇

Peace at Home

"No Mincing of Words"

WASHINGTON WAS A TUMULTUOUS CITY in the early autumn of 1945. It reflected with burning intensity the nation's compulsion to be done with the war and all its suffering, anxieties, and great and petty inconveniences. The elation of military victory, like a fourth martini, added a jolt of recklessness to the national consciousness. There was a contagious mood of "to hell with duty, let's have some fun." And "fun" meant different things to different people.

To millions of wives and parents it meant "bring the boys back home."

To millions of consumers it meant more beef for their tables, more gas for their automobiles.

To millions of factory workers it meant a boost in wages to catch up with the cost of living.

To millions of businessmen it meant getting free of the shackles of production controls and the cost-price squeeze.

To the politicians it meant a frantic effort to propitiate all these competing clamors at one time. And to Republican politicians in particular it meant riding this irrational wave of discontent to its rational consequence—toppling the Democrats from the seat of national power that they had monopolized for a decade and a half.

But to the politicians at the top of the heap—President Truman and his family of chief advisers and administrators—the sense of "fun" was heavily diluted. The sudden transition from war to peace, they knew, could be as convulsive to the national welfare as the transition from peace to war. The American economy in five years had become a monster of productivity, which, even as the war ended, was roaring ahead under tremendous momentum. To stop it in its tracks—to turn it about and head it in peaceful directions—involved the risk of a shattering collapse. The prospect of millions of jobless veterans and war workers overhung the planning counsels like a storm cloud. The leaders of government in those days, and the President particularly, had first-hand recollection of the melancholy depression years of the early 1930's. Another such disaster now would certainly be fatal to our world leadership; it might also be fatal to our national existence. Only by the most careful management could the disaster be avoided. This would require not "fun" but discipline. The challenge to Harry Truman was to lead an unwilling nation along this straight and narrow path of virtue.

Five years of war had done these things to the American economy:[1]

It had sunk more than $300 billion—a sum inconceivable to the human imagination—into guns, airplanes, warships, atomic bombs, soldiers' and sailors' pay, and the countless other appurtenances of warfare for itself and its allies.

The gross national product (the total of all goods and services produced in the national economy) had jumped from an annual rate of $101.4 billion in 1940 to $215.2 billion in 1945.

We were geared to make guns, not butter. In 1944 factory production lines turned out 95,272 military aircraft as against only 70,000 passenger automobiles. Five years before, the ratio had been the reverse: 3,700,000 autos, 6,000 airplanes.

Farmers harvested 813,000,000 bushels of wheat the year the war began; in its last year their yield was 1,123,000,000 bushels.

A total of 16,353,000 men had been drawn out of jobs and schools and put into uniform. On V-J Day there were still 12,123,000 in the Armed Forces, and the civilian labor force was at an all-time high of 53,140,000.

Average weekly earnings had almost doubled in five years, from $24.20 to $44.39, and the 48-hour work week was standard. Scarcities plus price controls had held a lid on living costs, with the result that at war's end there was an unheard-of nest egg of $136.4 billion of personal savings in banks and government bonds itching to be spent.

And therein lay the hot fuse of a disastrous inflation—too much money bidding for too few houses, refrigerators, automobiles, overcoats, nylon stockings, sirloin steaks, steel girders, plumbing fixtures, and just about everything else. A classic economic theorem reads: Abundant dollars chasing scarce commodities equals spiraling prices; *ergo,* boom and bust.

In mid-August the director of the Office of War Mobilization and Reconversion, John W. Snyder, put a report on Mr. Truman's desk that charted the dangers ahead. It said:

The outlook for this peacetime victory [on the home front] is bright but it will not be won easily or immediately. There should be no mincing of words. The sudden termination of the major portion of war contracts will cause an immediate and large dislocation in our economy. Our nation will undergo the shock of considerable but temporary unemployment (five million within three months, eight million by next spring). In a sense, we have exchanged lives which would have been lost in battle for sharp unemployment at home. It is a very welcome swap, but . . .

The report was a detailed strategic blueprint for easing the national economy down from a wartime peak to a peacetime plateau. There would be some slippages and rockslides in the process, but by careful management the casualties could be held to tolerable limits. The steps consisted essentially of a *gradual* relaxation of controls over production, wages, and prices until supply and demand in the starved consumers' marketplace could be brought into reasonable balance. The estimated time required was eighteen months.

On August 18 President Truman put most of Mr. Snyder's detailed recommendations into effect through an Executive order. It became known as the "hold-the-line order." Then, on September 4, he called Congress, which had adjourned in July, back into special session. He staggered the lawmakers with a 16,000-word message (only Theodore Roosevelt had produced a longer one) containing a 21-point program of domestic legislation. His program called for immediate statutory underpinning for some of his reconversion directives (several of the stabilization agencies were to expire automatically six months after the end of the war) and the initiation of basic social and economic reforms reaching far into the future. Among his recommendations were proposals for a full year's extension of the War Powers and Stabilization acts; a sweeping reorganization of the executive branch of the government; enactment of "full employment" and "fair employment practices" bills; federal control of the unemployment compensation program and an increase from

40 cents to 65 cents in the minimum wage; a housing program aimed at 15,000,000 new homes in ten years; and a vast extension of natural-resources development. As sweeteners, he included a modest tax reduction and a boost in congressional pay from $12,500 to $20,000 annually. Though the phrase had not been coined at the time, Mr. Truman laid down in this message to Congress in the late summer of 1945 the basic pattern of the Fair Deal.

There was a roar of protest from Republicans and from business leaders generally. Joe Martin, House Minority Leader, groused: "Not even President Roosevelt asked for so much at one sitting. It's just a plain case of out-dealing the New Deal." And his politically minded deputy, Indiana's Charley Halleck, proclaimed: "This is the kick-off. This begins the campaign of 1946." Business columnist Leo Wolman, surveying the "hold-the-line order" and the legislative program as parts of a whole, wrote in the Washington *Post* that they contained "the most far-reaching collection of economic policies ever promulgated by a public authority in the United States in peace time. It is hard to see how some of these policies can be dropped within any reasonable period of time." In conservative eyes, Truman was now revealed as not only determined to carry on in the social-welfare tradition of his predecessor, but, what was worse, also scheming to use his wartime economic powers to perpetuate the government's control over business.

This was the hostile climate in which the new President was to wage the first of his two major battles to secure peace at home.

Hold That Line: Prices

The battle to "hold the line" against inflation was essentially a battle over the Office of Price Administration.

OPA was the keystone of the whole cluster of special boards and bureaus created, beginning in 1941, to channel the total productive energy of the nation into the war effort—men, raw materials, factories, fuel, transport, food, medicines, wearing apparel, consumer credit, rent, cigarettes—everything that goes into the making of a national economy. These agencies had proliferated like mushrooms in a new lawn. They sprang suddenly into being to meet a newly discovered emergency and disappeared almost as rapidly, usually by amoeba-like division or by merger with still another of its kind.

They were peopled by tens of thousands of eager, confused, hastily recruited workers (the Federal civilian payroll tripled between 1940 and 1945), who inhabited scores of dilapidated "tempos," warehouses, and hastily evacuated apartment houses all over Washington, and throughout the nation as well.

Rules and regulations, each with the force of law, were spewed forth in a paper torrent—on wage levels, hours of work, and the right to strike (prohibited); on the allocation of steel, rubber, chemicals, electric power ("dimouts" were common in many cities), building materials, newsprint, and thousands of other commercial products; on the prices at which virtually everything was to be sold, from pig iron to pork chops; and on the quantity that any purchaser, from General Motors to Mrs. Grundy, could buy. To call the roll on only a few of these emergency bureaucracies is to evoke memories of the hectic war years on the civilian front: War Manpower Commission, War Production Board, Solid Fuels Administration, Office of Economic Stabilization, Office of War Mobilization and Reconversion, and, of course, OPA.

The OPA was the most familiar of all, for its ubiquitous hand (and the effort to dodge it) was a part of everyone's daily experience. It had the impossible task of rationing the supply of some eight million different commodities and services among the civilian population and setting the prices at which they could be sold. Its rent controls covered more than 15,000,000 hotel rooms, apartments, and houses. It devised a new currency—red, green, and other types of ration stamps—without which the coin of the realm was almost worthless. Seventy-nine cents and five red stamps would buy a pound of medium-grade sirloin, provided you could find a store that had sirloin. Or you could pay $2 and no stamps to a shady black marketeer, and run the risk that both of you would go to jail. At its peak, around V-E Day, OPA had 73,000 employees and an office in every city and hamlet in the land. It issued a total of 130,000,000 books of ration stamps to people who queued up, with varying degrees of impatience, for as much as half a day for their turn.

It was the ultimate in regimentation ever imposed on the American public. Nobody liked it. It inspired a devious, illicit sort of gamesmanship not unlike that of the prohibition era, with black marketers taking the place of the bootleggers. But the majority of people went grudgingly along, because they knew it was the only sane course to follow. The testament of OPA is read in the fact that consumer prices rose only 30 percent over their 1939 levels in the five years of World War II. In the three years of World War I, with no equivalent of OPA on the statute books, prices shot above 100 percent and the word "profiteer" entered the vocabulary.

But why price controls in peacetime?

Thousands of shopkeepers, merchants, landlords, manufacturers, and others in the business community grew apoplectic asking the question after V-J Day. Millions of consumers with money clenched in their fists were figuratively storming business doors, willing to pay $5 for a pair of $1.98 nylons, $20 for a recapped auto tire, or a $100 "bonus" for the privilege of renting a $75 apartment. Not only were the inventories of most consumer goods already low, but thousands of manufacturers and producers held back new supplies from the market in the hope of pressuring the government into granting them higher price ceilings, or abandoning controls altogether. Stock growers went on strike in the hope of forcing a rise in beef and pork prices. A swelling, angry chorus of trade association executives proclaimed OPA a "socialistic" bottleneck that was strangling production, employment, and the very heart of the free enterprise system. Drop all controls, they said, and the "natural forces of the marketplace" will soon produce abundance and low prices. These voices found a ready echo in Congress, with Senator Taft, that stern apostle of Republican righteousness, wielding the baton.

Even within his own administration, Harry Truman was caught in a crossfire of conflicting advice. His reconversion director, John Snyder, who viewed the world through the coldly pragmatic eyes of a banker, urged a breaching of the price line here and there where the pressures were most intense. His OPA director, Chester Bowles, whose businessman's *bona fides* were the equal of Snyder's but who wore the "stigma" of a New Dealer, urged the President to stand firm. Breach the line at one point, Bowles said, and the whole anti-inflation front would topple like a line of dominoes.

In February 1946 Snyder made an end run around Bowles to give the steel companies a $5-a-ton increase in prices, which they had been demanding in exchange for an 18½-cents-an-hour wage boost with which to get steel workers, who had gone out on strike, back to the furnaces. Bowles, furious, handed in his resignation. The President cooled him off by reviving the almost-expired Office of Economic Stabilization—a wartime superagency with somewhat ambiguous powers over both prices and production—and moving the disconsolate Bowles upstairs to be its director. Mr. Truman glossed over the steel pact as being no more than a "bulge in the line," and

said that the fight to hold firm on prices and wages would continue
without abatement. To replace Bowles at OPA, he reached into the
Federal Communications Commission for Chairman Paul A. Porter,
a handsome, bustling lawyer-bureaucrat with a demonstrated knack
for getting along with Congress. But the shuffling of manpower in
the economic agencies did little to relieve the dilemmas and conflicts the President faced.

Congress, before adjourning its 1945 special session at Christmas,
granted a grudging six-months reprieve to OPA, which otherwise
would have gone out of existence at midnight on New Year's Eve.
This threw the major battle over price controls into the new Congress which assembled on January 14, 1946. In his State of the
Union message, the President asked for a full additional year's authority to regulate prices and to ration scarce commodities, promising to relax these controls, item by item, as supply and demand
leveled off. Bills to accomplish this were introduced in both Houses
in February. The committee hearings, which went on for weeks
thereafter, provided one of the greatest carnivals of mass lobbying
and political manipulation Washington had ever seen.

The opposition forces in the Senate were under the skilled guidance of Taft and Kenneth S. Wherry, the brassy Nebraska under-
taker who had recently unseated the veteran liberal George Norris;
and in the House, under John Taber and Charles Halleck. Behind
them were the massed forces of business as represented by the U.S.
Chamber of Commerce, the National Association of Manufacturers,
and scores of specialized trade organizations. Day after day dozens
of the nation's top industrialists, merchandisers, and bankers paraded
across the witness stand in the Senate's marbled Caucus Room.
Their statements were backed up with charts, statistics, and the
testimonials of bankrupt businessmen to drive home the evils of a
regimented economy.

Away from Washington, scores of business groups held conventions and protest meetings and deluged Congress with resolutions
denouncing OPA. Housewives, doctors, teachers, and ministers were
proselytized through elaborate "educational campaigns" to do the
same thing. Millions were spent on newspaper, magazine, and radio
advertisements urging people to write their Congressmen to vote to
"strike the shackles from American business" and to "save the free
enterprise system." It was the most massive and concerted campaign
by the business community since the assault on the National Recovery Administration (NRA) ten years earlier.

The field commanders for the administration were Bowles, now director of Economic Stabilization, and Porter, who had succeeded him at OPA. Bowles, as the senior officer, led the troops in defending the administration's cause before the predominantly hostile committeemen. A hulking, erudite Yale man with an engrossing quirk of talking out of the side of his mouth, he had made a fortune in advertising before the war and then turned with the passion of a New Deal dogmatist to government service. He had run the OPA for two years as though it were composed of equal parts of economics and social service. Now he was engaged in what became almost a holy crusade to protect the defenseless consumer against the greed and avarice of "big business." Marshaled behind him were most (but by no means all) of the Cabinet, the full research and publicity resources of the government, scores of top labor leaders and spokesmen for consumer groups, women's clubs, and *ad hoc* committees of workers, mothers, housewives, whatnot. More passionate but less well organized and financed than the business lobby, they employed many of the same frenetic techniques in defense of the OPA.

Rarely has Washington seen such a propaganda battle as raged on through the late winter and into the spring of 1946. The following eyewitness account from the New York *Times* of April 20 gives an idea of what it was like:

A spectacle reminiscent of the late pre-war months when pacifist agitation reached its dizziest heights occurred in Washington this week when more than a thousand housewives, gathered from all parts of the country, marched up Capitol Hill to buttonhole protesting members of Congress and demand a full year's extension of OPA "without crippling amendments." . . .

[The demonstration] served to emphasize that the fight over OPA, in and out of Congress, has reached proportions of bitterness, stridency and obfuscation which have not been matched in years. . . .

The "March of the Housewives" earlier this week was the climax of but a single episode in a [consumers'] crusade. . . . The NAM has spearheaded the fight against OPA with the [equally] enthusiastic assistance of associations representing the meat industry, retail trade, real estate and others. . . .

As the battle has grown each side has became progressively more voluble, they have started calling each other names, and a few blows have been struck below the belt. Those who have watched the fight from the ringside are convinced that reasoned conviction ceased to be a factor after the first couple of rounds.

Mr. Truman had told Congress in January that orderly planning made it necessary that he have a new OPA bill by April 1. It was late in June—one week before OPA's authority would expire—when a thoroughly mangled compromise of the original measure was laid on his desk. It did provide for a full year's extension, but it included a tangle of "crippling amendments" aimed squarely at undercutting effective enforcement. The most drastic was the so-called "Taft amendment," which stipulated that OPA should issue no new price schedule which did not reflect a manufacturer's profit on each item covered—manifestly an administrative and bookkeeping monstrosity. Chester Bowles handed in his resignation as Economic Stabilizer, and this time made it stick. "Clearly," he told the President, "I cannot remain here to administer the inflationary bill which Congress has presented for your signature."

Mr. Truman's dilemma was acute. If he signed the bill, he would be saddled with the responsibility for checking inflation but would be deprived of the tools to do it with. If he did not sign it, all price controls would go out of the window at midnight June 30—only a week away—and inflation would pour in. He called his Cabinet into special session on the morning of Friday, the 28th. He was urged to sign the bill as "better than nothing" by every one except Henry Wallace, the Secretary of Commerce, and Julius Krug, at Interior. They held out for a veto.

That afternoon, Alben Barkley, his Senate Majority Leader, and Sam Rayburn, Speaker of the House, came to see him. In the Cabinet room, next door, Porter and Clark Clifford (a new addition to the White House staff) were writing a draft of a veto message which they hoped, but did not much believe, they could persuade the President to adopt. Mr. Truman called them in to listen to the report of the legislative leaders. At the end of half an hour, the kindly Barkley, who had been a mentor to Truman for ten years, walked around the desk and put his hand on the President's shoulder.

"Harry," he said, "you've got to sign this bill. Whether you like it or not, it's the best bill we can get out of this Congress, and it's the only one you're going to get."

The President's face was drawn, his lips thin and tight as he bade his visitors good-bye. "We'll see, Alben; we'll see," he said noncommittally. As he returned to his desk, he spied Porter and Clifford, as if for the first time.

"You heard all of that?" he asked them.

"Yes, Mr. President," Porter said haltingly. "And I really feel I ought to tell you that if you do sign this bill, I don't feel I could honestly stay on as OPA administrator."

The thin lips spread in the familiar, puckish smile.

"What the hell makes you think I'm going to sign it? You fellows are writing a veto message, aren't you? Well, get to it. And I want a thirty-minute speech to go on the radio with tomorrow night to tell the people *why* I vetoed it."

Save for a few death rattles, that was the end of OPA as an effective instrument for controlling prices. Truman had lost the fight to "hold the line" against inflation, but he came out of the battle with some medals on his chest. Two years later, when he would be stumping the country for reelection, millions of common folk were to look at those dusty medals and remember how he had won them. OPA was to live on as a symbol, if not much of a reality.

After the veto, prices soared just as Truman had predicted they would. Veal cutlets in New York went from 50 cents to 95 cents a pound in the first few days, and milk from 16 cents to 20 cents a quart. Now it was consumers who went on strike. In Princeton, New Jersey, housewives banded together in "The Militant Marketers" to boycott food shops with inflated prices. In mid-July every production line in Detroit shut down for a day while thousands of auto workers swarmed into Cadillac Square "to terrorize the profiteers." Congress, feeling the hot wind on its neck but still not converted, whipped through a new price control bill in August. It had been stripped of the "Taft amendment," but in some ways it was even flimsier than the bill that had been vetoed. Truman, feeling that he had made his point on where responsibility for high prices lay, let the new bill, with all of its Republican contrived defects, become law. But the hiatus had wrecked the price control machinery. About all that was left for OPA, now that it had little authority to *control* prices, was to *decontrol* them officially.

This was made emphatic late in October when the President, yielding to the deafening public and political clamor over meat shortages (the midterm election campaign was under way), ordered all price controls over beef dropped. This was less a retreat than a strategic withdrawal. Republicans, lining up with the striking cattlemen, promised they would make the decontrol of beef the first order of legislative business in the new Congress, in which they said they would have a majority. Truman knew he would not have the votes to block such a move, so he beat them to the punch—a week before the election. Thus, the last major battlement in the price line was abandoned. OPA thereupon became, in Porter's irreverent mind at least, the "Office for Cessation of Rationing and Priorities," or, more pointedly, OCRAP.

In a few months OPA, unloved and unmourned at the end, would go out of business for good. One December day, as Porter sat at his desk in the old Census Building from which he presided over this bleak dissolution, he was handed a White House envelope. Inside was a scrap of yellow paper torn from the United Press news ticker. It was a routine three-line report noting that his office that day had abolished, among scores of other items, price controls on Hawaiian sleigh bells and canned octopus. Beneath it in a familiar blue-ink scrawl was this personal message:

"Great work, men. Decisions like this will carry us to the top. —H.S.T."

Hold That Line: Wages

It was principally on the urging of organized labor that Harry Truman reached the Vice Presidency (and thence the White House). But before his first year as President was out, he was locked in one of the bitterest battles with labor in history. Truman knew well how vital to his program and to his own political survival was the backing of such titans as John L. Lewis of the miners, Philip Murray of the steel workers, and A. F. Whitney of the railmen, among others. But when they tried to buck him in the midst of his struggles with reconversion, he took them on in a series of bare-knuckle encounters such as the country had rarely seen. The verdict was not always clear-cut, but he scored at least one knockout and a long-count decision in the others.

As in other great encounters during his Presidential career, it was Truman's fate to collide with labor at a historical peak in its march to power. Its Magna Carta—the 1935 Wagner Labor Act, which set labor on the road to political and economic potency—had been in effect only about five years when the war broke out. The unions' enormous energies were immediately suppressed, like a boiling tea-kettle with the lid held down, by the War Labor Act of 1942 and the "little steel formula," which granted only minimal and grudging wage adjustments. Now, five years and a war later, this pent-up force was seeking release. Labor saw its postwar goal as an equal voice in the national dialogue with organized business. It felt that it had been discriminated against in the application of wartime controls as compared with businessmen and farmers. It wanted not only a bigger bite out of the postwar pie, but compensation for past deprivations as well. Coupled with these bread-and-butter aims was the larger vision that labor's moment of destiny was at hand: that, as it regained its freedom of action, it would start out on a higher plateau of power and influence than it had ever occupied before.

Concomitantly, many business leaders took the view that if the forward thrust of organized labor was ever to be checked, the time was now. Late in 1945 a small, select group representing steel, motors, food processing, and the electrical industry met secretly in New York with Ira Mosher, then president of the NAM, to pledge that they would fight to the mat before yielding to the rising tide of labor's demands. Truman, a few weeks earlier, had alarmed and angered the business community by proposing that management should open its books in collective bargaining as a means of determining a company's ability or inability to meet a union's contract demands. The businessmen responded with a roar that this was an attack at the very vitals of the free enterprise system. In a sense it was, and Mr. Truman, victimized by bad advice and his own snap judgment, quickly backed away from his proposal. But the businessmen were convinced that they now faced a double enemy—labor *and* government—and they locked arms for a showdown.

Truman was in the middle of a fight for which he had no taste, but he had no intention of walking away from it. His political interests and his native philosophy predisposed him in general toward labor's point of view. But it was equally a part of his philosophy that labor was not a sacred cow with special privileges and immunities unenjoyed by the rest of society, and when it kicked over the traces of public responsibility, it was as subject to the lash as business or anybody else. Truman has said:

My attitude toward labor has consistently been one of sympathy and support. I was deeply aware of the serious problems that were certain to confront labor when the war came to an end and in the period of industrial reconversion that followed. But it was also my responsibility as Chief Executive to see that the public was not injured by private fights between labor and management or among the unions themselves.[2]

The nub of the controversy was this: Should management be permitted to raise prices in order to compensate for the wage increases demanded by labor? Management obviously said Yes. The administration said No, except for unusual hardship cases which the government would mediate. Profits accumulated in wartime, it argued, were in most cases adequate to meet "reasonable" wage demands. Labor sided with the administration in theory, but set out pragmatically on its own to wring the most it could out of each employer. It had some extra weaponry on its side, for, while management was caught under the statutory price ceiling, labor's right to strike had been restored through expiration of the War Labor Act.

With this high-octane seasoning, the labor-management pot came to a boil late in 1945. The dire forecasts of massive unemployment had not materialized. The highest it reached in the twelve months after V-J Day was a shade over three million. But wave upon wave of strikes shut down one major segment of industry after another as workers battled management for peacetime wages to match their wartime earnings and for pensions, welfare funds, union security, and other fringe benefits. As the new year of 1946 opened, 900,000 workers, led by Walter Reuther's auto workers, were already on strike. Within weeks they were followed by 700,000 steel workers, 263,000 packinghouse workers, 200,000 electrical workers, 50,000 communications workers. Picketers battled police before the Chicago stockyards; overturned and burned the autos of white collar workers trying to get to their offices at the big General Motors plant in Detroit; hurled stones through the windows of an electrical plant in St. Louis. Never before had the nation been faced with such a workers' revolt. The year was to register a total of 116,000,000 mandays of work lost due to strikes, which was three times higher than it ever had been before (and twice as high as in any year since then). In February, an even more menacing prospect darkened the picture—a threatened walkout by the 400,000 soft coal miners and a general strike on the nation's railroads.

Truman's battle with the miners and the railmen erupted simultaneously, but the rail strike was the first to reach a showdown.

Months of fruitless negotiation between the twenty powerful rail brotherhoods and railroad management reached a final impasse on April 18. An arbitration board had proposed to settle the unions' demand for a $2.20-a-day wage increase at $1.28 and to defer decision on work rules for a year. The carriers accepted and the unions rejected the proposal. Eighteen of the brotherhoods agreed to further negotiation, but the Brotherhood of Locomotive Engineers, headed by Alvanley Johnston, and the Brotherhood of Railroad

Trainmen, whose president was A. F. Whitney, said they were
through with negotiation and called a strike of their members in
thirty days—for May 18.

Both Johnston and Whitney, paunchy, shrewd old veterans of the
labor wars going back to the turn of the century, were old political
friends of the President. They had given him a boost in his 1940
campaign for reelection to the Senate and were among his strongest
backers for the Vice Presidential nomination. Up to the time of the
impasse on April 18, their defiance of Truman's arm's-length effort
to compose their differences with the carriers had been conducted in
good spirits. Now their attitude was to stiffen in cold hostility.

The President's mediator in the beginning had been his Labor
Secretary, Lewis B. Schwellenbach, an old Senate crony and former
judge in the State of Washington, who was distinguished mainly by
his amiable ineptitude. To strengthen Schwellenbach's hand, when
the going began to get rough, the President had recruited John R.
Steelman, chief of the Conciliation Service, and put him on the
White House staff as a "labor consultant." Steelman, a horse of a
man weighing well over two hundred pounds and with energy to
match, had the scrubbed, bright-eyed appearance and the brisk
geniality of an Eagle Scout. He knew the leaders of the labor movement and the devious maneuverings of the bargaining table in a way
that Schwellenbach could never match.

With the collapse of bargaining negotiations in April, President
Truman took the rail dispute into his own hands and put Steelman
to work on the problem as his personal representative. Weeks of
consultation and wheedling followed, but to no avail. On Wednesday, May 15, three days before the strike deadline, the President
summoned the management representatives and the leaders of the
twenty brotherhoods to his office. He talked to them like a Dutch
uncle, and when it was over found that leaders of eighteen of the
unions were willing to settle on the basis of the $1.28 arbitration
award. But not Whitney and Johnston. Between them, they could
bring every wheel on the railroads to a stop, and that was what they
proposed to do. Peering coldly through his thick glasses at his two
old friends, the President said:

"If you think I'm going to sit here and let you tie up this whole
country, you're crazy as hell."

"We've got to go through with it, Mr. President," Whitney said.
"Our men are demanding it."

Truman got up from his desk, ending the conference. "All right,

I'm going to give you the gun. You've got just 48 hours—until Thursday at this time—to reach a settlement. If you don't I'm going to take over the railroads in the name of the government."

By now, an angry uproar from Congress and the press was arising from all across the country. Lewis had already slowed the flow of coal to a trickle, causing a shutdown of thousands of factories and a resumption of wartime "dimouts" in many cities. Now the threat of paralysis in the transportation system seemed intolerable.

When the Thursday deadline came without a break in the dead-lock, Truman called the railroad leaders again to his office to watch —and to be on public view to the news photographers—as he signed an Executive order carrying out his threat of seizure of the railroads. Whitney and Johnston, bending only slightly to the winds of protest—much of it now generated by their brethren in the other rail unions—grudgingly agreed to postpone their strike for five days, but not an instant longer. That made the new and final dead-line 4 o'clock on the afternoon of Saturday, May 25. On Thursday, Steelman called the leaders in for another all-day session at the White House. When it was over, Whitney and Johnston continued to hold out. That night they wrote the President a curt letter saying: "We have told you many times that the present agitation among the men is extremely serious and their demands cannot be abandoned. Therefore your offer is unacceptable.".

When Harry Truman's mad is up, his eyes glint coldly behind his spectacles, his mouth is a thin, hard line pulled down at the corners, and his carriage has the brittleness of a bamboo reed. This was the image, as one remembers it, as he stalked into a specially called meeting of his Cabinet that Friday morning. In the manner of Lin-coln and the Emancipation Proclamation, he had summoned them not to solicit their views but to tell them what he was going to do. He was going to Congress in person the next day and demand the stiffest labor law in history—one that would give him authority to draft strikers into the armed services without respect to age or de-pendency when their strike threatened to bring on a national emer-gency. When Attorney General Tom C. Clark raised a question about the Constitutionality of such a move, the President brushed him aside peremptorily. "We'll draft 'em first and think about the law later," he said.

Next, he turned to Charley Ross, his press secretary, and told him to arrange a coast-to-coast radio hookup for him that night so that he could explain to the people what he was about to do. He pulled from his pocket and slapped on the table a bundle of twelve small sheets of ruled tablet paper such as schoolchildren use. They were closely written in ink—and spleen.

"Here's what I'm going to say," he snapped. "Get it typed up. I'm going to take the hide right off those so-and-so's."

Ross's blood pressure rocketed as he read what possibly will stand for all time as the angriest public message ever written in a President's own hand. It accused the labor leaders of having tried to sabotage the war effort while America's young men faced death on the battlefield; now they were sabotaging the peace by "holding a gun to the head of the government." He called on the ex-soldiers who had been his comrades in arms to help "eliminate the Lewises, the Whitneys and the Johnstons," and to "hang a few traitors and make our country safe for democracy."*

It is hard to conjecture what might have happened if this blast of invective had reached the public. Happily, Charley Ross was the kind of old friend who could go to the President and say, "Look, Harry, this just won't do." Which is substantially what he did, and with the help of Clark Clifford a greatly toned-down version of the

* Here is the full text of the proposed speech as written in Mr. Truman's own hand:

"In World War Two our young men were drafted for service and they faced bullets, bombs and disease to win the victory. At home those of us who had the country's welfare at heart worked day and night.

"But some people worked neither day nor night and some tried to sabotage the war effort entirely. John L. Lewis called two strikes in war time to satisfy his ego, two strikes that were worse than bullets in the backs of our soldiers. He held a gun at the head of the government. The rail unions did exactly the same thing.

"Now these same union leaders told your President on VJ-Day that they would cooperate with him one hundred percent to reconvert to peacetime production. They all lied to him.

"First came the threatened automobile strike. Your President asked for legislation to cool off and consider the situation. A weak-kneed Congress didn't have the intestinal fortitude to pass the bill. Mr. Murray and his communist friends had a conniption fit and Congress had labor jitters. Nothing happened. Then came the electrical workers' strike, the steel strike, the coal strike and now the rail tie-up.

"Every single one of the strikers and their demigog [sic] leaders have been living in luxury, working when they pleased and drawing from four to forty times the pay of a fighting soldier.

"I am tired of the government's being flouted, vilified and misrepresented.

"Now I want you men who are my comrades in arms, you men who fought the battles to save the nation just as I did 25 years ago, to come with me and eliminate the Lewises, the Whitneys and the Johnstons; the communist Bridges [of the maritime unions] and the Russian Senators and Representatives and really make this a government of, by and for the people.

"I think no more of the Wall Street crowd than I do of Lewis and Whitney. Let's give the country back to the people. Let's put transportation and production back to work, hang a few traitors and make our own country safe for democracy.

"Come on boys, let's do the job!"[3]

speech was hammered out before the President went on the air at 10 o'clock that night.

Even so, that speech was one of the most emphatic indictments of a group of individuals by a President that has ever been uttered. In it Mr. Truman, speaking in tones of sober indignation, said:

My fellow countrymen—I come before the American people tonight at a time of great crisis.

The crisis of Pearl Harbor was the result of action by a foreign enemy. The crisis tonight is caused by a group of men within our own country who place their private interests above the welfare of the Nation. . . .

I assume that these two men [Johnston and Whitney] know the havoc which their decision has caused, and the even more extreme suffering which will result in the future. . . . This is no contest between labor and management. This is a contest between a small group of men and their government. . . .

If sufficient workers to operate the trains have not returned by 4 P.M. tomorrow, as head of your government I have no alternative but to operate the trains by using every means within my power. . . .

This emergency is so acute and the issue is so vital that I have requested the Congress to be in session tomorrow at 4 P.M. and I shall appear before a joint session of the Congress to deliver a message on this subject.

Saturday—the next day—was as packed with drama as a Hollywood cliffhanger. Steelman was locked in a room at the Statler Hotel with Whitney and Johnston in a last-ditch effort to make them relent. Clifford and Sam Rosenman, in the Cabinet room at the White House, were battling against both time and uncertainty trying to draft the President's speech to Congress. Would, or would not, the strike be settled by the time the President got to the Capitol? Steelman telephoned Clifford that an agreement might be signed any minute, but he couldn't be certain.

"That was going to put us in a hell of a fix if it were settled at the last minute, and we had this speech," Clifford recalled. So he and Rosenman wrote out a couple of alternative pages that might be substituted at the last minute. The President had already left for the Capitol with the original text when they finished. Hatless, Clifford set out in pursuit, only to find on arrival at the office of Speaker Sam Rayburn that the President had already entered the House Chamber and was about to begin his speech.

Five minutes later, Clifford got a call through to Steelman at the Statler, who told him breathlessly: "It's signed!"

Clifford scribbled a note on a scrap of paper: "Mr. President, agreement signed, strike over," and gave it to Leslie Biffle, the Secretary of the Senate. Biffle scurried across the corridor and into the House Chamber and thrust the note on top of the text from which the President had already begun to read. Truman halted in midsentence and then looked up with a grin:

"Gentlemen, the strike has been settled," he said. There was a boisterous outbreak of applause and shouts from the packed Chamber.

There is a brief epilogue to this drama. Truman went through with his speech, demanding the right to draft workers as a guarantee against future strikes endangering the national security. The House passed it with a whoop that same evening by a vote of 306 to 13. Taft blocked the Senate from going on a similar stampede, and ultimately the bill was defeated. The effort cost Truman a shrill blast of condemnation from labor, the most severe he had ever experienced. Whitney promised that the entire $47,000,000 in his union's treasury would be used to defeat Truman in 1948, and a CIO conference in New York branded the President as the nation's "No. 1 Strikebreaker."

Like most stratagems conceived in anger, this one would have been disastrous had it been consummated, and it would almost certainly have been struck down in time as unconstitutional. As an instance of dangerous impetuosity, it does not enhance Mr. Truman's stature with the historians. But it had its short-term compensations: It *did* avert a major catastrophe at a moment of deep domestic crisis, and it *did* put a shine on Harry Truman's image as a tough, determined, to-hell-with-where-the-chips-may-fall fighter for what he believed to be right. He reaped the political dividends of his daring in 1948, when even Whitney and the trainmen were back in his corner.

While President Truman was fighting the railroad workers with one hand, he was fending off John L. Lewis and his coal miners with the other. On the very day—Tuesday, May 21, 1946—that Whitney and Johnston curtly told the President they would not call off their strike, he signed an order seizing the coal mines to end a forty-day work stoppage in the bituminous fields. In many respects this was to be the longer and the tougher of the two battles.

For one thing, if the ultimate showdown with the two rail unions had come, it would have been possible for the government to maintain at least a semblance of rail service with crews from the various military transportation units. But when Lewis said, "You can't mine coal with bayonets," he knew he was right, and the President knew it too. Coal in those days was the economic lifeblood of the nation. It drove 95 percent of all locomotives and provided 55 percent of all industrial energy and 62 percent of all electric power.

For another thing, Whitney and Johnston did not have the full backing of the other rail brotherhoods, nor of labor in general. But John Llewellyn Lewis, a miner and the son of miners, had been the undisputed boss of his United Mine Workers of America for almost thirty years. He needed no man's backing.

Lewis was a figure of almost unbelievable power and picturesqueness. He was a man of ponderous and majestic bearing with a billowing crown of gray hair and dark, baleful eyes peering from under immense eyebrows. His scowl had an Olympian ferocity, and his speech the cavernous tone and the measured cadence of a nineteenth-century Thespian. Vain, arrogant, confident of his authority, he had crushed his enemies within the union but had won the fanatic loyalty of the rank and file, for whom he had wrought a veritable revolution in pay and working conditions.

Singlehandedly, he could control the flow of the nation's coal supply as easily as manipulating a bathroom faucet. And he was contemptuous of any power that stood in his way, not excluding that of Presidents of the United States. "Truman doubts the legality of our demands?" he once roared to a reporter. "What does Truman know about the legality of anything?"

As the coal crisis deepened, many of the President's advisers urged him not to risk a showdown with this mighty tyrant of the coalpits. Better, they said, to seek a compromise on Lewis' terms than to gamble on a public bloodying of the Presidential nose. Clark Clifford recalls the circumstances this way:

> We were split right down the middle on this one. Steelman and some of the others were really afraid that the President would be licked if he locked horns in public with John L. on this issue. The rest of us argued that the President would have to take him on sooner or later, and that the longer it was put off, the worse it would be.
>
> Mr. Truman was really in a hell of a quandary at this time. His natural sympathies were on the side of labor; even of the miners, although he had no use for Lewis. But he felt that labor had let him down in the whole reconversion effort. He felt that they were acting irresponsibly in a period of real crisis, and that they needed a shaking up.

Well, the upshot was, he tried it both ways. First, he tried to appease Lewis. And when this didn't work, he hauled off and let him have it right between the eyes.

If the heat in industry's furnaces went down, it soared to the boiling point in the furnaces of public opinion as the coal shortage worsened. In a blast of outrage from Capitol Hill, Congress demanded immediate punitive action against the miners' chief and sharpened the teeth of a score of restrictive labor bills then in the legislative hopper. Truman was excoriated for timidity in dealing with the labor bosses (this was before his demand for the right to draft strikers) and for weakness in his leadership. Across the country, editorialists raged at the spectacle of labor leaders thumbing their noses at the national welfare, and irate citizens by the thousands took pen in hand to belabor the President. The New York *Sun* proclaimed in a front-page editorial on May 9:

The time has come for the nation to talk turkey to President Truman, the national administration and to the Congress of the United States. The President has dodged and hedged and shilly-shallied with the problem of industrial unrest. What he has actually done about it can be summed up in one word—nothing.

Typical of thousands of letters that poured into the White House was this one from businessman Clyde M. Allen, of Richmond, Virginia:

Dear Mr. President—How much longer are you going to sit idly by and allow business and industry to close down for the want of coal? This strike is now in its 39th day, and so far as the public has been informed, your administration has not turned a hand to effectuate a settlement. Why not draft the miners and put them on army pay to dig coal? And this goes for their chief, too. . . .[4]

The coal controversy began to take shape in January 1946, when Lewis presented the mine operators with a revolutionary new contract demand—a ten-cent royalty on every ton of coal mined to be put into a welfare fund to provide medical and old-age care for the miners. This, God knows, was a meritorious concept, for there are few more hazardous occupations, and none that are more exhausting to the human body and spirit. Scattered in the debris around every abandoned coal tipple are the ambulant shells of abandoned coal miners and their scrawny families. Lewis demanded new wage and hour provisions, too, but it was the welfare royalty that stopped the mine owners in their tracks. They refused to budge, and when the old contract expired on March 30, the miners walked out—400,000 of them in twenty-one states.

The economic impact was not immediately felt. There was a 30-day supply of coal above ground when the pits shut down. But as April wore on into May, the smoke began to disappear from factory chimneys, rail schedules were cut, and scores of cities returned to the wartime "dimout" to conserve dwindling supplies of fuel.

On May 15, President Truman summoned Lewis and Charles O'Neill, the operators' representative, to the first of a long series of conferences with himself and Steelman. Efforts to get collective bargaining moving again were fruitless, and on the 21st the President ordered seizure of the mines and put them under the direction of his Secretary of the Interior, Julius A. Krug, a barrel-chested, hard-nosed New Dealer who had understudied Harold Ickes in the job. A week later, Krug and Lewis signed a contract that gave the miners just about what they had asked for, including a five-cent—instead of a ten-cent—royalty on each ton of coal to underwrite their ambitious welfare program. O'Neill and the operators were outraged, but there was nothing they could do about it as long as their seat at the bargaining table was occupied by the government.

Truman had bought time but not peace in his appeasement of Lewis. He had not taken the vaulting ambitions of the mine chief into his calculations.

Labor's postwar thrust for status was accompanied by a desperate power struggle between William Green of the AFL, Philip Murray of the aggressively upstart Congress of Industrial Organizations (CIO), and Lewis and the UMWA. Lewis had been in and out of both the other camps and now stood contemptuously aloof as a third force. He decided on a bold stroke that would land him at the top of the pyramid: He would match his power against that of the government.

Late in October he announced his displeasure over a minor provision in his contract with the government, one that had to do with vacation pay, and demanded that the whole contract be reopened. When Krug refused, Lewis said, Very well, the miners would cancel it themselves effective in thirty days, or November 20—and, of course, "no contract, no work."

The President was vacationing in Key West as the mid-November deadline approached. When there was no retraction forthcoming

from Lewis, he summoned half a dozen of his top aides, including
Steelman, to fly down for a hasty conference. He opened the proceedings by telling them in effect, "This time I mean to slap that so-
and-so down for good. Now you fellows tell me the best way to do
it."

The strategy that was adopted was less dramatic than in the rail
case but just as drastic and inflammatory to the men of organized
labor. It reverted to the use of the most hated weapon in the anti-
labor arsenal—the injunction.

In the turbulent early decades of the labor movement, the injunction was a favorite device of employers to break strikes. Contracts
that were enforceable by court injunction were called by the union-
ists "yellow-dog contracts," and thousands of protesters had their
heads cracked or went to jail when they defied the court's orders
against striking. In the Norris-LaGuardia Act of 1932, Federal courts
were prohibited from granting injunctions in labor-management disputes, and this prohibition was further strengthened in the Wagner
Act of 1935. This was one of the greatest victories for labor in the
New Deal era. In the liberal decalogue of the period, the "yellow-
dog contract" belonged in the chamber of horrors along with the
iron collar and the whipping post. Now Harry Truman, labor's friend
and the heir of Franklin Roosevelt, was about to bring this hated
scourge out of the closet again.

It was argued within the White House that the prohibition
against injunctions applied only to disputes between a union and a
private employer, and did not apply when, as in the present case,
the government was the employer. But this interpretation had never
been tested. Would it stand up in court? And if it did, would the
miners obediently go back to digging coal? And if not, where would
the President and the government be then?

There was no certain answer to these questions as the conference
in Key West broke up, but President Truman had made his decision
and it was going to be carried out.

On Monday, November 18—two days before Lewis' contract can-
cellation was to take effect—Attorney General Tom C. Clark strode
into the Washington courtroom of Federal District Judge T. Alan
Goldsborough and asked that a temporary injunction be issued restraining the miners' chief from abrogating his union's contract with
the government. The order was issued and served on Lewis that
afternoon at his office in the old City Club building at Fifteenth and
I Streets. But already, in one bleak, soot-covered mining camp

after another throughout Pennsylvania, West Virginia, and Kentucky, miners by the tens, fifties, and hundreds had failed to report in for their shifts as if in anticipation of their leader's purpose. No contrary orders reached them from Washington. By the Wednesday midnight deadline the ritualistic phrase "no contract, no work" had penetrated along the farthest hollow and railroad spur in the Appalachian coal fields. By morning, virtually every soft coal mine in the country was shut down.

Now began a brief but historic series of court maneuvers. On Thursday, November 21, Justice Goldsborough cited Lewis and the mine union for contempt of court in having ignored his restraining order. The following Monday, Lewis and his attorneys, Joseph A. Padway and Welly K. Hopkins, filed briefs challenging the court's authority to issue the injunction, citing the Norris-LaGuardia Act. Assistant Attorney General John F. Sonnett, heading the government's legal battery, contended that the Act was not intended to apply to disputes between the union and the government. Moreover, he argued, the point at issue was not labor's rights but the national safety.

The court weighed these contentions for three days, and then, on Friday, ruled across the board in the government's favor. Judge Goldsborough ordered Lewis and the union to stand trial on the contempt charges, beginning Monday.

Washington dug in for what looked like a long and gaudy display of legal fireworks. Reporters and photographers clustered around the union's headquarters on Fifteenth Street, and trailed the glowering, taciturn Lewis to his luncheon table in the nearby Carlton Hotel and in the evening to his stately home in Alexandria. They got color but no quotes. In the face of a steadily worsening coal shortage, the government embargoed all unnecessary rail travel, and scores of cities reimposed wartime restrictions on electrical consumption. President Truman, back in the White House from his Key West vacation, heightened the air of suspense by refusing to make any comment on the coal controversy.

The trial opened on Monday, December 2. To the hundreds of spectators who crowded the chamber and the adjacent corridors, it was a disappointment, for the hoped-for fireworks did not develop until the very end. No witnesses were called by either side, and the opposing lawyers narrowed their arguments down to legalistic interpretations of the Norris-LaGuardia and related acts. By midday of Tuesday, the second day of the trial, all the evidence was in.

Justice Goldsborough, a tall ascetic-appearing man in his black robes, then pronounced his verdict in an unemotional monotone: ". . . The defendant John L. Lewis [and the United Mine Workers of America] has beyond a reasonable doubt committed and continues to commit a civil [and criminal] contempt of this Court."

There was a tense silence in the mahogany-paneled room as the Judge spoke. When he finished, Lewis, who had sat in controlled, white-faced anger during the recitation, rose ponderously to his feet and asked leave to address the court. In the sepulchral tones and rolling cadence of a Lear, he said:

The history of the labor injunction prior to 1932 is a sordid one. . . . Speaking and acting in my official capacity as President of the United Mine Workers of America, I cannot by action or inaction acquiesce in what must be described as the ugly recrudescence of "government by injunction." I cannot disavow labor's principles or policies, nor am I disposed to adopt a course which will inevitably amount to a betrayal of labor's constitutional rights. . . .

So saying, he stalked with elephantine dignity out of the courtroom.

Was Lewis about to defy the court? Was he, in the tradition of Debs and Gompers, inviting jail and martyrdom?

The enigma persisted through the next day, when the principals were summoned to court again to hear the sentence: smashing fines of $3,500,000 against the union and of $10,000 against Lewis personally, the stiffest penalties ever imposed in a labor contempt case.

"This day will live in infamy, Sir," Welly Hopkins cried out, and Lewis accused the court of attempting to bankrupt the union. The Judge cautioned him to be careful of his words. "Sir, I have already been adjudged in contempt of your court," the old Thespian thundered in reply. He obviously had more to say, but Hopkins got him into his seat before he could compound his offense.

The union moved an appeal directly to the Supreme Court. Lewis gave no sign of repentance. He did nothing to get the miners back to work. On Saturday morning the White House announced that President Truman would go on the air that night in a direct appeal to the miners over their chieftain's head, urging them to go back to work. It was a desperate, last-ditch stratagem with the prestige of the Presidency laid squarely on the line.

The denouement of this tense drama came unexpectedly at 4 o'clock that Saturday afternoon. Lewis called a special press conference in the paneled conference room of his headquarters. When nearly a hundred reporters and photographers were securely locked in, he entered ceremonially from a side entrance with, as one reporter recalled, "the dignity and panoply of a one-man processional." Taking his seat on the platform, and looking worn and weary, he read in measured tones from a prepared statement:

> The administration's "yellow dog" injunction has reached the Supreme Court. The issues before the Court are fateful for our Republic. . . . These weighty considerations and the fitting respect due the dignity of this high tribunal imperatively require that during its period of deliberation the court should be free from public pressure superinduced by the hysteria of an economic crisis. . . .
> [Accordingly] all mines in all districts will resume production of coal immediately. . . . Each member is directed to return to work immediately under the wages and conditions of employment in existence on and before November 20, 1946.

Lewis' capitulation was complete, and Truman's desperate gamble had paid off. He had staked his own shaky prestige in the Presidency, recently battered by his party's defeat in the congressional elections, against the stubborn pride of the nation's most powerful labor dictator. He had won, and the sense of victory gave him an enormous surge of confidence. Clark Clifford said of the event some years later:

> I think you can put your finger on winning this showdown with Lewis as the moment when Truman finally and irrevocably stepped out from the shadow of FDR to become President in his own right. . . .
> When he saw that compromise was not going to work, he decided to meet the issue in the really characteristic Truman fashion—the way he met things as a young fellow in Independence, as a county judge, as a Senator—head on, with his sleeves rolled up, and to hell with the consequences.
> I can tell you, there was a big difference in the Old Man from then on. He was his own boss at last.

The future historian who tries to follow the thread of Harry Truman's labor policies during the early years of his administration will surely be baffled unless he comprehends the basic consistency in the man's apparent inconsistency.

In the railroad and mine cases, Truman fostered two of the most punitive attacks on labor organizations in this century. But literally at the same time, and against tremendous political pressures, he vetoed the Case bill, which would have hardened into statutory law antistrike weapons of a less deadly nature than those he, himself, had just invoked. And he followed this up in 1947 with a veto of the Taft-Hartley bill, which was even less extreme than the Case bill. What Truman sought was a basic mechanism by which the inherent conflicts of labor and management could be reconciled on a basis of equity to both sides and to the public interest as well. In his pragmatic, uncomplicated view every such issue could be resolved ultimately by simply deciding on which side of the scales the weight of the public interest belonged, and then putting it there—by decree if necessary. He did not believe that labor should be shorn of any of its hard-won rights. But he did think that strong rules of fair conduct for resolving labor disputes should be set up, and that there should at all times be a hickory stick behind the White House door to enforce those rules when necessary.

This was the essence of his own labor-management bill, which he submitted to Congress in December 1945. It was modeled on the highly successful Railway Labor Act of 1926. In addition he asked for the creation of a topflight commission to restudy the whole field of labor-management relations and to come up with recommendations for a new basic labor act designed with the needs of the postwar world in mind. Congress ignored his request. It was in a punitive, not a conciliatory, mood toward labor. It passed the Case bill instead. When that was vetoed (in June 1946), Congress went on a year later to enact the Taft-Hartley bill and to make it stick in spite of a veto.

Hold That Line: Politics

After a year and a half in office in the closing weeks of 1946, Harry Truman must have concluded that Peace at Home was a no less illusive goal than Peace in the World. He had striven for much and had gained little. The Congress, in which he had so long served and which he so much loved, had turned out to be his costliest battlefield. And as "a man of the people" he had failed conspicuously to rally the people to his support. They had been tired of war when he came into office, and now they were tired of Democrats too.

In his major endeavor—to hold the line on prices and wages—he had been a loser. The crippling of OPA and final emasculation of the other economic controls fueled a rampant inflation. The cost-of-living index, which normally fluctuates not more than a couple of points from year to year, leaped from 76.9 at the end of 1945 to 83.4 a year later and was on its uninterrupted way to a peak of 102.8 by 1948. Each round of price increases brought a new round of wage increases. Strikes and slowdowns, setting an all-time record, fouled the production lines and fanned the public anger. Ordinary consumers, caught in the spiraling price squeeze and bedeviled by continuing shortages of meat, automobiles, housing, and other needs, turned their ire on the most obvious scapegoat, the President and his administration.

There were some pluses on the scorecard, to be sure. He had won the right to reorganize some major functions of the executive branch. He had won enactment of the Employment Act of 1946, which revitalized the machinery for economic planning. He had won enactment of the Atomic Energy Act of 1946, which put the control of this awesome new power in civilian rather than military hands and as a monopoly of the government. And he had made a substantial beginning toward unification of the nation's Armed Forces.

These were substantial gains. In the perspective of history, they loom larger than the debacle of OPA and the brawling with organized labor. But it was strikes and high prices and black markets and rent gougers and "government by crony" and a score of other annoyances, large and small, real and imagined, that set the public mood of disaffection in those first Truman years. The man was a bungler, people said, or he lacked the experience or the talent for leadership. "Among the members of his own party," the New York Times reported late in 1946, "the prevailing attitude toward the President is one of simple despair and futility. Most seem to think he has done the best he could, but that his best simply was not good enough."

As the midterm election campaign of that autumn warmed up, the Republicans channeled this galloping discontent to their own uses. With rare genius they compressed the national mood into two words—"Had Enough?"—to coin one of the most devastating campaign slogans of all time.

Election Day was November 5. When it was over, the Republicans had taken control of Congress for the first time in sixteen years, picking up eleven seats in the Senate and fifty-four in the House.

Anticipating a period of national paralysis, Senator J. William Fulbright of Arkansas, an immature first-termer in those days, suggested that Mr. Truman should step aside and let a Republican successor take over.* The Truman luck had hit bottom.

But, as time would prove, it's hard to keep a good man down.

---

* Thereafter Mr. Truman could only pronounce the Arkansan's name as "Senator Halfbright."

CHAPTER 6

◇◇◇◇◇◇◇◇◇◇◇◇◇◇◇◇◇◇◇◇◇◇

Politician in the White House

A President Is Many Men

IT TOOK the American people a couple of years to find out what sort of man they had in the Presidency in Harry Truman. The picture they formed was not so much a portrait as a montage.

• *He was brassy and full of corn when he got away from the White House.*

"Mr. Truman did everything except have himself shot from the mouth of a cannon."

Edward T. Folliard in the Washington *Post* on Mr. Truman enjoying himself at an American Legion convention in Caruthersville, Mo., in October 1945.

• *He was guided by devout and uncomplicated moral precepts.*

"Mr. Truman has long cherished Solomon as the model of a public man. . . . Because he endeavors constantly to govern his conduct by a passage in I Kings 3: 7-9 . . . it should be set down in any study of Mr. Truman. Accordingly, it follows:

"'And now, O Lord my God, thou has made thy servant king instead of David my father; and I am but a little child; I know not how to go out or come in.

" 'And thy servant is in the midst of thy people which thou hast chosen, a great people, that cannot be numbered nor counted for multitude.

" 'Give therefore thy servant an understanding heart to judge thy people, that I may discern between good and bad; for who is able to judge this thy so great people?'

"He holds that to be the most desirable and necessary quality in a President of the United States. Though modest rather than humble, Mr. Truman is reasonably sure he shares this blessing with the great King."

—Arthur Krock, the New York
Times magazine, April 7, 1946.

• *He had a strong sense of duty and the courage to fight for what he thought was right.*

"The President's reputation for insisting on principles has been strengthened by his first nine months in the White House. Repeatedly, he has insisted on legislation which, from a national point of view, could only be considered as an invitation to a rebuff. . . . It is not unusual for a President to be rebuffed by Congress. What is a little unusual is for a Chief Executive, repeatedly rebuffed, to refuse to change his tactics."

—Felix Belair, Jr., in the New
York *Times*, Dec. 22, 1945.

• *He was often given to snap judgments and wound up with his foot in his mouth.*

"Q. (by William Mylander, Des Moines *Register and Tribune*): In the middle of the speech (by Henry A. Wallace, Secretary of Commerce) are these words: 'When President Truman read these words he said they represented the policy of this Administration.'

"The President: That is correct.

"Q. My question is, does that apply just for that paragraph or to the whole speech?

"The President: I approved the whole speech.

"Q. (by Raymond P. Brandt, St. Louis *Post-Dispatch*): Mr. President, do you regard Wallace's speech as a departure from [Secretary of State] Byrnes' policy?

"The President: I do not. They are exactly in line."

> —Transcript of press conference, Sept. 4, 1945, one week before Wallace was fired for a speech delivered at Madison Square Garden in New York at a pro-Soviet rally.

He tackled his job conscientiously and had the ability to make up his mind and the courage to act.

"During the years, I acquired the greatest respect and admiration for the President's capacity to understand complex questions and to decide. This is one of the rarest qualities possessed by man. Too frequently the mind vacillates between unpleasant choices and escapes through procrastination. Mr. Truman did not do this. He read tirelessly the material given him; listened intently to the arguments; and then he decided, clearly and firmly. Once a matter was decided, he went on to new problems and had little time or inclination to rehash the old ones."

> —Dean G. Acheson, in interview with the writer, winter of 1962.

• *He was a "man of the people," plain, forthright, and without guile or pretensions.*

"Harry Truman's story is not average, but it is symbolic. It is unique in terms of the manner in which it has touched, in personal problems and private pain, all the difficulties of American life in our time. . . . He is both the product and the embodiment of the American faith which is set up more clearly now than ever as a faith for the world. He speaks that faith in the language of his countrymen. Moscow understands what he says, as well as Independence and Iowa, the steel towns, the Carolinas, and Wall Street."

> —Jonathan Daniels, in *The Man of Independence*, pp. 19-25.

• *He lacked brilliance but he had an abundance of guts, political intuition, and common sense.*

> ". . . These are some of the aspects of the man who will next week complete his first year as President of the United States. The portrait is not thrilling, but there is much of comfort and reassurance in it, and much to admire. Here is to be seen no flaming leadership, little of what could be called scholarship and no more that is profound. But it is very good and human and courageous. Common sense shines out of it, and political experience, the lack of which has been the downfall of Presidents."
>
> —Arthur Krock, the New York *Times* magazine, Apr. 7, 1946.

Harry Truman brought a new sense of bustle and physical vitality to the White House. While FDR had been a late riser who began the day with bedside conferences with his aides, the ex-farm boy from Missouri was up and wide awake by 6 o'clock every morning. Eschewing the services of a valet, he showered, shaved, and dressed meticulously in a haberdasher's good taste. He scanned three or four newspapers; scribbled a letter home or a couple of memos to his staff; and promptly, at 7 o'clock, took the family elevator down to the ground floor. There a brace of Secret Service men awaited his greeting, and together they stepped out into the fresh morning air to perform again one of the most celebrated pedestrian rituals of the day—the Truman prebreakfast walk. Often a reporter or two showed up; it was unfailingly a good opportunity for an informal chat with the President, though note-taking was impossible at his 120-paces-a-minute clip. Besides, the President preferred banter to serious conversation on these occasions. The route varied with the Presidential whim. One day he would strike across Lafayette Square, up Connecticut Avenue to Dupont Circle, down Massachusetts Avenue, and home. Another time he might choose a circuit of the Washington Monument grounds and the Lincoln Memorial, or a window-shopping tour along F and G Streets. By 7:45 he was back for breakfast, which he usually had with Mrs. Truman and Margaret. A few minutes after eight he would stride into his oval office, say a cheery Good Morning to Rose Conway, his secretary from Senatorial days, settle into the big black leather chair at his desk, and start another official day in the Presidency.

Truman was a tidy administrator without being a slave to routine or organization charts. His principal virtue lay in his abhorrence of procrastination. Whatever had to be done got done, and he drilled this rule of conduct into those who worked with him. He tightened up the loosely drawn staff organization of secretaries and special assistants inherited from Roosevelt but stopped short of compartmentalizing each man's duties. David D. Lloyd, who joined the White House staff in 1947, has recalled:

We had a free-wheeling but effective sort of system. We were divided up by job rather than on any functional basis. Assignments were parceled out more on the basis of who was available than who was the expert. I might be working on a labor problem one week and the defense budget the next.

That doesn't sound very efficient, but we were a pretty close-knit crew by and large, and it worked out quite well.

There were regular staff meetings each morning, rarely lasting much longer than 20 or 30 minutes with six or eight of the principal aides sitting around the President's desk. These were less for policy discussions than for progress reports and assignments. But the members were free to pop in on the President any time they wanted to between his regular appointments to discuss a point or to clarify their instructions.

Generally, the morning hours were given over to the "customers," as Truman called the procession of visitors who demanded to see him each day. These were screened by his appointments secretary. In an ordinary day, eight to a dozen legislators, politicians, businessmen, foreign dignitaries, old friends, friends of friends, and the promoters of causes that varied from National Cheese Week to the annual fund drive of the Red Cross filed past his desk and lingered for a few minutes to half an hour. He greeted them all with a crisp, smiling cordiality and a firm handshake. Most frequently he and Mrs. Truman lunched alone, and after a brief nap he was back in his office.

The afternoons were reserved for the serious business of government and briefings on specific problems: conferences with his Cabinet Secretaries, the Director of the Bureau of the Budget, staff members, and others. This was the time when policy was evolved. If Truman was not a profound thinker, he was a good listener, a sharp interrogator, and a conscientious student and digger for facts. He was blessed with a highly retentive memory, and his extensive reading of history often enabled him to draw parallels or to perceive contexts for current issues that helped greatly to illuminate them. It was no pain to his pride to acknowledge the supremacy of the experts in the many specialized fields of diplomacy, economics, and military affairs with which he had to deal. He delegated responsibility freely to the experts and accepted their advice after passing it through the sieve of his own common sense. When he thought he had the right answer, he acted on it then and there.

The following incident is worth recording to document Mr. Truman's prodigious memory for historical detail. When the late William Hillman was interviewing him for the book *Mr. President,* in 1951, Mr. Truman expounded at some length on Alexander the Great, one of his heroes, who, he said, made the mistake of overreaching himself.

"And then the people around him," he told Hillman, "made him think he was immortal, and he found that thirty-three quarts of wine was too much for any man, and it killed him at Babylon."

Working over the proofs of his book later, Hillman paused to puzzle over the President's mention of the thirty-three quarts of wine. Obviously, he thought, it was some sort of allegory; he, himself, had never heard of it, nor was he sure what it meant. He called the Library of Congress and asked their scholarly assistance in running the item down. A few days later they called back to say, sorry, they could find no link, real or poetic, between Alexander and the thirty-three quarts of wine. Hillman was convinced that the President had mixed either his metaphors or his kings and was about to challenge him on it when, a few days later, he received another call from the researcher at the Library. In the manner of librarians everywhere, this one had not given up the search after the first admission of failure. He had pursued his quarry behind the locked doors of the Rare Books Section, and into an obscure and long-out-of-print volume on the history of the ancient Greeks, and by golly, the President was right after all!

"And you know what?" the researcher added. "That book has been checked out of the shelves only twice in the last twenty years, and the last time was for Senator Harry Truman in 1939."[1]

It took something more than a year for the Truman staff—the inner corps of White House aides who are a President's extra eyes, ears, and hands—to shake down into a relatively stable pattern. The three principal secretaries were Ross, for press; Matthew J. Connelly, an alert, politically shrewd Irishman from Massachusetts who had worked on the Truman investigation committee in the Senate, for appointments; and amiable William D. Hassett, a former newspaperman whose head was stacked with Washington lore, for correspondence, a job he had performed for many years under Roosevelt.

Below the secretarial level, another holdover from Roosevelt's day was Samuel I. Rosenman, a brilliant New York lawyer, and later a judge, whose profound command of liberal dialectics graced many Presidential speeches and public papers before he retired to private life in January 1946.

The job of Special Counsel was filled by a handsome but obscure young naval officer and former St. Louis lawyer, Clark M. Clifford. Clifford's gifts, it soon developed, were many and varied. He was urbane, gracious, and socially talented. He had a mind of extraordinary scope and analytical capacity, and he expressed himself with easy, unpretentious clarity. He brought to his job of Presidential aide an intelligence and creativity that sensed the loopholes and detours by which the obstacles to Presidential initiative could be surmounted. For a Chief Executive geared to action rather than deliberation, such as Truman was, Clifford came close to being the ideal No. 2 man, the how-to-do-it man.

John R. Steelman, who acquired in time the resounding and unique title "*The* Assistant to the President," never quite measured up to it in either performance or personal relationship. A 220-pound Alabamian with an overwhelming heartiness, he had served for years as a top-ranking member of the Labor Department's Conciliation Service before coming to the White House. In addition to his role as the principal liaison man between the administration and organized labor, he was also the chief conduit between the White House and the operating levels of the executive departments, prodding them to action, receiving their reports, and adjudicating their lesser disputes. He was a principal buffer against the tide of administrative detail that beats constantly against a President's door.

The name of Brigadier General Harry Hawkins Vaughan would be worth hardly more than a footnote in this roster were it not for the fact that he epitomized, almost painfully, the softest spot in Truman's executive armor—a stubborn sentimentality about old friends that often blunted his judgment.

Harry Vaughan was a big, jovial extrovert who had been a First World War buddy of the President and served later with him in the

Missouri Organized Reserves and the American Legion. A man of minimal talents and of modest attainments, he had worked in Truman's 1940 reelection campaign and then came on to Washington to serve on the Senator's staff. When Truman moved to the White House, he took his yarn-swapping, poker-playing, old-shoe crony with him. To the astonishment of just about everyone, and to the outrage of the Old School traditionalists in the Pentagon, he boosted Vaughan's Reserve rank of Colonel to Brigadier General and made him his Military Aide.

This sudden eminence went to Harry Vaughan's head like a draught of strong booze. He began to make speeches and to give press interviews. His White House office became a hangout for a gaudy assortment of new-found friends and political hacks who used his easy hospitality and his prestige for their own dubious ends. His gaucheries and his heavy-handed intrusions into areas of the bureaucracy where he had no business soon became the talk of Washington. The President was not ignorant of this, and several times he dressed Vaughan down in the Army language they both understood, but he would countenance no criticism of his old friend from others.

Except for his role as a kind of court jester, Vaughan made no constructive contribution to the Presidency of Harry Truman. Instead, he was the all-too-visible symbol of "government by crony" and "the mess in Washington" with which millions of citizens would for years identify the Truman administration.

A few other names are sufficient to round out the list of principal members of the White House staff during the first Truman administration. David Niles, a soft-spoken Boston social worker held over from the Roosevelt days, was the listener-in-chief to the complaints of organized Jews, Negroes, Poles, and other minority groups. Charles Murphy, David Lloyd, and George Elsey, able and conscientious technicians, were general utility men in the field of speech-writing, legislative research, and fact-finding. Donald Dawson, a lawyer and Pendergast man from Kansas City, took care of patronage and lesser political chores. James E. Webb, a competent but largely unknown career man, was moved up to head the Bureau of the Budget when the holdover from the previous administration, Harold Smith, resigned late in 1945.

On the whole, and in comparison with the high intellectual octane of such former White House stars as Tugwell, Corcoran,

Cohen, *et al.*, the Truman team was generally lacking in luster—competent but pedestrian, conscientious but unimaginative. The striking exception was Clark Clifford. Every administration has its "inner circle"—a clique that may contain legislators, Cabinet ministers, professors, bankers, astrologers, old friends, or the President's own hired hands. In the Truman inner circle, Clifford stood among the top half-dozen who gave constructive meaning and direction to the Truman Presidency.

Family life in the White House, once the novelty had worn off, was something of a wrench for the Trumans. They were an affectionate, close-knit trio who had always orbited comfortably in a large constellation of kinfolk and friendly neighbors centered mainly on Independence, Missouri. Even under the comparative affluence of a Senatorial salary of $10,000, and briefly $15,000 as Vice President, they had lived an ordinary and unspectacular social life in their five-room apartment on Washington's upper Connecticut Avenue.

Bess Truman, a plump, strong-willed, and not overly gregarious matron, did most of the housework, played bridge and canasta with a small coterie of Senate and Missouri wives, and never yearned for the glitter of the more pretentious salons of the city. Margaret, a gangling and overprotected little girl of ten when her family first came to Washington, was a high-spirited, fragilely pretty George Washington University sophomore when her father became President.

Before that awesome event, father and daughter used often to set out together on the bus in the morning, she with an armload of books and he with a battered brown briefcase stuffed with committee reports. At night they all reassembled around the dinner table to swap news of their varied experiences of the day, to quarrel briefly and sporadically, to laugh a good deal, and to bask in the security and warmth of a well-adjusted middle-class family.

Margie, as she was called, was the apple of her father's eye. On one of her first big romantic experiences, a bid to a dance at the Military Academy at West Point, Senator Truman suddenly found it necessary to go up on the same train to "inspect" the establishment. A few years later he was to make his much publicized threat to commit mayhem on a Washington music critic, Paul Hume, because of his unsympathetic opinion of Margaret's performance as a professional singer.

But Bess Truman was also the apple of Harry Truman's eye. He

came perilously close to creating a major international incident soon
after he became President for what he construed as a slight to her.

On the day of his first big diplomatic reception, the Russian Embassy called at 5 o'clock in the afternoon to say that Ambassador
Novikov was ill and would be unable to attend. A quiet check by the
protocol officer revealed that the Ambassador's indisposition was
political rather than physical (he was miffed because the representative of a government-in-exile which the Soviet Union had recently
gobbled up was also to attend).

Before 9 o'clock the next morning the outraged husband-President
summoned his acting Secretary of State, Dean Acheson, to his office.
He demanded that the Russian Ambassador's credentials be lifted
immediately. His rudeness in absenting himself from the reception,
the President stormed, "is not only an insult to the country, it is an
insult to my wife."

The emanations of his fury must have penetrated to the second-
floor living quarters of the White House. For while a badly shaken
Acheson was fencing for time, Bess Truman rang the Presidential
phone. What dialogue took place is not recorded, but slowly the
steam appeared to go out of the Presidential boiler, and after a few
minutes he put down the phone with a small grin of resignation.

"Well," he said, "if I've got both you and 'the Boss' against me, I
guess I'm licked."

"Maybe you think I'm silly about this, Dean," he went on soberly,
"but I want to show you something."

He took from his desk a faded snapshot of a young girl in an old
filigreed gold frame. He pulled a couple of pins at the back and took
out a calling card of Miss Virginia Elizabeth Wallace. Written on it
was a 1917 date and this message: "Dear Harry: I hope this picture
will see you safely to France and back again."

Said the President of the United States: "Any so-and-so who is
rude to that girl is in trouble with me."

As much as they could, the Trumans separated their official life
from their family life, but it was hard going. The ubiquitous Secret
Service shadowed each of them wherever they went. A summer trip
home to Independence meant a private railroad car and a monster
reception at the station when they got there. Their social life was
dictated by a relentless bureaucratic machinery. However they
moved furniture about in their living quarters, changed the
draperies, rehung the pictures, the place still had the aspect of a

museum. Even when they took their dinners alone on the south balcony, they were spied on by the curious with binoculars and cameras with long-range lenses. Bess Truman did what she had to do as First Lady—the dedications, the receptions and teas, the honorary chairmanships and such—but no more. She never held a press conference, or gave a private interview, or lobbied for a government program while she was in the White House. The Trumans invited old friends in occasionally for an evening card game or for a private showing of a movie. Members of their families from Independence visited often, and Mrs. Wallace became in time a permanent member of the household. But the free-and-easy visiting was out; so were the shopping trips downtown. Margaret had a hard time attracting new beaux. In her lively book of reminiscences, *Souvenir*, she wrote:

One of the unexpected things about my new life was the interest that was suddenly generated in my romantic affairs, which up to then had bothered nobody but me, and maybe Mother! . . . As anybody who can read English must know, the press yearned to get me married, or at least engaged, while I was a tenant of the White House.

While I am not silly enough to suppose that being watched over by the Secret Service had any real effect on romance, I ask you to consider the effect of saying good night to a boy at the door of the White House in a blaze of floodlights with a Secret Service man in attendance. There is not much you can do except shake hands, and that's no way to get engaged.[2]

In his public life Truman was cocky, self-confident, always on his toes. In his private life he had his moments of doubt and introspection, and, by his own admission, was "a damned sentimentalist— what an old fool I am."

Bess' and Margaret's occasional absences from the White House left him desolate with loneliness. After working hours, he poked aimlessly about the big old mausoleum, adjusting the clocks, poking into closets, exploring the attic and basement, ruminating about the giants who had preceded him, and continuing to indulge that awe-struck wonder that he, himself, should now be standing in their stead. The mystique of the Presidency and his self-identification with it burned always like a tiny light in the back of his mind. In the erratic diaries he kept, he wrote one evening during his temporary tenancy of Blair-Lee House while the White House was undergoing repairs:

Had dinner by myself tonight. Worked in the Lee House office until dinner time. A butler came very formally and said, "Mr. President, dinner is served." I walk into the dining room in the Blair House. Barnett in

white tie and tails pulls out my chair, pushes me up to the table. John in
white tie and tails brings me a fruit cup. Barnett takes away the empty
cup. John brings me a plate, Barnett brings me a tenderloin. John brings
me asparagus, Barnett brings me carrots and beets. I have to eat alone
and in silence and candlelight. I ring. Barnett takes the plates and butter
plates. John comes in with a napkin and silver crumb tray—there are no
crumbs but John has to brush them off the table anyway. Barnett brings
me a plate with a finger bowl and a doily on it. I remove the finger bowl
and doily and John puts a glass saucer and a little bowl on the plate.
Barnett brings me some chocolate custard. John brings me a demitasse
(at home a little cup of coffee—about two good gulps) and my dinner is
over. I take a hand bath in the finger bowl and go back to work. What a
life![3]

Few men have chafed less under the personal restraints of the
Presidency than Truman. Behind his many touching protests about
the weight of responsibility and the restrictions of office, he actually
enjoyed the job. His whole life's training had conditioned him to
welcome responsibility. He had the normal appetite of any ambitious, outgoing man for the sense of power that derives from
command. He was blessed with a tough hide and a secure conscience, so that he could roll with the punches of political adversity.
And, with healthily uncomplicated vanity, he responded with simple and exuberant delight to the flattery and deference that were
showered upon him wherever he went in public. This accounted in
large part for the fact that he was among the most peripatetic of
Presidents. He seized every opportunity he could to get out into the
country to make speeches, attend conventions, cut ribbons, take
well-publicized vacations, and especially to touch the familiar and
reassuring bases of Kansas City, Independence, and Grandview,
where his mother lived. He was a man of the people, a man of the
grass roots. He felt himself to be one of the multitude, but one whom
fate had inexplicably chosen to catch the big brass ring. He fancied
himself, quite accurately indeed, as a sensitive barometer to what
the multitude felt, believed in, and aspired to.

It was the away-from-Washington Truman who revealed most
sharply his public profile etched as a carefree, fun-loving, irrepressi-
ble, and, to many, undignified person. He liked, he often said, "to get
away from that goldfish bowl and unbend." He did, and with a zest
that was sometimes breathtaking.

Escorting Winston Churchill to Fulton, Missouri, in 1946, where
Churchill made his famous Iron Curtain speech, the President
climbed into the cab of the big diesel locomotive at a way-stop,

donned an engineer's blue cap and red bandanna, and manned the controls for a 25-mile run. He was as pleased as a 10-year-old boy.

In October 1945 he turned up in Caruthersville, Missouri, for the state American Legion Convention, an event he had not missed in twelve years. He held open court in the little hotel lobby, out on the street, and in the corner drugstore; signed hundreds of autographs on everything from paper napkins to blank checks; walked down to the banks of the Mississippi River to perform the traditional rite of spitting into it; hopped into the cab of the Legionnaires' jerry-built "40 & 8" locomotive and tugged away at the bell cord for the delighted photographers; judged the horse races at the county fair and looked in on a couple of the tent shows; misplayed a Chopin étude for an impromptu stand-up audience that overflowed the hotel dining room; and stayed up half the night playing poker in his room with some of his old buddies.

On a parade in Kansas City, he spied his old barber, Frank Spina, among the sidewalk crowd. He pointed meaningfully to his head, and two hours later showed up at Spina's shop for one of the most publicized haircuts on record. On another visit home he led his entourage of reporters into Eddie Jacobson's haberdashery "to pick up a couple of shirts." When it developed that Jacobson did not have the President's correct size (15½ x 33), the word was flashed to the four corners of the country. For a month thereafter the White House mail room was deluged with shirts of every shape, shade, and size as gifts, and spoofs, for the shirtless President.

Truman put Key West, a tiny island at the tip of Florida, on the tourist map by his frequent vacations there. It had many advantages. The naval base there is on a large, fenced reservation, which provided privacy as well as security. The President and his staff were housed in the commandant's large but unpretentious quarters. There was an adequate airport for the Presidential plane, the *Sacred Cow*, and a special communications ship was tied up to one of the piers to maintain contact with Washington. David Lloyd has recalled those Key West days:

Truman loved that place. He'd work a little, rest a lot and play a lot. It did him a world of good. He'd get into one of those crazy-colored shirts he liked, put on a white cap, pick up his cane and walk all over the place—through the shipyards, the shops, into the officers' and the enlisted men's mess, sometimes even into the town. He'd talk, talk, talk with any and everybody he ran into.

There was a nice little stretch of beach there, too, and Mr. Truman would go in swimming almost every day. He wasn't much of a swimmer. He had a funny kind of stroke that we used to call a "side-arm Missouri crawl." He wasn't much of a fisherman, either, although he would go out occasionally more to please the Navy or some visitor than to satisfy any sporting instinct of his own.

I remember one occasion when they took the Old Man and a party of us out about ten miles in what was supposed to be one of the greatest deep sea fishing spots anywhere around. The Commandant had supplied the President with the finest and most complicated set of fishing gear you ever saw. But nobody got so much as a nibble, and you could see that Mr. Truman was getting a little restless and fed up.

Finally, he said: "To hell with all this fancy stuff. Give me a handline and some bait, and I'll show you how we used to catch catfish in the Kaw River back home."

Well, believe it or not, he threw that handline over the side of the boat and in almost no time at all he had hooked a fish. I've forgotten what kind it was; I believe it was some inedible variety that real deep sea fishermen usually throw back. But Mr. Truman was as pleased as Punch, and he kidded everybody at Key West for a week, saying he was the only fisherman in the lot.[4]

The ten or twenty reporters who usually accompanied the President to Key West put up at the Casa Marina, which at that time offered the peak in luxury on the island—a quite modest peak by Miami standards. Ross held a daily briefing for them at the Naval Station at noon to fill them in on whatever business had been transacted during the morning. The President was usually available for an impromptu interview or press conference.

Inevitably, the press copy that was filed daily out of Key West during these sojourns was heavily loaded with the bright and sometimes exasperating trivia of a President at play. Felix Belair, White House correspondent for the New York *Times* at this period, has recalled:

This was before the Eisenhower boys thought up the gimmick of the "work and play" vacation.

Mr. Truman would get his work done, all right. He'd put in three or four hours at his desk every morning before most of us were even up. And every day or so some delegation would fly down from Washington for a conference. Some really important pieces of business were transacted there at "The Little White House" in Key West.[5]

The Navy yacht *Williamsburg* was another chief source of Presidential relaxation. Kept tied up at Washington's Naval Gun Factory during weekdays, she was used by the President for many enjoyable weekend cruises when the weather was good. During his first term in particular, he would often take six or eight of his advisers, and even occasionally some newsmen, or members of Congress, aboard Friday nights. Usually this was to work on some immediate problem of government, but there would also be a couple of sessions of poker and enough bourbon to keep things properly lubricated. They would put back into port sometime during the night Saturday. On Sunday mornings the original party would disembark, and Mrs. Truman, Margaret, and a group of family friends would come aboard for another cruise down the Potomac and back. Edward T. Folliard, the veteran White House correspondent for the Washington *Post,* has said:

There was always a lot of gossip about Mr. Truman's poker playing and his addiction to "bourbon and branch water." Most of it was inaccurate, and some of it was downright scurrilous.

Mr. Truman loved to play poker. It was his favorite relaxation, and it took the place of golf, quail shooting, sailing, and even hacking around with loose women, which is what some other Presidents have done in their off hours.

He didn't care whether it was a nickel-and-dime game or one for big stakes; what he liked was the tug of wits and skill and luck. If he figured somebody was getting in over his head, he'd insist on "poverty poker." But if he figured the other fellow could stand it, he wasn't above taking him for a sucker—or getting taken himself. Churchill took him for a few shillings on the train ride back from Fulton, Missouri. Truman didn't find out until the game was over that old Winston had learned the rudiments in the Boer War.* But on the *Williamsburg* one time he let Joe Short, of the Baltimore *Sun,* drop $400 in a game. He figured—and I might say quite mistakenly—that all of us reporters were on unlimited expense accounts.

Now about the drinking. There were more lies told on him about that than anything else. I *know!*

Mr. Truman was not a heavy drinker. In fact he was a sparing drinker, and a social drinker at that. He liked a shot of bourbon and water when he was having a good time with his friends. I remember his squinting at the sun from the deck of the *Williamsburg* one morning and saying: "It must be noon somewhere in the world. Boy! Bring the bourbon."

But I've seen him nurse a single, soggy highball through a whole eve-

---

* Clark Clifford, who also accompanied the President on this trip, has a different recollection of the poker episode. "Churchill was rather an indifferent poker player," he said, "and had such a rough time that night that the President cautioned those in the game the next day to 'go easy on old Winnie, boys. I don't think he's in our league.'"

ning of talk and poker. And he was not a ritual drinker nor a cocktail-before-dinner man. In fact, he always thought it was the worst of bad manners to drink in the presence of ladies, and I believe he still thinks so.[6]

"To Err Is Truman"

Much can be told about a President by the kind of people he has around him, particularly those whom he appoints to high and confidential positions. In the earlier years at least, the Truman bag was a mixed one. The White House staff, the Cabinet, and other principal lieutenants of his administration were marked less by "cronyism" than by mediocrity, a level that was kept from being no worse than it was by a few outstanding exceptions. The poor impression was heightened, however, by a number of unseemly personal conflicts.

Truman had a three-way dilemma in staffing the top echelons of his administration. First, most of the Roosevelt holdovers, idolators of the former chief, were dubious in their loyalty to and appreciation of the new chief. He was not of their clan and kidney, a distinction which Truman sensed as well as they. Second, he seemed to be riding a downward curve of history and of personal fortune. After the high drama of the war years, the postwar years seemed tame and uninviting, while Truman himself seemed to many to have no political future beyond that of caretaker for the balance of FDR's fourth term. Hence, there was a dearth of volunteers who were both eager and able to take over the field command posts in the new Truman army. Finally, Truman did not have the broad acquaintance among the nation's elite—the leaders of finance, industry, public affairs, the law—that would enable him to summon "the best brains in the country" to his side. His social and intellectual orbit had been pretty much limited to the United States Senate, the state of Missouri, and the top layer of professional politicians in perhaps a dozen states where he had campaigned as candidate for the Vice Presidency.

For all these reasons, the new President was obliged to grope uncertainly as through a mist for the help he needed; to impose on old friends responsibilities that overtaxed their competence; and to accept uncritically the recommendations of others. The wonder, indeed, is that he did not do worse in building his administration, that the clash of personalities and ambitions did not flame higher than it did.

Mr. Truman was to find, as Jonathan Daniels wrote, "the same sort of Cabinet contentions which began with Jefferson and Hamilton at the table of George Washington. He was to discover that some who accepted places as his subordinates did so with no lapse of their sense of superiority. No other President in history ever had at his table two men who so deeply felt that somehow they had been cheated out of his chair." The two, of course, were James F. Byrnes and Henry Wallace.

By the end of his first ninety days in office, the President had gone a long way toward replacing the Roosevelt Cabinet with men of his own choice. Byrnes had succeeded Edward R. Stettinius at State; Fred M. Vinson had replaced Henry Morgenthau, Jr., at the Treasury; Tom C. Clark had taken over from Francis Biddle as Attorney General; Clinton P. Anderson was the new Secretary of Agriculture, replacing Claude Wickard; Lewis B. Schwellenbach had taken over the Labor post from Miss Frances Perkins; and Robert E. Hannegan, chairman of the Democratic National Committee, had become Postmaster General in place of Frank Walker.

Thus, James Forrestal, at Navy (he later was to become the first Secretary of Defense) was the only Roosevelt Cabinet holdover to go the full route of the first Truman administration—and beyond. And of Truman's own first batch of appointees, only two—Attorney General Clark and Interior Secretary Krug—remained in their slots as the second administration began. Throughout the seven and one-half years of his tenure, President Truman had a total of twenty-four different men in his Cabinet, as compared, for example, with President Eisenhower's sixteen. The second and third waves of Truman appointees, many of them with long experience in the departments they were chosen to head, showed a marked improvement over the first.

Truman was faced with some awkward situations in forming his first Cabinet, and his handling of several of the appointments did not add to his luster. Each of the incumbent Secretaries, as a matter of protocol, had submitted his resignation to the new President shortly after he was sworn in. He asked them all to remain in office for the time being, but each understood, without rancor, that a replacement probably would be designated in due course.

One of these was Francis Biddle, the Attorney General. He knew

the President only slightly, and not under the most propitious circumstances, for he had opposed Senator Truman on the appointment of a District Attorney in Missouri in 1944. But Biddle was not
prepared for the abrupt manner in which his offer to resign was
picked up. It came late in May in a telephone call from Steve Early,
the holdover Press Secretary, who told the Attorney General that his
resignation was accepted as of "day after tomorrow."

Biddle, a lanky Philadelphia aristocrat with a waspish temper,
exploded.

"Dammit, Steve, I expected my resignation to be accepted sooner
or later, but at the least I think I should have the courtesy of a
personal request for it from the President."

Early agreed, and within an hour Biddle was summoned to the
Oval Office. The confrontation was stiff but not acrimonious. When
the civilities had been disposed of and each had managed a smile
and a handshake, Biddle asked the President if he minded telling
him who his successor would be.

"Not a bit, General, and I know it's one you will approve of,"
Truman said. "He's a man from your own department, Tom Clark."

Biddle was aghast. Clark, an amiable, easy-going Texan, had been
in the Justice Department for a number of years and currently was
serving as head of the Criminal Division. He had reached this eminence less because of his legal talents than because of the insistent
pressures of the powerful Texas bloc in Congress, chiefly Speaker
Sam Rayburn and Senator Tom Connally.

"Unhappily, Mr. President, I do not approve of your choice,"
Biddle said. "And I most urgently suggest that you study this matter
further before making up your mind."[7]

Clark was, of course, appointed, and in 1949 he was moved up to
the Supreme Court.

Most of the details of this episode were known in Washington at
the time, but strangely Mr. Truman gives a totally different version
of it in his memoirs. He has written that Biddle *asked* to be relieved,
and that it was Biddle who recommended Clark as his successor.

Jimmy Byrnes was President Truman's first choice for a Cabinet
appointment—and the first he decided to dispense with. He told
his former Senate colleague that he wanted him to become Secretary of State as they rode the train back to Washington from Hyde
Park after Roosevelt's funeral. The appointment actually came on
July 1, after the resignation of Edward Stettinius. By December,
only six months later, the President knew he had made a poor choice

and determined to get out of it. But it was January 1947 before
Byrnes was separated from the job and the man whom Truman
wanted most of all, General George C. Marshall, could move in.

The personal relationship between Truman and Byrnes was a
strained and difficult one: envy and disdain on the part of Byrnes,
distrust and wounded vanity on the part of Truman. Byrnes had a
substantial following among the press and the politicians in Washington. He was shrewd, competent, and aggressive. He had been a
Congressman, a Senator, a Supreme Court Justice, and "Assistant
President" under Roosevelt, in charge of war mobilization. He, instead of Truman, might well have been Roosevelt's successor
had not the fact of Byrnes' dissociation from the Catholic Church
ruled him out of the Vice Presidential nomination in 1944. Byrnes,
and a big segment of the press and public as well, thought
he would have made a better President than "the little man from
Missouri." This Byrnes could not conceal. So when the little man
chose the big man as his first deputy, people said the little man
showed proper humility and wisdom. All, that is, except some very
knowledgeable professionals in the area of foreign affairs. One distinguished member of that group, whose service began under
Roosevelt and continued under Kennedy, told the writer: "Of all the
Secretaries of State I know something about, Jimmy Byrnes was the
poorest of them all."

In spite of the personal friction between them and the rupture of
their relations in later years, Truman did not share this low estimate
of Byrnes' capacity. He felt, for example, that Byrnes did as well as
could be expected in the long, tedious negotiations leading to the
peace treaties with Italy and the other satellite nations in 1946. But
he felt also that Byrnes' ambition and arrogance often got in the
way of his effectiveness as Secretary of State.

In his memoirs Mr. Truman gives a colorful account of a dressing
down he is supposed to have given Byrnes in December 1945 because of the Secretary's failure to keep the President informed on
the progress of the Foreign Ministers' Conference in Moscow.

"I read him the riot act," Mr. Truman said in later years. "A
Secretary of State should never have the illusion that he is President
of the United States."

Byrnes, in his memoirs, doesn't remember it that way. On the day
he returned from Moscow, he was invited to join the President on
board the *Williamsburg* to give a firsthand report, not to get a dressing down. "The fact is," he wrote, "the President did not on that

occasion nor at any other time express to me disapproval of any position I took at the meeting of Foreign Ministers . . . nor of any statements I made on our foreign policy."

In any event, Jimmy Byrnes was certainly guilty in Moscow in the winter of 1945, and possibly on other occasions, of giving the brush-off to Presidential authority. Averell Harriman, who was U.S. Ambassador to Moscow at the time, recalls that after the first day's session of the Foreign Ministers, he offered to help the Secretary draft the customary telegraphic summary to Washington.

"I'm not going to send any daily reports," Byrnes replied. "I don't trust the White House. It leaks. And I don't want any of this coming out in the papers until I get home."

And he did not report until, en route home on December 27, he wired the President a vague and reassuring summary of the conference and said he expected to make a full report to the nation by radio the day after his arrival. Bluntly, Truman shot back an answer saying that the Secretary was to report to his President before he reported to anybody else, and reminding him that he had had no word whatever from his emissary since Byrnes' departure for the conference on the 17th.

As the diplomat's plane put down in Washington, another picked him up and flew him to Quantico, Virginia, where the Presidential yacht was tied up. Whatever then transpired in the confrontation between President and Secretary, the fact is that Byrnes thereafter was a somewhat more tractable subordinate, at least in public. But the relationship between the two men was visibly frayed. It was the subject of much gossip and speculation in the Capital, with Truman, as usual, getting somewhat the worst of it. In April 1946, Byrnes handed in his resignation, pending completion of the peace treaties. Truman accepted, but it was the following January before Jimmy Byrnes, still nursing his hurt pride and thwarted ambition, went home for good to South Carolina.

The most egregious blunder in Harry Truman's White House career came in the manner of his firing of Henry A. Wallace, his inherited Secretary of Commerce. The President was totally justified in his action. In fact, he should have done it sooner. But both the timing and the towering ineptitude of its consummation cast a shadow over his judgment which time has not relieved.

The Wallace family of Iowa is synonymous with all that is good and fruitful and inspiring in the story of American agriculture. The third Henry of that distinguished line was picked by Roosevelt in 1933 to lead the American farmer into the mainstream of the New Deal deliverance. Wallace did this with such boldness and imagination that FDR, to protect his Secretary of Agriculture from being shot down by political guerrillas, elevated him to the Vice Presidency in 1940. Four years later he dumped Wallace from his fourth-term ticket in favor of the less controversial Truman. In an incomprehensible act of atonement, Roosevelt then rewarded Wallace with the job of Secretary of Commerce. And so it was as a member of the Cabinet that Wallace, feeling no doubt that "There but for the hand of fate, go I," welcomed the new President in that somber ceremony at the White House on the evening of April 13, 1945.

Henry Wallace was a large, rumpled, sad-faced man with pale blue eyes that always seemed to be fixed on some distant troubled horizon of the mind. He was a passionate humanitarian, a mystic, and on occasion a demagogue. As the liberal dynamic of the New Deal withered under the pressures of the war, he remained its one high priest within the temple. In the scramble for political reidentification that surged up like a geyser in the aftermath of the war, he became the apostle of the left-wing utopians, of "the Century of the Common Man." Few people really understood Wallace, least of all Harry Truman. But he was a man of powerful magnetism: He seemed to have polarized the political left when most other elements in the Democratic Party were shunning it, and Truman decided, on practical grounds, to leave him where he was. Moreover, the President had some of the same misguided sense of *noblesse oblige* toward his disappointed competitor that he felt toward Byrnes.

A principal thesis of Wallace (as it had been with Hopkins and other close associates of Roosevelt almost to the end) was that the new world of peace and plenty could only be built through trustful cooperation between the United States and the Soviet Union—a consummation that required major concessions, both ideological and practical, by capitalist America. All secrets of the atom bomb, he argued before a Cabinet meeting in the autumn of 1945, should be shared with our Russian allies. And he warned at another time that this country had no more right to interfere with Russia's iron-fisted "pacification" of Hungary and Rumania than the Soviets had of interjecting themselves into some dispute of ours with Mexico or Brazil. Truman and most of those in the Cabinet dismissed such wrongheaded advocacy by the Secretary of Commerce as a harmless aberration.

In September 1946 Secretary Byrnes was in Paris for another meeting of the foreign ministers. It was a particularly critical session, in which the American and British delegates had begun to challenge, with unusual obstinacy, the self-serving assumptions of Comrade Molotov about the political integrity of the former satellite states. On the afternoon of Tuesday, the 10th, Wallace came to the White House with a speech he planned to deliver in New York two nights later before a rally for Soviet–U.S. friendship. In a brief and pleasant chat, he told the President generally what he planned to say, and that he was going to take a more critical line toward the Russians than he had in the past. As they talked, the President thumbed through the pages of the manuscript. No problems were raised.

Then the two men talked on for a while. The President told his Secretary of Commerce he hoped he would continue his efforts to rally liberal and left-wing support for the Democratic congressional candidates in the coming election. The New York speech, he observed, ought to boost the prospects of the Herbert Lehman–James M. Meade ticket for Governor and Senator, in particular. Wallace left the Oval Office "bouncing," according to *Newsweek*, and answered reporters' inquiries on what he and the President had talked about with the cryptic suggestion that they read his forthcoming speech.

Reread today, there is no doubt that the speech carried criticisms of greater severity against the Russians than Wallace had uttered before. But it reiterated, too, and in a more compelling context, some other things Wallace had been saying about the failure of the Western Powers to recognize and accommodate themselves to Russia's innate suspicions of the capitalist world. While Truman and Byrnes had been trying belatedly to hammer out a new "get tough" policy to counter Russian belligerency, Wallace was prepared to tell the world that the United States and Great Britain should keep their hands out of the affairs of Eastern Europe, and that they should abandon, unilaterally if necessary, the buildup of postwar armaments and the United States' monopoly of atomic energy. The whole scheme of a Western consortium was evil, Wallace said, adding with plausible and provocative irrelevance: "To make Britain the key to our foreign policy would, in my judgment, be the height of folly. Make no mistake about it: the British imperialist policy in the Near

East alone, combined with Russian retaliation, would lead the United States straight to war."

Then there followed the fateful words: "I am neither anti-British nor pro-British; neither anti-Russian nor pro-Russian. And just two days ago, when President Truman read these words, he said they represented the policy of his administration."*

The speech was scheduled for delivery at 7 o'clock on the evening of Thursday, September 12. At 4 o'clock that afternoon, the President held his customary press conference. Most of the reporters had got the advance Wallace text. When they asked the President if he had approved it, and if it accurately reflected his administraton's policy, he answered firmly that it did.

One thing about Mr. Truman was that he never indulged (often to his sorrow) in fuzzy circumlocution: Yes meant yes, not yes-but or yes-maybe, or possibly no. He clearly meant to convey the impression that he had read the speech (which he had not done with any thoroughness); that he had approved it (which by the bulk of subsequent testimony he had); and that it represented no departure from established foreign policy (which it most certainly did). From these questions he passed blithely to other subjects, and that night went to a stag dinner at the home of Clark Clifford, quite unaware that in a colloquy of less than two minutes he had launched a major controversy.

The first internal alert on the implications of the Wallace speech was sounded by Acting Secretary of State Will Clayton. A copy reached his hands from an aide shortly before 6 o'clock Thursday evening. There was a hurried and angry conference around the Secretary's desk. "This will cut the ground right out from under Jimmy at Paris," Clayton groaned. It was agreed that if there was any way of shutting Wallace up, it ought to be done. Clayton called Ross at the White House, but the Press Chief argued that the President already had committed himself on the speech and it was too late for a turnabout.

The newspapers the next morning, reporting Wallace's speech, blazoned the "fact" of an about-face in U.S. policy vis-à-vis Russia on their front pages and in their editorial columns. The word was flashed to Europe, and a flabbergasted Byrnes first learned of the "new direction" he was presumed to follow from the correspondent

---

* This last sentence appears in the mimeographed copies of the speech distributed to reporters in advance of delivery. It seems probable that they were written in by Wallace immediately after his conference with the President.

of a British newspaper. Republican Senator Arthur Vandenberg, a member of the delegation brought along to Paris to dramatize the sturdy bipartisanship in American aims, issued an indignant statement saying, "I can cooperate with only one Secretary of State at a time."

In Washington, meanwhile, there was a series of hectic conferences in the White House and the State Department. The confusion had to be untangled and the President extricated from the hole into which he had stumbled. The unhappy conclusion was that the President could not now deny or retract his endorsement of the Wallace speech, but only "clarify" it. Saturday morning, reporters were called into his office to hear a statement read, not to ask questions about it. Mr. Truman, looking deceptively chipper and undismayed, went right to the point.

"There has been a natural misunderstanding," he said, "regarding the answer I made to a question asked at the press conference on Thursday, September 12, with reference to the speech of the Secretary of Commerce delivered in New York later that day. The question was answered extemporaneously and my answer did not convey the thought that I intended it to convey. It was my intention to express the thought that I approved the right of the Secretary of Commerce to deliver the speech. I did not intend to indicate that I approved the speech as indicating a statement of the foreign policy of this country. There has been no change in the established foreign policy of our government. . . ."

This transparent fabrication, though it might have served the uses of diplomacy, fanned the flames of adverse public opinion at home. *Time* magazine called it "a clumsy lie."

On Monday, Henry Wallace, from his sandstone fortress flanking the southeast corner of the White House backyard, announced: "I stand upon my New York speech. Feeling as I do that most Americans are concerned about and willing to work for peace . . . I shall within the near future speak on this subject again."

In Paris, the volatile Jimmy Byrnes could contain himself no longer. For days, he had been avoiding informal confrontations with the members of the other delegations because he did not want to have to answer their embarrassing questions. He had had no word of rectification or consolation from the White House. Finally, on Tuesday evening, he sent a bristling message to his chief:

If it is not possible for you for any reason to keep Mr. Wallace, a member of your Cabinet, from speaking on foreign affairs, it would be a grave mistake from every point of view for me to continue in office, even temporarily. Therefore, if it is not completely clear in your own mind that Mr. Wallace should be asked to refrain from criticizing the foreign policy of the United States while he is a member of your Cabinet, I must ask you to accept my resignation immediately. . . .[8]

This ultimatum hit the Oval Office like a brick tossed through the window. Byrnes was telling his chief, "It's Henry or me."

There followed two more days of backing and filling, of secret White House conferences and transatlantic dialogues, of compromises and countercompromises.

At last the President reached the conclusion that there was no way out but to fire Wallace. He wrote his decision in longhand and dispatched it to the Secretary of Commerce by messenger. No one in the White House knew of this letter until Wallace, in a mild state of shock, called Charley Ross. The letter was so intemperate and bitter, Wallace said, that he doubted, for the sake of propriety, it should even go into the archives, much less be made public. When it was read to him over the telephone, Ross unhappily concurred. In what seems under the circumstances to have been an act of magnanimity, Wallace returned the offending document to Ross, who destroyed it.

The end result was the same, however. On the morning of Friday, September 20, President Truman telephoned Wallace and said in briefer and more civil terms what he had said in the letter: that he wanted the Secretary's resignation.

Wallace replied humbly: "If that's your decision, Mr. President, I'm happy to comply."

Two hours later the reporters were called into the Oval Office for a denouement they all knew was coming. As they crowded in around the President's desk, Bill Simmons, the Chief Usher, urged them to move "a little to the left, gentlemen, a little to the left," which was greeted with a burst of nervous laguhter. Mr. Truman, laughing with them, picked up a single typed sheet and began to read:

The foreign policy of this country is the most important question confronting us today. . . . The people of the United States may disagree freely . . . but the government of the United States must stand as a unit in its relations with the rest of the world.

I have today asked Mr. Wallace to resign from the Cabinet. It had become clear that between his views on foreign policy and those of the administration . . . there was a fundamental conflict. We could not permit this difference to jeopardize our position in relation to other countries.

I deeply regret the breaking of a long and pleasant association, but . . .*

The President's performance in the Wallace affair was almost totally bad, and that of his staff as well. Clifford and Ross took prompt steps to see that there would not be a repetition: They persuaded the President that he should never again give offhand approval to a speech until the staff had combed it for bugs. He accepted their dictum meekly. But outwardly he never betrayed any sign of contrition or even of awareness that he had pulled a monumental boner in plain public view. One of his talents was that he could put such episodes, once they were irretrievably done, out of his mind, and not keep them around to haunt his sleep. That same Saturday night, in fact, he dashed off a breezy letter to the home folks that disposed of the matter in these words:[9]

Dear Mama and Mary:

Well, I had to fire Henry today, and of course I hated to do it. . . . Henry is one of the most peculiar fellows I ever came in contact with. I spent two and a half hours with him Wednesday afternoon arguing with him to make no speeches on foreign policy. . . . Well, he answered questions and told his gang over at Commerce all that had taken place in our interview. It was all in the afternoon Washington News yesterday, and I was never so exasperated since Chicago. . . .

Well, now he's out, and the crackpots are having conniption fits. I'm glad they are. It convinces me I'm right.

Love to you both,

Harry

Wallace had been booted out of the Cabinet, belatedly and awkwardly, but Truman was not shut of him by any means. As Messiah of the Radical Left, Wallace was to come marching back at the head

* There are many published versions of Henry Wallace's dismissal from the Cabinet, none of which agree in all details. The account given here is reconstructed from several of these sources and from interviews with a number of persons who were in a position at the time to know what went on. I submitted it to Mr. Wallace for his comment. On May 31, 1963, he wrote me that the account contained "the essential truth" but added this qualification: "The difference was that I called up President Truman himself and suggested that he might not like to have a letter of the type he had written on the record. He agreed, thanked me, and sent a messenger over for it at once. I do not have a copy of the letter." Mr. Truman gives a very different account of the affair and includes no mention of a letter to Wallace (Memoirs, vol. 1, pp. 555-61).

of a "Gideon's Army" to lay siege to the Presidency in 1948. The attack would come uncomfortably close to costing Truman his political life.

President Truman did make some wise and successful choices for his first-term Cabinet. The most distinguished by far was Fred M. Vinson, whom he moved into the Treasury fast upon the heels of Roosevelt's Henry Morgenthau, Jr. Vinson, a big, shaggy, gentle Kentuckian with an orderly and well-stocked mind, already had a distinguished public career behind him. He had served fourteen years in the House of Representatives, had been a judge of the Circuit Court of Appeals, had served FDR as Federal Loan Administrator and then as Director of Economic Stabilization, which was the post he held when Truman became President. The two men had known each other only casually during their concurrent terms of service in Congress. But when the overawed Missourian moved into the White House, he found the warm and sagacious Vinson already a fixture there, a steady anchor to whom he could cling with confidence.

The two men had much in common: a middle-class heritage rooted in the old frontier across the Appalachians; a simple, nondoctrinaire liberalism that equated well with intense Democratic partisanship; an ingrained sense of responsibility that surmounted personal ambition; a lively interest in history; and a fondness for poker at any hour and in most of its variants. But beyond congeniality, Vinson had much to offer the new President. Through long service on the House Ways and Means Committee, plus subsequent administrative experience, he was expert in a field in which Truman was deficient—namely, government finance and taxation. Moreover, he commanded wide respect on Capitol Hill and throughout the government for personal integrity and soundness of judgment.

Vinson quickly became the strong man of the first Truman Cabinet, counseling the President not only on economic affairs but on broad issues of domestic policy generally. But Truman's admiration for him at last outran his best judgment. When Chief Justice Harlan Fiske Stone died in April 1946, the President elevated his Treasury Secretary to the high court vacancy. It was an excellent choice by most standards, but one that left a gaping hole in the inner circle of the White House, where, for the next couple of years at least, Vinson's talents might have been better employed. Their close relationship continued, but on a personal rather than on an official basis.

In 1951 Truman did his unavailing best to persuade his old friend to accept the Democratic nomination for President.

Vinson lent more stature and dignity to that first Truman Cabinet than any of the President's other appointees. Years later, Truman was to say of him: "Vinson was gifted with a sense of personal and political loyalty seldom found among the top men in Washington. Too often loyalties are breached in Washington in the rivalries for political advantage. Not so with Vinson. I developed a great respect for him."

John W. Snyder was not in the first wave of Cabinet appointments —he followed Vinson as Secretary of the Treasury in June 1946— but he deserves to be considered with that initial group because of the special coloration he lent Truman's first term. From the very outset he was one of the President's closest and most controversial advisers, and he remained such right up to January 20, 1953. As a Missourian, he epitomized the "Missouri influence" in the first Truman administration and lent verisimilitude, at least, to the charge of "government by crony." He was, indeed, a "crony," for he and Harry Truman and their families had been close friends since their Army days together. He had grown up in the banking business in St. Louis, and in the early forties gravitated to Washington. He was an assistant to Jesse Jones at the Reconstruction Finance Corportation when, in the first batch of Presidential appointments, Truman picked him to head the Federal Loan Administration. Three months later Snyder took over the reconversion job vacated by Fred Vinson's elevation to the Treasury post.

His advisory orbit was the same as Vinson's—namely, fiscal affairs. But Snyder lacked both the depth and the breadth of the Kentuckian's perception. His was the commercial banker's approach —cautious, orthodox, and conservative. A contemporary profile of him in the New York *Times Magazine* described him as "prim and restrained as a deacon . . . with a slack and unwilling hand on the economic reins of the country [during] the switch from a military to a civilian economy. . . . To many, he gives the impression of being acutely uncomfortable in the tempestuous atmosphere of Washington; of being the unhappy middleman in a free-for-all the issues of which are not entirely clear to him."

Inevitably, Mr. Snyder was the target of much abuse from the liberals and leftover New Dealers in the new administration. They were particularly incensed when, in the steel crisis of February 1946, for example, he made an end run around OPA Administrator

Chester Bowles to grant the steel companies a $5-a-ton price increase in exchange for a wage settlement with the steel workers' union. In many such controversies, he came down on the side of industry, finance, and the advocates of "business as usual" in ways that appeared to contradict and even to negate positions that the President had previously taken. Yet, no audible conflict ever erupted between the two men. And the reason may have been that, in addition to the bonds of friendship, Mr. Truman welcomed within his inner circle at least one top aide upon whom the accolade of "soundness" was bestowed by such conservative foes as Senator Taft and Columnist David Lawrence.

The remaining faces in the group portrait of the first Truman Cabinet can be identified without much more ado. Harold Ickes, the professional "Old Curmudgeon" who had held down the Interior Post since the inception of the New Deal, stormed out early in 1946 in an undignified dispute with the President over a patronage appointment. His place was taken by a less gifted technician, Julius A. Krug. Henry L. Stimson, the distinguished Secretary of War, stepped aside, as he long had planned to do, once the war with Japan was successfully concluded. He was succeeded by another New York Republican of almost equal distinction, Robert P. Patterson. James Forrestal retained his post as civilian chief of the Navy and gave belated but effective support to Truman's subsequent effort to unify the armed services. Clinton P. Anderson, a New Mexico Congressman who had served well on the House Agriculture Committee, took command of the Department of Agriculture. Lewis B. Schwellenbach, a former Senator and Federal judge from Washington State proved to be a most indifferent Secretary of Labor. The chief political post, that of Postmaster General, was filled by a beefy, hard-boiled graduate of St. Louis ward politics, Robert E. Hannegan, who doubled characteristically as chairman of the Democratic National Committee. His stock sank after the party's defeats in the 1946 congressional elections, although it would have taken a greater genius than his to have averted that outcome.

Truman made few of the mistakes in his second- and third-wave Cabinet appointments that he had made in the first. Experience had taught him much. He now had a higher sophistication in equating a man's qualifications with the job at hand. Many of the most important appointees brought in between mid-1946 and the period around the 1948 election.

The outstanding one, at least from the President's point of view, was General George C. Marshall, who succeeded Byrnes as Secretary of State early in 1947. Though he was not skilled in diplomacy, and though many professionals in that field continue today to minimize his performance, the taciturn, straight-laced, soldier-statesman was a man of great wisdom and force of character who provided a substantial forward thrust in the new direction that American foreign policy was taking under Truman. And in Truman's eyes, Marshall always partook of the history-book heroes of his youth.

Averell Harriman's brief sojourn at the Department of Commerce was an interlude in a career directed mainly toward international troubleshooting, in which he excelled. He had been Ambassador to Moscow when Truman came in, and the President later shifted him to London—the two top diplomatic assignments in the book. Harriman—tall, loose-jointed, and with a perpetually troubled look—was the heir to one of the great American family fortunes. He and "the little man from Missouri" seemed an improbable pair of collaborators, but a few weeks of intimacy forged an enduring bond of mutual affection and admiration. Harriman continued to the end to serve the Truman administration in a variety of top-level diplomatic and administrative jobs. As with Vinson, Truman tried to pay Harriman back by securing the Democratic Presidential nomination for him in 1956, a generous but ill-conceived gambit that failed dismally.

In a number of instances, President Truman reached down into the professional ranks of the departments for the men he wanted to head them, and nearly always with good results. One such was Oscar Chapman, who succeeded the politically fainthearted Krug at the Department of Interior shortly after the 1948 election. Another was Charles E. Brannan, Anderson's 1948 successor at Agriculture. And a third was Jesse Donaldson, an ex-letter carrier who assumed the Postmaster Generalship (but not its political function) when Bob Hannegan resigned in 1947. Each of these served effectively, if not always with distinction, for the duration.

One appointment at the sub-Cabinet level during this period is particularly worthy of note, for its recipient was to affect the direction and shaping of the Truman Presidency more profoundly than any other individual save Harry Truman himself. This was Dean Gooderham Acheson, confirmed as Under Secretary of State on September 26, 1946, after almost a year of procrastination by the Senate. If ever a man was born to a Foreign Minister's portfolio, it

was the tall, impeccably aristocratic and brilliantly intellectual
Dean Acheson, who was to succeed Marshall in January 1949. But a
great deal more about him later.

Viewed collectively, the Truman Cabinet (or Cabinets) was a
competent if not a very exciting group of men. It contained a few
outstanding individuals, such as Acheson, Marshall, Vinson, and
Forrestal, and a few dreary misfits. Between these extremes, it was
peopled by men with varying degrees of ability who were, for the
most part, knowledgeable and industrious but unimaginative. Such
incidents as the insubordination of the Messrs. Wallace, Byrnes, and
Ickes should never have been allowed to happen. They came at a
time, of course, when Truman was feeling his way uncertainly, and
in the midst of national and international crises that would have
challenged even a Roosevelt. There was little tendency at the time,
however, to excuse the new President because of his inexperience.
These events strongly colored public opinion about him and contributed directly to the Democrats' disastrous defeat in the 1946
congressional elections. The second- and third-wave appointees
were a more stable and more competent lot. And there was one
distinguishing characteristic about them: They were, and they remain today, intensely loyal to Truman. The accidental leader began
at last to get a following, and it multiplied in both numbers and
devotion year after year.

"Nerve and a Program"

A President without an instinctive feeling for politics will have an
unhappy time of it in the White House, as Wilson did, or an ineffectual time, as Eisenhower did. Whatever his other shortcomings,
Harry Truman had no such disability. He was, as the saying goes, "a
natural."

The President and Mrs. Truman went home to Independence to
vote in the congressional election on November 5, 1946. When they
stepped off the train in Washington's Union Station on their return
the next morning, only one member of the administration—Under
Secretary of State Dean Acheson—was on hand to greet them.
While this typified Acheson's affection and loyalty to his chief, his
solitary gesture symbolized something far more pointed and poig-

nant: Harry Truman's political fortunes had hit a new low, and he was a very lonely man.

In the biggest off-year turnout since 1938, voters in every part of the country had emphatically repudiated Truman and the Democratic Party. For the first time in seventeen years, the Republicans took substantial control of both Houses of Congress and a majority of the state governorships. One big city Democratic machine after another crumpled before the Republican onslaught—Chicago, Jersey City, New York, Detroit. Even Mr. Truman's effort to purge his own unsympathetic Democratic Congressman, Roger C. Slaughter, of Kansas City, misfired. His handpicked candidate, Enos Axtell, lost by 6,000 votes to Republican Albert L. Reeves. In New York State, Governor Tom Dewey won reelection by a whopping margin of 680,000, piling up a Republican majority in New York City for the first time in any statewide election since 1928. And, in a contest scarcely noted at the time, a liberal Democratic Congressman in Los Angeles, Jerry Voorhis, was swamped by a vibrant young Republican just out of naval uniform: Richard M. Nixon.

An "in" party normally loses some ground in an off-year election, but rarely by such landslide proportions as occurred in 1946. There were a number of reasons. The Democrats had been in power overlong: the pendulum was due for a swing. There was a weariness with war and an impatience with the frictions and annoyances of readjusting back to peace. The Roosevelt coalition of southern conservatives, big-city machines, labor, and minority groups, which had been cemented together in the first place by the largesse of the New Deal and held together by the necessities of war, were beginning to come unstuck. And finally, there were the accumulated mishaps and missteps which befell the Truman administration: constant warfare between labor and management, a procession of strikes, slowdowns and lockouts; inflation, black markets, and a disintegrating price control apparatus; a frustrating war of nerves with the Russians over a prostrate Europe; the spectacle of a new President seemingly unable to cope with a strife-torn Cabinet or a sullen and rebellious Congress. All this the Republicans adroitly dramatized and personalized in a taunting campaign slogan, "Had Enough?"

Here was the shape of the Truman dilemma as Walter Lippmann saw it:

It is not, I think, an exaggeration to say that the condition of the Truman administration is a grave problem for the nation. How are the affairs of the country to be conducted by a President who not only has lost the support of his party but is not in control of his own administration? . . . Mr. Truman is not performing, and gives no evidence of his ability to perform, the functions of the Commander in Chief. At the very center of the Truman administration . . . there is a vacuum of responsibility and authority.

Probably no President since Andrew Johnson had run out of prestige and leadership more thoroughly than had Harry Truman when he returned almost unnoticed to Washington on that bleak, misty November morning in 1946.

A successful politician knows how to take the good with the bad, the bitter with the sweet. Harry Truman is a successful politician. He also has more guts than guile. A favorite aphorism of his is, "When you're at the bottom you've got no place to go but up." So he started up.

Before the month was over, he had locked in combat with John L. Lewis of the mine workers' union. This revived his spirits, and also his rating on the public opinion polls. In January he sent a strong State of the Union message to the new Republican Congress and laid out a budget of $37.5 billion. He renewed his demand for some of his more controversial programs of the past, including compulsory health insurance, civil rights, and a national fair employment practices act. He also called for unification of the armed services, a massive housing program, and a complete overhaul of existing labor legislation. Later he was to ask approval of the revolutionary Truman Doctrine for aid to Greece and Turkey.

This was the Eightieth Congress, a Congress whose place in history Truman was to assure by labeling it "that no-account, do-nothing Eightieth Congress" at whistlestops all across the country during the 1948 campaign. (Many years later he was to admit that it was a pretty good Congress.) The Republicans were in firm and exuberant control—a margin of 6 in the Senate, 57 in the House— under the personal command of Mr. Republican himself, Robert A. Taft.

This was to be a joyous feast of retribution dispensed by the GOP. For seventeen years they had had to live off the crumbs from the Democrats' table, and they had seen the whole balance of government initiative shift from Congress to the White House. Now they had two years in which to roll back the iniquities which Roosevelt and his upstart successor had imposed upon the nation, and beyond lay the shining promise of recapturing the Presidency itself.

Truman had made the appropriate gestures of conciliation to the

victors, offered cooperation, and warned that the nation would be
the loser if Congress and the White House locked in partisan warfare. But he was too much of a realist to expect much quarter, and
too much of a fighter not to know that an offense is the best defense.
"Any good politician with nerve and a program that is right can win
in the face of the stiffest opposition," he often said. Applying this
principle now, he stood by his program, peppered Congress with
fresh demands and sharp rebukes and took his case directly to the
people in frequent speeches over the radio. He was at his best in a
fight. This was a fight for political survival, one of the toughest of
his career, and he came out on top.

It was out of this ordeal, indeed, that the distinctive Truman
trademark, the Fair Deal, took on substance as an identifiable political program. Its genesis is one of the most significant developments
of the Truman era. It is pieced together here from the personal
testimony of several members of an extraordinary "palace guard,"
which operated quietly and almost invisibly during 1947 and 1948 to
create a positive and distinctive identity for the Truman Presidency.
Their short-range objective was to try to assure Mr. Truman's reelection in 1948, to which he had not at the time committed himself.
But in the long run they sought, also, to shape the social and political development of the nation in accordance with their liberal philosophy.

The nucleus of this group was composed of Oscar R. Ewing, Director of the Federal Security Agency; Clark Clifford, Special Counsel to the President; Leon Keyserling, member of the Council of
Economic Advisers; C. Girard ("Jebby") Davidson, Assistant Secretary of the Interior; David A. Morse, Assistant Secretary of Labor,
and Charles S. Murphy, an administrative assistant to the President.
Read today, these names do no suggest a "junta" of revolutionary
potency. But each man had power in his own corner of the Federal
bureaucracy, and each could enlist support as it was needed among
other constituencies. Their collective influence could make itself felt
in practically every important agency of the executive establishment.

The rationale of their undertaking was as follows:

Truman, in his first eighteen months in office, had labored under
the assumed obligation of carrying out the policies of Roosevelt and
the New Deal. But the dynamic of the New Deal had lost much of
its meaning by the interruption of the war. New and different imperatives had been imposed by the postwar readjustment.

These imperatives called for a liberal approach to the domestic problems of the nation. But this was not a liberalism focused on poverty and inequality, as in the New Deal. Rather, it was a liberalism focused on the creation and equitable distribution of abundance, which now loomed as an attainable reality. What this group sought, in a word, was political implementation of the theory of a constantly expanding economy.

This was a daring concept in 1947. It collided squarely with the orthodox conservative view that the rate and direction of economic growth could be determined only in the marketplace, uncontaminated by the hand of government.

This was the core of the politico-economic debate of the postwar years. Most of the nation's press and business leaders, most of the Republican spokesmen in Congress as well as the more conservative Democrats, and most of the Truman Cabinet held to the conservative view. Among the latter in particular, John Snyder, James Forrestal, Jimmy Byrnes, and Chairman Edwin G. Nourse of the Council of Economic Advisers, argued persuasively that the country had had enough of liberal experimentation under the New Deal; that the time had come for retrenchment and consolidation. The words "back to normalcy" may not have been used, but the philosophy of these advocates was not far from that imposed on President Harding in an earlier postwar era.

Where did Truman stand in this ideological crossfire? No one was quite certain, including Truman himself. His instincts were liberal, and he had a good pro-New Deal voting record in the Senate. But it was an intuitive, nonspecific sort of liberalism rooted in his frontier heritage. His Senate friends had been among the moderates, like Joe O'Mahoney, Sherman Minton, and Carl Hatch, and rarely among those of the progressive wing, like Wagner of New York and Pepper of Florida. In his first year and a half as President he had wavered frequently between a strong and a moderate liberal course. He had failed to identify himself either one way or the other.

Clark Clifford tells the story:

That was a stinging defeat in 1946. It pointed up more clearly than anything else could that there just was no clear direction, no political cohesion to the Truman program—at least not in the minds of the politicians and the people. And it pointed to two more years of frustration and final defeat for Mr. Truman in 1948.

I think it was Jack [Oscar] Ewing who first suggested the idea that a few of us get together from time to time to try to plot a coherent political

course for the administration. Our interest was to be exclusively on domestic affairs, not foreign. We wanted to try to develop not only policies
that would be good for the country, but especially those that would have
a high political appeal. We wanted to create a set of goals that truly met
the deepest and greatest needs of the people, and we wanted to build a
liberal, forward-moving program around those goals that could be recognized as a *Truman* program.

The idea was that the six or eight of us would try to come to an
understanding among ourselves on what direction we would like the President to take on any given issue. And then, quietly and unobtrusively,
each in his own way, we would try to steer the President in that direction.

Naturally, we were up against tough competition. Most of the Cabinet
and the congressional leaders were urging Mr. Truman to go slow, to veer
a little closer to the conservative line. They held the image of Bob Taft
before him like a bogeyman. We were pushing him the other way, urging
him to boldness and to strike out for new, high ground. He wasn't going
to pacify that Republican Congress, whatever he did.

Well, it was two forces fighting for the mind of the President, that's
really what it was. It was completely unpublicized, and I don't think Mr.
Truman ever realized it was going on. But it was an unceasing struggle
during those two years, and it got to the point where no quarter was
asked and none was given.[10]

The group materialized late in 1946. They met each Monday evening in Ewing's apartment at the Wardman Park Hotel. They would
have dinner at about 6 o'clock and then discuss and argue until close
to midnight. No notes were taken, no records were kept, and no leaks
were permitted to the press. The agenda usually was restricted to
one or two topics, issues currently, or soon to come, before the
President for decision. Clifford and Keyserling, because of their strategic location in the White House, could aim their influence directly
on target—the President. The others worked at a distance, but effectively nevertheless.

Keyserling has recalled:

One of our early major projects was to have the President veto the Taft-
Hartley bill. We worked this over for several sessions, because not all of
us were together on this at the outset. I was clear in my own mind that it
was bad legislation and ought to be vetoed. I also felt that on purely
political grounds this was the most beneficial course for the President to
take.

Well, we thrashed this out for two or three meetings, and in time we all
came to see it the same way. The President was getting tremendous

pressure from his congressional leaders to sign the bill, also from every member of his Cabinet except one, the Secretary of Labor. For a time, I think the President was inclined to go along with them. But in time our viewpoint prevailed and he did veto the bill.

Of course, the veto was overridden. But I never had any doubt—and I'm sure the President never did either—that the veto was the correct thing both substantively and politically.[11]

The Ewing-Clifford strategy board dissolved after the victorious 1948 election, its major mission accomplished. It had imparted a much-needed element of liberal consistency to the Truman program that was to make the Fair Deal a distinctive and distinguished chapter in the history of the Presidency.

CHAPTER 7

❖❖❖❖❖❖❖❖❖❖❖❖❖❖❖❖❖❖❖❖❖❖❖❖

"A Measure Short of War"

The Truman Doctrine

LATE ON THE AFTERNOON of Friday, February 21, 1947, two minor diplomats, one American and one British, sitting in a bleak office of the old State, War and Navy Building across the street from the White House, took the decisive first step by which Great Britain handed over virtually the last of her responsibility for perserving the world balance of power to the United States. Their brief discussion set in train one of the most momentous events in international political relations of this century.

The initiative in this undertaking fell more or less by accident to the Englishman, H. M. Sichell, First Secretary of the British Embassy. His chief, Lord Inverchapel, the Ambassador, had telephoned the State Department earlier to ask if he might come to pay an emergency call on the Secretary of State, General George Catlett Marshall, and was told that the General had departed less than an hour before for Princeton University, where he was to deliver an address. The Undersecretary of State, Dean Acheson, asked whether the matter could wait until Monday. The Ambassador said it obviously would have to, but meanwhile he would like to have the substance of his communication put into the working channels of the State Department with the least possible delay, pending a more formal presentation of the subject on Monday. This was promptly agreed to, and Mr. Sichell was dispatched to the State Department in an Embassy staff car to be received by his approximate opposite number, Loy Henderson, Director of the Office of Near Eastern and African Affairs.

These two veteran diplomats had known one another well for years, and there was no need for preliminary palaver between them. Mr. Sichell took from his dispatch case two brief documents, handed them over to Mr. Henderson, and then began to explain their background and significance.[1]

By agreement stemming from the last weeks of the war in Europe, Britain and the United States had shared a mutual responsibility to preserve the political integrity of Greece and Turkey. Britain's side of the bargain, by far the preponderant one, was chiefly military, while the United States had an almost wholly economic role. But constant and massive Communist pressure on the two Mediterranean powers now threatened both with collapse. Indeed, a crisis in the tottering Greek Government was imminent. If Greece fell, Turkey would be drawn under with her; and if Turkey fell, the fate of Greece was automatically sealed. And once Communist power broke through these political barricades into the Mediterranean, all of the Middle East, India, North Africa, and even Italy would be in jeopardy—and so, also, would be the concept of a free-world counterforce to Communist aggression.

To avert such a disaster, Mr. Sichell pointed out, both immediate and long-range assistance to these two countries, on a scale far exceeding present commitments, was essential. In the case of Greece alone, he said, a sum on the order of $250,000,000 was needed in the current year to avert starvation of the populace and to re-arm the Greek armed forces for a now-or-never assault against the Communist guerrillas in the northern provinces. Turkey's needs were only slightly less pressing.

With most of these facts Mr. Henderson was quite as familiar as Mr. Sichell. What he was not prepared for was the clincher to Mr. Sichell's presentation: His Majesty's Government would be forced to pull out of Greece and Turkey as of March 31, next, a little more than a month away. Thereafter, if this bastion were to be held, the United States would have to hold it.

Almost until this very hour the foreign policy of the United States had historically been based on the *Pax Britannica*—the power of the British Navy to rule the waves and the economic power of the British Empire to impose a relative degree of stability on the turbulent

political life of Europe, Africa, and Asia. In the century from 1815
to 1914 the world enjoyed an almost unparalleled freedom from
large-scale international warfare at the same time that the industrial
revolution opened up new vistas of material abundance for mankind. This era bore the largely benevolent and seemingly indestructible imprint of the British Crown. Thus sheltered, and with the
additional advantage of wide ocean barriers east and west, the
United States grew and prospered in untroubled isolation, its foreign policy postulated on the simple doctrine of "no entangling alliances."

That doctrine was breached, of course, in the First World War,
and the same whirlwind which pulled the United States into that
vortex worked powerfully to undermine the primacy of Britain as
the mainstay of Europe's political edifice. The extent of its weakening became shockingly apparent in the initial blasts of World War
II when it was revealed that the initiative in world politics, and the
military strength to back it up, had been snatched from the British
by the rampaging dictatorships of Germany, Japan, and Russia.

American intervention averted the imminent collapse of the old
British-oriented power structure. By the end of World War II,
though the victory had been won by the Western Allies, little more
than the façade of Britain's world power remained. Internally, she
was exhausted and spent, her economy on the verge of ruin. Her
empire was crumbling. And the imposing sea power on which her
diplomacy had been based for two hundred years had become at
best a feeble anachronism in the new age of air power, of which she
had virtually none. Similarly on the continent, the Western European nations, which had long been the unwilling accomplices of
Britain's hegemony, were crushed and impotent.

In all this vast political void of Europe, then, only the Soviet
Union, though crippled in part, was left with the strength and will
of a conqueror. And a conqueror she meant to be: to erect out of the
war rubble the world dictatorship of the proletariat prophesied by
Marx and Lenin. The only power left in the world with a potential
great enough to challenge Russia's dream of empire was the United
States.

This new balancing of international power between Russia in one
hemisphere and the United States in another was but vaguely seen
by the men of Yalta when they met to plan the postwar world. The
shifting tides of history can be seen only in retrospect. But while
Stalin, at Yalta, had clearly in mind the dynamic of Marxian expan-

sionism as the wave of the future, Roosevelt—and, somewhat skeptically, Churchill—had his eye fixed on a new world order based on the benign cooperation of the great powers through the United Nations. The partnership of war, he believed, would become the partnership of peace.

Thus the foreign policy that Roosevelt passed on to Harry Truman was predicated on mutual trust between Russia and the West, on strict adherence to all agreements, and on the substitution of collaborative for unilateral action wherever the international community was affected.

Faith in this altruistic concept had already begun to wear thin in Washington by the autumn of 1945, for the seeds of the cold war had begun to sprout—in Poland, in Yugoslavia, in Germany, and at the formative UN conference in San Francisco. Now, in 1946 and early 1947, they bore their first fruit. Russia was pushing toward her own goals of a communized Europe and Middle East without reference to her former allies, and with cold contempt for the slogans of "democracy" and "freedom" as the West understood them. Averell Harriman, U.S. Ambassador in Moscow, had sensed the true dimensions of Russia's designs, and in a long report to President Truman he likened it to "a new barbarian invasion of Europe."

An immediate objective of this Soviet power thrust was a breakthrough into the Mediterranean, and from there into the oil-rich Middle East and the beckoning political turmoil of Africa and South Asia. Turkey offered the most likely path of conquest, and Greece another. At Yalta, Stalin had spoken almost casually of hoping to share with Turkey, after the war, control of the Dardanelles, the narrow bottleneck through which the Black Sea empties into the Mediterranean. In anything but casual terms, Churchill told him No, to which Roosevelt added his endorsement. The matter was dropped for the time being. But in August 1946, Stalin again turned covetous eyes on Turkey, and this time he meant business. In a note to the government at Ankara he proposed a revision of the long-standing Montreux Convention by which Turkey had exercised exclusive control over the Straits. He suggested that in its place "a new regime" be established in which Turkey and the Soviet Union would jointly share control of the waterway. He suggested further that Russia would undertake to "protect" the waterway through the establishment of naval and air bases on Turkish soil. This was by now a familiar and ominous pattern of Soviet conquest.

Turkish authorities turned in near panic to London and Washington for "advice." President Truman hastily convened his war cabinet, composed of the Secretaries of War, Navy, and State, and told them he needed a fast rundown on the implications of the Soviet threat and some proposals on a course of action. In four days—on August 15—they were back in the President's office. It was their unanimous opinion, they said, that the Soviet intention was to swallow up Turkey just as Rumania and Bulgaria had been swallowed and that this was a danger that the United States and other Western Powers clearly could not tolerate. The sternest diplomatic and military measures would be justified in thwarting the Soviet scheme.

Truman agreed so readily with this drastic interpretation that General Eisenhower, sitting in as Army Chief of Staff, hesitantly and anxiously raised the question of whether the President fully understood and appreciated all the implications of his decision. Dean Acheson recalls that Truman took a well-worn map of the region from his desk drawer and, using it as a guide, delivered a ten-minute dissertation on the historical significance of the Dardanelles and the eastern Mediterranean, "stretching from Tamerlane to the day before yesterday."

When the President had finished, he looked up with a smile and asked: "Does that satisfy you, General?" There was good-natured laughter all around as Eisenhower admiringly replied: "It sure does, Mr. President. Strike my question from the record."[2]

The next day, Acheson, as Acting Secretary of State, after coordinating his actions with his opposite number in London, told the Turks to stand firm. To the Soviet Ambassador in Washington he handed a polite but diplomatically loaded note which said:

It is the firm opinion of this government that Turkey should continue to be primarily responsible for the defense of the Straits. Should the Straits become the object of attack or threat of attack by an aggressor, the resulting situation would constitute a threat to international security and could clearly be a matter for action on the part of the Security Council of the United Nations.[3]

Near the end of August an imposing naval task force, composed of the new aircraft carrier *Franklin D. Roosevelt* and half a dozen destroyers, steamed past Gibraltar en route to "routine training maneuvers" in the eastern Mediterranean, conveniently in view of the Turkish coast.

The heat was off for the time being, but no one doubted that it would turn up again at Moscow's convenience. Turkey was of strategic importance to Western designs for "containment" of the Soviet Union. Besides, Turkey was esteemed in Washington and London as a nation striving desperately to shake off a tyrannical past and to take its place with the democratic societies of the world. Its present government was authoritarian, but it was a stable government dedicated to gradual social reform. Its 19,000,000 people enjoyed a tolerably decent scale of living by Middle Eastern standards. But with much of Turkey's border exposed to Soviet aggression, the maintenance of its 600,000-man army was a bankrupting necessity. The U.S. Ambassador at Ankara warned the President in a note late in 1946: "Turkey will not be able to maintain indefinitely a defensive posture against the Soviet Union. The burden is too great for the nation's economy to carry much longer."[4]

Unlike Turkey, Greece had been plundered and ravaged by Nazi occupation during the war. King George had fled to London to set up a paper government-in-exile. British and American agents had infiltrated the peninsula and helped to organize thousands of natives into roving bands of guerrillas and partisans to fight the invaders. Communist agents flowed across the borders from Albania and Bulgaria to lend a hand in this guerrilla warfare against the Nazis. But long before the Germans began to withdraw in 1944, the native irregulars had splintered into mutually hostile ideological groups and began fighting among themselves for political control of the country when liberation should come. The dominant band was the Communist-oriented ELAS (Peoples National Army of Liberation), with an army estimated at about 20,000. Opposing it was a substantially weaker rightist army led by General Zervas. Britain had moved some of its forces into Greece behind the retreating Germans in the hope of averting a disastrous civil war until such time as the Greek King could be returned to his throne. But the monarchy, which had been plagued in the past by corruption and reaction, was not a popular symbol, and warfare between the partisan bands and the forces of the tottering provisional government in Athens raged on with stubborn, exhausting violence. At the same time, Greece's Communist satellite neighbors to the north kept up a drumfire of propaganda against King George and the Athens government and fed arms and supplies across the borders to the Communist partisans. Under a British-supervised truce, a plebescite of sorts was held in March 1946, in which the King was shakily restored to his even shakier throne. He was sustained almost entirely by British soldiers and the largesse of the United Nations Relief and Rehabilitation Administration (UNRRA). The Greek Government made desperate appeals to the United States for direct assistance in the form of long-term loans, but in its shattered, unstable condition it could not meet the minimal credit requirements of the only source of such loans then available, the Export-Import Bank. Moreover, UNRRA, which had pumped some $700,000,000 of goods and money into Greece since the close of the war, was due soon to go out of business.

As a partial substitute, President Truman, in January 1947, dispatched Paul A. Porter (former chief of OPA) to Greece at the head of a technical mission to see what order, if any, could be retrieved from the prevailing chaos and under what circumstances direct assistance might be proffered. Late in February, within days of British First Secretary Sichell's urgent call on Loy Henderson in the State Department in Washington, Porter, in company with U.S. Ambassador Lincoln McVeagh in Athens, advised the President that the Greek Government probably could not survive another two weeks without an instant and massive grant of American funds to provide food for the starving city masses, arms and ammunition for the sorely pressed Greek national army, and a measure of hope and encouragement for Greek morale. Collapse of the government of King George and Prime Minister Constantin Tsaldaris, they pointed out, would inevitably and swiftly lead to a Communist take-over in Greece and the country's absorption into the growing ring of Soviet satellites.

Another dreary scene complicated the picture. In July 1946, after many months of negotiation, President Truman signed a bill authorizing the Treasury to extend a fifty-year loan of $3,750,000,000 to the government of Great Britain. This was to have been a financial lifesaver. At the end of the war, Britain's gold reserves were all but gone, and she was staggering under a deficit of more than $3,000,000,000 in her international balance of payments. The rebuilding of her war-blasted economy was being hindered by shortages of raw materials and coal. There was a clamorous public demand for housing, for more consumer goods, and for food at lower prices. The Attlee government had instituted its "austerity" program of limiting imports to bare essentials and pumping as much as possible of domestic production into the export trade. The armed forces were cut by nearly half a million men. Consumption of electricity was tightly rationed between domestic and industrial consumers. The American loan of 1946 had *not* halted Britain's slide toward the abyss—not, at least, by February 21, 1947, the day of Mr. Sichell's visit to the State Department in Washington. For on that day there was issued from Whitehall an official white paper titled, prosaically, "Economic Survey for 1947," which predicted even worse things to come in the year ahead. The London *Times* said that it was "the most disturbing statement ever made by a British government."

This was the background of the crisis that came to a head with Lord Inverchapel's telephone call to the State Department on Friday, February 21, 1947. The Russians were about to force the stopper out of the bottle which contained them north of the Mediterranean. Greece and Turkey, essential bastions to the maintenance of free governments from Italy eastward into the Levant, were threatened with extinction. Britain, the traditional protector of Western interests in the region, was forced to give up. If the most devastating *coup* of Communist imperialism to date was to be blocked, the United States would have to block it.

Inverchapel and Marshall had their conference on the morning of Monday, February 24, in an atmosphere of anticlimax. Over the weekend, Acheson, Henderson, and others in the State Department had pulled most of the relevant facts together in a preliminary position paper, and the search for solutions was already on. That afternoon the Secretary of State laid the problem before President Truman, who immediately sensed the urgency of the crisis. They agreed on the spot that there was no alternative to the United States moving promptly and with determination into the breach. The only question was how, and that was turned over to the State-War-Navy Coordinating Committee, the nearest thing extant to a central planning board.

President Truman has described the situation as follows:

America could not and should not let these free countries stand unaided. To do so would carry the clearest implications in the Middle East and in Italy, Germany, and France. The ideals and the traditions of our nation demanded that we come to the aid of Greece and Turkey, and that we put the world on notice that it would be our policy to support the cause of freedom wherever it was threatened.[5]

This was a fateful and historic decision, matching in significance the Monroe Doctrine. It meant a great deal more than picking up the tab for Great Britain in Greece and Turkey. The commitment to defend freedom wherever in the world it was threatened set a new course for American foreign policy which has prevailed ever since.

Many days of intensive preparation and staff work followed. Twice, the President called congressional leaders of both parties to the White House to tell them what was going on and to prepare them for the eventual demands that would be made upon Congress. They were shocked at the disclosure that Great Britain had reached the end of the line in its ability to preserve its traditional role of monitor in the Mediterranean and the Middle East. Some, initially, like Senator Taft, querulously took the position that we simply were being euchred into pulling Britain's chestnuts out of the fire. But Senator Vandenberg expressed the prevalent view when he told a colleague: "I sense enough of the facts to realize that the problem of Greece cannot be isolated by itself. On the contrary, it is probably symbolic of the worldwide ideological clash between Eastern communism and Western democracy; and it may easily be the thing which requires us to make some very fateful and far-reaching decisions."

In the midst of it all, President Truman had to leave for a long-planned state visit to Mexico—the first by an American President. On his return, plans were perfected for what was to become known as the Greek-Turkish Aid Program, or, more popularly, the Truman Doctrine. On March 12 he went before a joint session of Congress— a particularly sober, thoughtful, and responsive one, considering that it was dominated by his political opposition and that he was later to excoriate it from one end of the land to the other as a "do-nothing Congress"—and laid the problem before it in these words:

The very existence of the Greek government is threatened by the terrorist activities of several thousand armed men, led by Communists, who defy the government's authority. The Greek Government is unable to cope with the situation. Greece must have assistance if it is to become a self-supporting democracy. . . . The future of Turkey as an independent and economically sound State is no less important to the free world than the future of Greece. . . . Should we fail to aid Greece and Turkey in this fateful hour the effect will be far-reaching to the West as well as to the East. . . . The free peoples of the world look to us for support in maintaining their freedoms. If we falter in our leadership, we may endanger the peace of the world—and we shall surely endanger the welfare of our own nation.

Concretely, he asked Congress to appropriate $400,000,000 for military and economic aid: $250,000,000 for Greece, $150,000,000 for Turkey. He also asked authority to send both civil and military missions to each country to supervise the operations of the programs and to assist the two countries in putting their governments, their economies, and their armed forces in order. This was a significant departure from the postwar relief and aid programs of the past. So pressing was the emergency, the President said, that it was essential that Congress act before March 31, the deadline for Britain's withdrawal from the area. This, obviously, was a bit more than Congress could accommodate. The President had placed a large order before the world's greatest deliberative body, and it insisted, rightly, on a degree of deliberation. When it became apparent that the deadline would pass without action, the President gained consent for an interim loan of $100,000,000 from the Reconstruction Finance Corporation to get the aid program under way. Congressional action was concluded early in May, when the House passed the Greek-Turkish aid bill by a vote of 287 to 107, and the Senate by a vote of 67 to 23. Mr. Truman signed the bill into law from his temporary office in the Muehlebach Hotel, at Kansas City, on May 22. America had taken a giant step into the unknown.

The Marshall Plan

The Truman Doctrine was the prologue to a drama called "foreign aid" that is still unfolding.

In the two years following V-E Day, the United States loaned and gave away close to $6 billion, directly and through such international bodies as the United Nations Relief and Rehabilitation Administration—UNRRA—to feed the world's hungry and to shore up the sagging economies of war-torn governments, friendly as well as hostile. This aid was given on a piecemeal basis, like a gigantic charitable enterprise, without pattern and without much effort to reach the cause of poverty and dependency among the recipients. The United States was suffering from a massive guilt complex, since, unlike most of the other combatants in World War II, it had suffered no physical damage to her land, and, in a material sense, had prospered mightily. Even the aid to Greece and Turkey, though it contained the vital new concept that we would defend freedom wherever it was threatened, did not look far beyond the immediate crisis in those two countries.

To a good many people in government, however, it was becoming apparent that what Europe really needed was not relief but reconstruction—the kind of help that would enable her eventually to take care of her own needs. By mid-1946 it was obvious, except to such inveterate altruists as Henry Wallace, that the Soviet Union was exploiting the despair and domestic turmoil of Europe for its own political ends. All the diplomatic protests in the world would not suffice to save Hungary, Rumania, and Czechoslovakia from a Communist take-over whenever Stalin felt the time was ripe to strike. Nor was there much reason to think that Italy, France, the Low Countries, and Scandinavia would be spared in the long run. Only if these governments and their people could be put back on their feet—economically, politically, and spiritually—could they ever develop the strength to defend their own interests, and, in a sense, the larger interests of the United States. To do this would require a long-range program of rehabilitation, at a staggering cost.

Some gauge of the magnitude of the job was suggested late in 1946 by Paul Nitze, a brilliant international scholar who was an assistant to the Under Secretary of State for Economic Affairs, Will Clayton. It was Nitze's idea that the United States surplus of the world balance of payments—the extent to which we were absorbing the gold and foreign exchange of other people—was a pretty reliable guide to the depth of the trouble they were in. His calculations showed this figure to be in the neighborhood of $5 billion a year, and he suggested that an aid program at about that level over a five-year period might get the rest of the world's productive machinery going again on a self-sustaining basis. He elaborated this in a memorandum for Mr. Clayton, who was setting out on a fact-finding trip of his own to Europe.

When the Under Secretary returned six weeks later, he brought the President and Secretary Marshall an alarming and eye-opening report on the extent to which Europe's physical resources—factories, mines, farms, transportation facilities—and its fiscal structure —had either been destroyed outright by the war or rendered impotent by political disruption and financial ruin. Most of Europe's cities and towns, he said, were stagnant pools of hunger, joblessness, and despair, and the farmers and peasants were only little better off. The situation was worsening daily, he said, and political collapse threatened in several capitals, Rome and Paris among them. The only means of averting such a disaster, he argued, was through an immediate massive program of rebuilding Europe's economy. It would take at least five years to do it, he said, and the cost would be in the range of Nitze's estimate of $5 billion a year.

Some others in the Department, among them Acheson and George Kennan, had arrived independently at approximately the same conclusion. But it was Clayton's disturbing report to the President and Secretary Marshall that lighted a match under this intellectual broth and set it to bubbling. The newly formed Policy Planning Staff, which Marshall had just set up in State under Kennan's able chairmanship, was directed to get busy on the problem. The Planning Staff were told that there were two facets to their assignment: (1) to conceive a workable plan for rebuilding Europe's economy; and (2) in some way to invest the plan with a dramatic psychological impact that would give the European peoples an immediate burst of hope and confidence. In the state of affairs then existing, the second consideration was almost as important as the first.

This was in the late winter and spring of 1947, while Congress was still trying to digest the Greek-Turkish aid bill. Late in April, the President asked Under Secretary Acheson to substitute for him at a long-standing speaking engagement which he had with the Delta Agricultural Council at Cleveland, Mississippi, on May 8. Acheson accepted with alacrity. He had been looking for an opportunity to spell out publicly the state of Europe's depression and the necessity for some broad-based program of relief. The little town of Cleveland, Mississippi, did not seem to be a very promising pad from which to launch a major foreign policy pronouncement, Acheson has recalled, but it was the only one available at the moment, and time was pressing. He and the President agreed that this should be the first public intimation of the administration's thinking on a new approach to Europe's problems, and the substance of his speech was discussed carefully at the White House and among the Cabinet.

"I wanted every one to understand," Acheson said some years later, "that I was putting a ball in the air and that we had all better be prepared to field it when it came down, because if it just landed, *plunk!* on the ground, it would be a very bad thing."[6]

The urbane and mustachioed Under Secretary arrived in Greenville, Mississippi, on the evening before he was to make his talk. He was the overnight guest of one of the community's leading citizens.

The next morning they drove through the lush cattle and cotton country of the lower Mississippi Delta and arrived about noon at the campus of the State Teachers College, at Cleveland. Hundreds of guests of the Delta Council had arrived beforehand. In shirt-sleeves and summer dresses, they were disposed at tables set up under the trees for a traditional fried-chicken dinner. Chairs had been set up in the gymnasium for the speaking, and for any overflow of guests there were loudspeakers outside. Less than half a dozen reporters, representing the regional press and the wire services, were on hand.

Acheson placed his rural audience in the mainstream of international affairs with his opening words:

You who live and work in this rich agricultural region, whose daily lives are concerned with the growth and the marketing of cotton and corn and other agricultural products, must derive a certain satisfaction from the fact that the greatest affairs of state never get very far from the soil.

When Secretary of State Marshall returned from the recent meeting of the Council of Foreign Ministers in Moscow he did not talk to us about ideologies and armies. He talked about food and fuel and their relation to industrial production, and the relation of industrial production to the organization of Europe, and the relation of the organization of Europe to the peace of the world.

The devastation of war has brought us back to elementals, to the point where we see clearly how short is the distance from food and fuel either to peace or to anarchy.

He then gave an account, with stark explicitness, of the human and economic desolation of Europe and Asia, induced by war but aggravated by financial and political chaos and by two years of summer droughts and winter storms of uncommon severity. These grim developments, he said, "have produced a disparity between production in the United States and production in the rest of the world that is staggering in its proportions." The United States has tried to correct this cruel imbalance, he said, through great outlays for direct relief, for loans to impoverished governments, and through financing various international organizations. But while the world's wants are expressed in monetary terms, it is *things*—wheat and coal and steel and meat and clothing and medicines—of which the world is in such crying need. At its utmost effort, the United States could not supply all these needs; they can only be supplied in adequate quantity when these needy nations are able to produce for themselves. "The war will not be over," Acheson said, "until the

people of the world can again feed and clothe themselves and face
the future with some degree of confidence."

He then posed the question of what these facts of international
life meant for the United States. They mean, first, he said, that we
must take as large a volume of imports from abroad as possible "in
order that the financial gap between what the world needs and what
it can pay for can be narrowed." They mean, second, that we will
have to continue to finance these foreign purchases heavily in order
to sustain life abroad while the broken economies are being restored. Acheson went on:

> European recovery cannot be complete until the various parts of Eu-
> rope's economy are working together in a harmonious whole. And the
> achievement of a coordinated European economy remains a fundamental
> objective of our foreign policy. . . .
>
> Last winter's blizzard [in northern Europe] showed up the extremely
> narrow margins of human and national subsistence which prevail in the
> world today, margins so narrow that a blizzard can threaten populations
> with starvation and nations with bankruptcy and loss of independence.
>
> Not only do human beings and nations exist in narrow economic mar-
> gins, but also human dignity, human freedom and democratic institutions.

And then he stated, as succinctly as it ever has been phrased, the
terms of a new American doctrine:

> It is one of the principal aims of our foreign policy today to use our
> economic and financial resources to widen these margins. It is necessary if
> we are to preserve our own freedoms and our own democratic institu-
> tions. It is necessary for our national security. And it is our duty and
> privilege as human beings.[7]

The audience at Cleveland gave the Under Secretary a warm
ovation. Whether it perceived the deep implications of his message
is not known. The American press, however, seems not to have
fielded the ball he put into the air until the second bounce. The New
York *Times* was one of the few major papers to give it a front-page
play the following morning, with a perceptive Washington sidebar
inside by its diplomatic correspondent, James Reston. The British
press was considerably more alert to what Acheson was talking
about, and European papers made something of a furore over the
speech. This in turn got American editorialists and columnists
stirred up a day or two later. Now it was beginning to be sensed that
a major turn in foreign policy was gestating.

But neither Dean Acheson nor any one else had at that time a clear conception of just how the new policy was to be worked out. All that was known for sure was that a major crisis in the affairs of Europe impended, and that the United States alone had the capability, and the urgent obligation, to meet it. In long sessions of the Policy Planning Staff and in conferences around the President's desk it was agreed that the United States must be prepared to invest very large sums of money continuously over a number of years in a truly Herculean effort to revitalize the world's ailing economy. Gradually there emerged some fixed points around which positive planning could be done.

First, this new enterprise should not take the form of a fight *against* communism, but a fight *for* economic recovery and political freedom.

Second, it should not be administered as a shot in anybody's arm but as a sustained course of *curative* treatment.

Third, for maximum effect, the effort should initially be concentrated where the prospects of success were most promising, and this meant Europe.

A final and most important postulate was supplied by Secretary Marshall—namely, that the initiative in this effort and the responsibility for making it work must come from the nations who expected to benefit from it. The time was past, he argued, for either openhanded doles or arbitrarily imposed plans for rehabilitation. To succeed, this must be a truly cooperative effort in which Europe would devise its own scheme of salvation—collectively, not on narrow, nationalistic lines—and we would help with the money and the goods to make it work.

This, it soon came to be realized, was the heart of the matter. The plan would succeed only as the nations of Europe together willed and strove to make it succeed.

Now there was a concept, cohesive and well buttoned up in its various parts. It was novel, it was daring, and it was staggering in its scope. (Winston Churchill was later to describe it as "the most unsordid act in history.") It would be buffeted by the unruly waves of public opinion at home, and if the Europeans turned out to be unequal to its great challenge, it would fall with a sickening thud. To minimize these risks, the introduction of the idea had to be achieved with great skill and dramatic finesse. The President was its logical expositor, but his popularity at home was in a period of eclipse, and the Republican-controlled Eightieth Congress, with

which he was having his troubles, would undoubtedly have projected its disdain for him onto a scheme of such radical design
issuing from his lips. So the choice fell upon Secretary Marshall,
whose standing both at home and abroad was above partisan
cavil. Moreover, he had available a featured role in an impeccable
forum: the commencement exercises at Harvard University on
June 5.

Acheson not only worked on the text of the speech, along with
Kennan, Clayton, Bohlen, and others (few such literary accouche-
ments in State Department annals have been attended by so many
anxious midwives), but also undertook the role of publicity flack.
Distrustful of the capacity of most American reporters to get the full
impact of what Marshall was to say (just as he had been prior to his
own speech at Cleveland), he carefully and secretly briefed a few
chosen correspondents in advance. Also, he called in three favorites
of the British press corps in Washington. The Marshall speech the
next day, he told them, would be "it"—the development in detail of
the program at which he had broadly hinted in his Delta Council
speech only a month ago.

"Don't waste time trying to write about it," he counseled them.
"As soon as you get your hands on a copy telephone the whole thing
to London. And one of you must ask your editor to see that Ernie
Bevin [the British Foreign Minister] gets a full copy of the text at
once. It will not matter what hour of the night it is; wake Ernie up
and put a copy in his hand." (This quite unconventional tub-
thumping by the distinguished Under Secretary of State paid off
handsomely.)[8]

General Marshall was not an electrifying orator. His delivery was
dry and colorless, and he had no knack for the artful gesture or the
dramatic pause. But in the brilliant, warm sunlight of that afternoon
of June 5, standing erect and dignified before the colorful multitude
assembled in the Harvard Yard, he epitomized the responsible and
compassionate world statesman embarked upon a serious mission.

His address was concise and to the point, and it took him a scant
fifteen minutes to say all that he had to say. He began with a brief
review of the physical and spiritual disaster which the war had left
behind in Europe. The destruction, he said, had affected people and
institutions, and "the whole fabric of the European economy" had
been torn apart. Its reconstruction would require a far greater effort
than had been foreseen. Then he turned to the means in these
words:

The remedy lies in breaking the vicious circle and restoring the confidence of the European people in the economic future of their own countries and of Europe as a whole. . . . It is logical that the United States should do whatever it is able to do to assist in the return of normal economic health in the world, without which there can be no political stability and no assured peace.

Our policy is directed not against any country or doctrine but against hunger, poverty, desperation and chaos. . . . Such assistance, I am convinced, must not be on a piece-meal basis as various crises develop. Any assistance this country may render in the future should provide a cure rather than a mere palliative. Any government that is willing to assist in the task of recovery will find full cooperation, I am sure, on the part of the United States Government. Any government which maneuvers to block the recovery of other countries cannot expect help from us.

Here, the Secretary knew, he was venturing into a treacherous bog. One of the stickiest points that had been debated back and forth in the planning sessions in Washington was whether to make this an invitation to all the governments of Europe, irrespective of their politics, or just to those which were, or might become, oriented toward the West. And if it was an open-ended invitation, what would happen if Russia elected to accept? Russia's vast, spongelike appetite would almost certainly wreck any program that was feasible for passage through Congress. On the other hand, it was worth trying to lure her satellites and prospective satellites, such as Czechoslovakia, into the cooperative spider's web in the hope that the Communist grip on those countries might be loosened.

"We decided to leave it vague and hope for the best," Paul Nitze recalled some years later. "It was a calculated risk, because at that point we really didn't know what we would do if the Russians came in."

Concluding his Harvard talk, Marshall openly tossed the ball to the Europeans, saying, in effect, "Your serve!"

It is already evident that before the United States can proceed much further in its efforts to alleviate the situation . . . there must be some agreement among the countries of Europe as to the requirements of the situation and the part those countries themselves will take. . . . It would be neither fitting nor efficacious for this government to undertake to draw up unilaterally a program designed to place Europe on its feet economically. This is the business of the Europeans. The initiative, I think, must come from Europe. The role of this country should consist of friendly aid in the drafting of a European program and of later support of such a program so far as it may be practical for us to do so. The program should be a joint one, agreed to by a number of, if not all, European nations. . . .[9]

Mr. Acheson, as the whilom PR man for the nascent Marshall Plan, wrought better than he had hoped. The American press and radio gave the Secretary's speech quite respectful attention: the New York *Times* featured it under a three-column banner on the front page along with a story on the Communist coup in Hungary. In the European press, the speech was a minor sensation. A messenger from the London *Daily Telegraph* did, indeed, pedal his bicycle up to the door of Foreign Minister Ernest Bevin that night with a flimsy of the story dictated by transatlantic telephone an hour earlier by correspondent Malcolm Muggeridge, in Washington. The American Ambassadors in London, Paris, and elsewhere on the continent were unaware of the speech until they read about it in their local newspapers the next morning. And there was no question of the impact it made in high governmental quarters all the way from Moscow to Madrid.

Bevin is reported to have been so elated over the news that he started immediately to phone his Ambassador in Washington for confirmation, and then decided impulsively not to. He did not want to risk having this splendid illusion destroyed. Instead, the next day he laid the Marshall proposal before an emergency session of his Foreign Office colleagues and then arranged a hasty conference with the French Foreign Minister to lay the groundwork for the convening of European authorities, which the proposal obviously called for.

President Truman had shrewdly not neglected his own most critical segment of public relations at home. Acheson's speech to the Delta Council back in May had excited the curiosity of such foreign policy leaders as Senators Arthur Vandenberg and Tom Connally, and Representative Charles A. Eaton, chairman of the House Foreign Affairs Committee. Congress was still in heated debate over the revolutionary Greek-Turkish aid bill, which these stalwarts were backing mightily, and now something even bigger and costlier seemed to be in the works. What was afoot?

The President invited these congressional leaders and a couple of his top advisers from the State Department for a quiet cup of tea at Blair House one afternoon. The legislators were given a confidential recital of the crisis in Europe and of the plans being devised for meeting it. To men who lived daily with the cautiousness, the prejudices, and the partisan obtuseness of Capitol Hill, a development of such proportions at this particular time was studded with barbs.

But there was an inexorableness about the problem that could not be denied, and the legislators were won over, with certain tentative reservations. In the end, Chairman Vandenberg assigned one of his top staff men from the Foreign Relations Committee, Francis Wilcox, as liaison with the special task force in the State Department, to keep the others informed.

The President had thus lined up his most important support before the battle started. In his *Memoirs* he paid tribute to these allies in these words:

Credit is due to Republican Senator Arthur H. Vandenberg and to Republican Representative Charles A. Eaton, the chairmen respectively of the Senate Committee on Foreign Relations and the Committee on Foreign Affairs of the House of Representatives. In a Congress dedicated to tax reduction and the pruning of governmental expenditures, they championed this program in a truly bi-partisan manner.[10]

Bevin and Georges Bidault, the French Foreign Minister, set a preliminary meeting of the conference of European nations to consider the Marshall Plan for July 17, in Paris. Somewhat to their dismay—and to the consternation of many in Washington—V. M. Molotov and a team of aides turned up representing the Soviet Union. Did this mean that the Russians were going to drain the well before any one else could lower a bucket? The Czech provisional government, already under heavy Communist influence, had indicated its eagerness to get into the program, and so, somewhat more tentatively, had the Communist overlords of Poland and Rumania.

The Paris meeting went on for four inconclusive days trying to set up an agenda for the all-European conference that was to follow. The Russian delegate was his usual intransigent self, picking at details and expressing his suspicions of a dark, capitalist plot, although he seemed determined to join the program in the end. On the fifth day, an aide, in obvious agitation, brought a telegram to Molotov at the conference table. An American observer who was on hand later described the tableau as follows:

Molotov, you know, has a little bump in the middle of his forehead, and when he gets excited this thing swells and pulsates as though he had bumped his head. Well, when he read this telegram, the bump swelled up to half the size of a golf ball, and there was a lot of heated whispering among all the Russians present. Then Molotov got up very abruptly from his chair, swept up his papers, and announced that Russia was withdrawing forthwith, and the same would go for Poland and Czechoslovakia as well. And as for the Marshall Plan, he said it was nothing but a vicious American scheme for using dollars to buy its way into the internal affairs of European countries.[11]

This probably was as grievous a blunder as that wily old Bolshevik ever made, although his order to pull out of the conference came from Stalin. At all events, it is now clear that if the Russians *had* decided to join the Marshall Plan, along with their hungry satellites, and then proceeded in their familiar fashion to dynamite it, very probably they would have succeeded. Instead, they tried to create a pale imitation of it—the Molotov Plan, it was called— among their captive adherents, and failed. But the Marshall Plan, as we now know, succeeded magnificently to do just what Molotov most feared.

Sixteen nations responded to Bevin and Bidault's invitation for a full European conference on implementation of the Marshall Plan— Austria, Belgium, Denmark, France, Greece, Iceland, Ireland, Italy, Luxembourg, The Netherlands, Norway, Portugal, Sweden, Switzerland, Turkey, and the United Kingdom. West Germany and Spain were the only nonsatellite nations of Western Europe excluded, although the Germans were brought in later. The sessions began on July 12, 1947, and on September 22 they sent to Secretary Marshall their first comprehensive report on Europe's needs and goals. They called themselves the Conference for European Economic Cooperation (CEEC), and they spelled out what major steps they planned, jointly and severally, to attain economic viability during the next four years, and the measure of help they hoped to get from the United States.

Some of the highlights of that report are of interest in showing where Europe was at the time, and where it hoped to get. For example: Production of *bread grains* in the normal prewar year of 1938 had been 34 million tons; in 1947 it was down to 28.3 million; by 1951 they planned to boost it back to 34 million tons. *Coal* production had been 552 million tons; it was now down to 439 million tons; the goal was 584 million tons. *Steel* production had been 45.5 million tons; it was now down to 30.3 million tons; the goal was 55.4 million tons. And so on. To finance this ambitious program, they asked the United States for $21.8 billion over the four-year period 1948–1952.[12] Both the goals and the request were unrealistic and would have to be scaled down, but the fuse of Europe's reconstruction and recovery had unmistakably been lighted. And it was not to sputter out.

While Europe was measuring its capacity to receive, this country was measuring its capacity to give. To this end, President Truman in the summer of 1947 set up three special committees of prominent private and public citizens to advise him. The first, headed by Averell Harriman, then Secretary of Commerce, was to measure in broad terms the fiscal, economic, and political limits within which the country could safely undertake this vast experiment. The second, headed by Julius A. Krug, Secretary of the Interior, was to study the question of the drain on our natural resources (agricultural products, minerals, fuels, etc.). The third, headed by Dr. Edwin G. Nourse, chairman of the new Council of Economic Advisers, was to gauge the probable impact of such an effort on the national economy.

Most important of all, probably, Mr. Truman persuaded the Republican leadership of the House of Representatives, which had shown the most stubborn resistance to foreign spending, to send its own fact-finding commission abroad to see if all the things being said about Europe's plight were true. This eighteen-member bipartisan group, whose chairman was the scholarly and dignified Representative Christian A. Herter of Massachusetts (he succeeded John Foster Dulles as Secretary of State in the second Eisenhower administration) sailed on the *Queen Mary* on the last day of August 1947 and returned a month and a half later. Even such a hard-core isolationist as Chicago's Representative (the future Republican Minority Leader in the Senate) Everett McKinley Dirksen became a practicing convert to the cause of the Marshall Plan, as did most of the other members of the group.

This was one of the most important gambits in the battle to get the Marshall Plan onto the statute books, and it proved again Harry Truman's political acuity. Wherever he thought he could get his opponent's backfield off balance before the ball was snapped, he was likely to do it.

Two unrelated events that occurred during the critical early phase of Marshall Plan negotiations in July 1947 were to affect adversely President Truman's ability to deal with the matter.

The first, and lesser, of these was the resignation of Dean Acheson as Under Secretary of State. He had been a power in the State Department continuously since 1941, and its No. 2 man since

shortly after Mr. Truman's accession in 1945. Now he wanted to get
back to the practice of law. A great affection and respect had grown
up between the two men, and in the many long absences of Secretary Marshall from the country, the President had come to depend
greatly on Acheson's counsel. Acheson was succeeded by Robert A.
Lovett, also a man of great charm and ability. But it is no deroga-
tion of Mr. Lovett to say that neither he nor any one else could
adequately take Dean Acheson's place in President Truman's
esteem. Within eighteen months, Acheson was to be back in office,
this time as Secretary of State.

The second event was the death, on July 26, of Martha Ellen
Truman, the President's mother. Until only a few weeks before her
passing, at the age of 94, she had maintained an incredible physical
and mental vigor. Martha Truman was one of the vanishing generation of pioneer women in whom simple piety, honest dealing, and
a hardheaded pragmatism were the dominant character traits. She
communicated these qualities in generous measure to her son. He
adored her and leaned upon her throughout her life, not just for
affection (she was sparing in such displays) but for strength and
inspiration. Hardly a week passed during his adult life away from
home, even in the midst of great crises, when he did not write her a
"Dear Mamma" letter, full of the spontaneous and intimate chitchat
of a loving and dutiful son. Often such a letter, handwritten on
White House stationary or bearing a postmark that identified it with
some world-shaking event of current history, betrayed a beguiling,
naïve pride that what he was doing would make his mother proud
of him. There can be little question that this impulse toward mater-
nal approbation churned somewhere in the back of Harry Truman's
mind in every important decision he made. Martha Truman's death
left a void in her son's life.

Congress adjourned in July, while the forces that were generating
the need for a recovery program for Europe were speeding inexorably toward their conjunction. Now something called "the Marshall
gap" evolved—the problem of keeping the European nations afloat
until the Marshall Plan could be perfected and sent to their rescue.
Early in September, Under Secretary Lovett warned that unless the
United States moved swiftly to close "the Marshall gap" some democratic governments on the continent would crumble. He said that
Europe's economy was sliding downhill much faster than people in
this country realized, that the need for food and fuel throughout the

continent was desperate, that supplies were available only from the United States, and that the dollar loans which the various governments had received were running out and would be gone by the end of the year. Britain, Mr. Lovett pointed out, had only about $400 million of her original $3.75 billion U.S. loan left and had had to cut off all foreign food imports to conserve her dwindling dollar reserves. France was relying almost entirely on monthly credits from a $25 million loan from the International Monetary Fund. Italy was living a hand-to-mouth existence on the vanishing proceeds of a $75 million U.S. relief grant of the previous June, and was planning another cut in the bread ration of its politically volatile masses.

In both France and Italy, Communist minorities were capitalizing on the prevalent despair and making serious inroads on the existing governments. Late in September, Harold Callendear, the New York *Times* correspondent in Paris, cabled his paper: "Sober observers here believe that the bread shortage, plus unemployment (if allowed to worsen) would so undermine the French economy and the existing government that social chaos would open the door to a communist-dominated regime." And from Arnaldo Cortesi, the same paper's correspondent in Rome, came this somber warning in respect to Italy: "If the food ration is further cut almost anything can happen. The communists . . . with their registered membership of 2,500,000 are a formidable party. But they are not so formidable that the de Gasperi government cannot meet their challenge if [domestic] conditions are half-way favorable . . . But if food shortages get much worse, few would bet on the ability of the present government to survive."

Meanwhile, the debate here at home on whether and how to meet Europe's problem was livening up. In September, the President made public the three economic studies he had ordered, each of which concluded that the United States was capable of making—indeed, obligated by self-interest to make—a massive effort for Europe's reconstruction. To a great many orthodox Republicans this whole developing situation was a nuisance and a menace. Their party was in control of Congress for the first time in sixteen years, and if ever they were to make good their incessant demands for a cutback in government expenses and a contraction of government activity, this, surely, was the time to do it. Now they were faced with a demand for a program unprecedented in peacetime in both cost and scope.

Their prevailing frustration was expressed by Senator Robert A.

Taft, who that autumn was on a feeling-out expedition around the country to test his prospects in the Presidential contest upcoming in the next year. To an audience in Tacoma, Washington, early in October, he said:

Certainly we wish to help, but an international WPA would fail to solve the problem. . . . We cannot afford to go on lending money on a global scale. I believe our loans should be made to specific countries for specific purposes and only to pay for goods shipped from the United States.

This was a pretty narrow view of the matter. Taft was to back away from it later, but he amassed a considerable amount of public support in behalf of his position during the late months of 1947. Other opinion leaders, almost equal to Taft in stature, were, of course, propounding the opposite viewpoint.

The problems of "the Marshall gap" had become so insistent by mid-October that President Truman reluctantly called a special session of Congress to convene on November 17 to deal with it. His reluctance was due to the growing virulence of the general Republican attack on him. (The scent of possible victory in the 1948 Presidential elections was causing Republican noses to twitch impatiently, and the President was an inviting target any time he showed his head.) Mr. Truman debated seriously with his aides whether, under the circumstances, he should risk a setback or defeat for the European recovery program by calling a special session, or wait until the regular session convened in January. In the end, he decided that the urgency of the need outran the risk, and the call was issued.

He first asked Congress for an immediate appropriation of $597 million of stopgap aid to get Europe through the rigors of winter. He then asked for a package of economic and credit control laws to shore up the American economy against an onrushing inflation and to cushion the eventual shock of full-scale operations of the Marshall Plan. On the latter request he received short shrift, but on the interim aid measure Congress was surprisingly cooperative. By very substantial margins in both Houses it voted late in December a total of $540 million for stopgap foreign aid, with $100 million earmarked for China, which the President had not asked for and the wisdom of which he questioned.

The ease with which the aid bill went through a violently partisan Congress in special session was a tribute to the towering influence of Senator Vandenberg and of the eighteen-man Herter committee of the House, which had made the on-the-spot inspection tour of Europe a couple of months earlier.

On December 19, while the aid bill was nearing passage, Mr. Truman sent to Congress a special message containing the first full-dress presentation of the Marshall Plan. By now the nature of the problem and the pattern of our expected answer to it were widely known. The hospitable reaction to the interim aid bill was a favorable augury for the success of the longer-range plan. Even so, the scope of the proposal—$17 billion of U.S. tax money to finance the economic recovery of Britain and half of Europe in a commitment that would run at least four years and probably longer—had a shock effect. Never had this nation, or any other nation, been asked in peacetime to assume so great and so altruistic a burden. The President's message read:

We must now make a grave and significant decision relating to our further efforts to create the conditions of peace. We must decide whether or not we will complete the job of helping the free nations of Europe recover from the devastation of war. Our decision will determine in large part the future of the people of the continent. It will also determine in large part whether the free nations of the world can look forward with hope to a peaceful and prosperous future as independent states, or whether they must live in poverty and in fear of selfish totalitarian aggression. . . .

Our deepest concern with European recovery, however, is that it is essential to the maintenance of the civilization in which the American way of life is rooted. . . . If Europe fails to recover, the peoples of those countries might be driven to the philosophy of despair—the philosophy which contends that their basic wants can be met only by the surrender of their basic rights to totalitarian control.

Such a turn of events would constitute a shattering blow to peace and stability in the world. It might well force us to modify our own economic system and to forgo, for the sake of our own security, the enjoyment of many of our freedoms and privileges. . . .

Concretely, the President's request boiled down to three basic proposals: (1) authorization for the expenditure of $17 billion in support of European recovery from April 1, 1948, to June 30, 1952; (2) an immediate appropriation of $6.8 billion to carry the program for its first fifteen months, from April 1, 1948, to June 30, 1949; (3) authorization to create an Economic Cooperation Administration, an independent agency answerable to the President, to administer the program.

Concluding his long and detailed presentation, the President said:

I know that the Congress will, as it should, consider with great care the legislation necessary to put the program into effect. This consideration should proceed as rapidly as possible in order that the program may become effective by April 1, 1948. It is for this reason that I am presenting my recommendations to the Congress now, rather than awaiting its reconvening in January.

I recommend this program . . . in full confidence of its wisdom and necessity as a major step in our nation's quest for a just and lasting peace.

Mr. Truman's historic message was received with sober approval by most of the nation's press and by most members of Congress. However, some of the Republican stalwarts could not resist a critical shaft or two. Senator Taft said a program of such a magnitude should only be tried on a year to year basis, and that a commitment for four years should be withheld. Senator Joseph R. McCarthy of Wisconsin argued that for every dollar spent the nation should receive a dollar's worth for foreign bases and strategic supplies. And Senator Homer Ferguson of Michigan deplored the whole idea as "a global WPA" that would discourage the Europeans from buckling down to help themselves.

But there was never much doubt that the President would get from Congress substantially what he asked for to bring the Marshall Plan alive. Most responsible leaders agreed, however reluctantly, that the free world had reached an inevitable turning point in its quest for survival, and that only the United States had the means and the will to lead it along this new path toward salvation.

If any additional impetus for this realization were needed, it was obligingly and dramatically supplied by the Soviet Union. Late in February 1948, the U.S.S.R. engineered a starkly cynical coup in Czechoslovakia, finally forcing that struggling democracy behind the Iron Curtain. At almost the same time Stalin presented Finland with an "invitation" to enter into a joint defense pact with Russia. Late in March, the Russians began a new campaign of harassment against the West by clamping restrictions on rail and road access to West Berlin. These were all parts of a pattern frankly described by A. A. Zhnadov, a member of the Politburo in Moscow, as designed to see that "the Marshall Plan is not realized."

But the Marshall Plan *was* realized, on April 2, 1948, when the House approved it by a vote of 318 to 75 and the Senate by an overwhelming voice vote, and the measure was sent to the White House for the President's signature.

Felix Belair, Jr., wrote two days later in the New York *Times:*

What was to have been a measure of economic aid to Europe changed unnoticed to "a measure short of war" to counteract Russian influence. . . . Never before in peacetime had Congress acted with such despatch on such important legislation. But rarely ever before had there been such a threat to the world's free institutions.

The legislative journey for the European Recovery Program (ERP) was not all clear sailing, of course. There were those who denounced it as "operation rathole," and others questioned its implications with more restraint and a good deal more wisdom. Congress gave the President $5.3 billion instead of the $6.8 billion he had asked for, but it added on $563 million for China and $275 million to keep the Greek-Turkish aid program going. It required that he come back each year for additional appropriations, and hemmed the program about with some minor "nuisance" restrictions. When a few days later the President sent up the nomination of Paul G. Hoffman, a prominent Republican businessman (he was then President of Studebaker Motors), to be the first administrator of the Economic Cooperation Administration (ECA), approval was prompt and enthusiastic.

On April 14, eleven days after the ERP became law, the freighter *John H. Quick* steamed out of Galveston Harbor with 9,000 long tons of wheat for Bordeaux, the first of a fleet of six vessels to sail in a week with emergency food cargoes for France. The Marshall Plan was a going concern.

The Truman Doctrine saved Greece and Turkey (they were subsequently incorporated in the ERP) and all of the Mediterranean. The Marshall Plan saved Western Europe. The fact may be attested in cold statistics. Using 1938 as a base (100), the index of industrial production for the ERP area showed the following growth in the 1947-51 four-year period:[13]

	1947	1949	1951	Percent Increase 1947-51
All participating countries	87	112	135	55
United Kingdom	110	129	145	32
France	99	122	138	39
Italy	93	109	143	54
Greece	69	90	130	88
West Germany	34	72	106	312

Political stability in the ERP world grew along with economic stability, although a good deal more unevenly. At all events—and this was a primary consideration in 1947—no Communist regime has been established in the area, and it seems highly unlikely now (almost two decades later) that one will be. In 1948, for example, Italy seemed to be hanging onto democratic forms by her fingernails. The parliamentary elections scheduled for April 18 that year had been designated a primary target by world communism, a make-or-break effort to crash through the democratic cordon of Western Europe. But ERP had become a dramatic reality almost three weeks before, and tens of thousands of Italian-Americans wrote and cabled their kinsmen, "In the name of Mary and the Saints, hold on!" And they did, by millions: anti-Communist parties received 69 percent of the popular vote in that crucial test.

The Marshall Plan cost the United States less than was expected. The total through 1951, when ERP as such expired, came to $12.5 billion. It did not, as present-day critics of foreign aid correctly contend, buy for us the friendship and affection of the world. Nor has it materially lessened the anxieties of the cold war. But it *did* save free and independent governments in Western Europe; it *did* put Europe on the road to a now-booming industrial prosperity; and it *did* make impossible (up to this date) the convulsive explosion of a hot war out of a cold war. It is also comforting to note that should a hot war still erupt between the free and Communist worlds (a specter that haunts most men's minds these days), we here are not likely to be isolated in a lonely and insecure "fortress America." The Marshall Plan "cured" the economic and spiritual disintegration of Western Europe, and today we have strength on our side—more than enough, collectively, to match the strength of the world of communism.

The Marshall Plan was a logical extension of the Truman Doctrine. Together they have formed the philosophical core of American foreign policy of the last decade and a half and probably for decades to come. They have provided the substance and the sinew of America's free-world leadership. They have contained European communism within its 1948 boundaries. And stemming directly from them have come other makeweights in the desperate struggle for a balance of power between the East and the West: the Military Assistance Program, the North Atlantic Treaty Organization, the European Common Market.

War, it is said, is the ultimate extension of diplomacy. A measure short of war, when it succeeds, is diplomacy at its best.

CHAPTER 8

<><><><><><><><><><><><><><><><><><><>

1948—The Preliminaries

"A Gone Goose"

IF EVER a successful political campaign was patched together with scissors and paste and sheer bravado, it was that incredible effort of 1948 when Harry Truman upset not only his Republican rivals but the massed forces of the nation's press, public opinion polls, and political experts, including his handlers and seconds. He was seeking vindication of his record by winning the Presidency in his own right. Not only did he have a host of issues raised against him by the Republicans, but he faced a two-pronged revolt within his own party—the Wallace Progressives on the left and the Thurmond Dixiecrats on the right. Moreover, a sense of defeat overhung the Democratic organization from coast to coast like a paralyzing miasma. The party's morale was shot and its treasury worse than broke. In the final week before election day, Mr. Truman was the deadest of ducks to just about everybody except candidate Truman himself. Because he stubbornly refused to lie down, he wrought the greatest coup d'état in all the history of Presidential politics.

When and how did he decide to take this riskiest of gambles? In his many recollections about it, Truman leaves the impression that from 1947 onward his mind was made up, however reluctantly, to run. There was still "unfinished business" from sixteen years of Democratic reforms to be completed, he has said, and the Republi-

cans in the Eightieth Congress had demonstrated both their dis-
inclination and their inability to carry them out or even to deal
adequately with the newly arising problems at home and abroad.
He was not blind to the mountainous obstacles in his way, but "I
was not brought up to run away from a fight when the fight is for
what is right. Supposedly scientific predictions that I could not win
did not worry me one bit."

Two other little-known circumstances may have had a bearing on
that decision.

The first one: Truman offered, as late as the autumn of 1947, to
step aside for Eisenhower if the General would accept the Democratic nomination, while Truman would take the No. 2 position on
the ticket as Vice President.

Ever since the 1946 election, Eisenhower's name had acquired a
growing and irresistible magic to the politicians of both parties. The
General's preference as between the GOP elephant and the Democratic donkey was unknown, but in the declining light of Truman's
popularity he looked like a sure winner on any ticket for 1948, and
he was assiduously courted by emissaries from both sides. This
courtship grew in ardor as 1947 wore on.

One day in the fall of that year Kenneth C. Royall, Secretary of
the Army, came to see the President. With some trepidation he told
Mr. Truman that, if Eisenhower, who was then Chief of Staff, did
become a candidate under either party's banner, he could not, in
conscience, work against the General, whom he so greatly admired.
The Secretary asked, Would it not be the best thing for him to
resign quietly now before the issue had to be faced?

Not a bit of it, the President replied. On the contrary, he had a
countersuggestion to offer. He would like to have Royall go in deepest confidence to Ike and tell him that, if he were receptive to the
Democratic nomination for President, he, Truman, would not only
help him get it but would offer to be his running mate as Vice
President.

The incredulous Secretary did as he was bidden. He had some
difficulty in persuading the equally incredulous General that the
President was in earnest. But Eisenhower at that time was just as
earnest about staying out of politics as others were to get him in,
and this message was then conveyed back to the White House with,
of course, hearty expressions of gratitude.

The implication of this incident is clearly that Truman, even in
the later months of 1947, doubted his ability to win reelection and

possibly even the nomination. But rather than forfeit the Presidency to the Republicans he was willing to make a personal sacrifice such as no President before him had ever ventured. When his strange gambit failed, he was ready to go it on his own.*

The second circumstance: Mr. Truman's decision was ultimately shaped by the cogent and persuasive reasoning of Clark Clifford and the secret political strategy board. Late in November of 1947, Clifford put in the President's hands a 40-page analysis of the status of Truman and the Democratic party that should rank as one of the great dissertations on the art of politics. It did not promise Mr. Truman he could win. What it did do was to cut down to size some of the mountainous imponderables of his situation and to suggest that he did not have to lose.

As an extraordinary example of the kind of political perception that underpins a Presidential election campaign, this study is worth summarizing at some length.

The aim of the memorandum was "to outline a course of political conduct for the administration extending from November 1947 to November 1948." Its basic premise, as stated, was "That the Democratic Party is an unhappy alliance of Southern conservatives, Western progressives, and big city labor. . . . The success or failure of the Democratic leadership can be precisely measured by its ability to lead enough members of these misfit groups to the polls" on election day of 1948.

What were the "probabilities" of the opposition to be encountered in that effort?

First of all, Dewey was almost certain to be the Republican nominee—"a resourceful, intelligent, and highly dangerous candidate . . . with an extremely efficient group of men around him."

Second, the only safe assumption to make about Wallace was that he would run as a third-party candidate, in spite of all the talk about the "futility" of such a gesture. If he should do so, and then draw 5 to 10 percent of the vote in a few key states, this might throw the

---

* This incident is published here for the first time. The writer submitted the facts to the three principals involved and received the following comments: Secretary Royall wrote that the account was "substantially correct" but denied that he was unprepared to support Mr. Truman if he should become the candidate. He adds: "Mr. Truman was a realist and from time to time doubted whether he could win in 1948. But he never gave up trying." General Eisenhower wrote: "Your letter involves an action by an individual who is still alive and active. It is my conviction that in writing about words or actions of such a person, you should contact him directly." Mr. Truman wrote: "That story about which you wrote me has been going around and around. I never agreed to help Ike get the Democratic nomination. There is nothing to the story."

victory to the Republicans. There was no question about the strong
Communist influence at work in the Wallace ranks, or that Moscow
would delight in seeing the Truman administration pulled down.
"The best way it can achieve that result and hasten disintegration of
the American economy is to split the independent and labor vote
between Truman and Wallace, and thus assure the Republican candidate's election." To ignore the Wallace threat would be "extremely
unrealistic." Every effort should be made to dissuade him from running, and if that fails, "to identify him and isolate him in the public
mind with the Communists."

Third, "The South, as always, can be considered safely Democratic." That (mis)calculation left the administration free to concentrate on the large bloc of western states that the party had carried in 1944. The two blocs, combined, should yield 216 of the
required 266 electoral votes, leaving only 50 to be picked up in
doubtful states of the Middle West and East. If that could be
brought off, "We could lose New York, Pennsylvania, Massachusetts, Ohio, and Illinois—all the big states—and still win." (Clifford
was looking into his crystal ball three months before the submission
of Truman's 1948 civil rights program, which galvanized the Dixiecrat revolt. But the other half of his postulate was correct.)

There then followed a long analysis of the major voting blocs. The
No. 1 priority should be the farmers, who were enjoying a high rate
of prosperity and whose Republican moorings were already loosen-
ing. The labor vote was crucial in most big states, and it almost
certainly would suffer some inroads from the Wallaceites. The same
was true of the Negroes, and strong emphasis on civil rights would
be necessary to hold them in line. Jews held the key to New York,
and the key to the Jewish votes was what the administration would
do about Palestine.*

As to issues, the President had a majority of the people with him
on his handling of foreign policy, the degree of assent fluctuating
pretty much in accordance with the fever chart of U.S.–Soviet relations. On domestic problems, the Republican Congress would almost certainly block him on every major maneuver, so that Congress
itself became the overriding issue for the President.

Finally, the Clifford memo urged a prompt and drastic overhaul
of the Democratic Party organization. "The blunt fact is that
the party has been so long in power that it is fat, tired, and even a

* On direct orders of President Truman, United States recognition was extended to
Israel eleven minutes after it proclaimed itself a government on May 14, 1948.

bit senile." A new chairman should be brought in to start rebuilding "from the ground up." Moreover, the Truman "image" could stand a little face lifting. To add a new dimension to the popular conception of him as "a man of the people trying to do his best," he might consider an occasionally well-publicized lunch "with an Einstein or a Henry Ford, or to speak out now and then about an important current book he is reading."

Above all, he should get out of Washington more, to be seen and heard by the people in the flesh.

Since he is President, he cannot be conspicuously active politically until well after the convention. So a President who is also a candidate must resort to subterfuge. He cannot sit silent; he must be in the limelight. . . . He must resort to the kind of trip Roosevelt made famous in the 1940 campaign—the "inspection tour." . . . No matter how much the opposition and the press pointed out the political overtones of those trips, the people paid little attention, for what they saw was the Head of State performing his duties.

What direct effect this document had on Truman's ultimate decision to take the plunge in 1948 has never been stated. But that its influence was substantial, and perhaps decisive, can hardly be doubted.

Weighing against all the negative political snares that lay in Truman's path were two positive factors of his own temperament and personality. First, his instinctive response to a challenge was to fight back; he was not, in this case, going to take repudiation lying down. Second, he was convinced that the forces arrayed against him, Democratic as well as Republican, were intent on rolling back the liberal accomplishments of his and the Roosevelt administrations. And his belief that he alone could thwart that design grew in direct proportion as the campaign to deny him the opportunity intensified.

Given these subjective compulsions "to show those s.o.b.'s who's right," the Clifford memo provided Harry Truman with a practical rationale and a strategy to underpin his natural impulse. It resolved whatever misgivings he was still harboring as 1947 drew to a close and the year of decision dawned. And its traces are strikingly evident in all that he did subsequently.

The State of the Union message, sent to Congress in January 1948 was a bold, almost defiant, reaffirmation of the Fair Deal policies Truman had advocated before. There were no retreats to appease anybody, right or left. It was, indeed, and it was so intended, the framework for a Democratic platform to be written at the Philadelphia convention in July. It called for a "poor man's" tax reduction of $3.2 billion; enactment of a ten-point program for combating inflation which a special session of Congress had rejected only two months previously; a whopping housing program; enactment of new civil rights legislation (for which a later special message was promised); extension of unemployment and Social Security benefits, plus national health insurance; and a starting appropriation of $6.8 billion to get the Marshall Plan going.

His special message on civil rights, sent to Congress in February, turned high the burners under the already simmering Dixiecrat revolt. In April, when Truman vetoed a "rich man's" tax bill that Congress had substituted for his "poor man's" bill, the stampede to override showed only 88 Democrats in the House and 10 in the Senate sticking by their President.

The President's plummeting prestige within his own party at this period brought this grim commentary from Arthur Krock in the New York *Times* on April 4, 1948:

The Democratic Party is imperiling the President's effectiveness as no major party in this country has done since the Republican radicals impeached Andrew Johnson. . . . A President whose defeat at the next poll is generally prophesied faces difficulties in performing his office that conceivably bring disaster. . . . At this writing, the President's influence is weaker than any President's has been in modern history.

This bleak mood not only infected the President's party in Congress but sapped the juices of the working organization as well. Jake Arvey, in Chicago, and New York's Mayor William O'Dwyer, satraps of two of the nation's mightiest Democratic machines, publicly announced their readiness to "dump" Truman for almost any other candidate. James Roosevelt, in California, and Senator Claude Pepper in Florida, were openly flirting with a "draft Eisenhower" movement. The Democratic National Committee, starved of cash for even day-to-day operations, found its usual sources of funds drying up. Left-wing contributors were funneling their money to Wallace. In the South, contributors were building a war chest for the Dixiecrats. Big Jewish contributors from the retail and entertaining industries were keeping their wallets zipped tight until the administration showed how it was going to jump on the Palestine issue. Big business, which usually hedged its bets by helping both parties in equal amounts, felt safe in ignoring the Democrats this time. When the new National Chairman, J. Howard McGarth, tried to arrange a quiet dinner in New York for a score of "fat cats" who had always come to the aid of the party in the past, only three accepted the invitation, and he had to call off the affair.

If there ever was an office-seeking politician with the chips stacked against him, it was Harry Truman in those early months of 1948. Late in February he went off for a two-week Caribbean cruise.

Breaks of this sort were important to Truman. They broke the oppressive continuity of Washington's hostilities and allowed his natural self-confidence and optimism to take command of his spirit. He came back looking tan, rested, and full of fight. On the afternoon of Monday, March 8, he called Chairman McGrath to his office. An hour and a half later the usually dour McGrath, now with a flicker of a smile on his face, walked into a swarm of reporters in the White House lobby.

"The President," he told them, "has authorized me to say that if nominated by the Democratic National Convention he will accept and run."

Henry Wallace, leading the attack on Truman's left flank, was the first candidate in the field in the 1948 campaign. In an emotional nationwide broadcast from Chicago on the night of December 29, 1947, he sounded the trumpet to rally a "Gideon's Army" that would wrest the country from the hands of the tired, reactionary, and corrupt old parties that were blindly leading it, he said, into another world war. The Republicans he dismissed as being "beyond hope." And the Democrats under Truman's leadership he condemned as "a party of war and depression" which had abandoned the New Deal theology and concocted a Marshall Plan whose only result could be to drive a permanent wedge between Russia and the West.

As he reached his peroration that night, Wallace's voice rose in pitch and fervor. He declared:

When the old parties rot, the people have a right to be heard through a new party; a chance to vote for the greater good, and not just for the lesser evil. . . . And so I announce to you tonight that I shall run as an independent candidate for President of the United States in 1948.

The history of third parties during this century has been a dismal one. Only one materially affected the outcome of an election and that was the Republican Bull Moose revolt in 1912, which paved the way to victory for Woodrow Wilson, a Democrat. The LaFollette Progressives who sought in 1924 to deny a full term to another

President-by-succession, Calvin Coolidge, were swamped by an
avalanche of regular Republican votes. Obliteration even more profound overtook the Union Party of William Lemke, which was also
a Republican splinter, in the memorable year of 1936, when FDR
swept every state in the Union except Maine and Vermont into the
Democratic column.

Every such rebellion is fueled at the start by emotion. The Wallace venture was no different. It was a mixture of religious fervor,
dogmatic humanitarianism, and, as time was to tell, of Marxian opportunism. He had begun to lay the foundations for his third party
almost from the time he stepped out of the Truman Cabinet. Almost
at once Wallace was offered the editorship of the *New Republic*, a
liberal weekly that gave him a respectable journalistic pulpit for his
views. In addition, he took to the international lecture circuit. He
made a dozen speeches in Europe during the spring of 1947, and
scores of them throughout the United States in the remainder of the
year, denouncing this country's anti-Russian foreign policy, and
demanding a new round of liberal reforms in civil rights, social
welfare, and labor legislation. The uncertainty and anxiety of the
times made a fertile seedbed for his ideas.

The base of Wallace's political support evolved through a new
organization called the Progressive Citizens of America (PCA). At
its core were the political actionists in the trade union movement, in
particular those identified with the Political Action Committee of
the CIO. Another constituent was the Citizens Committee for the
Arts and Sciences, a crucible for the political discontent of left-wing
intellectuals, particularly the physical scientists, whose sudden
fright over the implications of atomic energy had made them among
the most vocal "peacemongers" of the nation. The PCA had also
attracted a sizable contingent of New Deal Democrats who had
despaired of Truman's liberalism and who shared, to some degree at
least, Wallace's belief that the Truman foreign policy carried the
fuse of another world war. The Communist Party did not openly
embrace the PCA, but hundreds of its members joined as individuals and worked their way up to positions of power within the local
chapters and in the national organization. Scattered through the
roster, and occasionally speaking or writing under the aegis of PCA,
were a few names that lent it intellectual status: Rexford Tugwell,
for example, one of the "greats" of the New Deal; Dr. Frank Kingdom, the liberal New York cleric; Bartley Crum, C. B. Baldwin, and
others. Philip Murray of the CIO was one of its early vice presidents.

By late 1947, PCA was recognized as the organized "left" of the American political edifice. It claimed a national membership of 100,000, with chapters in twenty-five states. By mutual adoption Wallace became its *de facto* leader. It sponsored his Chicago speech in December, and later officially transformed itself into the Progressive Party, committed to the candidacy of Henry Wallace for President and Glen H. Taylor, a flamboyant freshman Senator from Idaho, as Vice President.

But the infant party was afflicted with the virus of disintegration almost from the start. Some of the more prominent sponsors of the PCA, such as Chester Bowles and Mrs. Eleanor Roosevelt, had envisioned it only as a liberalizing influence on the Democratic Party, not as a separatist movement. Scores of members pulled out and cast their lot with the newly formed Americans for Democratic Action (ADA), which was avowedly anti-Communist and committed to working within the established two-party system. The mounting Communist influence within PCA also brought the defection of some of its more powerful labor constituents, including the Amalgamated Clothing Workers in New York and many of the CIO unions. James Roosevelt, son of the former President and now leader of a major Democratic faction in Southern California, had welcomed Wallace and the PCA in Los Angeles as a scourge to the faltering Truman, but now he wanted no part of Wallace and his Progressive Party.

The result was that as the moment of transition from a political *committee* to a political *party* arrived, the base of the Wallace movement had shrunk to a hard core of radical left-wingers with a strongly Communist orientation. Political observers wrote it off as a political force in its own right, but gave it high marks as a diversionary tactic to secure the defeat of President Truman and of the Democratic ticket. The new party had acquired a certain amount of momentum, and Wallace's zeal was undiminished.

Even if election were out of reach, as Wallace realized it would be, the role of a dominant "third force" beckoned invitingly. "Gideon's Army" set off to get itself on the ballot in as many states as possible (the total was to reach forty-four by November) and to swell its ranks with recruits wherever it could find them. In the process it wrote one of the most bizarre chapters in the annals of American political folklore.

Henry Wallace barnstormed the country in those middle months of 1948 like an impecunious tent evangelist. He scrounged the money in one town to move on to the next. He rode the day coaches in preference to the higher-priced airlines. He put his traveling party up in second-class hotels and held his rallies in dingy union halls or public parks because he could not afford the high-rent auditoriums. His entourage consisted of not more than half a dozen aides and speech writers, plus a variable corps of traveling newsmen. His arrival in a new town was heralded by little fanfare—no bands at the station or airport; no banners flung across the streets; no public welcome from the Mayor or the Governor. The local committee in charge of a Wallace meeting was likely to be a group of political amateurs from the unions or the campuses, high on enthusiasm but low on know-how, and probably suspect among their neighbors as crackpots and radicals.

But what the local managers lacked in expertise was more than offset by some of the candidate's own handlers. They were young, talented, suave, hard-driving. Their political ties were obscure, but their ideologies were hard left. They were adept at the arts of dialectics, showmanship, and mass psychology. All they asked was that a crowd be turned out for a meeting, and they would take over from there. By prayer, exhortation, and mass singing of familiar proletarian tunes, they converted these gatherings into evangelistic orgies, building up step by step to the climactic, spotlighted entrance upon the platform by Wallace. Wearing a rumpled suit and his hair in a tousle over his right eye, he would stride purposefully out of the wings, grinning and waving his arms in answer to the tumultuous greetings.

The crowds at a Wallace rally were predominantly working class, with a heavy representation of Negroes, at least several of whom were always accorded a place on the platform. Always, too, there was a heavy turnout of youngsters of the college or GI set, with bristly crew cuts and open-neck sport shirts, their girls in bobby socks and dirndls. More often than not there were contingents of hecklers at these meetings, yelling mock Communist slogans at the speakers. Wallace was several times on the receiving end of a thrown egg or tomato.

A set part of the proceedings was a wring-out of the audience for contributions, anything from a dollar up, to keep "Gideon's Army" on the march. This was accomplished not by a passing of the hat but by the deft, relentless wheedling and bullying of a master pitchman, William Gailmore. At the climax of his nightly routine a forest of hands would be raised, each waving a dollar or two, and sometimes a ten or twenty, to be harvested by the ushers.

Wallace, who was a man of quite substantial means, financed much of this early campaigning himself. The Progressive Party had a few "angels" among well-to-do liberals in New York and Chicago who contributed modestly, as did the political adjuncts of some labor unions. But without the nightly exertions of the hypnotically persuasive Gailmore, an ex-rabbi from Brooklyn who had gone into public relations, "Gideon's Army" would have been stranded somewhere on the plains of Kansas or Iowa in that spring of 1948 for lack of train fare and the money to pay hotel bills.

The Communist tinge of the new party became steadily more evident as its crusade crisscrossed the country. No avowed Communists held conspicuous posts in the organization at the start, but prominent fellow travelers were easily identifiable, even among those closest to the two candidates. There were many touches of familiar Communist dialectics in speeches and literature bearing the Progressive label, and the left-wing press, the *Daily Worker* in particular, gave the party unrestrained praise. Wallace appeared to be the captive of forces which he either did not recognize or whose effect he underestimated. He grew resentful and evasive when questioned about it. He publicly denied that Communists controlled his party but said he welcomed their support. Democratic strategists did their Machiavellian best to fix the Communist label on the Wallaceites. In a New York speech during March, President Truman proclaimed, "These are days of high prices for everything, but any price for [the support of] Henry Wallace and his Communists is too high a price for me. I'm not buying." Mrs. Eleanor Roosevelt chided Wallace in her newspaper column for making common cause with the radicals of the left. Some important figures on the Progressive roster, such as Dr. Frank Kingdon and Bartley Crum, resigned in protest.

However, "Gideon's Army" rolled on in its antic, unpredictable way into the summer of 1948, garnering enthusiastic if not overwhelming crowds wherever it made a stand, and posing an ever more worrisome enigma for Harry Truman and the Democrats. Henry Wallace could not be elected, that they knew, but every labor, Negro, Jewish, or left-wing vote he got he would take from the Democrats, chiefly in the crucial big-city precincts. Candidate Truman was not going to have many votes to spare come November.

In an odd sort of way there was a connection between the Wallace revolt on the left and the Dixiecrat revolt on the right. As things turned out, the latter proved a greater threat to Mr. Truman than the former, although this was the reverse of his expectations.

The President's civil rights message, sent to Congress on February 2, was one of the most sweeping of its kind. It was based on a study prepared by a special Presidential commission headed by Charles E. Wilson, President of General Electric. It set out to correct at one legislative stroke a host of injustices borne by the Negro since his emancipation from slavery. It proposed the establishment of a permanent Federal commission on civil rights; a permanent Fair Employment Practices Commission to abolish discrimination in hiring; the outlawing of "Jim Crow" in schools, transportation, and public service facilities such as theaters and restaurants; and a Federal statute against lynching.*

While Mr. Truman, as an individual, undoubtedly believed that each of these reforms was desirable, as a politician he knew that the timing of his request made their enactment impossible. But there are good reasons for believing that, as a politician, he picked this timing deliberately—to undercut the appeal of Wallace to the Negro voters in particular, and to Northern white liberals in general. The Truman strategy board feared Wallace's inroads in the big-city precincts, where the Negro vote is decisive, far more than they feared defections in the South. Regardless of the provocations, they reasoned, the South would retain its historic Democratic solidarity. They turned out to be wrong. It was the civil rights gambit, aimed at Wallace, that triggered the biggest Southern revolt since 1928.

Southern reaction to the President's February message was immediate and angry. Senator James O. Eastland of Mississippi accused the President of trying "to mongrelize the South." Representative Ed Gossett of Texas said the President was "kissing the feet of the minorities," and Representative "Gene" Cox of Georgia wondered out loud "whether Wallace was such a bad fellow after all." In Wakulla Springs, Florida, where the annual meeting of the Southern Governors' Conference was under way, its lethargic proceedings were suddenly vitalized as if another Sherman had been discovered marching toward the sea. Oratory flamed. There was talk of bolting the Democratic party, or of finding ways of denying Truman as its candidate the 116 electoral votes of the old Confederacy. A six-man delegation headed by South Carolina's Governor

---

* The Truman program anticipated not only the Supreme Court's antisegregation decision of 1954 but most of the civil rights legislation of the Kennedy and Johnson administrations through 1964.

Strom Thurmond was named to go to Washington to plumb the true depth and meaning of this assault on Southern Democracy. Two weeks later the Governors' delegation met for an hour and a half with Chairman McGrath at Democratic headquarters in the May-flower Hotel. Thurmond, tense and coldly formal, put the ultimate question to McGrath in these words:

"Will you now, at a time when national unity is so vital to the solution of the problems of peace in the world, use your influence as chairman of the Democratic National Committee to have the highly controversial civil rights legislation, which tends to divide our people, withdrawn from consideration by the Congress?"

McGrath's answer, was a firm and simple No.

The Governors stalked out and later that day issued a formal statement to the press: "The present leadership of the Democratic party will soon realize that the South is no longer 'in the bag.'"

Secessionist talk like this has long been a familiar feature of the political dialectic in the South, but this time there was an uneasy feeling in Washington that there was more than just talk involved. At the big Jefferson–Jackson Day dinner at the Mayflower in March, in place of the customary levity of a Democratic clambake the atmosphere was notably strained—a circumstance enhanced by the conspicuously empty table of South Carolina's Senator Olin B. Johnston immediately in front of the lectern from which Truman spoke. At a similar gathering in Little Rock the same night, half the diners rose noisily from their seats and walked out as the President's speech began to come in over the radio loudspeakers. More significantly, Virginia's Governor William M. Tuck, whose every move was dictated by the South's most influential elder statesman, Senator Harry Flood Byrd, proposed to his legislature a bill to keep the name of the Democratic Presidential candidate off the ballot in Virginia. Shortly afterward, Alabama voters elected a slate of "free" Presidential electors pledged to withhold their ballots from a civil rights candidate.

On May 10 a conference of "States' Rights Democrats" brought approximately one thousand public officials, politicians, and onlookers from seven Deep South States to Jackson, Mississippi. The city's main street was alive with Confederate flags and noisy with the refrains of Dixie played by school bands. The host was Governor Fielding L. Wright, who had found occasion, only the day before, to tell the Negroes of his state that if they expected "equality" they had better "move to some state other than Mississippi." The affair was not quite the barn-burning that Thurmond, Wright, and other sponsors had hoped for. An air of caution had dampened some of the rebel spirit of the delegates from Virginia, North Carolina, and Georgia. An outright bolt against the sacrosanct Democratic Party had begun to acquire some of the bitter and sobering tinge of heresy. To connive at a Republican victory would deprive Southern politicians of their patronage and powerful chairmanships in Congress.

These second thoughts did not reduce by much Southern resentment against Truman but did impose a period of reflection on strategy. The consensus was, first, to try to block Truman's nomination with a convention bolt to a Southerner of the stature of Dick Russell or Harry Byrd. In the probable event of the failure of this tactic, they would call a separate convention of "States Rights' Democrats" immediately after the regular Democratic convention to field a slate of "true" Democratic candidates. By this stratagem, it was reasoned, neither Truman nor his Republican opponent could get a majority of the electoral vote, and the issue would be thrown into the House of Representatives. Then, with each state having but a single vote, and the Southerners holding the balance of power, they could dictate their choice of a Democratic President.

There were a number of holes in this argument, the most conspicuous being that it was predicated on the recapture of control of the House by the Democrats, in spite of their badly fractured condition. To most observers in the early summer of 1948, this seemed as unlikely a prospect as Truman capturing the Presidency. At all events, the States' Righters left Jackson firm in their determination to "stop Truman." They deferred the details to a convention to be called in Birmingham after the regular Democratic convention, should Truman become its nominee.

The Jackson meeting had one positive and long-lasting result. It brought the word "Dixiecrat" into the vocabulary, the invention of a copy editor on the Charlotte (North Carolina) News who needed a headline abbreviation for the States' Rights Democratic Party. A shorter-range but more pointed result was that it gave the "Trumancrats" a good deal more to worry about as the convention approached than they had bargained for. A fracture in the Solid South was now a genuine possibility.

More humiliating to the President than the Wallace attack from the left or the Dixiecrat attack from the right was the boom for

General Eisenhower, which was aimed at the dead center of Truman's support in the Democratic Party. It was designed to deny him the almost inviolable right of a President to have his party's nomination for a second term if he wants it. As this movement began to snowball in the late winter and spring of 1948, it became clear that it was more than a rash of scattered defections. It was an organized repudiation of Truman as a man and as a leader—an ill-tempered verdict of "You won't do!" It was all the more galling to Truman in that it was utterly irrational.

First, not even an Eisenhower could have been elected under the banner of a Democratic party that had so emphatically rejected its own record of the past four years as well as the man who made that record. To dump Truman would simply have meant to give the victory to the Republicans by default.

Second, the willingness of Southern conservatives and Northern liberals to rally together behind a man whose views on the most divisive issue of the day—civil rights—was totally unknown, betrayed a panic born of desperation. This unrealistic rationale was defined by the *New Republic* in these words: "Democratic politicians are not concerned about Eisenhower's views. What they want is a winning candidate who will carry local candidates to victory."

Unrealistic or not, the drive was to generate enough momentum to alarm Truman's small but loyal cadre of backers. It was a threat for which no counterattack had been devised in the Clifford strategical plan.

Up to the beginning of 1948, the Republicans had been Eisenhower's most relentless pursuers. Their fascination with the glamorous war hero had caused confusion and indecision within their own stable of orthodox aspirants, such as Senator Taft, New York's Governor Thomas E. Dewey, Harold E. Stassen (the former "boy wonder" Governor of Minnesota), and the liberal California Governor Earl Warren. Late in January, on the eve of his resignation as Chief of Staff, General Eisenhower sought sincerely to choke off further speculation about his availability.

His name was about to be entered as a Republican in the New Hampshire preferential primary, the first of the season and therefore one with a psychological significance greater than its electoral significance. To scotch this and similar designs (he hoped), the General wrote Publisher Leonard W. Finder of the Manchester *Union Leader,* one of his most determined admirers, in these seemingly unequivocal terms:

I am not available for and could not accept nomination for high public office. My decision is definite and positive.

The necessary and wise subordination of the military to civilian power will be best sustained when life-long professional soldiers abstain from seeking high political office. I would regard it as unalloyed tragedy for our country if the day should come when military commanders might be selected with an eye to their future potentiality in the political field.

This manifesto was convincing to the Republican leaders, and it threw the barn doors wide open to their team of light and dark horses, who had been impatiently pawing in their stalls. But the anti-Truman Democrats chose to read it another way: "He only said he didn't want the *Republican* nomination. Maybe he's a Democrat after all." On this slender thread of hope, they took off in hot and disorderly pursuit.

The Eisenhower obsession struck indiscriminately at many elements in the Democratic Party. It felled a score of leaders in the South, Dixiecrat and non-Dixiecrat alike. It hit hard-nosed old machine bosses in the North, like Mayor Frank Hague, of Jersey City, and Boss Jake Arvey, of Chicago. It hypnotized scores of New Deal liberals like Leon Henderson, head of the militant Americans for Democratic Action, and Elliott and James Roosevelt, sons of FDR. The Liberal Party in New York, after having said in March that it would stick with Truman, reversed itself in April and plumped for Eisenhower. A Democratic rally in Los Angeles was thrown into an uproar when Chairman McGrath, the principal speaker, was booed at his first mention of Truman. The meeting had been secretly rigged by Jimmy Roosevelt, leader of a major Democratic faction in Southern California, to be suddenly turned into a "spontaneous" demonstration for Ike. Hugh Mitchell, Democratic leader in the State of Washington, concocted the crowning indignity by sending the President a wire urging him to assume leadership of the movement to "draft" Eisenhower for the Democratic nomination.

On through the spring and into the summer, the Eisenhower bandwagon rolled with an ever-increasing din and clatter. Jimmy Roosevelt was in charge of it in the West, and Florida's red-hot New Dealing Senator Claude Pepper in the East. Its passenger list grew impressively: Senator Dick Russell, of Georgia; Kentucky's ebullient Governor A. B. ("Happy") Chandler; Paul H. Douglas, reform candidate for Senator from Illinois; John M. Bailey, state chairman for Connecticut; Governor Jim Nance McCord, of Tennessee;

Mayor Edward J. Kelley, of Chicago; Mayor William O'Dwyer, of New York; Senators Lister Hill and John J. Sparkman, of Alabama; the bouncy new Mayor of Minneapolis, Hubert Humphrey, who was destined to play a leading role in the forthcoming convention; Walter Reuther, of the CIO; Leon Henderson, Chester Bowles, and Wilson Wyatt, of the top hierarchy of ADA, and scores of others. It was a mixed, rowdy, and thoroughly uncongenial lot, held together by a panicky distrust of Truman and an infantile belief in miracles.

But the miracle was not about to happen. With the convention scheduled to open in Philadelphia on Monday, July 12, Roosevelt and Pepper, early in the month, wired each of the 1,592 delegates inviting them to a special caucus in the city on the Saturday preceding the opening. Their summons did not mention Eisenhower. It said only that the purpose was "to pick the ablest and strongest man available" for the nomination, and adding with transparent subtlety, "It is our belief that no man in these critical days can refuse the call to duty and leadership implicit in the nomination and virtual election to the Presidency of the United States."

Meanwhile, the absence of so much as a glance of recognition for their efforts from Eisenhower began to seem not only ominous but sinister. He was President of Columbia University and shut himself off from politicians and reporters alike. George E. Allen, the professional friend of Presidents and Generals, was sent to Morningside Heights early in July on a do-or-die assignment to break Ike's silence. Allen's failure plunged the managers of the draft in gloom. In a final desperate effort, Pepper, two days before the caucus was due to assemble, wired the General that his name would be put before the convention with or without his permission. To this, Eisenhower replied in terms as closely approximating those of General Sherman as any present-day politician has used: "I would refuse to accept the nomination under any conditions, terms, or premises."

That ended the Eisenhower boom of 1948. For a time it had looked like a near thing for Mr. Truman, and indeed it was. If anyone could have stampeded that restless, uncertain, anxiety-ridden corral of delegates—the Democratic national convention—it was the amiably enigmatic General Ike. He had a charm of universal appeal, and no one knew enough about him politically to be against him, while nearly everyone seemed to have something against Truman.

Although Truman by early June had amassed enough delegate

pledges to assure him a winning margin, no matter whom the Southern rebels might pit against him, it is unlikely that those pledges would have been proof against a massive, Willkie-type stampede on the convention floor for so popular a figure as Eisenhower. So it was not until Eisenhower took himself finally and irrevocably out of the running two days before the convention that the Truman forces were sure they had the nomination in the bag.

Truman's confidence in the face of all the noisy conspiracies going on around him reached back to a sound political investment he had made weeks earlier, his famous "nonpolitical" whistlestop tour to the West Coast and back. Such a trip had been prescribed in the Clifford memorandum. Truman was anxious to undertake it for a special personal reason. While all the machinations of the left, right, and center were monopolizing the newspapers, he had a hunch that "everybody was against me except the people." He wanted to test that hunch. If it proved out, he would go the whole course to try to win the election. If it didn't, well, maybe he would try anyway.

The immediate problem for the political strategists at the White House was to find a plausible excuse for sending the President on a cross-country tour. The congressional session was drawing to a close, with a lot of important legislation pending. The President would do himself more harm than good by absenting himself for such trivial reasons as a convention of his war buddies or to dedicate a few dams and reclamation projects. A solution dropped unexpectedly one day into the lap of Oscar Chapman, the Interior Secretary and a member of the political strategy board. Late in April he received a telephone call from an old friend, Robert Gordon Sproul, president of the University of California, at Berkeley. Dr. Sproul asked Chapman if he thought the President would be receptive to an invitation to address the commencement exercises at the Berkeley campus in June. Chapman later recalled:

I jumped two feet out of my chair. I told him to hold the line, that I thought I could get him an answer right away. With Sproul on the "hold button" I picked up my direct line to the White House and got through to the President. I told him this was just the thing we were looking for; that here was an unassailable prestige invitation that would take him all the way to the West Coast.

The President seemed pretty pleased, too. I asked him to speak directly to Sproul. He agreed, so I just switched the call from my phone to the

President. He and Sproul completed the deal right on the spot, with an honorary LL.D. for the President thrown in.

That's how that first whistlestop trip got started.

A great deal of undisguised fudging was necessary to give this journey a nonpolitical overwash. It had to be labeled as nonpolitical —first, for strategic reasons, and second for financial reasons, since the Democratic Committee did not have the money to pay for it even if it had wished to do so. So the expense was charged up to the President's official travel fund—to the fury of Senator Taft, Chairman Carroll B. Reece of the Republican National Committee, and most other leading Republicans. The chief concession made in stressing the nonpolitical character of the trip was the refusal to include Chairman McGrath or any of his Democratic Committee people on the passenger list.

But the dissembling ended there. When the sixteen-car "Presidential Special" pulled out of Washington's Union Station at 11:30 on the night of Thursday, June 3, with a White House party of twenty and approximately one hundred reporters and photographers aboard, the most naïve knew that a political junket was under way. Candidate Truman was out to test the water.

The itinerary called for five major speeches—at Chicago, Omaha, Portland, the University of California campus just outside San Francisco, and Los Angeles. But there were scores of stops with rear platform appearances, and brief detours through the towns en route to each of these points. Chapman had set out a week ahead of the official party as advance man, making contact with local Democratic leaders to assure a proper reception and turnout for the President. Many times he had to pick his way cautiously between warring local factions to find a pro-Truman leader to handle arrangements. Some towns he had to strike from the itinerary when no such loyalists were available. Some local candidates even declined Chapman's offer of the traditional benediction of getting aboard the President's train as it entered their state and spending a day of public politicking with him from the rear platform.

But from the very first stop—at Crestline, Ohio, on Friday morning, where more than a thousand people spilled over the station platform and the adjacent tracks to have a ten-minute look at their President and to shout a welcome—it was apparent that this was going to be a triumphal tour. The President, jaunty and at his wisecracking best, "poured it on" the Congress, the Republicans, and the stay-at-home Democrats who, "because they stayed at home and didn't vote last year, got just the kind of Congress they deserve." At Omaha, he jumped out of his official car and led a parade of veterans of the 35th Division on foot, waving to the cheering crowds right and left. At Grand Island, Nebraska, he held up a pair of gold spurs someone had given him at the trainside welcoming, and said:

"When I get these on, I can take Congress to town."

At Pocatello, Idaho, center of a region desperately concerned about its water resources, he lashed the Republican Congress for having cut reclamation funds.

"We have some people," he told them, "who would like to restore the Insull era when they put the welfare of a few promoters above the welfare of the people." There was a roar of assent.

More and more, Congress became the eye of Truman's target. "You've got the worst Congress you've ever had," he said in Spokane. And time after time he reminded his listeners why he was there: to dispel "the lies and the misinformation" his opponents had been spreading about him. "I am coming out here," he said, "so you can look at me and hear what I have to say, and then make up your mind as to whether you believe some of the things that have been said about your President."

There had been some dreadful gaffes along the way. A foul-up in arrangements for his major night speech in Omaha brought a skimpy audience of 1,000 into the cavernous Ak-Sar-Ben auditorium with its 12,000 seats. Hundreds of papers the next day ran pictures of the acres of emptiness surrounding the President and his handful of listeners. At Carey, Idaho, his briefing went awry, and he dedicated an airport named for a young girl who had been killed in a private plane crash to "the brave boy who died fighting for his country." And in Spokane, his offhand remark, "I like old Joe Stalin," was seized by the Republicans as an evidence that he was "soft on communism," an issue that was to loom large in the campaign later.

But Truman's buoyancy and optimism were an easy match for such setbacks. The crowds were big, friendly, and good-naturedly boisterous. Truman caught their mood and reflected it back to them in his warm, sparkling grin, in his genial, unpretentious manner, in his flat earthy prose. He was one of them. He spoke the language of the courthouse steps, the Baptist Church, the businessmen's table at the Busy Bee Café. He was fighting their battle with high prices, with a stubborn Congress, with Russian communism. There were no tricks about this fellow; he was down to earth, on the level, called a spade a spade. They warmed up to him.

"Give 'em hell, Harry," they yelled. "Pour it on!" Harry warmed up to them in return and yelled back: "If you send another Republican Congress to Washington, you're a bigger bunch of suckers than I think you are!" They loved it.

Eastern editorialists haughtily deplored the crassness of the President's speech and conduct, ignoring or misreading what their reporters on the scene were writing about the political shock waves he was sending through the Western grass roots. George Elsey, a White House staff man remaining on duty in Washington, sent Clifford a long telegraphic memo saying that the President was getting an almost solidly adverse reaction in the major newspapers of the country.

In Philadelphia, Senator Taft petulantly complained to the Union League Club about the spectacle of an American President "blackguarding Congress at whistlestops all across the country." McGrath and his publicity man, Jack Redding, pounced gleefully on Taft's semantic blunder. They wired the Mayors of thirty-five towns and cities through which the President had passed, asking if they agreed with the Senator's pejorative designation of their communities as "whistlestops."

"Must have wrong city," Mayor Earl McNutt, of Eugene, Oregon, responded.

"Characteristically, Senator Taft is confused," the President of the Laramie, Wyoming, Chamber of Commerce wired back.

"Very poor taste," said the Mayor of Gary, Indiana.

In any event, Taft had put a new word in the political vocabulary.

The "Presidential Special" was gathering political momentum as it rolled into Oregon and on down into California. At Berkeley, the ultimate destination of this meandering journey, the streets were decked with flags and bunting. Fifty thousand people, a gathering twice the size of any previous commencement audience, crowded into the university stadium to hear the President deliver a sober, carefully-thought-out address on foreign policy. He received an ovation at the end, and wide commendation in most of the nation's press the next day. The abrupt change of pace from the rip-snorting partisan oratory of the previous days had its effect in presenting a more balanced image of the President, of statesman as well as politician.

The effect was visible two days later when he arrived in Los

Angeles and attended the biggest, noisiest, and most prolonged reception he had received on the entire trip. An estimated one million people packed the sidewalks along the five-mile parade route, throwing confetti and waving flags, while jet aircraft flew past and a skywriter wrote "Welcome President Truman" in mile-high letters overhead. The President was "thrilled," according to the New York *Times*. He held court jubilantly that afternoon in his suite at the Ambassador Hotel for a procession of Democratic potentates, including the now somewhat chastened Jimmy Roosevelt. In his speech that night to the Los Angeles Press Club, he returned with relish to the attack on Congress.

His hosts at the banquet gave him as a souvenir an oversized eight ball, the Press Club emblem and a traditional symbol of hard luck. Accepting it, Mr. Truman said: "A President is always behind the eight ball."

But he clearly did not mean it that night. Instead, he felt about as chesty and confident as he ever had felt in his life. He had run the only kind of test he knew on his political standing, and he had come through it with colors flying. He had gone to the people and said: "Here I am, look me over." And the people had said: "You're OK, Harry, give 'em hell." Intuitively, he knew what the experts and the pollsters and the editorial writers did not know—that what he, Truman, believed in and wanted for the country was what the common people of America also wanted. As he headed homeward— there were a few stops yet along the way before he would reach Washington on Sunday, June 20—he was confident that he could be elected if he could see and talk to enough of the people before November. That few others shared his optimism bothered him not at all.

While all this was going on, the Republicans, of course, had been narrowing down their own field of candidates. The first to be eliminated was General Douglas MacArthur who, with a sort of Olympian magnanimity, had indicated from far-off Tokyo his readiness to hang the Presidency from his trophy belt if enough people wanted him to do so. His name went on the ballot in the April 6 primary in Wisconsin, which claimed him as a native son. The General won only 8 out of 27 delegates, and this finished his political career for good.

The surprise winner in Wisconsin was a young newcomer on the national scene, 39-year-old Harold Stassen, of Minnesota, who picked up the other 19 delegates and suddenly became "the man to beat" for the Republican nomination. Well backed with money and organizational skill, Stassen's was an exciting new face in the GOP gallery, a progressive out of the Middle West in the old Populist tradition, or so it seemed.

Ranged against him were New York's Governor Thomas E. Dewey, a suavely automated product of Eastern Republicanism and the party's nominee in 1944; Senator Robert Taft, of Ohio, the doggedly uncompromising champion of Republican orthodoxy; Governor Earl Warren, of California, a handsome neo-New Dealer; and, with somewhat less serious intent, Senator Arthur Vandenberg, of Michigan, who had virtually invented bipartisanship in foreign policy, and Speaker Joe Martin, Massachusetts' gift to the House of Representatives. This large and varied field of aspirants testified to the almost universal belief that whoever won the Republican nomination in 1948 would be the next President of the United States. Not in twenty years had the prospect been so alluring, nor the scramble for preferment so intense.

Stassen went on from Wisconsin to win handsome primary victories in Nebraska and the Dakotas. Taft finally checked his momentum in Ohio, whose primary the Minnesotan had dared, against sound advice, to enter early in May. And Dewey all but finished Stassen off in a memorable radio debate in Portland, Oregon, on May 17. The topic was "Should the Communist Party Be Outlawed?" From the outset, the sharp-witted former prosecutor of the New York underworld had his adversary floundering in a sea of constitutional legalisms and a confused, unintended defense of communism. The debate was a disaster for Stassen, and his campaign lost steam from then on.

The Republican convention met in Philadelphia on Monday, June 21, only two days after the adjournment of Congress. Dewey, Taft, and Stassen were the front-runners, in that order. But with a handful of favorite sons cluttering up the field, none of the three had enough votes for a first-ballot victory. Thus for the first couple of days there was a frantic procession of secret conferences, negotiations, bargaining, and wheeling and dealing, as each tried to beg, borrow, or steal some of the opposition support for a second-ballot "blitz." The Dewey forces, sharper and better organized, outmaneuvered the others. His lead on the first ballot was 434 to Taft's 224 and Stassen's 157, with 257 ballots scattered. On the second roll call, Dewey pulled up within 33 of the necessary majority of 548, and the battle was over, for on the next pool all the dissenters joined in to make his choice unanimous. The next day, Earl Warren was picked for the Vice Presidency by acclamation.

It was a strong ticket, and it looked like a sure winner. "Truman," said Connecticut's Clare Boothe Luce, "is a gone goose," and most of the country, it seemed, agreed with her.

The Democratic convention opened on a note of despair, but it ended on a wholly unexpected upbeat of enthusiasm and even of hope. When the opening gavel fell at noon on Monday, July 12, in Philadelphia's Convention Hall (the bunting and flags left over from the Republican convention were still in place), the last obstacle to Mr. Truman's nomination had evaporated. By the sheer working of the laws of machine politics, he had the votes in hand to assure his winning. But it would be a victory without triumph—a victory that would lead the party through a mutinous discontent to what seemed almost certain defeat in the larger battle at the polls.

Liberal columnists such as Max Lerner scorned the whole proceeding as a fraud. Many important labor leaders showed their disdain by refusing to attend. Southern conservatives made clear their intention to boycott any ticket with Truman on it. Even among the President's most loyal aides there was a tendency to regard the nomination as the end of the road—a hollow token whose greatest value would be to spare their chief the humiliation of rejection.

"None of us," Clark Clifford said later, "really felt at the time that the nomination meant very much. Our aim was just to get the President nominated. Because it would have been an unconscionable reflection upon him if, after four years, the party had turned him down and gone for somebody else."

With Truman's nomination foreordained, the resulting boredom of the convention proceedings was relieved by two events.

On Monday night, Alben Barkley, the revered Senate Majority Leader, delivered a keynote address redolent with the clichés and the oratorical melodrama so dear to the heart of the professional politician. He evoked the past glories of the New Deal and the saintly image of FDR and wrapped them about the figure of Harry Truman. Then, with that good-natured raillery at which he was adept, he turned to a dissection of Republican claims:

The Republican nominee has announced that he proposes to clean the cobwebs from the government in Washington.

I am not an expert on cobwebs, but if memory does not betray me, when the Democratic party took over the government sixteen years ago, even the spiders were so weak from starvation that they could not weave a cobweb in any department of the government in Washington.

Barkley's speech, a jewel of old-fashioned political oratory, warmed every heart in the hall and was met with a bedlam of cheers and applause. It broke the ice of apathy and made the delegates feel that they were at a convention, and not at a wake.

On Wednesday, a fight that had been going on behind the scenes in the platform committee broke out spectacularly on the convention floor. It concerned the plank on civil rights. Most of the committee, still hopeful of mollifying the Southerners, wanted simply to repeat the modest and ambiguous civil rights language of the 1944 platform. It was believed that most of the Southern delegates would accept this, and that the President, too, would be content with it. But a band of liberal rebels led by the passionate and vociferous young Mayor of Minneapolis, Hubert Humphrey, held out for a flat endorsement, item by item, of the program which Truman had put before Congress in January.

The debate on adoption of the platform raged through the afternoon and into the evening with the advantage seesawing back and forth between the Young Turks of the left and the standpatters of the center and right. Then, one after another of the big-city bosses switched their support to the liberals, persuaded that nothing could save the national ticket in November anyway and that a strong civil rights stand would win Negro support for local candidates in their own bailiwicks.

When the issue went to a final vote, the Humphrey forces won a decisive victory, 651½ to 582½. When the result was announced, all of the Mississippi delegation and half of those from Alabama (thirty-five in all) rose from their seats, assembled in ranks in the center aisle, and strode from the hall and into the pouring rain outside, followed by a wave of boos from the galleries. But the mass walkout the Dixiecrat leaders had threatened did not materialize, and the other Southern delegates remained resolutely if glumly in their seats.

Meanwhile, the maneuverings to agree on a Vice Presidential candidate were coming to a head. Truman had hoped to have a bona fide young liberal share the ticket with him, preferably one from the West. His choice settled on Supreme Court Justice William O. Douglas, and emissaries were sent to sound him out. When their reports indicated a lack of interest, the President, through Clark

Clifford, induced Mrs. Roosevelt to telephone the Justice at his vacation retreat, in Washington State. In addition, some casual consideration was give to Senator Joseph O'Mahoney, Paul V. McNutt, Wilson W. Wyatt, and others. It was not until the opening day of the convention, however, that Douglas told the President definitely that he preferred to stay on the Court rather than gamble his future on the election.

The buildup for Senator Barkley had already been set quietly in motion by Leslie Biffle, the Secretary of the Senate, who now occupied the strategic position of convention sergeant-at-arms. He worked with the delegates rather than with Chairman McGrath and the White House group, because the President was known to feel that both Barkley's age (70) and his border-state residence (Kentucky) would add little strength to the ticket. Biffle's cause was greatly aided by the enthusiasm which Barkley's keynote speech had aroused. When it was learned late on Monday that Douglas had refused the Vice Presidential offer, the last serious obstacle to Barkley appeared to have been removed. Thus it fell to McGrath on Wednesday to tell the President that the choice of a running mate had virtually been made for him by the delegates themselves. The President assented to the choice but withheld any great enthusiasm.

The President's special train brought him from Washington to Philadelphia early on the evening of Wednesday, July 14. His presence was unavoidable, but awkward and inconvenient. The convention hall was insufferably hot and humid, and as chaotic as an anthill under enemy attack. It would be indecorous for the candidate-to-be to show himself to those on the floor. The only space that afforded a modicum of privacy and an occasional breath of fresh air was a small bare room beneath the platform with a tiny balcony overlooking an alley. Here the President waited out, much of the time alone, the last fervid scenes in the battle over the civil rights plank and the nearly four hours of oratory that preceded his final selection as his party's candidate. His isolation was not a deliberate affront, as it often has been reported to be, but a consequence of poor planning by the convention managers. Few people knew the President was there at all, and those who did know were so busy on and about the platform that they had little time for visiting.

Senator Dick Russell's name was put in nomination as the candidate of the States Rights' delegates. When the long and tedious round of seconding speeches was over, Governor Phil M. Donnelly of Missouri offered "the name of a soldier, patriot, and statesman whose splendid courage has never faltered in war or in peace, and who is today leading the nation to a new and greater destiny—the President of the United States, Harry S. Truman!"

Though the hour was late (it was well past midnight) and impatience and irritability had sprouted from the fatigue of the delegates, this climax to an ancient ritual brought a flickering resurgence of life to the wilted multitude.

The inevitable floor demonstration developed a sudden spontaneity; the whoops and rebel yells sounded real; delegates who had listlessly kept their seats while others paraded up and down the aisles picked up their banners and noisemakers and joined the aimless snake dance. Reporters standing on their benches in the press bank looked at one another in disbelief and said, "This looks like it is for real."

And strangely enough, it was. A drama had unfolded and reached a climax that only the most jaded member of that political audience could ignore. Harry Truman, a stubborn underdog, had proved his mettle and faced down a colossal mutiny in his ranks. He had completely routed the Eisenhower forces; he had discredited the Wallace left-wingers; he had asserted his contempt for the bolting Dixiecrats; and against all these overwhelming odds he had collected enough delegate pledges to assure nomination. It was a tour de force in almost the classic mold. Whatever the delegates felt about him personally or as a candidate, they could not but admire his courage and his style. Only the Southerners remained stonily unmoved.

There was but one ballot that night. With 607 needed for a majority, Truman got 948 and Russell 263. The entire bloc of Southern votes, except for 12 from North Carolina, went to Russell, and the Truman managers prudently decided against any repolling in an effort to achieve the customary unanimity. The effort would have failed in any event.

Barkley's nomination for the Vice Presidency was then approved by acclamation.

It was 1:45 Thursday morning when Truman, looking crisp in a white linen suit and cockily self-assured, strode onto the platform to accept the nomination. According to the New York *Times*, his acceptance speech "set the convention on fire." When the noisy demonstration set off by his appearance quieted down, he led off with a typically Truman gambit: "Senator Barkley and I will win this election and make those Republicans like it—don't you forget that!"

The hall erupted again with cheers and yells. The smog of apathy and discouragement which the delegates had endured since they came to Philadelphia, even the sweaty weariness of their long confinement in the convention hall that night, began to peel away as the President's flat but vibrant voice, abounding in courage and confidence, rang out.

Speaking from notes instead of from a script, chopping the air with quick, awkward gestures of his hand, Truman recited the accomplishments of his administration in the hallowed tradition of the New Deal: gains for the farmers, for the working man, for the poor and underprivileged. He excoriated the Republicans, and the Republican-controlled Congress in particular, as the enemies of progress, who had thwarted his best efforts "for the common everyday man." He listed their opposition to price controls, better housing, medical care, and aid to education, and censured their favoritism for the rich in tax legislation and power development. He noted that at their recent convention in this same hall they had adopted a platform promising to do many of the things which, as the party of opposition controlling Congress, they had prevented his administration from doing. Then he let go with his well-concealed Sunday punch:

On the 26th day of July, which out in Missouri we call "Turnip Day," I am going to call that Congress back in session, and I am going to ask them to pass some of these laws they say they are for in their platform.

Now, my friends, if there is any reality behind that Republican platform, we ought to get some action from a short session of the Eightieth Congress. They can do this job in fifteen days if they want to do it, and they will still have time to go out and run for office.

Truman's words were uttered against a rising din of cheers and yells. He had to shout into the microphone at the end to make himself heard.

"They are going to try to dodge this responsibility," he said, "but what that 'worst' Eightieth Congress does in this special session will be the test of whether they mean what they say."

Rarely has there been a more audacious exercise of a President's power for partisan political ends than this. Truman conceded later that he knew the session would be fruitless as far as legislation was concerned—as it was, of course—and he justified it solely on the grounds of calling the Republicans' bluff. But his promise that night lifted the Democratic convention to its feet and put the glow of life into a Democratic campaign that practically everybody had believed would be stillborn. Editorial reaction was almost solidly adverse at the time. But Truman's attack was a stroke of political genius, for it focused the Democrats' fire for 1948 precisely on the target they had chosen—the "do-nothing Eightieth Congress."

The Progressive Party moved into Philadelphia a week behind the Democrats for the formality of confirming the candidacies of Henry Wallace and Glen Taylor. By now the Communists and fellow travelers had become conspicuous in the organization. Lee Pressman, the former general counsel of the CIO, and Representative Vito Marcantonio, both noted for their open Communist connections, were the principal drafters of the platform, which closely paralleled that of the Communist Party of America. Wallace went out of his way in Philadelphia to welcome Communist support, telling a press conference, "They support me because I say we can have peace with the Russians." Political writers had now substantially reduced their estimates of the vote-getting potential of the Wallaceites, but they still credited the new party with the power to hurt, and possibly to kill, Truman's narrow victory prospects in such big cities as New York, Chicago, and Los Angeles.

The Dixiecrats held a one-day convention in Birmingham the day after the adjournment of the Democratic convention in Philadelphia. It was a rousing affair, with some 6,000 flag-waving, slogan-shouting Southern patriots on hand. But it was notably short on politicians of stature from the states of the old Confederacy except for Alabama and Mississippi. Georgia's Dick Russell and Virginia's Harry Byrd, both of whom were vigorously pressed to stand for nomination, not only stayed away but refused to let any of their henchmen attend. Governor Ben Laney of Arkansas, one of the initiators of the revolt, got as far as a hotel room in Birmingham but never showed up at the meeting. The nominations thereupon went, almost by default, to the other two prime movers, Governor J. Strom Thurmond of South Carolina, and Governor Fielding L. Wright of Mississippi. Before adjourning, the leaders set another convention for mid-October, to which the yet-to-be-chosen Presidential electors of the Southern states were to be summoned. If for any reason the electors could not cast their ballots for the Thurmond-Wright ticket, they would be pledged to withhold them from the Truman-Barkley ticket in any event. This, it was hoped, would throw the final choice of a President into the House of Representatives.

It was apparent at Birmingham that much of the steam had gone out of the Dixiecrat revolt since its organizational meeting in Jackson in May. But that it would rupture the Solid South in ways that had not happened since 1928 was becoming clear to everyone. This was the vital contingency which Truman had not prepared for. The Clifford memorandum and all the other White House strategy had been built on the assumption that, come what may, the 117 electoral votes of the old Confederacy were in the bag. Now the bag was leaking.

CHAPTER 9

✧✧✧✧✧✧✧✧✧✧✧✧✧✧✧✧✧✧✧✧✧✧✧

1948—The Main Event

Up Hill All The Way

"Nice guys don't win ball games," Leo Durocher, the baseball philosopher, once observed. The same is often true of the game of politics, and never has it been more eloquently documented than in the Presidential election campaign of 1948.

Republican Thomas E. Dewey, with deliberate calculation, chose the high road for his campaign. His effort was as tidy as a new pin, abundantly financed, and organized with the meticulous efficiency of an electronic computer. Computers of a sort, in fact, told the Dewey team that they could not lose, so they campaigned not to win an election but to set up the guideposts and stage props of a new administration. The candidate, with his crisp executive manner and his rich commanding baritone, exuded so much confidence that he put his followers to sleep.

Democrat Harry S. Truman, no less deliberately, chose the low road. It was a choice of necessity. No one believed he could win, and many had told him so. His party treasury was broke, the party organization was in chaos, and, although he was a sitting President, he was on the defensive as a candidate. So he fought with the heedless, slambang ferocity of the underdog who knows there is only one way out—and set the public imagination on fire.

The "Turnip Session" of Congress was as much a part of Truman's election strategy as campaign buttons and whistlestops. Late in June, Clifford had put before him a memorandum from the political strategy board, which said in part:

This election can only be won by bold and daring steps calculated to reverse the powerful trend now running against us. The boldest and most popular step the President could possibly take would be to call a special session of Congress early in August. This would: (1) focus attention on the rotten record of the Eightieth Congress, which the Republicans and the press will try to make the country forget; (2) force Dewey and Warren to defend the actions of Congress and make them accept Congress as a basic issue; (3) keep the steady glare of publicity on the Neanderthal men of the Republican party, who will embarrass Dewey and Warren; (4) split the Republicans on how to deal with such major issues as housing, inflation, foreign policy, etc., and (5) give President Truman a chance to follow through on the fighting start he made on his western tour.

This course may be hazardous politically, but we cannot shut our eyes to the fact that President Truman faces an uphill fight to win the coming election.

The special session opened on Monday, July 26, with much editorial grumbling and offended congressional dignity. The President went up the next day to lay out his program in person. He got a chilly reception. There was scattered, perfunctory applause only six times during his thirty-minute speech. Some members, to emphasize their resentment, did not even rise from their seats as the President entered and left the chamber. But Truman could not have cared less. During the preceding week he had stolen another march on the opposition. Instead of adhering to the usual practice of keeping secret a Presidential message to Congress until the moment of its delivery, Charley Ross, the White House press secretary, had arranged a series of strategic leaks of its contents all during the week. Thus the Truman program got double exposure in the nation's press, first in the provocative form of "dope stories," and again when the message was made officially public. As a publicity gimmick, it was a small triumph.

What the President asked for was an eight-point program that contained such politically flammable legislation as controls on inflation, civil rights, an increase in minimum wages, extension of Social Security coverage, and public housing. All this he had asked for before and been denied. Most of the items had been endorsed with appropriate ambiguity in the Republican platform only six weeks earlier. Particularly nettlesome for the Republicans was the item on housing, for Senator Taft had sponsored a housing bill that had passed the Senate during the regular session but had been bottled up by the conservative oligarchy on the House Rules Committee. What the President was asking in this instance was that the Republican Congress pass a bill bearing the name of its most distinguished Republican leader. A neat ploy, indeed!

The session lasted twelve days, six of which were spent in a filibuster precipitated by Southern Democrats to block Senate consideration of an anti-poll-tax bill. The legislative results were meager, as everyone expected them to be. A $65,000,000 loan to the United Nations for its headquarters building was the session's most substantial and noncontroversial achievement. Its token gesture toward anti-inflation legislation was a limited curb on consumer credit. Its reluctant bow toward housing was a bill that omitted slum clearance and low-cost public housing development—a far cry from the Taft bill. This grudging compromise put the Ohio Senator in a box and played neatly into the hands of the Truman strategists.

The special session was a farce, and it was characterized at the end by the New York *Times* in these words: "Who has put whom on the spot?" The verdict at the time was that it had been a standoff. The Republicans had gained nothing, because their attitude throughout had been defiant and negative. Truman's advantage, if any, was supposedly canceled out by popular resentment over the crassness of his motives in convening the session in the first place. But this was a false supposition, as the next few weeks would prove.

One event that occurred in Congress during this fortnight was to have an immediate effect on the campaign and a long-range impact on the whole political climate of the country for the next decade.

On Friday, July 30, a dumpy, plain-looking woman in her middle thirties took the witness chair before a subcommittee of the Senate Committee on Expenditures in the Executive Departments, gave her name as Elizabeth T. Bentley, and began to unfold a spectacular tale of Communist espionage that reached into the upper levels of the Federal government. Within a week, she and a subsequent witness before the House Un-American Activities Committee—a paunchy, desolate former editor of *Time* magazine named Whittaker Chambers—had hung the label of "spy" or "collaborator" on a score of present and former government officials, including William T. Remington, of the Department of Commerce; Lauchlin Currie, once a White House economic adviser; and Alger Hiss, a principal State Department technician in the formation of the United Nations.

Thus the haunting specter of "Communists in government" first cast its dark shadow across the political landscape, and the seeds of a mass hysteria later to be known as "McCarthyism" were sown. Asked at his press conference on Thursday, August 5, what he thought of the spy hearings, President Truman snapped:

"They are simply a red herring. They (the Republicans) are using this as a red herring as an excuse to keep from doing what they ought to do.

"Yes, you can quote me."

The Democrats opened their campaign headquarters on two floors of New York's Biltmore Hotel in mid-August. In charge was Chairman J. Howard McGrath, who was also Senator from Rhode Island. His principal aide and director of publicity was Jack Redding, a jut-jawed former Army Colonel and reporter with the audacity of a carnival pitchman. The committee's Washington operation, concerned mainly with campaign logistics and White House liaison, was in charge of William M. Boyle, Jr., a deceptively bland and soft-spoken product of Kansas City ward politics. The financial wizard of the operation was Louis Johnson, a ruggedly built West Virginian who had begun to accumulate a postwar fortune as a Washington attorney. He took the job of finance chairman after it had been turned down by half a dozen better-known nominees, including Bernard Baruch and Cornelius Whitney. (Subsequently his efforts won for him the appointment as Defense Secretary.) Few men could have prospected more profitably in the arid wastes of the Democratic financial desert than Louis Johnson. He knew which arms to stroke and which to twist; and when the till actually ran dry, he put up his own money to tide the party over. Oscar Chapman took leave of his post as Interior Under Secretary to take charge of field operations. Throughout the campaign he acted as advance man to set the stage for each of the President's trips and the important stops en route.

Truman was not a man to concede that another might know more about the art of politics than he, nor was anyone likely to dispute his assumption. In a real sense, he ran his own show in the 1948 campaign, but he was wise enough to take good counsel when he could get it.

Clustered around the candidate and accompanying him on all his trips was a cadre of the White House "brain trust": Clark Clifford had the role of chief of staff; Jonathan Daniels had been brought back from his newspapers in Raleigh to lend a hand with the speech-writing; Charley Ross, in his gentle, patient way, handled the clamorous demands of the scores of reporters and photographers who accompanied the President wherever he went; and Matt Connelly cast his trained and skeptical eye on the local dignitaries and politicos who pushed and scratched to get a few minutes of the candidate's time or to be photographed in his company whenever his train paused.

The anchor men in Washington while the President's party was on tour were principally Federal Security Administrator Oscar Ewing, one of the masterminds of the political strategy board, and Charles Murphy, Clifford's chief White House assistant. There was almost constant communication between the traveling unit and home base.

Truman's election campaign was to be a life-size version of the experimental whistlestop tour of the previous June. In the view of most of his team, the tour had been a huge success. It created the kind of environment in which the President showed to his best advantage, and it apparently appealed to the public. But a few changes were made. For one thing, prepared speeches would be avoided wherever possible. The President was a poor reader, and his delivery from text was stiff and unconvincing. But in ad-libbing, his natural warmth and sincerity came through splendidly. So his staff avoided scripts for all but the big speeches and provided him with a series of topical cards, each containing only a few highlight sentences to serve as oratorical pump primers. As another precaution, they worked out an elaborate series of "tour books" for each state, containing, for each stop of whatever duration, a brief précis of the local who's who, history, politics, and prevailing taboos and interests. Thus, instead of dedicating an airport to a nonexistent local hero, as he had done in June, he could compliment a trainside audience in Iowa on the fine new sausage factory that had just been opened in their town. These two devices—the natural, homespun speeches and the accurate and intimate hometown lore he was able to put into them—had an important bearing on the outcome of the campaign.

Two other factors which were going for Candidate Truman in September did not exist in June. Most of organized labor had swung its big guns into his campaign, including the militant Political Action Committee of the CIO and even his erstwhile sworn enemy, A. F. Whitney of the Brotherhood of Railway Trainmen. It is always problematical how many votes labor leaders can deliver at the polls. But what they usually can deliver, and did in 1948, is cash and an enormous amount of manpower to do the spadework of electioneering at the precinct level.

The second factor was a revitalized Democratic National Committee, which, in spite of continuing financial and organizational deficiencies, managed to pump new life into the party organization across most parts of the country, the Deep South excepted. A network of Truman-Barkley Clubs was organized to raise money and to interest the disinterested. A Women's Division, under the skilled guidance of India Edwards, worked among the housewives and women's clubs. A Negro Division and a Minorities Division went to work in the big-city melting pots, aiming chiefly at stemming the drift of the dispossessed toward Wallace.

The great obstacle still was apathy and a pervasive disenchantment with Truman among organization Democrats, plus a conviction that he was beaten before he started. But McGrath and his team, playing every chord on the organ of party loyalty and political self-interest (with an occasional resort to what in any other pursuit than politics would be called blackmail), whipped many of the reluctant troops into the battle line. McGrath, for example, sent cablegrams to every United States Ambassador abroad, inquiring with the subtlety of a traffic summons, "What if any financial assistance you might be able to secure for the national committee to assist the President in his campaign." And Jack Redding talked a delegation of Hollywood movie producers into the free gift of a Truman campaign film matching one they had prepared for the Dewey forces for a fee of $30,000.

Truman launched his campaign with a Labor Day speech at Detroit, which has become a ritual for Democratic candidates ever since. The event set a pattern that he was to follow almost without deviation for the next eight weeks.

The "Truman Special," with eighty-odd reporters and photographers, details of Secret Service and Signal Corps men, a dozen White House aides and secretaries, and the President and his daughter, Margaret, aboard (Mrs. Truman was attending a christening in Denver), pulled out of Washington's Union Station at 3:40

on the afternoon of Sunday, September 5. It was a sixteen-car train with sleeping and dining cars, a work car for the reporters, a communications car for the Signal Corps and Western Union, and, at the end, the *Ferdinand Magellan,* a Pullman specially adapted for Presidential use in the days of FDR. The *Magellan* contained its own galley and dining area, two spacious bedrooms, and a combination salon and office. An oversized platform at the rear, with a protective striped canopy and a public address system, served as a stage for the endless repetition of a seriocomic folk drama with which hundreds of thousands of Americans were to become familiar in the next two months. A typical day went like this:

The "Truman Special" rolled onto a siding at the station in Grand Rapids, Michigan, shortly before 7 o'clock on a Monday morning. Several hundred people lined the station platform, cheering and shouting a welcome. The local leaders and politicians—among them an ambitious newcomer to Democratic politics in Michigan, one G. Mennen Williams,* who was running for the governorship—packed into the President's car for handshakes and coffee, and then into open automobiles for a parade to the town square. Although it was the breakfast hour and Grand Rapids was a heavily Republican city, 25,000 people jammed into the area to hear and see the President and to give him a warm welcome.

Within an hour the train was under way again. At crossings and way stations knots of people were on hand to wave to the President as he whizzed by and get a wave in return. Several times the train stopped briefly at stations where crowds of a few hundred to a few thousand had assembled, and the President stepped out on the back platform to speak for four or five minutes and to shake some of the scores of hands thrust up eagerly toward him. He was genial and good-natured, full of quips and folksiness, and even when he warned them of the perils of sending another Republican Congress to Washington, or electing another Republican governor of Michigan, it was in a joshing, half-serious vein free of venom. Everywhere the people responded warmly, sometimes enthusiastically, occasionally with shouts and whistles of genuine fervor.

Detroit, where the party arrived about noon, wore a carnival aspect, with marching bands, flags flying, and masses of cheering people along the streets. This was labor's city, labor's holiday, and labor's candidate, and approximately a quarter million working men

---

* No one thought he had much of a chance in his campaign, but he won that year and four successive terms as well—a Michigan record.

and their wives and children were packed in Cadillac Square to give
the President a noisy workingman's greeting. And he gave them
what they had come to hear.

Two years ago, he said, the people had dropped their guard and
elected a Republican Congress.

"The Republicans promptly voted themselves a cut in taxes and
voted you a cut in freedom. They put a dangerous weapon in the
hands of the big corporations, in the shape of the Taft-Hartley law.
I vetoed it, but they passed it over my veto."

If the same forces that created Taft-Hartley, he went on, are
allowed to stay in power and to elect a Republican President, "labor
can expect to be hit by a series of body blows—and if you stay at
home as you did in 1946, and keep these reactionaries in power, you
deserve every blow you get."

There were roars of assent and shouts of "Pour it on," "Give 'em
hell, Harry!" The crowd was with him as he went on to excoriate
"that do-nothing Eightieth Republican Congress" for high prices
and for blocking minimum wage and Social Security improvements
and low-cost housing legislation. He lambasted the "gluttons of privilege" in the Republican Party, and, making it clear he had Dewey
in mind, said they were men "with a calculating machine where the
heart ought to be."

The yells and applause coming wave upon wave filled Cadillac
Square and rattled from radio sets in living rooms, union halls, tav-
erns, and picnic grounds all across the United States. This was not
just another Labor Day speech by a President. It was the opening
attack in a go-for-broke election campaign. It *had* to be good. It *had*
to go over. And it was aimed as much at New York, Pittsburgh,
Dallas, and Seattle as it was at Detroit. In the anxiety-ridden Democratic strategy, this was *it*.

But it was only by a narrow, nerve-shattering squeak that the
President had a live microphone to talk into that day.

Oscar Chapman, the advance man, had spent the preceding week
in Detroit perfecting plans for the President's appearance. Everything seemed to be in apple-pie order. But Saturday morning the
radio network that was to broadcast the speech nationally told him
they would have to have their fee of $50,000 in full before the day
was out or they would cancel the Monday broadcast. Chapman was
stunned. He called McGrath in New York.

"My God, Oscar," the chairman told him, "we haven't got that
kind of money. If the labor boys out there can't raise it, you'll just
have to cancel."

Chapman had already put his problem to the local CIO-PAC leaders, and they were as powerless as McGrath to help on such short notice. But to cancel the broadcast, to lose the nationwide impact of what promised to be a rousing kickoff for an otherwise shaky campaign, was unthinkable. Oscar Chapman sat brooding for an hour in his hotel room and then he was struck by an inspiration. Governor Roy Turner of Oklahoma, an old friend of Chapman's, was not only a loyal Truman Democrat (he was president of the national Truman-Barkley Club) but also a personally wealthy man, and he had a lot of oil-wealthy friends. Chapman put through a long-distance call to him at 3 o'clock that afternoon.

"Governor," he said, "I'm in the tightest spot I've ever been in in my life." He said that he either had to lay $50,000 on the line before midnight or cancel the most important broadcast of the entire Truman campaign.

"Of course you can't cancel," Turner boomed reassuringly. "Stay in your room and I'll call you back in an hour."

Two hours later he called back.

"You're in business, Oscar," the Governor said. "I've just cleared the whole thing with the network. I've laid down $50,000 with their station here, and everything is checked out all the way up the line. You tell those sons of bitches there that if they don't put this show on the air Monday, I'll wreck this damn station of theirs here before sundown."

The broadcast did, of course, go off without a hitch and Truman's Labor Day performance was one of the highlights of the campaign.

The Republicans tipped their hand the next day to the casual, aloof strategy that was to cost them dearly before the campaign ended. Governor Dewey chose to ignore the Truman attack and instead sent Harold Stassen to Detroit to "answer" the President. There was no hope or expectation of matching the huge labor turnout in Cadillac Square of the day before. But the fact that Stassen's indoor audience reached only about 3,000, made up predominantly of Republican business and professional people, and that he concentrated on a defense of the Taft-Hartley Act, created a striking contrast in vitality with the Democratic effort, which every newspaper in the country noted.

This revealed a deliberate Republican strategy, a conscious change of pace. In his 1944 campaign against Roosevelt, Dewey had employed the aggressive cut-and-thrust tactics of the courtroom

prosecutor. In his quest for the 1948 nomination, he had slammed
and slandered the domestic and foreign policies of the Truman administration with scant reserve. But now, in the election campaign,
he chose to give Truman the silent treatment, and to concentrate
on elucidating the larger issues of statecraft and creating an air of
harmony within Republican ranks.

The rationale for this decision was simply this: Within the Republican Party there was a chronic division of power between the
conservative and progressive wings. As a progressive, Dewey's ideas
on foreign policy, minimum wages, public housing, and economic
controls came a great deal closer to Truman's than they did to such
GOP fundamentalists as Styles Bridges and John Taber. But it
would do no good to offend their sensibilities by openly espousing
his New Dealish views on these issues during the campaign. Moreover, it was reasoned, since Truman was a dead duck anyway, why
should Dewey bother trying to trade him punch for punch? It would
be a useless and undignified brawl that might inhibit the next
President's freedom of action. So it was decided to let Truman make
a spectacle of himself shadowboxing against the Eightieth Congress
and the outdated ogres of the 1930s, while Dewey declaimed with
lofty earnestness on the broad policies of his forthcoming administration.

The principal architects of the Dewey campaign strategy were
Herbert Brownell, his campaign manager; Russell Sprague, a long-
time power in New York Republican politics; Hugh Scott, a young
Congressman from Pennsylvania; and, above all, Elliott Bell, a Wall
Street economist whom Dewey had named State Superintendent of
Banking. Bell, a former newsman, was brilliant, articulate, and un-
compromisingly self-assured. He had managed Dewey's two successful campaigns for the governership and enjoyed Dewey's un-
stinted admiration and friendship. In manner and outlook they were
as alike as a matched pair of Swiss watches—and just as purpose-
ful.

Governor Warren had little or no part in the strategy. He was
counted on mainly to keep California and the Far West safely in
line. Senator Taft was counted on to pick up any stray electoral
votes that might be floating around in the South. Stassen was an all-
purpose troubleshooter and the chief adjutant for the Middle West,
although that faithfully Republican farm region was confidently expected to take care of itself.

Thus the main thrust of the Republican campaign was directed toward the intellectual and economic interests of the urbanized Northeast. When its directors sniffed the first scents of danger from the grass roots beyond the Appalachians, it was too late to change direction.

President Truman opened the first of two transcontinental tours he was to make with a memorable appearance at the National Plowing Contest outside Dexter, Iowa, in the broiling midday sun of Saturday, September 18. This occasion was memorable because he uncorked a ploy that had as much to do with winning him the Midwestern farm vote in November as any other factor in the campaign: hanging on the Eightieth Congress responsibility for failing to provide sufficient government storage bins for the year's bumper crop of corn and wheat.

Under the farm price support program, the Commodity Credit Corporation (CCC) lent grain growers 90 percent of parity on their surplus crops. These surpluses, which had run as high as 300,000 bushels a year shortly after the end of World War II, were stored under government control until such time as the market might absorb them. In renewing the CCC authorization in the spring of 1948, Congress failed (apparently without any notable protest from the Democrats) to provide for the acquisition of additional storage bins. (Clusters of these low, silo-like structures, made of corrugated metal, are a familiar feature of the landscape in the corn and wheat country.) The 1948 crop, however, was to be one of historic abundance and therefore one of large surpluses and sliding prices. Between January and September, for example, corn was to drop from $2.46 to $1.78 a bushel, and wheat from $2.81 to $1.97. Without proper storage capacity to hold this enormous yield, many farmers would be unable to get their CCC loans and would have to sell at the depressed market price.

This lapse seems not to have been discovered by the Truman strategists until just before the first major farm speech of the campaign, at Dexter. As the Presidential party was getting ready to leave Washington on September 17, Matt Connelly handed Clifford a brief and disingenuous memo which read: "Charlie Brannan [the new Secretary of Agriculture] suggests that at platform stops in the western area we may be able to develop the following with respect to farmers—failure of Congress to provide storage bins. This action was the responsibility of the Banking and Currency Committee of the House."

Seventy-five thousand farmers (and their wives and children), bankers, mortgage holders, equipment sellers, and produce buyers stood in ankle-deep dust under a 90-degree sun as President Truman mounted the wooden platform on the prairie outside Dexter a few minutes after noon that Saturday. He reminded them that he had been a dirt farmer himself, back in Missouri, and added that he could plow as straight a furrow behind a pair of mules as the next man. He joked them about how well they had prospered under Democratic administrations, as evidenced by the fifty private planes, tied down in an adjacent field, in which many of them had flown to the plowing contest that day. Then he got down to business:

This Republican Congress has already stuck a pitchfork in the farmers' backs. They have already done their best to keep price supports from working.

When the Republican Congress rewrote the charter of the Commodity Credit Corporation this year, there were certain lobbyists in Washington representing the speculative grain trade. These big business lobbyists and speculators persuaded the Congress not to provide storage bins for you farmers. They tied the hands of the administration. They are preventing us from setting up the storage bins that you will need in order to get the support price for your grain.

And when you have to sell your grain below the support price because you have no place to store it, you can thank this same Republican Congress.

There was no sudden cry for revenge from the sweaty multitude at Dexter. This was the very heartland of Republicanism, and many in the crowd sensed that this Democratic President was probably just politicking with his talk about unnamed lobbyists and speculators having subverted the Congress. But they were friendly and responsive, and by God, they conceded, Truman was right about the storage-bin business. This was already hitting a lot of them in the pocketbook, and the shortage was going to get worse as the weeks wore on. Moreover, they remembered, it was only about a week ago that Harold Stassen, speaking presumably for Governor Dewey, had talked disparagingly about farm price supports being responsible for high food prices. Was it a fact, as Truman was now telling them, that the Republicans were out to scuttle the whole farm price support system? It was not too hard to believe.

Truman's well-poisoning operation had worked to perfection. Suspicion over the Republicans' farm policy seeped through the crowd at Dexter that day, and in the days following it raced like a contagion throughout the Farm Belt.

In the press car of the "Truman Special," as it rolled across Iowa that evening, a score of reporters wrote for their papers that the Democratic candidate appeared to have "hit the mark," or that he had "touched a sensitive nerve," in his first big farm speech of the campaign. The country was to hear a lot more about grain storage bins between then and November.

The Truman campaign consisted of two major transcontinental tours of about ten days each, a tour into the Northeast, and a number of lesser forays of one or two days' duration to various parts of the country. In eight weeks he would cover 32,000 miles, make more than 250 speeches, and be seen and heard in the flesh by an estimated 6,000,000 people—a record up to that time for personal campaigning.

For nearly everyone—except, apparently, the candidate himself— it was a bruising, bone-wearying ordeal. The days and the crowds and the scenery and the speeches; the endless succession of high school bands and flag-draped platforms and madly careening motorcades; the ulcerous tensions of successive deadlines, of too little sleep, of cold dinners and warm drinks, and of too many people living too close together for too long—all of these seemed to coagulate into an unintelligible montage for the reporters and the staff men and the flunkies who made up the supporting cast in this extravaganza. But there is a special octane in the bloodstream of a political candidate like Harry Truman that enables him to survive, even to thrive upon, the unconscionable stresses of a campaign. He, after all, has a gambler's stake in each word spoken, each hand shaken, each smile conferred. Every audience is a fresh challenge to his courage or a new boost to his vanity, and the sound of his own voice never palls, even when the setting and the words have been blurred unrecognizably by repetition.

Harry Truman seemed never to flag in those arduous autumn weeks of 1948. He was as brisk and sassy at midnight as he had been eighteen hours and a dozen whistlestops earlier. But the troops behind him—the aides, the secretaries, the flacks, and the grousing minions of the press and radio—existed in a state of perpetual wilt and rebelliousness. Not one of them, however, would willingly have given up his ringside seat at this epic carnival in spite of his exhaustion and exasperation. There just isn't anything in human experience quite like a Presidential campaign, and a campaign *train* is its quintessence.

The pattern of the days on the road varied but little. As the "Truman Special" rolled to its first stop in a state, usually between 6 and 8 o'clock in the morning, it would be boarded by a delegation of local politicians: the Governor, Senators, and a Congressman or two, if they happened to be Democrats, or the Democratic candidates for these and other major offices; the state and local party chairmen; a handful of important contributors; possibly a wartime buddy of the President (the veterans of his World War I artillery outfit were discovered to have a geographical distribution approximating that of the English starling); and whoever else among the local population could assert a real or imagined claim to be numbered among the President's "guests." Often the leading statewide candidates would stay aboard for the remainder of the day to gain what advantage they could, in their own bid for votes, by being seen at the various stops in the Presidential presence, or by introducing him to the local audiences.

On most days there would be one or two outdoor rallies, or even a major speech, to which the Presidential party would be whirled in a motorcade with screaming police sirens. Afterwards there would be another traffic-stopping dash back to the schedule-bound train. As the train rolled across the countryside, it would pause at station after station where crowds had gathered. Men, women, and children would crowd out onto the tracks at the rear of the train or climb nearby roofs and signal towers for a better view. As the local band struggled through "Hail to the Chief," the "Missouri Waltz," or the state anthem, the President and half a dozen others would step out onto the back platform to be met by cheers and applause—sometimes merely perfunctory, but more often spontaneous and friendly. One of the accompanying guests would introduce the President, not omitting, usually, a plug for his own political interests. Then the President, bareheaded and beaming with a bright smile, would take the microphone and say:

Every time I come out this way, I feel again the tremendous vitality of the West [or of New England or Oregon or Texas]. This is straight-from-the-shoulder country and it has produced a great breed of fighting men.

I am going to call upon your fighting qualities. For you and I have a fight on our hands, a fight for the future of the country and for the welfare of the people of the United States.

If Truman's words, read today, sound corny, the impression is correct. They *were* corny. But it was a natural, and not a contrived, sort of corn. His words reflected the way he thought and felt, and they sounded right in his flat, unpolished Missouri accents. And because they sounded right, people were moved to yell approvingly, "Give 'em hell, Harry" to this plain, unpretentious man who was their President.

There might follow a brief allusion to a nearby dam or conservation project or other Federal benefaction from which the locality had gained, and a reminder that this and most other blessings carried Democratic labels. Then, a note of indignation coming into his voice, Truman would say:

Republicans in Washington have a habit of becoming curiously deaf to the voice of the people. But they have no trouble at all in hearing what Wall Street is saying. They are able to catch the slightest hint from Big Business.

When I talk to you here today about Republicans, I am talking to you about the party that gets most of its campaign funds from Wall Street and Big Business. I am talking to you about the party that gave us the phony Wall Street boom of the nineteen twenties and the Hoover depression that followed. I am talking to you about the party [and here he spaced his words for emphasis] that gave us that no-account do-nothing Republican Eightieth Congress.

Flogging Congress is a safe ploy in almost any political climate. As Mr. Truman did it, it was always good for fresh outbursts of whoops and yells from the crowd. "Give 'em hell, Harry!"

"And now," he would say at the end, "I want you to meet the Boss." Turning proudly, he would reach into the doorway of the car and lead Mrs. Truman out by the hand. Plump and motherly, she would acknowledge the applause with a smile and a wave.

"And here's the one who bosses her," the President would say as Margaret, young, radiant, and usually with an armful of roses, stepped onto the scene. Her appearance always set off the loudest response of all, liberally spiced with wolf whistles from the boys and young men.

As Margaret tossed a rose or two into the crowd, the President would bend down over the railing to grasp a few of the scores of hands thrust toward him and to swap good-natured jibes with whoever could make himself heard over the uproar. The local band would strike up another tune, the engineer would give a warning toot on his whistle, the reporters would scamper down the platform toward the press car, and the "Truman Special" would begin to pull slowly away. The whole event would not have lasted more than fifteen or twenty minutes. But Fence Post, Nebraska, would have a red-letter day to talk about and to mark down in its memory book, and Harry Truman would have done again the one thing he knew best how to do, personal politicking. The same routine would be repeated fifty miles down the line, and again and again until midnight or exhaustion put an end to the day.

The Truman odyssey zigzagged across the map like a giant medicine show. Just as the bearded "Doctor" in those gaslit spectaculars evoked symptoms of dread ailments in the imagination of his startled audiences, so Truman conjured up images of a reckless, reactionary, and greedy Republicanism in the minds of his listeners.

In Denver, 50,000 people lined his parade route, and 20,000 more stood on the lawn of the Capitol to hear him berate the GOP on the subject closest to their hearts and to their pocketbooks: irrigation and power development. Husky-voiced from a cold but full of fire, he told them, "As soon as the Republican Party gained control of Congress it began to tear down the whole Western development program. The Republicans slashed funds right and left, they cut back projects to bring water to the land and electric power to industry."

In Sacramento he talked about the control of the Republican Party by "Eastern mossbacks," who would stifle the economy of the West. "The Republicans," he said, "work for the benefit of the few bloodsuckers who have offices in Wall Street. This is a crusade of the people against the special interests, a crusade to keep the country from going to the dogs. You back me up and we'll win that crusade."

In Los Angeles, a hotbed of Democratic liberalism where Wallace was believed to be making serious inroads, Truman lashed out at the third party's Communist ties. He warned those wavering liberals "to think again. The fact that the Communists are using and guiding the third party shows that this party does not represent American ideals. A vote for the third party plays directly into the hands of the Republican forces of reaction, whose aims are directly opposed to the aims of American liberalism."

In Oklahoma City, at the end of a thirteen-speech day that had begun with a 6:30 whistlestop, he mounted his major attack against Republican charges that his administration had "coddled the Communists in its midst." This was one of a handful of issues on which the Dewey forces were explicit and hard-hitting, and it was being documented almost daily by the splashing headlines produced by the Un-American Activities Committee hearings in Washington, where Elizabeth Bentley was telling her story. Truman's speech that night was one of the few during his campaign which was broadcast nationally. He argued vehemently that the government had not been endangered by Communist infiltration, and that his administration had taken all necessary precautions against such a danger. He wound up with a series of indictments against the Republicans, charging that their exploitation of the issue was doing more to undermine national security than all the Communist espionage that had been uncovered to date.

To a cheering throng of 50,000 packed in the War Memorial Plaza at Indianapolis, Truman said that the Republicans had been too busy "playing political checkers" to pay any attention to runaway prices. Time and time again, he said, he had asked the Eightieth Congress to take concrete steps to check the rocketing inflation. But "they figured that maybe the fire of inflation would burn itself out, or that it was un-American to put water on the flames."

In Toledo he said that Dewey as President could not build a strong military defense for the United States "because the Republicans [in Congress] would not let him take those steps that are necessary to develop and maintain the strength of this great nation."

In Buffalo he made it clear that his indictment of the Republican Eightieth Congress included the Republican candidate for President as well. "Make no mistake," he told an overflow crowd in Eagles Hall (a stadium rally for 20,000 had been rained out), "when we talk of the failure of the Eightieth Congress we are talking about the policies of the Republican candidate. They are tarred with the same brush—the brush that big business uses to brush off the needs and the claims of the people."

And so the Truman cavalcade went rocketing up and down the land, laying down a barrage of political hyperbole, accusation, and ridicule. Much of it was nonsense and some of it was shameful, but there was a seed of truth in most of what he said and an element of low-keyed heroics in the way he said it. This, probably, was what counted most: the impression he created of the game, undaunted underdog. Dewey collaborated unwittingly to enhance this impression.

For the first four or five weeks of the campaign, Dewey and his men behaved almost as if Truman did not exist. They ignored the

President's taunts, challenges, and specific allegations, and talked instead in wholesome but bloodless generalities.

"I pledge you," Dewey told a midwestern farm audience, "that your next administration will cooperate with the farmers of the country to protect all people from the tragedy of another dust bowl." Nobody was worried about dust bowls, but farmers were worried about storage bins. And in the Far West Dewey said, "I propose that we develop a national policy that will really save our forests through Federal, state, and local cooperation."

Reporting from the "Dewey Victory Special" as it rolled through California late in September, Leo Egan wrote in the New York *Times:*

Governor Dewey [as candidate] is acting like a man who has already been elected and is merely marking time, waiting to take office. In his speeches and in his manner there is an attitude that the election will be a mere formality to confirm a decision already made.

The basic theme of Mr. Dewey's campaign is that only the election of a Republican President and a Republican Congress can provide the country with the unity it needs to insure peace in a troubled world. Factional divisions within the Democratic party have been referred to but not emphasized. Henry Wallace's third party has been mentioned only once. Governor Thurmond and his States' Rights party have not even been mentioned.

Governor Dewey is deliberately avoiding any sharp controversy with the Democratic incumbent.

The Dewey campaign organization (and this was possibly symptomatic of what was wrong) worked with the awesome efficiency of a computer but it lacked the lively distractions of error, surprise, and human warmth. Schedules were rigorously met. Enough automobiles were always available at trainside to accommodate the traveling party. Speech texts were always ready in advance for the reporters. The candidate was always shielded from rude interlopers by ranks of subordinates. A jerky start of the train from one wayside stop was so unusual as to cause the candidate to expostulate: "What's wrong with that damn fool engineer?" It was *that* kind of mistake that happened on the Dewey train, and this one turned out to be a magnificent blooper. In the skilled hands of Democratic propagandists, it became overnight a jeering anti-Dewey slogan in railroad roundhouses and Union halls all across the country.

In contrast, the Truman entourage lived in a continuing chaos of late arrivals and unexpected departures, overnight shifts in plans, and sudden discoveries that no plan for the next six hours existed. Speech texts, so vital to newspaper coverage in a campaign that rarely could afford radio and television broadcasts, often were unavailable until the hour of delivery. One major speech, on soil conservation, was by some unexplained foul-up delivered to an audience of industrial workers who had come to boo the Taft-Hartley law. The whole campaign came close to folding on the night of September 29 when, according to Jack Redding, the railroad refused to move the "Truman Special" out of the station in Oklahoma City until past charges for transportation were settled. A hasty passing of the hat among oil-rich Democrats in the state averted this humiliating disaster. "For a time," Redding wrote "it seemed possible the whole party might have to alight and get back to Washington the best way they could."

If the Dewey party lived in a cloudland of euphoria, the Truman camp was pitched in the slough of despond. As their train rattled back and forth across the country, the men around the President came increasingly to feel—up to the last couple of weeks, at least—that they were just going through the motions of campaigning. What kept them going was their loyalty to Truman, whose spirits, as far as the eye could detect, never flagged. Clark Clifford has recalled what he believes was the low point of the group's morale:

One day around the middle of October, somebody hopped off the train at some town out in the Middle West—I've forgotten where it was—and bought a current copy of *Newsweek* magazine. We knew they were going to publish this high-powered poll by fifty leading political writers around the country on the election outlook. We were pretty apprehensive, but we had to see it.

Well, there it was, in great big black type—"Fifty political experts unanimously"—get that, "unanimously"—"predict a Dewey victory." Not a one of them gave the Old Man a chance; the score was Dewey, 50, Truman zero. Boy . . . !*

We took it back and showed it to Mr. Truman. He blinked a little, but he didn't let it faze him. He gave us that big grin and said, "Oh, well,

* The poll was published in the October 11, 1948, issue of *Newsweek*. In addition to a unanimous prediction of a Dewey victory, the poll indicated that Dewey would receive 376 electoral votes, Truman 116, and Thurmond 39. It forecast that the Republicans would retain narrow control of the Senate and increase their majority in the House. Wallace, it was predicted, would receive 2,778,700 popular votes. As to the man "best qualified to be President," the experts voted 37 for Dewey, 7 for Truman, 1 for Thurmond, and 5 undecided. It is worth noting that the *Literary Digest* was sunk in 1936 under a scarcely more egregious load of error than this.

those damn fellows; they're always wrong anyway. Forget it, boys, and let's get on with the job."

So everybody takes a deep breath, squares his shoulders, and gets on with what really appeared to be a hopeless task.

I don't think Mrs. Truman and Margaret really thought he could win, and in his very deepest heart I suspect the President didn't think so, either. But he had too much experience and courage to ever let on, if he felt that way.

However, as the weeks wore on and November approached, spirits aboard the "Truman Special" began to lift. It was a subtle but exhilarating change. No one was quite sure what it was, but the motion and hubbub on the Truman train began to acquire a sense of purpose. The visible factor was that the crowds were getting larger, friendlier, and noisier. On a swing through hard-rock Republican Indiana, 25,000 people turned out at Kokomo to greet the President, 20,000 at Hammond, and more than 12,000 at Logansport. Dewey had been over the same route a week earlier and had not done as well. Five thousand people waited beside the tracks in a downpour of rain in Albany, New York, to greet the President's train when it rolled in at 8 o'clock one late October morning. Six thousand filled every available seat in the armory at Springfield, Illinois, and other hundreds gathered outside in this citadel of Republicanism to hear the Democratic candidate lambaste Dewey for not having a farm program. In St. Paul, he filled the 15,000-seat civic auditorium and three adjacent halls and drew applause forty-two times with his excoriation of the "do-nothing Eightieth Congress." Dewey drew only 7,000 in the same auditorium. At the traditional "Friday night before election rally" in the Brooklyn Academy of Music (some of its organizers had been prominent in the "dump Truman" drive at the convention) the crowd gave him a twelve-minute ovation when he rose to speak.

Something was in the air, all right: the biggest political upset in history. "We felt it, but we just couldn't believe it," Clark Clifford remembers. So did many of the reporters and political experts who had followed the campaign. Robert C. Albright, a veteran of the political staff of the Washington *Post*, wrote: "Now and then a particularly large crowd or a noisy ovation starts a mighty surge of hope in the rear staff car. Some of it filters forward to the press car, and hardbitten reporters ask themselves, 'Could we be wrong?'" Some began cautiously to hedge their predictions, but they could not trust their eyes above their judgment—or at least above the collective judgment of the journalists' tribe. They were trapped by professional timidity into going along with the consensus that Dewey was bound to win, and win big.* That was what the pros in the various states had told them; that was what they told one another in endless bull sessions in the press car; that was what all the polls told them.

The Gallup poll four days before election had it cold: Dewey, 49.5 percent of the popular vote, Truman 44.5 percent, the rest to Wallace, Thurmond, *et al.* The New York *Times* had it even colder. At great cost and earnest effort it had deployed a small battalion of reporters across the country for an entire month to take the national pulse. Its findings: Dewey, 29 states with 345 electoral votes (266 needed to win); Truman, 11 states with 105 electoral votes; Thurmond, 4 states with 38 votes; the rest "in doubt." Willard Kiplinger, one of Washington's most profound pundits, also had it cold. Publisher of a new weekly magazine, *Changing Times,* with an immovable Saturday deadline, he hit the newstands Monday, November 1, election eve, with a front cover proclaiming in inch-high type, WHAT DEWEY WILL DO.

Everybody had it cold, apparently, except Truman himself and Howard McGrath, his campaign chairman. On the Sunday before election, McGrath and Redding, sitting alone amidst the debris and overflowing ashtrays in their New York headquarters, telephoned a score of top Democratic state leaders across the country to get their last-minute estimates of the outlook. One after another they gave almost identical replies: "Things have been looking up in the last couple of weeks. We'll certainly carry the state for the Senator [or Governor or Congressman], but the President probably won't make it."

When the roundup was completed, McGrath looked at Redding and said: "You can't win all the things they say they're going to win and not elect a President too. After all, he's at the top of the ticket.

"We're either going to lose everything—every senatorial race, every congressional race, every courthouse—or we'll elect a President. I think we elect Truman."

In the folklore of the midsector of this century, two dates stand out so starkly in memory that it is still a popular parlor game to go around the room asking, "Where were you on . . . Pearl Harbor Day, or Election Night, 1948?" In each recital there is likely to be a high element of personal drama, suspense, and shock reaction. Both dates saw the utterly incredible come to pass.

This reporter had gone to New York on Tuesday, November 2,

---

* This reporter was no exception!—C.P.

1948, as an extra hand when and if needed in the city room of his newspaper to help with the election night coverage. But he turned out to be surplus, and, since there weren't any surprises in prospect, he went to the theater instead—the Lunts in something or other somewhere on 47th Street. At the second intermission, about 10:30 P.M., he strolled into a neighboring bar for refreshment. A news commentary was coming in over the radio, a jumble of vote totals, precinct numbers, and names of states. Then, with a swallow of Scotch just on its way past the windpipe, he heard one clear, intelligible phrase that caused him to gasp and strangle: "Truman's lead now looks almost unassailable. If he can hold his edge in Ohio . . ." Coughing and choking, he slapped a dollar on the bar and headed at a dead run for his office three blocks away. Halfway there, he suddenly remembered his new topcoat, dumped on his seat in the theater. He turned and ran back toward 47th Street. Then, as abruptly, he turned again. "To hell with it," he said, and sprinted on toward Times Square. The coat, a $47.50 job, was never retrieved.

This little yarn is significant only in that it typifies what happened to millions of Americans that night. All across the country men and women made a dutiful bedtime check of their radios and televisions, just to see how things were going—and then stayed glued to them past midnight, into the dawn, and even through the breakfast hour. Suddenly they were spectators at a contest as thrilling as that between David and Goliath, and containing the same dramatic ingredients.

Truman picked up an early lead in popular votes, and, though it expanded and narrowed harrowingly through the night, he never lost it. The commentators said at first this was to be expected. This was the city vote, they said, but wait until the rural precincts are heard from. But about midnight, Iowa—Iowa, the heartland of midwestern Republicanism—dropped irretrievably into the Democratic column. The commentators were not so sure any more, and they noted that the crowds had drifted away from the Dewey victory celebration at the Roosevelt Hotel, leaving a pall of apprehension and untouched cases of champagne behind them.

The electoral vote seesawed back and forth agonizingly as the hours ticked on. At 4:30 Wednesday morning, Jim Hagerty, Dewey's press man, broke a long and ominous silence to tell reporters, "We're still in there fighting." Then came the shocking news that Illinois had conceded—Democratic. At 6 o'clock, Truman had a commanding lead in both popular and electoral votes but not enough to win. His electoral score was 227 to 176 for Dewey. But a few states, including Ohio and California, were still out, and the experts had all said Ohio was a shoo-in for Dewey and that Governor Warren could hardly be expected to lose his home state.

Then, at 9:30, came the climax, a tension-snapping end to one of the most exhausting cliffhangers of all time. As idling teletypes in a hundred newsrooms across the nation suddenly began to chatter, bleary-eyed radio announcers grabbed their microphones to proclaim almost hysterically: "Ohio has gone Democratic! This puts Truman over the top with 270 electoral votes. Ladies and gentlemen, President Truman has won the election!"

What happened? How did this greatest of political miracles come to pass?

The Presidential vote statistics are as follows: *

Candidate	Popular Vote	Electoral Vote	States
Truman	24,045,052	304	28
Dewey	21,896,927	189	16
Wallace	1,137,957	—	—
Thurmond	1,168,687	38	4
Others	240,594	—	—
Total	48,489,217	531	48

The vote for Congress was as follows, with figures in parentheses showing the previous membership:

	Democratic		Republican	
Senate	54	(45)	42	(51)
House	263	(188)	171	(246)

It was the closest Presidential election since 1916. Truman's margin over Dewey was 2,148,125. He won by a plurality, not by a majority. His percentage of the popular vote was 49.5; Dewey's, 45.1. In a general way, each man lost where he assumed he was strongest, and won where his prospects seemed thinnest. Dewey swept all of the industrial Northeast, from Maryland through Maine, except for Massachusetts and Rhode Island. This was traditional Democratic territory. Truman captured many of the important farm states, most notably Wisconsin, Iowa, and Colorado, which were traditionally Republican. In addition, he swept the whole tier of eleven western states (excluding Oregon), in which,

* All figures from *The World Almanac, 1949.*

though they are traditionally Democratic, the Republicans had confidently expected to make important gains. Thurmond deprived Truman of four states in the once-solid South—South Carolina, Alabama, Mississippi, and Louisiana. And Wallace certainly robbed him of New York (the Progressive Party total there was approximately twice Dewey's winning margin), and probably of New Jersey.

What were the factors in this upset?

There were many, but in this writer's view the controlling one was this: Truman had, in the November 1947 memorandum by Clifford and the political strategy board, a basic campaign strategy that was unique to his needs and to his capacities, and he stuck with it. It was a strategy of go-for-broke; of recognizing that he was the underdog and that he had little to lose and much to gain; of seizing the initiative and pressing it with every weapon and against all risks. His banner was the New Deal; his targets were familiar and well defined; and the obstacles were starkly and realistically portrayed. The strategy called for courage and persistence, which Truman supplied in absolute measure. He did not deviate essentially from his master plan throughout the campaign. The result was that he knew what he was doing every step of the way.

Three voting blocs supplied the margin for Truman's victory: labor, Negro (plus other minorities), and farm. Throughout the campaign Truman had emphasized day after day his fights with the Eightieth Congress over civil rights for the Negroes, housing, minimum wages, and his veto of the Taft-Hartley Act. When the votes were counted, he had carried the thirteen largest industrial cities, where labor and Negro votes are decisive, some by pluralities greater than Roosevelt's in 1944. This swelled his popular vote score. It was not enough to outbalance the Republican "upstate" vote in places like New York, Pennsylvania, and Michigan, which gave their electoral votes to Dewey, but it was sufficient in Ohio and Illinois, and possibly in California.

The tradition of the eleven Great Lakes and Plains states—the nation's biggest grocery basket—is Republican. Seven went for Dewey in 1944, and six for Willkie in 1940. Dewey, presuming on a revulsion against New Deal and postwar regimentation of the farmer, expected to sweep them all with the possible exception of Illinois and Minnesota. Instead, he took only five—Indiana, North and South Dakota, Nebraska, and Kansas. Iowa's swing behind Truman was, psychologically, the most crushing blow of all to the

GOP. This was the very citadel of Republicanism, which had remained faithful since 1936. When Iowa defected to the Democrats in 1948, she took every other important farm and cattle state, except the aforementioned five, with her. It was a tribute to the efficacy of the grain-storage-bin issue and to a drastic mid-October break in farm prices. The farmers were riding a high crest of prosperity that year, but Truman frightened them into thinking that a Republican administration might take it away from them.

Another major factor was the contrast in campaign techniques and in the motivational appeals to the voters. The Truman campaign was positive, hard-hitting, and directed to the gut interests of the voters. He named names and places and gave chapter and verse (with whatever injury to the cause of accuracy) when he criticized something. And for every wrong and every fear, he had a palpable villain—the Eightieth Congress and, by extrapolation, Republican candidates and Republican officeholders in general. He gave the voters something to be "agin," which is the most powerful motivator of voter behavior.

By contrast, both Dewey's campaign and his personality were arid. He avoided direct controversy with his opponent. He was seldom specific or convincing when he elucidated the larger issues. Intellectually, his campaign was on a higher level than Truman's, just as it was in the matter of taste and decorum. By the same token it was overlaid with a palpable superciliousness. It was, said Clarence Buddington Kelland, national Republican committeeman from Arizona, "smug, arrogant, stupid. . . . It was a contemptuous campaign, contemptuous alike to our enemies and to our friends."

In fact, the demerits of the Dewey campaign technique may have bulked as large in the outcome as did the merits of the Truman technique. Jules Abels, in *Out of the Jaws of Victory*, pointed to what may have been a decisive and fatal factor in the Dewey operation in these words:

The election was not thrown away by indifference or lack of effort. Preparation and more preparation had always been the distinguishing characteristic of Dewey and his team throughout his career. . . . The truth is that the type of campaign was the result not of careless, but of too careful and painstaking calculation. The Dewey campaign line was frozen into inertia not because it had been underthought, but because it had been overthought.

The consequence of this, as Abels and others have pointed out, was that when the first turbulence of a Truman tide began to appear late in October, the Dewey crew, geared for smooth water only, were unable to trim sails in order to meet the rising seas.

Still another factor of importance was Truman's handling of the Russian blockade of Berlin. This had occurred in midsummer, and it had created an air of anxiety over the whole tenuous peace of Europe. The airlift that Truman had ordered seemed at first an act of desperation—which it probably was. But as the weeks wore on and tons of supplies continued to pour daily into Berlin, it became an act of defiance and of calling the Russian bluff. The country experienced a surge of pride, of which President Truman was the inevitable beneficiary. While foreign policy, per se, never became a flammable issue in the campaign, largely because of Dewey's forbearance, the dramatic success of the Berlin airlift greatly enhanced Truman's image as a leader.

Finally, in assessing the factors of the 1948 upset, there was the widespread miscalculation that the old New Deal dynamic had been buried in the grave with FDR. Dewey and his men believed that the concepts of the managerial revolution, so captivating to the Eastern elite in the postwar years, had captivated the rest of the country as well. In this new dogma the old political clichés, slogans, and alliances were written off as decadent, including particularly belief in the New Deal–forged coalition of labor, Negroes, city bosses, and Southern Bourbons. In its place was an aggressive, up-to-date, all-purpose conservatism of Republican hue with a base as wide as the continent.

They were wrong. Truman campaigned on an orthodox New Deal–Democratic platform. He held Dewey to a smaller proportion of the total vote (45.1 percent) than Dewey got running against Roosevelt in 1944 (45.8 percent). If the figures are recast to lump the essentially Democratic Wallace and Thurmond votes along with Truman's, the Democratic 1948 total becomes 54.9 percent, which is 1.6 percent above what FDR drew in 1944. In other words, it is clear that, instead of diminishing, the Democratic potential under Truman had grown.

Republican theorists in their postmortems attempted to explain Dewey's poor showing as attributable to Republican stay-at-homes who didn't bother to vote. Sam Lubbell, in an expert analysis of the campaign for the *Saturday Evening Post* two months* after the election, came to a quite different conclusion:

---

* Issue of January 22, 1949.

GOP victories in the industrial east were won less through new Republican adherents than by the apathy which kept much of the old FDR vote from the polls. Far from costing Dewey the election, the [Democratic] stay-at-homes may have saved him almost as crushing a defeat as Landon suffered in 1936.

At all events, Harry Truman was now President in his own right, his record was vindicated, and his leadership was open to no man's challenge. "You just have to take off your hat," the New York *Sun,* which rarely had said anything kind about him before, editorialized the day after election, "to a beaten man who refuses to stay licked! . . . The next few days will produce many long and labored explanations of what has happened. To us of the *Sun* there is no great mystery about it. Mr. Truman won because this is still a land which loves a scrapper, in which intestinal fortitude is still respected."

The President took all such accolades with becoming modesty. He set off for a rest at Key West—and within a week had summoned his aides to begin work on a new budget and State of the Union message.

CHAPTER 10

✧✧✧✧✧✧✧✧✧✧✧✧✧✧✧✧✧✧✧✧✧

New Directions in Foreign Policy

"We Live in Dangerous Times"

Dangers and crises arise with us not because the right policy or the right direction eludes us, but from the very nature of the situations we face. The idea that there is a right policy or a right action which will remove them and make all well is based upon the unspoken assumption that we could control the present situation if we only knew how.

We live in dangerous times because of the decisions of another power which are beyond the control of any or all of us. There is no formula which will exorcise these dangers. The decisions which create them will be affected by the facts which we are helping to forge from the unfolding future. The task calls for steady nerves and determined purpose. We are not doing badly.

—Dean G. Acheson, speech before
the Michigan Bar Association,
September 30, 1948

IN FIVE SHORT and perilous years between the summer of 1945 and the summer of 1950, the political structure of the world was upended and came to rest not on a balance of power, but on a balance of terror. This was the only visible alternative to either World War III or a world dominated by Communist Russia and her totalitarianism. A cold war is an unsatisfactory substitute for peace, but it is better than a hot war or surrender. Its primary weapons are economic and political, and its tactics are determined by the strategy of foreign policy. Devising a foreign policy to meet these new imperatives called for boldness and inventiveness in international relations such as this country had never ventured before, and for the virtual abandonment of many of the concepts of isolation and self-sufficiency which we had held sacred since the founding of the Republic. The foundations of this new policy were laid by President Truman, and they have not been substantially added to or subtracted from in all the years since. He projected the United States into a totally new role in world affairs.

When World War II ended, the vision of the world ahead still had, for most eyes, the roseate and optimistic glow imparted by Roosevelt's Grand Design—a democratic One World fellowship under the benign discipline of the United Nations. The leaders of the East and West had, in fact, toasted one another on this bright prospect (with some unexpressed misgivings) at Potsdam. War was to be forever outlawed. The chief aggressors, Germany and Japan, were to be militarily sterilized. The lesser enemy States were to be reconstituted as democratic sovereignties. And the major powers, renouncing selfish interests, would provide a sort of big brother guardianship for the rest of the world. As Secretary of State Byrnes put it in October 1945:

> The world system which we seek to create must be based on the principle of the sovereign equality of nations. That does not mean that all nations are equal in power and influence. . . . But it does mean equal respect for the individuality and sovereignty of nations, large and small. Nations, like individuals, should be equal before the law.[1]

No knowledgeable person believed wholly in this utopian, One World dream. But even as the guns fell silent and the first abrasions of the East-West conflict began to irritate, the Grand Design remained as a frame of reference, at least, for many of Washington's postwar planners. It was a shaky framework and destined before long to collapse. As President Truman came seriously to grips with postwar foreign policy at the beginning of 1946, this, roughly, was the world balance sheet that confronted him:

CAPITAL ASSETS

1. The Western Allies had won history's costliest and bloodiest war. Fascism had been crushed and its menace to human dignity and political freedom obliterated.

2. A forum for the peaceful settlement of future international disputes and for the worldwide propagation of the democratic way of life had become a reality in the United Nations. At least, it had survived the ordeal of birth and showed encouraging signs of vitality.

3. The United States, as leader of the free world cause, had come out of the war with its economy stronger than when it went in, and with the mightiest productive machine in all history.

4. The secret of atomic energy, believed to be both the ultimate weapon and the ultimate key to mankind's needs for physical energy (and probably much else besides), was an American monopoly.

ACCOUNTS RECEIVABLE

1. The great productive potential of Germany, to be reactivated under the Four Power guidance of its conquerors, was expected to nourish the economic revival of the rest of Europe.

2. Peace treaties in negotiation with Italy and the smaller enemy States from the Baltic to the North Sea were counted on to produce democratic stability in these historically turbulent and politically undependable countries.

3. A pliant Japan, docilely beating its swords into plowshares under the stern guardianship of General MacArthur would be, like Germany, an invigorating influence for good in the Far East.

LIABILITIES

1. Britain and all of Europe stood nakedly in the midst of their war-shattered economies and on the brink of fiscal ruin. Millions were jobless, homeless, without fuel, and hungry—not only because of exhausted reserves but also because of a disastrously poor harvest. In the Low Countries, and in France and Italy particularly, a surging Communist movement threatened to topple the existing governments.

2. The Republic of China clung to existence by a fraying thread. Mao Tse-tung's Communists controlled Manchuria and the northern provinces, while Chiang Kai-shek stood helplessly in the south, immobilized by weakness and confusion.

3. From Southeast Asia westward through India and Africa an

implacable tide of nationalism strained against the bonds of colonialism and second-class status.

4. The Soviet Union, in spite of heavy material and manpower losses during the war, remained the one cohesive and dynamic political force in most of Europe and Asia. It also had the biggest army in the world, with its outposts reaching like probing fingers toward the Atlantic, the Mediterranean, and the China Sea.

5. The United States, by contrast, was in the midst of a reckless, headlong dismantling of the most powerful military machine in history, spurred on by the irresistible clamor of public opinion.

What a reading of this balance sheet shows is that President Truman faced the task of rebuilding a war-torn world with a set of plans—the Grand Design—that was already obsolete. This truth was not widely recognized, nor always conceded when it was recognized. But the hard fact was that, at the end of 1945, the One World dream had deteriorated into a split-world reality. A new power struggle was inexorably forming, based on the opposing might of the United States and the Soviet Union. For the next two decades, men's minds were to be haunted by the fear of a showdown between these two giants.

At the outset, this country had an impressive margin of weight on its side. It had the A-bomb; it had overwhelming economic and industrial superiority; it had an aura of military invincibility. But for a number of reasons it could not, and did not, press its advantage.

For one thing, the United States was encumbered by its armor of moral principles, which looks fine on display but rather limits the wearer's freedom of action. At Yalta, at Potsdam, and at San Francisco we had solemnly covenanted with our allies in arms to bring about a peaceful and democratic world and to eschew military force and the devious implements of power politics. As the leader of the free world, we were determined to set an example of generosity, high purpose, and forbearance. We were dedicated to the proposition that good faith engenders good faith. It took time to learn that there is no such phrase in the Communist lexicon.

Another reason why we could not press our advantage was that we had robbed our diplomacy of its ultimate punch—the ability, when all else has failed, to back up our position with force. In international relations, the "ends and means" of a policy have to be in reasonable balance if a nation does not want to go over the brink in a test of brinkmanship. At the beginning of 1946, the Red Army could have swept into almost any part of Europe it chose, and we and the Western Allies together would not have had the guns or men to stop them. The armies of Britain and France were all but shattered, and in the United States the greatest fighting force ever assembled was being systematically dismantled in response to the clamorous cry, "Bring the boys back home." From a peak of 12 million men under arms at D-Day, we were down to 8 million when Japan surrendered, and 2 million by July 1946. As the mainstay of the non-Russian occupation forces in Germany, the United States had two and a half divisions, made up largely of replacements, with a combat efficiency about 50 percent of the wartime peak. "One prefers not to speculate," Lieutenant General Carl Spaatz, the Air Force Chief of Staff, recalled some years later, "on what might have happened only one year after V-J Day if our Air Force had been called upon to resist a new aggression or to repress a recurrence of combat in one of the occupied countries."

As the first year of the postwar era opened, the Truman administration was caught in a dilemma of confusion and contradictions about its role in the world. Across the map of Europe and the Far East there spread a pall of hunger, destitution, and political chaos. This was a challenge to the humanitarian impulse of the American people with their wealth and abundance virtually untouched. It was a challenge also to their convictions of political freedom and independence for all people. In the simplest term, this was what the war had been about. But the sheer magnitude of the humanitarian task seemed to defy solution. The political challenge seemed equally insoluble as long as we were bound in partnership to an ally whose idea of cooperation was to have his own way.

As Dean Acheson was to say, we were living in dangerous times indeed.

Containment

President Truman's first State of the Union message, on January 21, 1946, enunciated the nation's postwar foreign policy in disarmingly positive and confident terms. He told the Congress:

The great and dominant objective of United States foreign policy is to build and preserve a just peace. At a time when massive changes are occurring with lightning speed throughout the world, it is often difficult to perceive how this central objective is best served.

Despite this very real difficulty, there are certain basic propositions to which the United States adheres and to which we shall continue to adhere.

One proposition is that lasting peace requires genuine understanding and active cooperation among the most powerful nations.

Another is that even the support of the strongest nations cannot guarantee a peace unless it is infused with the quality of justice for all nations. . . .

And then, almost by way of warning, he added:

We may not always fully succeed in our objectives. There may be instances where the attainment of these objectives is delayed, but we'll not give our full sanction and approval to actions which fly in the face of these ideals. . . . When difficulties arise among us, the United States does not propose to remove them by sacrificing its ideals or its vital interests.

The President and his advisers were still rummaging in Roosevelt's old tool chest for the implements with which to create a postwar foreign policy that would cope with the emerging postwar realities. It was not a very rewarding search. Suddenly, enlightenment came from an unexpected quarter.

On February 9, 1946, Joseph Stalin addressed a monster gathering of Communist Party functionaries in Moscow as a prelude to the first election held in the Soviet Union in eight years. As a campaign speech it was negligible (there are no political campaigns in Russia), but as a definition of Communist goals and strategy in the postwar world it was historic.

There could be, Stalin said, no long-range collaboration between the young, dynamic world of communism and the dying, corrupt world of capitalism. The recent war had brought them together briefly as allies, but the war itself had been the result of convulsions in the capitalist system in fulfillment of the Marxian prophecy. The socialist system (he continued), despite its wounds and the loss of its manpower, had emerged from the conflict stronger than ever. Henceforth, the world revolution of the world proletariat would be pressed with new vigor everywhere, and to buttress that revolution the Soviet economy would embark on another great five-year plan that would triple the output of heavy industry above prewar levels.

"Only under such conditions," Stalin declared, "will our country be insured against any eventuality. Perhaps three five-year plans will be required to achieve this, but it can be done and we must do it."

What the Russian dictator was saying, in effect, was this: Let the Western Powers toy with their illusions of capitalist democracy if they want to, but we in the Communist world will press harder than ever toward the fulfillment of our historic revolutionary goals—and everyone else had better keep out of our way!

It took a little time for the full import of the Stalin speech to sink in in Washington. Secretary Byrnes and many in the State Department refused at first to attach great importance to it. Navy Secretary Forrestal and Ambassador Averell Harriman, on the other hand, took it at once for what it proved ultimately to be—a hard, new Communist Party line that proved the futility of counting upon Russian cooperation in the settlement of Europe's political affairs. To Justice William O. Douglas it was "the declaration of World War III."[2]

The full meaning of Stalin's words became more widely apparent in the ensuing weeks as they were read in the light of a long confidential memorandum from the U.S. Embassy in Moscow. The author was a brilliant but at that time little-known scholar of Russian history and psychology, George F. Kennan, who was our counselor of embassy there. His 8,000-word treatise, a thoughtful and expert analysis of contemporary Russian political philosophy, showed this philosophy to be not a rational system based on Western concepts, but a religion full of dogmas and demonology with strongly Oriental overtones. The West, he said, could no longer deal effectively with postwar communism on the basis of prewar notions and prejudices.

Kennan's thesis, which was to become so vital a factor in American diplomacy, is worth examining at length. He began by saying:

The political personality of Soviet power as we know it today is the product of ideology and circumstances: ideology inherited by the present Soviet leaders from the movement in which they had their political origin, and circumstances of the power which they now have exercised for nearly three decades in Russia.

This ideology, he continued, is based on three main postulates: (1) the central factor in man's life is the system by which goods are produced and exchanged; (2) the capitalist system of production is inefficient and is based on exploitation of the working class; and (3) capitalism contains the seeds of its own destruction, a process which must be fulfilled by the proletarian revolution.

The Russian revolution of 1916 was the first of these great up-heavals. But the teachings of Marx and Lenin, which concentrated on the seizure of power, were vague and impractical as to the exercise of power once it was gained. Beyond the nationalization of industry and the expropriation of private property, there was no agreed upon program. The harshness of the takeover by the Communist minority in Russia, and the social and economic chaos which followed it, made the establishment of dictatorial power a necessity. As Kennan wrote:

Their sense of insecurity was too great. Their particular brand of fanaticism, unmodified by any of the Anglo-Saxon traditions of compromise, was too fierce and too jealous to envisage any permanent sharing of power. . . . Outside of the Communist Party, Russian society was to have no rigidity. There were to be no forms of collective human activity or association which would not be dominated by the Party. And within the Party the same principle was to apply . . . the membership to be animated not by their own individual wills but by the awesome breath of the Party leadership and the overbrooding presence of "the word."

The process of political consolidation in the Soviet, Kennan continued, "has never been completed down to the present day." The leaders' efforts to secure their authority are directed not only against forces at home, but also against the outside world. Indeed, the image of a hostile outside world, intent upon the destruction of communism, has become a mainstay of Party doctrine, supporting the necessity for continued austerity, sacrifice, and belligerency.

He went on to say:

There is ample evidence that the stress laid in Moscow on the menace confronting Soviet society from the world outside its borders is founded not in the realities of foreign antagonism but in the necessity of explaining away the maintenance of dictatorial authority at home. . . . Today the major part of the structure of Soviet power is committed to the perfection of the dictatorship and to the maintenance of the concept of Russia as in a state of siege. . . . This fiction has been canonized in Soviet philosophy by the excesses already committed in its name; and it is now anchored in the Soviet structure of thought by bonds far greater than those of mere ideology. . . .

[This] means that there can never be on Moscow's side any sincere assumption of a community of aims between the Soviet Union and powers which are regarded as capitalist. It must invariably be assumed in Moscow that the aims of the capitalist world are antagonistic to the Soviet regime, and therefore to the interests of the people it controls. If the Soviet government occasionally sets its signature to a document which would indicate the contrary, this is to be regarded as a tactical maneuver permissible in dealing with the enemy and should be taken in the spirit of *caveat emptor*. Basically, the antagonism remains. It is postulated. And from it flow many of the phenomena which we find disturbing in the Kremlin's conduct of foreign policy: the secretiveness, the lack of frankness, the wary suspiciousness, the duplicity, and the basic unfriendliness of purpose. These phenomena are there to stay for the foreseeable future.

The Kremlin, like the Church, Kennan said, is under no compulsion to hurry. Lenin's teachings counseled caution, flexibility, patience, and deception in the pursuit of the ultimate Communist goal, and these precepts are fortified by the lessons of Russian history. Neither has it any compunction about retreating in the face of superior force. "Its political action is a fluid stream which moves constantly, wherever it is permitted to move, toward a given goal. Its main concern is to make sure it has filled every nook and cranny available to it in the basin of world power."

Kennan warned that the Russian leaders, being keen judges of human psychology, would not be diverted from their course by threats or bluster from the West. Effective opposition to the Kremlin requires coolness, persistency, and enough flexibility in demands to make compliance possible without too great a sacrifice of prestige. And then, coming to the heart of his argument, Kennan wrote:

In the light of the above it will be clearly seen that the Soviet pressure against the free institutions of the western world is something that can be contained by the adroit and vigilant application of counterforce at a series of constantly shifting geographical and political points, corresponding to the shifts and maneuvers of Soviet policy, but which cannot be talked or charmed out of existence. . . .

It is clear that the United States cannot expect in the foreseeable future to enjoy political intimacy with the Soviet regime. It must continue to regard the Soviet Union as a rival, not a partner, in the political arena. It must continue to expect that Soviet policies will reflect no abstract love of peace and stability . . . but rather a cautious, persistent pressure toward the disrupting and weakening of all rival influence and rival power.

Balanced against this are the facts that Russia, as opposed to the western world in general, is still by far the weaker party, that Soviet policy is highly flexible, and that Soviet society may well contain deficiencies which will eventually weaken its own total potential.

This would of itself warrant the United States entering with reasonable confidence upon a policy of firm containment, designed to confront the

Russians with unalterable counterforce at every point where they show
signs of encroaching upon the interests of a peaceful and stable world. . . .

It would be an exaggeration to say that American behavior, unassisted
and alone, could exercise a power of life and death over the Communist
movement and bring about the early fall of Soviet power in Russia. . . .
[But] no mystical, Messianic movement—and particularly not that of the
Kremlin—can face frustration indefinitely without eventually adjusting
itself in one way or another to the logic of that state of affairs. . . .*

What Kennan was saying was that Russian communism is not
merely a form of government but a pseudoreligion with fixed
dogmas and an unalterable mission to destroy the nonbelievers. It is
an ideological force without national or racial boundaries, impelled
by its very nature to flow into any political crevice from which it is
not forcibly excluded. It cannot be destroyed where it has taken
root, nor can it for long be appeased. But its spread can be checked.
It can be "contained" within the boundaries it already inhabits.

The Kennan thesis, coming on the heels of Stalin's speech, provided an intellectual stiffening for the spongy theories and postulates in which Washington's thinking about international communism had become bogged. Within a year a new strategic concept—
the policy of "containment"—had begun to guide American foreign
policy along a revolutionary path.

An Entangling Alliance: NATO

As the containment policy began to take form, its vast implications became gradually apparent. *First*, it meant an acceptance of
the fact of a bipolar world and a conflict of indefinite duration between the forces of communism and freedom. *Second*, it meant the
willingness of the United States to oppose the Soviet Union when
and wherever necessary, and by every means including the risk of
war. *Third*, it meant inducing other free nations to share these

* This résumé is based on "The Sources of Soviet Conduct," an article written by
Mr. Kennan under the pseudonym "X" and published in the July 1947 issue of
Foreign Affairs, the quarterly journal of the Foreign Policy Association. The editors
have kindly given permission for the extensive quotes used here. Mr. Kennan's
article is a paraphrase and condensation of the memorandum he wrote for the State
Department. In recent years he has modified somewhat the rigid tenets on which
he based his containment doctrine and speaks more hopefully of the possibilities of
coexistence. See his *On Dealing with the Communist World* (Harper & Row, 1963).

commitments and risks with us, and giving them the material assistance to make their cooperation effective.

In practical terms, containment meant throwing dams of political, economic, and, ultimately, military strength across whatever watercourse the Communist tide was likely to flow into. It was a pragmatic strategy to buy time rather than victory. Its tactical application during the next few years was to stretch from Europe and the Middle East to Korea. It began with the Truman Doctrine and the Marshall Plan, but its most enduring bulwark was to be the North Atlantic Treaty Organization. Time is still on the side of the free world and containment remains the core of its strategy.

Secretary Marshall's historic speech at Harvard in June 1947 had set in motion the first stirrings of cooperative activity among the nations of Western Europe to do something about their collective welfare. Assistance from the United States was promised on the condition that the Europeans themselves would plan and execute a realistic program for their own recovery.

The nations of Europe did get together to plan their economic future under the Marshall Plan. But even as they met, the fearsome shadows of Russian belligerence darkened their prospects. There were threats to force the Americans and British out of Germany. The satellite nations were forbidden to get in line for American aid. Moscow-controlled Communist parties in France and Italy openly fomented violence and registered victory after victory in important local and national elections. The Red Army appeared poised to move at any moment into Hungary and Czechoslovakia, and possibly elsewhere as well. If there was a promise of collective economic salvation for Western Europe in the air, there was only fear for its collective political and military security.

Early in 1948, Britain's Labor Foreign Minister, Ernest Bevin, conveyed to President Truman and Secretary Marshall a scheme he had proposed to the French, the Dutch, and the Belgians for a series of bilateral defense treaties against the threat of Russian aggression. The plan won the warm endorsement of the American leaders, and they sent an observer to Brussels for the formative sessions of what was to be called the Western Union.

Midway of the proceedings, on February 25, the shock waves of the Communist coup in Czechoslovakia rocked the Western world. It seemed clear now that Russia was embarked on a deliberate course of aggression—picking off the nations of central and Western

Europe one by one. Her course gave impetus to the Brussels powers to strengthen their pact, and it impressed upon the policy planners in Washington the inevitability of the United States joining such an alliance. How else could the free nations protect their freedom? They needed the productive and military strength of the United States.

The Brussels Pact—Western Union—was signed in the Belgian capital on March 17, 1948. It linked Great Britain, France, Belgium, The Netherlands, and Luxembourg into a fifty-year political, economic, and military alliance. On the same day, possibly by prearrangement, President Truman went before a joint session of the Republican-controlled Congress to plead for speedy enactment of the first appropriation for his European Recovery Program.

But he had another message, too, one that in time would lead these reluctant lawmakers to an even bolder adventure in internationalism than the one they were now about to consummate. He told the Congress:

> At the very moment I am addressing you, five nations of the European community, in Brussels, are signing a fifty-year agreement for economic cooperation and common defense against aggression. This action has great significance . . . for the preservation and protection of [Europe's] civilization. This deserves our full support. And I am confident that the United States will, by appropriate means, extend to the free nations the support which the situation deserves.
>
> Their determination will be matched by an equal determination on our part to help them to protect themselves.

There was a studied ambiguity in the President's words. While he and most of his advisers now recognized that the United States would have to become a partner in a larger alliance of Western Powers, he could not yet afford to show his hand. Congress was having a hard enough time digesting the request for a $6.8 billion European Recovery Program appropriation (it granted $5.3 billion), and it surely would balk at any other major new scheme in foreign policy. Moreover, the President's personal leadership had been weakened by a series of political mishaps, and he looked like a sure loser in the upcoming election, six months hence. For him to have broached a European alliance in the spring of 1948 would almost certainly have doomed it to rejection. Congress, largely dominated by Taft conservatives and quasi-isolationists, needed careful preparation before being confronted with such a challenge.

"I always kept in mind," Mr. Truman said later, "the lesson of Wilson's failure in 1920. I meant to have legislative cooperation."

For cooperation, Truman turned to an old and respected friend in the Senate, Republican Arthur Vandenberg, the senior Senator from Michigan. Vandenberg, once a howling isolationist, had, since the onset of the Second World War, been a wholly converted internationalist. He was a man of great stature in his party, President *pro tem* of the Senate, Chairman of the Foreign Relations Committee, and almost as powerful a leader in the area of foreign affairs as Robert Taft was in domestic affairs. Roosevelt had leaned on him in countless international conferences and crises during the war to lend bipartisan backing to administration policies, and Truman had made him a member of the official United States party at Potsdam in 1945 and a delegate to the Inter-American Conference of 1947, which wrote the Pact of Rio de Janeiro.

Truman, with the particular help of his Under Secretary of State, Robert M. Lovett, who was a close friend of Vandenberg's, impressed upon the Senator the critical need for a binding association among the nations of the Atlantic community, using the Western Union as a nucleus and with full participating membership by the United States. It could not be a showcase treaty; it had to be a working partnership capable of posing an invincible counterforce, both political and military, to Communist aggression throughout Western Europe. Vandenberg was soon persuaded, and he also agreed that the essential first step was to prepare the public mind, and the congressional mind in particular, for the jettisoning of the ancient American axiom of "no entangling alliances." For while the full shape of what was to become the North Atlantic Treaty was not yet clear in anyone's mind, it certainly would involve an "entangling alliance" and a total rejection of peacetime isolationism.

Vandenberg conceived the idea of a solemn Senate pronouncement of the basic premises of American foreign policy which would commit the faith and energies of the nation to the cause of world freedom. The "Vandenberg Resolution," which he and Lovett worked out in many evening meetings together in the Senator's apartment, is one of the great documents of American diplomacy.

It reaffirmed this country's faith in and support of the United Nations as the central guardian of world peace and proposed means to strengthen it. But it asserted at the same time the right of member nations to establish regional defense arrangements within the United Nations framework, and the intention of this country to join such arrangements "should any armed attack occur threatening its national security." The Resolution was offered as expressing "the sense of the Senate," and though it lacked the force of law, it imposed a strong moral obligation on the administration and on the American public.

Owing to the Senator's superb generalship, his Resolution achieved one of its main purposes: thumping bipartisan support. It was unanimously endorsed by the Senate Foreign Relations Committee, and when called up on the Senate floor on June 11, it was approved after a full day of debate by a vote of 64 to 4. Rarely has the Senate in a single day underwritten so emphatically a policy of such far-reaching importance as this.

From the Vandenberg Resolution to the North Atlantic Treaty was a direct step, though a delayed one. Within a week of the Senate vote, Under Secretary Lovett, on instructions from President Truman, began highly secret talks with the Ambassadors of the Brussels Pact nations and of Canada. By September they had reached a consensus that the compact should include not only the North Atlantic and Scandinavian nations but Portugal and Italy as well, and that the concept of military defense should have equal weight with that of political cooperation.

Tentative drafts of a proposed treaty were quietly distributed among the interested nations. All concurred in principle, though there were a number of individual reservations to be worked out. France wanted the treaty's protective blanket thrown over her North African possessions, and she wanted redoubled assurances that it would not lead to a rearming of Germany. Britain quibbled over the admission of Italy. The United States insisted that the mutual defense commitment be tempered by allowing some leeway short of war in assisting a member under attack, a device which had made the Rio Pact of 1947 (a similar regional treaty affecting the Western Hemisphere) acceptable to the Senate. All such objections were resolved, and the whole matter might have been concluded by winter had it not been for the uncertainties of the 1948 election. If there were to be a new President in Washington after November— and it seemed more than likely that there would be—he should not be tied down by the commitments of his predecessor.

There was, of course, no new President in Washington after November. A newly confident Harry Truman, in his second-term inaugural address on January 20, 1949, told the Congress and the nation that he planned to sign the North Atlantic Treaty, and that he would ask Congress for legislation to stiffen the compact with arms for the members of the alliance. He said:

The primary purpose is to provide unmistakable proof of the joint determination of the free nations to resist armed attack from any quarter. . . . If we can make it sufficiently clear, in advance, that any armed attack affecting our national security would be met with an overwhelming force, the armed attack might never occur.

The North Atlantic Treaty was signed on the afternoon of Monday, April 4, 1949, in the blue-and-gold splendor of the Departmental Auditorium on Constitution Avenue. (The Marine Band, with unintentional irreverence, included in its musical preface to the occasion such currently popular numbers as "It Ain't Necessarily So" and "I Got Plenty of Nothin'.") The foreign ministers of twelve nations put their signatures to the 1,500-word document. They represented the United States and Canada, for North America; Denmark, Iceland, and Portugal, which govern three strategic islands in the North Atlantic; and Britain, France, Italy, The Netherlands, Norway, Belgium, and Luxembourg in Western Europe. (Greece, Turkey, and West Germany were subsequently admitted.)

The signatory governments affirmed their faith in and allegiance to the United Nations and undertook to strengthen their free institutions, to encourage economic collaboration, and to consult together whenever the territorial integrity or political independence of any one of them was threatened. The key clause on which their hopes were centered and their greatest obligation rested was Article 5:

The Parties agree that an armed attack against one or more of them in Europe or North America shall be considered an attack against them all . . . and each of them . . . will assist the Party or Parties so attacked by taking forthwith, individually and in concert with the other parties, such action as it deems necessary, including the use of armed force to restore and maintain the security of the North Atlantic area.[3]

This was, indeed, an "entangling alliance"—the first of its sort ever to be initialed by the United States in a time of peace.

At the beginning of January 1949 a shift of considerable importance occurred in the top echelon of the Truman administration. George Catlett Marshall, after more than four decades of continuous service as soldier-statesman, stepped down as Secretary of State. To Harry Truman he was and always remained "the outstanding man" of the Second World War.[*] To replace Marshall, who had

---

[*] Robert M. Lovett, the Under Secretary, resigned at the same time. He was replaced by James E. Webb.

undergone surgery for a kidney ailment, President Truman recalled from private life another man who in terms of personal friendship and influence on national policy was destined in time to outweigh even the General. This was Dean Acheson, who had left the Under Secretaryship a year and a half earlier to return to his law practice. Now Acheson had the enormously difficult task of steering not only the North Atlantic Treaty but also its supplementary arms program through Congress.

The administration had tried without much luck to keep the treaty and the arms program separate in the public mind. Although legislation for the arms program was not to be asked for until after the treaty had been ratified, the planning for it in the State and Defense Departments had gone along simultaneously with the treaty preparations all during the winter and spring. It was common knowledge, and a matter of plain logic, that the two ideas were linked. But for the administration to have admitted such a warlike potential would, it was feared, have greatly prejudiced the prospects of the treaty. For psychological purposes both abroad and at home, a resoundingly favorable vote for ratification was essential. It took all of Acheson's great skill as lawyer, diplomat, and polemicist to deny the martial implications of the treaty and at the same time to protect its obvious military character.

Sixteen days of hearings on the North Atlantic Treaty were held by the Foreign Relations Committee during April and May, with Acheson as the principal administration witness. It was reported out unanimously and came up for Senate debate on July 5. During both the public committee hearings and the floor debate, opposition centered less on the treaty itself than on the treaty *cum* military aid package. Senator Taft demanded to know why a simple extension to Western Europe of the protective blanket of the Monroe Doctrine would not suffice. Senator Forrest Donnell of Missouri condemned the whole enterprise as a "moral commitment" that would draw the United States into fighting other peoples' wars. Still others denounced it for putting the right to declare war in the hands of the President and taking it away from Congress. A good deal of clamor from right-wing and "patriotic" groups around the country was focused on scuttling the whole program.

The floor debate was held in the congested old Supreme Court chamber of the Capitol, since the regular Senate chamber was undergoing repairs. The chief defense fell to Senator Vandenberg, since it was primarily members of his own party who were in opposition. It was to prove to be the last great parliamentary fight of his career (he would be incapacitated by illness in a few months) and one of his proudest victories. He himself had misgivings about the scope of the arms program, but the treaty he saw as an essential bulwark against a third world war. A vote for the treaty, he said, did not commit a Senator to vote for the arms bill also. The treaty contained, he added, "not one aggressive syllable. There is nothing but peace in its aspirations . . . the logical evolution of one of our greatest American idioms, 'United we stand, divided we fall.'"

But this argument did not hold water for Senator Taft and his determined little band of isolationists. He told the Senate:

I have come to the conclusion that I cannot vote in favor of ratifying the treaty because I think it carries with it an obligation to assist in arming, at our expense, the nations of Western Europe. With that obligation, I believe it will promote war in the world rather than peace.

Taft said he would accept the treaty only if it contained a reservation disclaiming any obligation to supply arms. He offered an amendment to that effect, which was soundly defeated.

Then came the vote on the ultimate question, "that the Senate advise and consent to the ratification of the North Atlantic Treaty." The answer was an overwhelming affirmation: 82 "yeas" to 13 "nays." The date was July 21, 1949. One month and three days later the North Atlantic Treaty Organization (NATO) became a living reality.

But the battle was not quite over. Two days after the ratification vote in the Senate, President Truman sent to Congress a bill titled "Mutual Defense Assistance Act of 1949." He asked an appropriation of $1.45 billion to provide military assistance to "nations which have joined with the United States in collective defense . . . and to other nations whose increased ability to defend themselves against aggression is important to the national interest of the United States." The "other nations," he indicated, were Greece, Turkey, and Iran, and on the other side of the world the Philippines and South Korea. For the first time the containment policy was to reach around the globe to the Far East.

The bulk of the aid, naturally, was for Western Europe, $1.09 billions of it. The size of the request shocked even the treaty's most ardent supporters, including Vandenberg and John Foster Dulles, the latter now sitting in the Senate on an interim appointment from

New York. They protested that the bipartisanship which had made collaboration on the NATO treaty so successful had been breached by the administration in formulating its arms program. Their disenchantment gave courage to the other dissenters, not only in the Senate but in the House, which would have an equal say this time since legislation rather than a treaty ratification was involved.

Again, Dean Acheson was the administration's chief ball carrier. He found himself in the anomalous position of now pleading the urgency of a cause which only weeks earlier he had attempted to minimize. He called to his support, in his marathon testimony before the congressional committees, the nation's chief military authorities and its leading European-based diplomats. The ensuing dialogue was, in most respects, a repetition of the arguments that had preceded the treaty ratification, with the exception that the critics now found themselves with stronger support. At one point only a tie vote in the House Armed Services Committee averted a 50 percent slash in the money authorization for the program.

It was Moscow, however, which supplied the decisive argument in support of the Mutual Defense Assistance Program (MDAP). On September 23, President Truman shocked the nation with this brief news bulletin: "We have evidence that within recent weeks an atomic explosion occurred in the U.S.S.R."

America's A-bomb monopoly was over. The shadow of communism's belligerent imperialism now lengthened not only across Europe, but across the rest of the world as well. Four days later, with heavy majorities in both houses, the military assistance bill had become law with a first-year appropriation of $1.3 billion, only $100 million less than the President had asked for. NATO was not only a political reality; it was a going concern.

With the implementation of the North Atlantic Treaty, the policy of containment had reached full maturity. Containment has continued to be the strategic core of this nation's foreign policy ever since, just as NATO has become its chief structural member. It is true of course, that NATO has never come up to its full expectations. Within the first two years it became evident that it probably never would achieve the sort of integrated military force capable, in itself, of repelling a determined invasion of Western Europe. Almost a decade and a half were to pass before, on its economic side, it produced a Common Market. On the other hand, it almost certainly created the deterrent effect that prevented an invasion from happening, and it is a fact that no boundary in Europe has changed, and the Iron Curtain has remained immobile there since 1948.

Meanwhile, the whole region has left far behind it the memories of economic disaster and political chaos that haunted it seventeen years ago. There are no longer many crevices in Europe, nor in the Middle East, for the Communist tide to flow into. Communism seeks its outlets in other, more distant, parts of the world. It may indeed be a tribute to the success of NATO that, in the mid-sixties, the European members of the compact are more concerned about asserting their independence of American leadership than in mutual defense against Communist aggression.

In evaluating this great innovation of the Truman foreign policy, it is enlightening to read the following editorial from the New York Times of April 4, 1964:

The NATO Success Story

Fifteen years ago today, in a historic departure from isolation, the United States signed the North Atlantic Treaty and entered in peacetime precisely the kind of "entangling alliance" against which George Washington had warned. It had taken two world wars, the emergence of the Soviet threat, the descent of the Iron Curtain, the Communist seizure of Czechoslovakia and the Berlin Blockade to make Americans realize that their future was inextricably linked with that of Europe. This is a lesson we can forget only at our peril, despite the many changes and new challenges the world has seen since 1949.

The greatest threat to the Atlantic Alliance now, ironically, is its own success. The attack it originally was designed to deter has been prevented. There is a temptation to relax, to pursue national rather than common interests. As President Johnson warned yesterday, "the danger has receded but not disappeared." Moreover, while the Atlantic agenda has changed, it remains heavy with problems neither the United States nor Europe alone can resolve.

The revival, behind NATO's shield, of Europe's economy and political confidence requires a basic change in Atlantic relationships. The United States now needs Europe's help to deal with the free world's pressing problems of trade, agricultural surpluses, monetary reform, economic growth and aid to the developing countries, as well as defense. Europe, in turn, wants a larger role in the decision-making processes. . . .

President Johnson yesterday rededicated the United States to support both the union of Europe and partnership across the Atlantic. He spoke not only of sharing the burdens of free world responsibility with the new Europe, but of sharing leadership and power "at every level." The future of the Atlantic community depends on how these commitments are fulfilled.

"Bold New Program": Point Four

The Point Four program was another significant Truman stratagem for the containment of communism. This was a novel plan to
use the leverage of American technical skills and know-how, rather
than its dollars, to pry the underdeveloped nations of the world into
the twentieth century—and, it was hoped, out of Moscow's reach.
Its birth was a happy accident rather than a planned addition to the
family, and it never quite stood on its own feet. But it was peculiarly Trumanesque in design—a dramatic and plausible mixture of
practical humanitarianism and economic self-interest—and it has
had a lasting influence on this country's foreign policy. Though the
Point Four label has long since been lost, the idea behind it has
become woven securely into our foreign aid program of the last
decade and a half, and it is the lineal ancestor of today's high-
priority Peace Corps.

A technical assistance program of some sort might have evolved
in any event out of the simple necessities of the world situation at
the time. But the immediate need that brought it to life was the
desire of President Truman's speech writers to invest his 1949
inaugural address with an exciting and dramatic punch line. The
genesis of the assistance program is worth recounting, not only because of its intrinsic importance, but as an illustration of the role
that happenstance so often plays in the arcane mechanics of national policy formulation. Clark Clifford recalls how Point Four
came about:

We were having a real problem during late December [1948] putting
the inaugural speech together. Our man had won a smashing and surprising victory at the polls, and he and all of us felt that when he stood up to
take the oath of office on January 20, he should have something big and
new and challenging to present to the country. Most of his program was
old hat, in a public relations sense, because it had been talked to death in
the campaign, including even the possibility of a North Atlantic Treaty.
We needed something fresh and provocative that would make people
think.

We all put our heads to it, Mr. Truman included. Then I remembered
a State Department memorandum that had crossed my desk a few weeks
or a few months earlier. A technical assistance program had been tried on
a very modest scale in Latin America, and this memo raised the question—not very hopefully as I recall—whether it might not be adapted to
the Far East as a sort of substitute for the ERP.

Freshman Senator Harry S. Truman attended his first Democratic convention in Philadelphia in June, 1936, where FDR was nominated for a second term. Truman is shown here with his political mentor Tom Pendergast, the famed Democratic boss of Kansas City. WIDE WORLD PHOTOS

Vice President-elect Truman was on hand to welcome President Roosevelt back to Washington after a brief post-election vacation on November 10, 1944. This was one of the very few occasions on which the two men appeared together in public. WIDE WORLD PHOTOS

Harry S. Truman, "politician by chance," was sworn in as the thirty-second President of the United States at 7:09 o'clock on the evening of Thursday, April 12, 1945. The oath was administered by Chief Justice Harlan F. Stone in the Cabinet Room of the White House. Mrs. Truman and Margaret were among the two-score witnesses to the brief and tense ceremony. HARRY GOODWIN, HARRY S. TRUMAN LIBRARY

Military men were high on Harry Truman's list of heroes. One whom he most admired
—for a time—was General of the Army Dwight D. Eisenhower. This early encounter
was at Brussels on July 15, 1945, as the President, with Secretary of State James F.
Byrnes (*right*), was en route to the Potsdam Conference. A few days later he was to
tell Ike that he would help him get the 1948 Presidential nomination if the General
wanted it. His estimate of Eisenhower had undergone an almost complete reversal
by 1952. U. S. ARMY PHOTOGRAPH

The Big Three Conference at Potsdam to assess the immediate problems of postwar
Europe was held in the great hall of Cecilienhof Palace. President Truman has noted
in connection with this photograph, made July 19, 1945, as the third day's session
broke up: "This is the place I told Stalin about the atom bomb which was exploded
July 16 in New Mexico. He didn't realize what I was talking about!" The probability
is, however, that Stalin had at least a notion of what it was about, thanks to his
efficient espionage network. Mr. Truman, center, with back to camera, is facing Stalin,
in light tunic. U. S. ARMY PHOTOGRAPH

This tripartite handshake between the Big Three leaders at Potsdam—Churchill, Truman, Stalin—suggests an atmosphere of harmony and optimism that none of them really felt. In truth, about the best they were able to do was to paper over some of the worst cracks in the wartime alliance. But for the new President, meeting his opposite numbers face to face for the first time, there was an invaluable gain in insight. "I had reached important conclusions in my own mind, and a realization of what I had to do in shaping future foreign policy," he said. U. S. ARMY PHOTOGRAPH

The center of the postwar battle against spiraling prices and runaway inflation was the Office of Price Administration—OPA. Businessmen wanted it abolished, consumers wanted it preserved and strengthened. As the Truman administration waged a desperate and losing fight in Congress to "hold the line" on prices during the summer of 1946, they were backed up by scores of popular demonstrations like this one in Trenton, New Jersey. ASSOCIATED PRESS PHOTOGRAPH

Holding the line on prices meant holding the line on wages, too. When railroad unions in the spring of 1946 rejected all White House pleas not to strike, President Truman told them, "All right, I'm going to give you the gun." On Saturday, May 25, only hours before the strike deadline, he went before a joint session of Congress to ask for legislation empowering him to draft striking railroad workers into the armed forces. A moment after he began his speech, Senate Secretary Leslie Biffle thrust a note before him: "Mr. President, agreement signed, strike over." UNITED PRESS INTERNATIONAL PHOTO

Truman was a friend of organized labor, but some of his lustiest battles during his first term were with labor chieftains who he thought were thwarting orderly reconversion. Here the mightiest chieftain of them all, John L. Lewis of the United Mine Workers, who had shut down the nations' soft-coal mines in the fall of 1946, faces photographers after being fined $3.5 million for contempt of court in refusing to call off the strike. It was the biggest fine of the sort ever assessed against a labor union. It was never paid, because Lewis purged himself the next day by ordering the miners back to work. HARRIS & EWING

Politics was an indispensable tool of statecraft, President Truman believed, and he valued his political advisers as highly as those in economics or foreign policy—indeed, their roles often overlapped. Clark M. Clifford, for example, at the right in this picture, was the President's principal administrative aide, but his nonprofessional political judgments carried almost as much weight as those of the professionals. Among the pros on whom the President relied heavily were J. Howard McGrath (*left*), Democratic chairman, and Leslie Biffle, veteran Secretary of the Senate. WIDE WORLD PHOTOS

Harry Truman understood grass-roots America because he was so instinctively and unreservedly a part of it. Getting out to mingle with the people was not for him a tiresome obligation but an exhilarating opportunity which he seized whenever he could. He particularly enjoyed the nostalgic comradery of veterans' functions, and here he is shown leading the parade of the 35th Division Reunion in Little Rock, Arkansas, on June 10, 1949. With him are, from left to right, Frank Spina, a sergeant in Captain Truman's World War I artillery company; Louis A. Johnson, Secretary of Defense; Governor Sid McMath, of Arkansas; and General Harry Vaughan, the President's military aide. HARRY S. TRUMAN LIBRARY

President Truman's favorite retreat away from Washington was Key West, Florida. There in unpretentious quarters at the U. S. Naval Station he established a "Little White House" and maintained a limited business routine interspersed with occasional fishing trips (for which he cared little), brisk walks about the old town and long sessions of no-nonsense poker. Informality prevailed, as this press conference on the lawn in April, 1950, indicates. Staff members, shown standing in the background, are, from left to right, Stephen J. Spingarn, Stanley Woodward, Donald S. Dawson, Matthew J. Connelly, Major General Harry H. Vaughan, Rear Admiral Robert L. Dennison and William D. Hassett. The reporter to the President's right, Merriman Smith of United Press, wears a sweat shirt with the legend "Truman Athletic Club." UNITED PRESS INTERNATIONAL PHOTO

Revolt on the Right: The States' Rights Democratic Party—the Dixiecrats—came formally into being at a convention in Birmingham, Alabama, on July 17, 1948, one day after the close of the regular Democratic convention in Philadelphia which had nominated Truman. Here the Presidential candidate Governor J. Strom Thurmond of South Carolina, and his running mate, Governor Fielding L. Wright of Mississippi, march to the platform to acknowledge their choice by acclamation. This was the death knell of the "solid South," and Truman was to be its first Democratic legatee. WIDE WORLD PHOTOS

The "whistle-stop" belongs as distinctively to Truman as the "fireside chat" belonged to Franklin Roosevelt. He perfected in 1948 the technique of the meandering campaign train that wandered back and forth and up and down the countryside with as many as fifteen or twenty pauses a day, from 6 A.M. to midnight, so that the people could see the candidate in the flesh and hear him with their own ears. Advance agents made certain that the local populace knew when to expect a Presidential visit. Almost without fail, they turned out en masse to welcome him, as this shot of a typical station-side crowd in a Middle Western town in September, 1948, shows. *The New York Times,* BY GEORGE TAMES

Big speeches cost a lot of money for national broadcast time, and the Democratic campaign committee in 1948, tied to deficit financing, picked the occasions with extreme care. One of their earliest investments was in the National Plowing Contest at Dexter, Iowa, where, on Saturday, September 18, President Truman addressed an estimated 75,000 farm people. It was here that he uncorked his attack on "that no-account, do-nothing Republican Congress" that was to be the theme of his campaign. He took Iowa and Wisconsin in the election and cut deeply into Republican majorities in other farm states. UNITED PRESS INTERNATIONAL PHOTO

There is little in the manner of the two men shown here at the dedication of the Idlewild Airport in New York on July 31, 1948, to suggest the contempt they held for one another. Truman regarded Governor Thomas E. Dewey, now the GOP candidate for President, as a shallow, pretentious upstart; the Governor thought the President a clumsy bumpkin who was leading the nation into waters beyond his depth. One conviction they shared in common was that Truman was the underdog in the forthcoming campaign—and that spelled the difference between them. HARRY S. TRUMAN LIBRARY

Revolt on the Left: Henry A. Wallace, Apostle of the Common Man, who had been ousted from the Vice Presidency in 1944 to make way for Truman, and then booted out of Truman's Cabinet, was the moving spirit and Presidential candidate of the Progressive Party of America in the 1948 campaign. This was an unstable compound of liberals and left-wingers that threatened for a time to deprive Truman of the vital labor and Negro vote. Its starkly Communist coloration drained the PCA of much of its effectiveness before election day. The picture above shows Wallace in a typical campaign posture at Charlotte, North Carolina, in August, 1948. WIDE WORLD PHOTOS

The pictorial classic of the 1948 campaign. The Chicago *Tribune* was bitterly contemptuous of Truman both as President and candidate. Faced with a 7:45 first-edition deadline on election night, with only scattered and incomplete returns, the editors yielded to impulse instead of judgment, with the disastrous results shown here. Truman was handed a copy of the paper when the train bearing him back to Washington reached St. Louis shortly before noon on the day after the election. Standing on the rear platform of his private car, he hoisted it aloft to the noisy delight of the thousands who jammed the station to cheer his victory.

UNITED PRESS INTERNATIONAL PHOTO

President Truman's choice of foreign policy advisers was stronger than in any other field. Here, on his return from the Wake Island conference with General MacArthur on October 18, 1950, he is being greeted by the three top members of his foreign policy "team." From left to right they are Averell Harriman, one-time Ambassador to Moscow and London and former Secretary of Commerce, now the special representative in Europe for the Economic Cooperation Administration, General George C. Marshall, formerly Chief of Staff, Secretary of State and special emmissary to China, now Secretary of Defense, and Dean G. Acheson, whom the President once described as "the greatest Secretary of State this country has ever had." *The New York Times,* BY GEORGE TAMES

President Truman and Vice President Barkley, winners of the biggest upset victory in the history of Presidential politics, respond to greetings as they watch the inaugural parade of January 20, 1949, from the reviewing stand in front of the White House. *The New York Times,* BY GEORGE TAMES

One of President Truman's most distinctive and enduring contributions to American foreign policy was the creation of the North Atlantic Treaty Organization. Through this pact the free powers of the West formed a political and military front with which to oppose the spread of Communist imperialism along the shores of the North Atlantic and the Mediterranean. He signed the instrument of ratification of the treaty at ceremonies in the White House on July 25, 1949, attended by, from left to right, Senator Walter F. George, chairman of the Finance Committee; Secretary of Defense Louis A. Johnson; Senator Scott Lucas, Majority Leader; Senator Tom Connally, chairman, and Senator J. William Fulbright, member, Foreign Relations Committee; Secretary of State Dean Acheson; Senator Claude Pepper, Foreign Relations Committee; Vice President Alben Barkley, and Senator Arthur H. Vandenberg, ranking Republican member of the Foreign Relations Committee and an indispensable force in winning Republican support for the treaty. WIDE WORLD PHOTOS

A rare grouping of the key leadership of the English-speaking world as the United States was moving into the political vacuum left by a withering British Empire. On the right of the President is Sir Winston Churchill, the British Prime Minister; on the far left is Sir Anthony Eden, the Foreign Minister, and next to him is Dean Acheson, the American Secretary of State. The visitors had come to Washington early in January, 1952, seeking an emergency loan of $300 million to prop up Britain's dangerously sagging economy. The President took them for a Potomac cruise aboard the S.S. *Williamsburg,* where this picture was made. HARRY S. TRUMAN LIBRARY

A sense of crisis and dismay hung over Washington in the early weeks of the Korean war as the slender U. S. forces dispatched from Japan to bolster the shattered ROK Army were sent reeling southward. Emergency conferences between the President and his military and civilian deputies were daily occurrences. Here a Cabinet meeting, early in July, 1950, reconvenes for a rump session on the White House lawn. Mr. Truman, back to the camera, is surrounded, left to right, by Cabinet Secretaries Charles F. Brannan, Agriculture; Jesse M. Donaldson, Postmaster General; Dean G. Acheson, State; Oscar L. Chapman, Interior, and Louis A. Johnson, Defense. The person immediately facing the President is unidentified. *The New York Times,* BY GEORGE TAMES

This is what "Truman's war" looked like to thousands of bone-weary, dispirited GI's in Korea in the early winter of 1951. This patrol of the 5th RCT, 24th Division, is combing a sector of the Korean highlands near the Han River shortly after the UN forces had been rolled back by the surprise intervention of Red China. It was "a war without banners or songs or poetry," a brutal test of the nation's morale and of President Truman's leadership. U. S. ARMY PHOTOGRAPH

Lieutenant General Matthew B. Ridgway was named commanding general of the U. S. Eighth Army in Korea in December, 1950, after the death of Lieutenant General Walton H. Walker in a jeep accident. Ridgway, "with the look of eagles about his strong-nosed face," was a veteran paratrooper of World War II, an imaginative, decisive and articulate leader, and just what the Eighth Army needed at this time to revive its battered morale. A few months later he would succeed General Douglas MacArthur as Far Eastern Commander. U. S. ARMY PHOTOGRAPH

In October, 1950, President Truman flew 4,700
miles to Wake Island for his first meeting with
his Far Eastern Commander, who was also in
command of the United Nations forces in
Korea. Vain and strong willed, Douglas
MacArthur was an authentic military hero
because of his generalship of the Pacific
campaign in World War II. Now he had
become something of a political hero as well to
Republicans who hoped to unseat Truman in
the next election. The two men greeted one
another with frosty suspicion on the air strip
at Wake Island, but when they parted six hours
later the President was unstinting in his praise
of the General. The "police action" in Korea, it
appeared, was about to be brought to a
successful conclusion—a gross miscalculation.

U. S. ARMY PHOTOGRAPH

The news on April 10, 1951, that President Truman ha
summarily relieved General MacArthur of his comma
had a shock reaction around the world. In governme
quarters abroad, the news was received generally wi
relief, for there was fear that MacArthur's belligeren
might spread the war beyond Korea. At home, the mo
conspicuous reaction (though it was far from universa
was outrage, directed chiefly at President Truman. Th
demonstration (*above*) in New York on April 1
was typical of scores that erupted in many par
of the country. Also typical was the restraine
consternation of many in high places who, li
General Eisenhower (*right*), then NATO Command
could not publicly express what they felt. Th
improbable comment attributed to Ike as he was give
the news at Coblenz, Germany, was, "Well, I'll
darned!" ABOVE: *The New York Times*, BY ARTH
BROWER / RIGHT: ASSOCIATED PRESS PHOT

With the war in a paralyzing stalemate and General MacArthur growing increasingly more truculent toward the civilian leadership in Washington, Secretary of the Army Frank Pace was the last of a succession of high-level emissaries whom President Truman sent to Tokyo to reason with the haughty Far Eastern Commander. The Secretary was met at Haneda Airbase by General MacArthur on April 9, 1951. Pace had been delegated to inform MacArthur of his recall, if such a decision should be reached. When the decision was made, less than twenty-four hours after this picture was made, the Secretary was on an airborne inspection of the Korean battle lines. The message went directly to MacArthur by army radio. HARRY S. TRUMAN LIBRARY

General MacArthur's return to the United States—his first in fourteen years—was a triumphal procession culminating in a dramatic address to a joint session of Congress on April 19, 1951. This was a stinging gesture of rebuke to President Truman engineered by Republicans and abetted by an emotional tide of public opinion, which Congressional Democrats were unwilling to oppose. The Senate investigation of the dismissal, which began a month later, put most of the facts of the case on the public record. This served to trim the General's stature down to more realistic proportions and to vindicate, in large measure, the President's judgment in recalling him. WIDE WORLD PHOTOS

Was Alger Hiss a traitor or a victim of bizarre circumstance? Fifteen years after his trial and conviction for perjury one can get an answer either way. He remains one of the great enigmas of the second half of the century—a well-born, highly educated and greatly respected government official against whom massive, though inconclusive, charges of Communist espionage were produced in a spectacular Congressional investigation. The courts rejected the espionage charges but sent him to prison for not telling the truth in his denial of the allegations. Hiss became the symbol of the "soft on Communism" charge with which President Truman was attacked throughout his second administration, and which was the forerunner of the era of McCarthyism. Hiss is shown here in one of his earliest appearances before the House Un-American Activities Committee in August, 1948. *The New York Times*, BY MEYER LEIBOWITZ

Senator Joseph R. McCarthy of Wisconsin wa[s] "in many ways the most gifted demagogue ever bred on these shores. No bolder seditio[n] ever moved among us—nor any politician wi[th] a swifter, surer access to the dark places of the American mind." One of the many victim[s] of McCarthy's unrelenting witch hunt for Communists in the government was Ambassa[dor] Philip C. Jessup. Here, in testimony before the Senate Foreign Relations Committee in October, 1951, he opposes Jessup's assignme[nt] to the United Nations on the grounds that h[e] had followed the Communist party line. WIDE WORLD PHOTOS

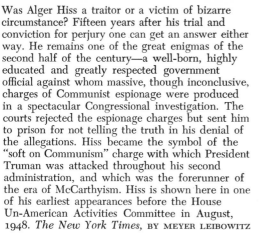

Truman's last years in the White House
afflicted by "the mess in Washington,"
h was not only a devastating Republican
n but a glaring and documented reality.
principal weakness as an administrator was
he so often ranked friendship and loyalty
e competence, putting his faith in small
incapable of bearing large responsibilities.
e then became the targets for a host of
ence peddlers and fixers trafficking for a
n government favors. One of the most
erable turned out to be the President's
l old friend from World War I whom he had
ted—and defiantly maintained in—the
igious rank of Military Aide. Vaughan is
n here while being questioned during a
te investigation of "five percenters" in
ist, 1949. *The New York Times,* BY
GE TAMES

Among the worst of the scandals contributing
to "the mess in Washington" was that involving
the Bureau of Internal Revenue, the
government's patronage-ridden tax collection
agency. A long and sensation-packed
investigatigation by the House Ways and
Means Committee during 1951–52 revealed an
incredible pattern of bribery and tax-fixing
that spilled over into the Justice Department.
Sixty-six persons, many of them top officials,
were fired from their jobs as a result of the
inquiry and nine eventually went to prison.
Among the culprits was the Assistant Attorney
General in charge of the Tax Division, Theron
Lamar Caudle, a flamboyant and loquacious
North Carolinian, shown here protesting his
innocence at a committee hearing in November,
1951. WIDE WORLD PHOTOS

Stevenson's reluctance to seek the
ocratic nomination in 1952 exasperated
angered President Truman to the point
e, late in the spring of that year, he
y contemplated taking the nomination
elf. The only active claimant for the honor
Senator Estes Kefauver, whom Truman
l not abide, but he stood to get the
nation by default if not opposed by
enson. When the Illinois Governor was
y drafted by the Democratic convention
30 A.M. on Saturday, July 26, the
dent's relief was genuine. "This is the
" he told the cheering delgates in the
e, "who will follow me into the White
se." But long before Stevenson was
lfed in the Eisenhower landslide, Truman
again become disillusioned as Stevenson
awkwardly and ineffectually to
sociate himself from the Truman record.
ED PRESS INTERNATIONAL PHOTO

It was a chilly ride, weatherwise and socially, as the President escorted the President-elect in the ceremonial procession to the Capitol for Eisenhower's oath-taking on January 20, 1953. Each had inflicted lasting scars on the other in the heat of the campaign battle and they had little to say to one another—then or later. It was a day of elation, but of poignancy as well, for "there had been losers as well as winners, and not only a Presidency but an era was coming to an end." *The New York Times.* BY GEORGE TAMES

The Trumans, going home to Independence, had expected to leave Washington quietly and all but unnoticed in the festive turmoil of Inauguration Day. Paraders were still streaming past the reviewing stand at the White House, in fact, and downtown Washington was gripped by a monster traffic jam when they arrived with a few friends at Union Station at five o'clock that afternoon to board their train. To their dismay the concourse was jammed with some 5,000 cheering, singing well-wishers who had come to bid the ex-First Family farewell. It was a tribute of affection that moved Mr. Truman as few experiences had done during all the time he was President. And it was a harbinger of an aspect of his career which was not to become visible until much later—that no President has grown so greatly in stature after leaving office as he. *The New York Times,* BY GEORGE TAMES

I checked this back with State and the Budget Bureau. I got the impression they thought the idea was OK, but that it needed a lot of work before it could be advanced as a policy. Maybe they were right, but time was pressing on us there at the White House.

Anyway, I took it to the Boss. Several of us kicked it around, sitting there at his desk. The more he thought about it, the more he liked it. You know, he never fooled around in making a decision. So after a bit he said: "This looks good. We'll use it. We can work out the operating details later."

The inaugural speech dealt almost entirely with foreign affairs, and near the end he enumerated the four props on which our foreign policy should rest. The first was the United Nations, the second was the Marshall Plan, the third was a North Atlantic Alliance, and the fourth was this "bold new plan," as he called it, for technical assistance.

He couldn't spell it out in any detail because nobody then quite knew what the details were. There wasn't even a name for it, although some of the newspapers began calling it the "World Fair Deal." Most of them just described it as "Point Four"—*sui generis*—and that's what it has been ever since.[4]

In its short-range objective at least, Point Four was an instant success. It had the quality of surprise and novelty and was generally acclaimed both here and abroad. As James Reston wrote from Washington in the New York *Times,* "While there is some criticism of the President for having shot first and questioned later, there is general approval of his colonial development program here." And William H. Stringer cabled the *Christian Science Monitor* from London, "President Truman's dedication of United States technological resources to improve the lot of the globe's less fortunate people has kindled the imagination of thinking people throughout Britain and Western Europe. It has stirred visions of a TVA on Palestine's Jordan River, and of boatloads of foreign students brought to the United States to learn production techniques." Senator Taft confined himself to an expression of only mild skepticism.

The Point Four idea was turned over to a working committee in the State Department to put the nuts and bolts in place. As it evolved, the program was to be a low-cost operation aimed at improving the cultural level and living standards of the people of backward nations. The United States was to supply the know-how and the technicians—engineers, teachers, public health experts, economists, agronomists, etc. The recipient nations, possibly with the help of various international bodies, were to supply the capital and other resources needed to carry out local improvement projects.

At some point, private capital from the West would, it was hoped, be induced to invest in these developing countries.

There was a twofold motivation behind the plan. The first was humanitarian and political: If the people of Asia and Africa could be helped out of their centuries-old rut of ignorance and poverty, they would become better world citizens and less likely pawns for Communist exploitation. The second was economic: As producers of much of the world's raw materials, the underdeveloped nations had become increasingly important to the reviving economies of the West. Not only was it desirable to protect these sources of supply, but also to offer a potential future market for the West's output.

The President sent his Point Four message to Congress in June 1949, asking the modest sum of $45 million to set the program in motion. Congress was heavily preoccupied all that summer and fall with the North Atlantic Treaty and MDAP. By that time, some of the gloss had worn off the "bold new program," and Congress and a good part of public opinion was beginning to wonder where the proliferation of this country's overseas obligations was going to end. It was not, in fact, until the following year, on June 5, 1950, that Congress got around to enacting the Point Four concept into law, with a hesitancy and with multiple restrictions that tended to vitiate the great propaganda value it had when President Truman first proposed it.

Operationally, Point Four became the Technical Cooperation Administration (TCA). Administratively, it was set up under the inhospitable wing of the Department of State. Secretary Acheson and his men were lukewarm about the feasibility of the program. Their department was not set up to handle operational problems involving public works, education, farming, and the like.

In spite of its stepchild status, TCA managed to float a number of projects, many of them highly useful. It built no TVA's on the Jordan River, but it dried up the malarial swamps around scores of Asian and Latin-American villages; it brought the first pure drinking water to dozens of others; it supplied the tractors and the technicians with which Egypt converted some three million acres of desert into farmland; and it gave Saudi Arabia a modern monetary and banking system. By fiscal 1953, TCA had a budget of $155.6 million and projects going in thirty-three countries. In that year, however, it began to lose its identity to the overshadowing Mutual Security Agency which was beginning to undertake large-scale economic and military aid to parts of the world outside Europe. In the first year of the Eisenhower administration, TCA was finally swallowed up in the overall foreign aid program.

Technical assistance has remained an integral part of foreign aid ever since, but the great humanitarian and propaganda banner of Point Four has long been furled and left gathering dust. Mr. Truman spoke fondly of it in his memoirs: "To call the undertaking a 'bold new program' was no exaggeration. It was an adventurous idea such as had never before been proposed by any country in the history of the world."

Disaster in the East: China

Compared with its triumph in Europe, the administration's search for a policy toward China was a dismal failure—a tale, as Herbert Feis described it, "of crumpled hopes and plans that went awry." The hope of making China the bulwark of postwar freedom in the Far East failed not so much through the Machiavellian interference of the Soviets as through the ineptness and bad luck of the Nationalist Government and its American ally. The Nationalist and U.S. governments allowed a political vacuum to develop into which Communist power flowed as hungrily as rainwater down a dry creek bed. In time the flood inundated the whole of China. Whether the United States might have stemmed this flow is a question that aroused one of the bitterest controversies of the Truman era—a controversy that still smolders and bursts periodically into flame two decades later.

China, in American textbooks a land of romance, mystery, and missionaries—a land of inscrutable little yellow men toward whom Americans always felt a benevolent superiority—is the ethnic and geographic colossus of Asia. Suffering from intense overpopulation and a feudal economy, China had been in the grip of a social revolution since the beginning of the century. This was intensified in 1927 with the first open break between a strong leftist minority led by Mao Tse-tung, a disciple of Lenin, and the dominant Kuomintang Party, which had been bequeathed by China's "liberator," Sun Yat-sen, to his brilliant brother-in-law, Chiang Kai-shek. The history of China from that date onward became one of almost continual civil war, interrupted (but never stilled) first by the Japanese aggression of 1937, which sliced away the whole of Manchuria, and then by World War II, in which she became the Eastern anchor of the anti-Fascist alliance.

In spite of massive support in money, weapons, and supplies from the United States, China proved to be an ineffectual ally in the war against Japan. The Nationalist government of the Kuomintang Party was shot through with corruption and dominated by the warlord mentality of many of its leading ministers and generals. Chiang, though a man of high aspirations and great patriotism, was never able to impose his ideals of purpose and integrity on his subordinates nor to win political authority over the Communist followers of Mao Tse-tung. There were, in effect, two hostile Chinese military and political commands toward the end of the war, and their effectiveness against the Japanese was largely dissipated as they carried out guerrilla raids and reprisals against each other. The war against the common enemy was subordinated to a civil war over the political control of China.

When Japan capitulated in August 1945, there were more than a million Japanese troops in China proper and an almost equal number in Manchuria. Russian troops had flooded in across the Soviet-Manchurian border in fulfillment of Moscow's commitment under the Yalta agreement. Chinese Communist forces were dispersed at key points in North China and in parts of Manchuria, while Chiang had been forced far to the southwest with his headquarters at Chungking. An immediate crisis in the Allied high command arose over how the surrender of the Japanese garrisons in China was to be handled. Chiang vehemently opposed allowing the Communists this honor on the realistic ground that they would not only acquire vast supplies of arms and other military equipment but would move their own governmental administrators right in behind the departing Japanese. The United States was apprehensive about delegating this function to the Russians where it could be avoided— that is, where the Chinese were not already in immediate contact with a Japanese command. The Russians seemed disposed to observe the terms of the Sino-Soviet Treaty, which they had entered into as a part of the Yalta package, and they acknowledged Chiang's Nationalist regime as the sole governmental power in China. But there was no certainty how long they would stay on their good behavior, or when they might decide to give more than passive support to Mao and his revolutionaries.

In addition to its burden of military and political chaos, the government of China was economically and materially bankrupt. Inflation had made its currency almost worthless (1,300 Chinese dollars to one American); 90 percent of its railroads were out of commission; highway and river transport were seriously crippled; manufactures had been heavily damaged; and conditions of near-famine existed in some parts of the country.

President Truman summarized the situation that his administration faced in China in the fall of 1945 in these words:

The problem of communism in China differed considerably from political problems elsewhere. Chiang Kai-shek was not confronted by a militant political minority scattered throughout the population, but by a rival government that controlled a definite part of the territory, with about one-fourth of the total population.

Our position in China offered us little choice. We could not simply wash our hands of the situation. There were still nearly three million Japanese in China, nearly one million of them military. Unless we made certain that these forces were eliminated, the Japanese, even in defeat, might gain control of China simply by their ability to tip the scales in the contest for power.

The other alternative was equally impracticable. That would have been to throw into China unlimited resources and large armies of American soldiers to defeat the communists, remove the Japanese from the mainland, and compel Russian withdrawal from Manchuria by force. The American people would never stand for such an undertaking.

We decided, therefore, that the only course of action open to us was to assist in every way the preservation of peace in China, to support the Generalissimo politically, economically, and, within limits, militarily. But we could not become involved in a fratricidal war in China.[5]

The job of trying to make a coherent blueprint for China fell mainly to Secretary of State Byrnes and Secretary of War Patterson, and through them to their principal deputies, Dean Acheson and Robert Lovett, respectively. Acheson described the problem this way before a Senate committee some years later:

The task which had to be solved was, in effect, how to create a nation, and how to have the authority of the Chinese government exercised throughout that nation.

Now, I do not say recreate a nation; I say advisedly create a nation, because for almost an infinite period of the past there had not been, in our sense, a nation in the territory which we call China . . . a nation in the sense of a government in control throughout that area.[6]

Starting from the assumption that the United States could not simply walk out of China and wash its hands of all interests and

responsibilities there, two alternative courses of action for stabiliz-
ing the area offered themselves.

One was to pour in vast new supplies of money, matériel, and
manpower—particularly manpower—and join the war with Chiang
Kai-shek against his Chinese Communist enemies. The Generalissimo greatly favored this plan. He could contemplate a unified
China only as a result of crushing Mao Tse-tung's Communists by
force of arms. This shortsightedly ignored the fact that his government had lost favor with large segments of the Chinese people other
than the Communists. It also ignored the fact that the United
States, in the midst of a headlong demobilization, no longer had the
military manpower for such a venture, and even less did it have the
will to become embroiled in a new war in Asia.

Finally, the futility of military collaboration with Chiang Kai-
shek on any such grandiose scale was clinched by our leading military man in the area. Lieutenant General Albert C. Wedemeyer,
commanding general of the China theater, warned Washington in a
report in November 1945 that Chiang could hold his own in South
China only if he accepted the help of foreign administrators and
technicians, cleaned up his own corrupt administration, and instituted some genuine social reforms. Chiang, he said, could not hope
to establish himself in North China "for months or perhaps even
years" without making a settlement with the Chinese Communists;
and that Manchuria should be controlled by an international trustee-
ship during the many years before Chiang could be expected to
extend his government there.[7]

Washington was left in the end, then, with this kind of dilemma:
It could *not countenance* a Communist regime anywhere in China.
It *was committed* to the support of the Nationalist regime. But it
was entirely clear that the Nationalists could not control more than
a fraction of China unless the Communists permitted them to. The
Communists were not, naturally, about to volunteer any such permission. Cooperation could be forced out of them only by the open
intervention of the United States. Such a scheme, from the American viewpoint, was politically repugnant and militarily next to impossible. It was equally unthinkable to wash our hands of China,
pick up our belongings, and go home.

The alternative course of action, then, was to try to make the
Nationalists and Communists come to terms on a coalition gov-
ernment—and on terms, inevitably, much more favorable to the
Nationalists than to the Communists. It was, in effect, a little like

putting the boy on the tiger's back and hoping he could ride home before the tiger ate him up.

Coalition had been the political goal of the United States in China since early in the war. President Roosevelt had sent Major General Patrick J. Hurley, an able but temperamental soldier-diplomat, as Ambassador to China in 1944, with coalition as his principal mission. Hurley had brought Chiang and Mao to the conference table on several occasions, but never with lasting results. In November 1945 he was back in Washington for consultation. In a sudden fit of pique and frustration, he resigned his post and went home to New Mexico, leaving in his wake a flurry of charges and innuendos highly critical of administration policies and personnel. The administration was just then on the verge of turning the screws down on Chiang to induce him to clean up his government and to make an honest effort to meet the minimal demands of the Communists for collaboration. With Hurley's exit, the President turned again to George Marshall, only a few weeks in retirement at his Virginia home, and asked him to go to China as the President's special emissary. The old soldier, tired but willing, arrived in Chungking on New Year's Day, 1946.

The General's mission to China has been described as "a long-drawn-out game of Chinese checkers in which each contestant jumped the other, play by play, and gradually eliminated from the board all the means by which the United States might have influenced the end result."[8]

His instructions from Washington were vague and gave him room for maneuver. He was to try to exact enough concessions from both Chiang Kai-shek and Mao Tse-tung to create a coalition government. This meant substantial social and economic reforms within the Nationalist administration and the acceptance of some Communist representation at the policy and executive levels. It also meant the yielding by the Communists of the military control they exercised in North China and their cooperation in extending Nationalist hegemony into Manchuria, where Russian armies stood in enigmatic passivity. Should there be promise of fulfillment of these goals, Marshall was told, he should authorize the use of United States planes and ships to transport enough Nationalist divisions north to accept the surrender of the Japanese garrisons and to effect military and political control of the areas held by Chinese troops loyal to Mao Tse-tung. Fifty thousand U.S. Marines still stationed in China were to be available to assist with the repatriation of the Japanese.

As leverage to be applied to both sides, President Truman told Marshall that he could promise a continuation of substantial economic and military aid to China if the proposals were carried out, and to threaten a cutoff if they were not. But there was a conditional stipulation in Truman's instructions: Come what may, the United States was not to abandon the Chiang regime. At any cost short of direct military intervention, the supremacy of the Generalissimo in any new political or military arrangement had to be preserved.

By February 1946 the Marshall mission had made an encouraging beginning. It had arranged for a cease-fire in the civil war and for the dispatching of a number of tripartite teams—Nationalist, Communist, and American—to police the truce in a score of spots where fighting was going on. It had also arranged for the convoking of a National Assembly to write a new constitution for China and for the establishment meanwhile of a provisional government with Communist representation, but with the reins of power held firmly in the hands of Chiang Kai-shek. Finally, it had arranged for a merging of Communist and Nationalist military forces into an army of sixty divisions, only ten of which would be under Communist control. These forces were to be strategically located throughout China, including Manchuria, to disarm and expel the Japanese and to maintain peace and back up the civil government. Whole divisions of Nationalist troops, complete with heavy weapons and equipment, were airlifted to North China in United States planes to effect this amalgamation. In the late winter months of 1946 it looked as though peace and tranquility were about to come once again to the land of the lotus.

That prospect began to fall apart in April. In spite of the truce teams, fighting erupted all over again in one key center after another. Communist troops in Manchuria took over huge stores of captured Japanese military supplies. Nationalists, instead of merging with their Communist "brothers," attempted to drive them by force from their strongholds. The National Assembly, convening in May, was soon disrupted as each side raised the ante for its cooperation. The Nationalists now settled on a policy of exterminating the Communists before considering political reforms and demanded heavy increases in United States military support. The Communists reacted in kind and threatened to invoke the aid of Russia. Both sides launched a heavy barrage of anti-American propaganda, and Marshall found himself stalemated at every turn.

Back in Washington, the disastrous course of events in China had fanned the fires of political partisanship. China was far away and sufficiently unknown to encourage a great deal of ill-informed and mischievous oratory by Republicans and Democrats alike. Moreover, General Hurley, in his hotheaded resignation, had cued in the suspicion that "subversives" in the State Department were secretly plotting a Communist victory in China. A particular Republican deity, General MacArthur, was obviously running a taut ship in Japan, and Republicans used this as a damaging object lesson to set against the Democrat-inspired chaos in China. Around the country a "China Lobby" was forming, controlled largely by zealots of the right, beating the gongs of public opinion to "save" China.

All these distractions, piled on top of the administration's own confusion about what to do in China, created an almost intolerable sense of frustration in the White House and State Department. Some years later, Mr. Truman said:

> The turn of events in China troubled me. The anti-American demonstrations by the Nationalist groups in such places as Nanking; the new policy of harshness against the liberals; Chiang Kai-shek's insistence on freedom of action in the military field—all these seemed to indicate that the Central Government was turning its back on my effort to preserve the peace in China.
>
> As I interpreted Marshall's reports, there were elements on both sides, among the Kuomintang and among the Communists, who were willing to work together on a peaceful solution. But on each side there were extremists who wanted no part of negotiation. The Generalissimo, himself, seemed to take a position between these two groups. In the spring, the influence of the moderates around him must have prevailed, and he agreed to concessions. Now, however, it appeared that the extreme military cliques had won out, and that he was no longer willing to listen to Marshall's counsel.[9]

On August 10, after much deliberation and many cable communications with his envoy in China, President Truman sent Chiang Kai-shek what sounded very much like an ultimatum.

> Since I sent General Marshall to you as my special envoy, I have followed closely the situation in China. It is with deep regret that I am forced to the conclusion that his efforts have apparently proved unavailing. . . .
>
> There exists in the United States an increasing body of opinion which holds that our entire policy toward China must be re-examined in the light of spreading strife . . . [the] tendency to suppress freedom of the press as well as the expression of liberal views . . . [the] assassination of distinguished Chinese liberals . . . [the settlement of] major social issues

by resort to force . . . a growing feeling that the aspirations of the Chinese
people are thwarted by militarists and a small group of reactionaries.

Such a state of affairs is violently repugnant to the American people.

Unless convincing proof is shortly forthcoming that genuine progress is
being made toward a peaceful solution of China's internal problems, it
must be expected that American opinion will not continue in its generous
attitude toward your nation.[10]

There was a brief period of repentance, but Chiang, in his reply
to the President, put all the blame for China's plight on the Communists. Within a few weeks he again embarked on a course of
trying to crush his enemies by military might before counseling with
them on a political settlement. In the process, he extended his forces
beyond any human capacity to support them.

In January 1947 President Truman made good his threat. The
Marshall mission, along with most other American personnel in
China, except for Ambassador John Leighton Stuart and his staff,
were called home. The General (soon to become Secretary of State)
submitted a final report to the President in which he said that the
problem of China could never be solved as long as the "overwhelming suspicion" between the Kuomintang and the Communists continued to exist. Pessimistically, he refrained from any speculation as
to when it would end.

The China tangle grew more complex and intractable as the
months went by. The Nationalists made temporary gains against
Communist strongholds in the North, but they were unable to consolidate them, and the Red tide began to push inexorably southward. As the pipelines of American aid began to dry up, Chiang
launched a propaganda offensive to have them refilled. The cry was
taken up in this country by the "China Lobby" and echoed through
the halls of Congress.

In July President Truman sent General Wedemeyer back to China
to see if any new circumstance had arisen that would warrant a
resumption of full-scale American cooperation. The General was as
pessimistic in 1947 as he had been in 1945. He reported:

In China today I find apathy and lethargy in many quarters. Instead of
seeking solutions of problems presented, considerable time and effort are
spent in blaming outside influences and seeking outside assistance . . .

To gain and maintain the confidence of the people, the Central Government will have to effect immediately drastic, far-reaching political and
economic reforms. Promises will no longer suffice. Performance is absolutely necessary. It should be accepted that military force in itself will not
eliminate communism.[11]

While the General despaired of a coalition government ever being formed, or of the Nationalists holding more than a small corner of China, he nevertheless recommended a resumption of substantial aid to China: military advisers and grants of $1.5 billion spread over a five-year period. This contradictory proposal created new consternation in Washington planning circles, already plunged deeply in confusion and divided counsel. One part of Wedemeyer's recommendations conformed to the prevalent administration view that the time had come to cut our losses in China and get out. Another part played directly into the hands of the "China Lobby" and a vocal Republican minority. To cover its own policy confusion, the administration had been less than frank in disclosing the true dimensions of the China situation to the American public. It now compounded the offense by suppressing the Wedemeyer report.

More in response to domestic pressures than to the rational needs of global policy, the administration did resume a program of limited military and economic aid to Chiang Kai-shek. Early in 1948 Congress approved a $400 million China aid bill. But Nationalist China was clearly beyond redemption. The morale of its people was undermined, governmental administrations faltered and collapsed, its soldiers laid down their arms and defected to the enemy.

On November 9, 1948, the same day that Chiang cabled a frantic appeal to President Truman for a massive increase in United States aid "to save the cause of democracy" in China, Ambassador Stuart sent the President a brief inventory of losses suffered by the Nationalist armies in the Changchun-Mukden campaign: eight U.S.-trained divisions with 85 percent U.S. equipment, totaling 84,000 men; one U.S.-trained division with 50 percent U.S. equipment totaling 15,000 men; two U.S.-trained divisions with 30 percent U.S. equipment, totaling 22,000 men.

At about the same time Major General David Barr, commanding the U.S. Military Advisory Group in China, reported to the Department of the Army:

I am convinced that the military situation has deteriorated to the point where only the active participation of United States troops could effect a remedy.

No battle has been lost since my arrival for lack of ammunition or equipment. Their military debacles, in my opinion, can all be attributed to the world's worst leadership and many other morale-destroying factors that led to a complete loss of will to fight.[12]

In January 1949 Chiang announced his resignation as President of the Republic of China and ostensibly turned the reins of power over to the Vice President, Li Tsung-jen. But it was a resignation of the title only. The Generalissimo continued to exert his powerful influence from his home in Fenghua, where he had sequestered most of the nation's treasury of $200 million in gold and silver. At the same time, the capital was moved for the fourth time in as many years, from Nanking, in the path of the advancing Communist armies, to Canton far in the south.

President Li put out numerous peace feelers, but Mao and his commanding general, Chu-Teh, were by now so confident of success that they upped their demands to what amounted to unconditional surrender and the handing over to Communist mercies of a long list of "war criminals," including Chiang Kai-shek. By April, an estimated one million Communist soldiers were poised on the north banks of the Yangtze River, which flows more than 2,000 miles westerly across China and which separated the few southern provinces still loyal to the Nationalist cause from the rest of China. Chiang, meanwhile, had secretly deployed the air force and the few gunboats of the Chinese navy to bases on the island of Formosa, to preserve them from capture by the Communists. Now he also arranged to have more than 200,000 of the best Nationalist troops pulled out of the line defending the south bank of the Yangtze to form a protective garrison around Shanghai.

On April 24, General Chu-Teh's battle-hardened troops swarmed across the Yangtze on a front hundreds of miles long, encountering scarcely any opposition from the demoralized Nationalists. Two weeks later Chiang and other principal leaders of the Kuomintang landed in Formosa to erect Nationalist China's last redoubt, bringing with them the Shanghai garrison as the nucleus of a promised but improbable army of "liberation." Nationalist elements on the mainland continued for a few months to offer fitful resistance to the triumphant Red army, mainly through guerrilla actions in an ever-narrowing sector in the south and west. But for all practical purposes, the struggle for China was over. Half a century of civil war to perfect the democratic revolution envisioned by Sun Yat-sen had ended in victory for Marxist totalitarianism. And Roosevelt's dream of China as the Eastern pivot of the Grand Alliance of free nations was smashed.

China was not only a military debacle, but a political debacle for the United States as well. The Truman administration unjustly bears the public onus for this, but no succeeding administration has had the wisdom to redress the error or the courage to do so if, indeed, it knew what to do. American foreign policy, in consequence, has been forced to walk awkwardly across the international stage, hobbled on the one hand by exaggerated bonds of loyalty to the anachronism of the Republic-of-China-on-Formosa, and on the other hand prevented by stubborn pride from acknowledging the reality of the Communist government that controls mainland China. It unhappily is as true today as it was nearly two decades ago that United States policy toward China is dictated more by the exigencies of domestic politics than by the realities of the world situation.

The disastrous course of events in postwar China gave Republican and other critics of the Truman administration their one secure handhold on a foreign policy issue. Many professed to see the beginning of an evil design to "betray" China in the Yalta agreement giving certain concessions to the Russians in exchange for their joining the war against Japan. Without reviving that ancient argument, the historical fact remains that the Soviets gave little direct help or encouragement to Mao and his Chinese Communists until the rout of the Nationalist armies was well on its way. Stalin distrusted Mao Tse-tung even before 1945, a fact that Khrushchev and Kosygin undoubtedly have brooded upon for most of the succeeding twenty years.

Some argue honestly, and others not so honestly, that Truman "sold Chiang down the river" by demanding that he take the Communists into his camp, and by shutting off the flow of American dollars and arms when he did not. General Marshall was misguided when he made this recommendation, it is contended, and it is freely asserted by some that he was led into this error by the wicked counsel of American Foreign Service officers who were secretly conspiring for a Communist victory. But the record is clear that more than $2 billion of American aid went to Chiang between V-J Day and the end of 1949, and that almost 75 percent of American-supplied arms and equipment wound up in Communist hands.

Mr. Truman and his aides in the State Department contributed to their own discomfiture by abandoning, as far as China was concerned, the bipartisanship that had lubricated so well their political efforts in respect to Europe. But this was dictated almost as much by necessity as by design. The fact was that during most of the period from 1945 to 1950, the administration had no hard, clear-cut policy toward China. It was dealing in an area where the choices were always between the lesser of several evils, and it played by ear instead of by note. It could hardly have won the Vandenbergs, the Dulleses, and the Deweys to a ringing support of its own indecision. The State Department published a 1,054-page white paper on China in 1950, which set a mass of facts in proper context but did not support the thesis that a rational and coherent policy for China was followed.

All these ingredients gave a virulence to the partisan debates over China that has seldom been matched either in intensity or longevity. Some portions of the suppressed Wedemeyer report lent themselves admirably to this purpose. From time to time, the oracular ambiguities of General MacArthur, uttered from his Olympian summit in Tokyo, were seized upon by the pro-Chiang forces in the United States as avidly as though they were bits of revealed Gospel. In October 1947, former Ambassador William Bullitt published in *Life* magazine a "Report on China" that restated with compelling plausibility all the arguments for virtually unlimited aid to the Nationalist cause. The thesis that it was the Truman-Acheson foreign policy that delivered China into the hands of the Communist infidels became almost an article of Republican faith in the late forties and early fifties, and it is still being repeated in the middle sixties.

But that some of this, at least, was a faith of convenience and partisan necessity is a conclusion hard to escape. Arthur Vandenberg, a man of great probity and responsibility, never came publicly to the defense of President Truman on the China issue. There was a strong prospect in 1948 that he might be Secretary of State in a Dewey administration and would have to pick up the China nettle in his own bare hands. But in that year he wrote privately to California's Republican Senator William F. Knowland, one of the first among the "China Firsters," in these cautionary words:

> The vital importance of saving China cannot be exaggerated. But there are limits to our resources and boundaries to our miracles. . . .
> Mr. Landon [Alfred M. Landon, the Republican sage of Topeka] may be of the opinion that we "gulled" Republicans should have yelled our heads off about China and the Generalissimo during the past year or two. But in my opinion it would only have precipitated and underscored a discussion of Chiang's weakness and nullified any remnant of his prestige. It is easy to sympathize with Chiang, as I always have and still do. But it is quite a different thing to plan resultful aid short of armed American intervention with American combat troops.
> I envy Mr. Landon's freedom to criticize what wasn't done and his freedom of responsibility for deciding specifically what should be done now. [But] when practically all of our American-trained and American-

equipped Chinese divisions surrender without firing a shot—where do we go from there?[13]

A good question, indeed. It was one that President Truman asked many times with quite discouraging results.

Harry Truman was never an expert in the esoteric disciplines of international affairs. He had little of the creative genius in this direction that Roosevelt and Churchill had, or even Joseph Stalin. Yet, as President he wrought the boldest and most far-reaching changes in United States foreign policy of any President in history—changes which have markedly affected the destiny of the world ever since.

As the present volume has tried to show, a part of the genius of Harry Truman as President lay in his ability to seek good advice and to act upon it when he got it. The most profound influence on his decisions in the field of international relations was supplied by Dean Gooderham Acheson, his last and greatest Secretary of State.

There could scarcely be two more dissimilar men—the one an Eastern aristocrat, the other a son of the proletarian Middle West. Yet there grew between them a bond of mutual respect and personal warmth that survived every vicissitude of public office and the cooling effects of many years of reflection. Their admiration for each other is undimmed today.

In the heyday of his official career, people used to say that Dean Acheson looked and acted too much like a Foreign Minister to be real. His erect, commanding figure, set off by a bristling, up-turned mustache and luxuriant eyebrows, his vast learning, his crisp, immaculate speech and lofty bearing—all conspired to impress his peers and to intimidate his inferiors, and to infuriate a good many of both.

A philosophical liberal nourished on the teachings of Theodore Roosevelt and Woodrow Wilson, he joined the first New Deal administration as Under Secretary of the Treasury. Within a year he had broken with FDR over monetary policies and returned in a magnificent huff to his Washington law firm. Roosevelt tried to tempt him out again in 1939 with the offer of a judgeship, which he declined. But in 1941 he accepted appointment as Assistant Secretary of State under Cordell Hull. Acheson remained in the State Department (with a lapse of eighteen months in 1947-48) until the Republicans took over in 1952. He had been Marshall's Under Secretary, and Truman named him Secretary on Marshall's retirement at the beginning of 1949.

As an American diplomat, Dean Acheson must be ranked as one of the greatest of the century. His hand was prominent in every major diplomatic negotiation and foreign policy formulation of the wartime and postwar years. Because of this, he was a prime target for the political foes of the administrations he served and of the Truman administration in particular. His situation was not helped by the fact that he plainly could not tolerate the bumptious self-importance or the slothful mentality of some of the members of Congress with whom he had to deal.

In consequence, Congress, frustrated and alarmed over the collapse of China, the saber-rattling of the Soviets, and the suspected infestation of the government by the Communists, aimed its angriest blows at Dean Acheson's head. This vendetta reached a height of absurdity in December 1949, when the Republicans in both Houses of Congress voted overwhelmingly to ask the President to dismiss Acheson as Secretary of State. Truman rejected their request with as much scorn as he could muster, which was considerable.

To Harry Truman, a sense of loyalty was as natural as breathing, and he used every opportunity to reiterate his faith in Dean Acheson. But the occasion recalled by Acheson with the most gratification was a handwritten "Memo to Dean Acheson" that he received near the end of the first month of the Korean crisis in the summer of 1950. The memo (it has never before been published) said:

Regarding June 24 and 25, your initiative in immediately calling the Security Council of the UN on Saturday night and notifying me was the key to what developed afterward. Had you not acted promptly in that direction, we would have had to go into Korea alone. The results attained thereafter show that you are a great Secretary of State and diplomat. Your handling of the situation since has been superb.

I am sending you this for your records.

H.S.T.

CHAPTER 11

◇◇◇◇◇◇◇◇◇◇◇◇◇◇◇◇◇◇◇◇◇◇◇◇◇◇◇◇◇

Korea

A Game of Chance

AT 2 O'CLOCK on the afternoon of Saturday, June 24, 1950, President Truman's private Air Force plane was just beginning to lose altitude for the long approach to the municipal airport at Kansas City, Missouri. It was a hot, humid day below, with ground temperatures close to 100 degrees. Above, tall columns of storm clouds reached into the sky. The President was homeward-bound to Independence for a weekend with his family and for some personal business with his brother, Vivian, at the old family farm near Grandview. A couple of hours earlier, the President had dedicated the new Friendship International Airport, at Baltimore, "to the cause of peace in the world," and he may have still been meditating on those words at that unsuspectedly historic hour of the early afternoon as he drew near his home.

Two o'clock of a Saturday afternoon in Kansas City, U.S.A., is four o'clock of a Sunday morning at the town of Hwach'on, just north of the 38th parallel of latitude, which separates the Republic of Korea, to the south, from the Democratic People's Republic of Korea, to the north. On that dark morning of Sunday, June 25, it was warm in Hwach'on and it was raining furiously, for it was the beginning of the monsoon season. Though the hour was unseemly, lights were burning in the headquarters of Senior Colonel Lee Hak Ku, Operations Officer of the Second Corps of the North Korean

People's Army (NKPA). His face and the other Oriental faces around him showed the evidence of strain. As the hands of his wrist watch reached the hour of four, Senior Colonel Lee Hak Ku brought his upraised arm down in a sharp gesture of command. As he did so, the purring, low-slung Russian tanks of the NKPA Seventh Division, ranged nearby, roared into life and churned southward through the mud. At the same time, the skies to the right and left of Colonel Lee's command post and across the greater part of the Korean Peninsula, burst with the thunder and flame of hundreds of cannon. Colonel Lee Hak Ku's meditations at that moment were on war, not peace.

Late on that drowsy Saturday afternoon in Washington, the telephones on the desk of the duty officer at the Department of State began to ring insistently. The press associations were getting reports of some sort of flare-up in Korea. Reporters were asking, "Does the Department know anything about this? Any word from MacArthur? [General Douglas MacArthur was Commander of Far Eastern forces, in Tokyo.] Or from Muccio? [John J. Muccio was U.S. Ambassador at Seoul.] Nothing? Anybody around the Department have any good guesses or comments about it? Well, try to locate somebody on the Far Eastern desk to give us a word or two on this thing, will you? Thanks."

About 9 o'clock that evening, Secretary of State Dean Acheson and Mrs. Acheson were sitting with visitors on the terrace of their quiet country home at Sandy Springs, Maryland, a few miles outside Washington, when the telephone rang. It was John D. Hickerson, Assistant Secretary of State for United Nations Affairs. He told Acheson that he and Assistant Secretary Dean Rusk had been at the Department for an hour because of persistent press reports of trouble in Korea, and that they had just received a message from Ambassador Muccio. It appeared that the trouble was, indeed, serious. North Korean troops had attacked or penetrated the border in force at a number of points all across the peninsula, and, the Ambassador had reported, "It would appear from the nature of the attack and the manner in which it was launched that it constitutes an all-out offensive against the Republic of Korea."

During the next half hour Acheson and his aides blocked out a preliminary course of action to protect the integrity of the Republic of Korea. Its principal feature was that there should be a prompt and unequivocal determination to block the aggression, with the full weight and authority of the United Nations backing up the effort.

Rusk and Hickerson rounded up members of their staffs and also brought into the action Ambassador-at-Large Philip Jessup and Ernest Gross of the UN delegation. Army Secretary Frank Pace was also alerted, since Defense Secretary Louis Johnson and General Omar Bradley, Chairman of the Joint Chiefs of Staff, were, at the moment, airborne somewhere over the Pacific, en route home from Tokyo. Around midnight, a call was put in to UN Secretary General Trygve Lie at his home on Long Island, asking that an emergency session of the UN Security Council be convened the next day, Sunday. Cables were then dispatched to United States embassies all over the world telling them of this country's proposed action in the UN and asking them to give it full support.

While this emergency course of action was being put in motion, Dean Acheson called the President at his home in Independence, and told him what had happened and asked his approval of the plans he had worked out with Rusk and the others. It was almost 11 o'clock and Mr. Truman's bedtime, but he said he would immediately fly back to Washington. Acheson told him this was hardly necessary, to get a good sleep, and that he would have another report for the President before noon the next day.

On Sunday, armed with additional reports from Korea and the promise of a UN Security Council meeting that afternoon, Acheson again communicated with the President. This time Mr. Truman told the Secretary to round up the chief State and Defense officials and to have them at Blair House for an emergency conference at 7 o'clock that night, and that he was returning to Washington at once.

As the President boarded his plane in Kansas City a couple of hours later, he gravely told the reporters accompanying him what he knew of the situation.

"Don't make it alarmist," he counseled them. "It could be dangerous, but I hope it isn't. There has been no formal declaration of war that I know of. I can't answer any more questions until I get all the facts."

Mr. Truman had concurred in full with the course of action proposed by his Secretary of State. In later years he would say:

In my generation, this was not the first occasion when the strong had attacked the weak. I recalled some earlier instances: Manchuria, Ethiopia, Austria. I remembered how each time that the democracies failed to act it had encouraged the aggressors to keep going ahead.

Communism was acting in Korea just as Hitler, Mussolini, and the

Japanese had acted ten, fifteen, and twenty years earlier. If this was allowed to go unchallenged it would mean a third world war. It was also clear to me that the foundations and principles of the United Nations were at stake unless this unprovoked attack on Korea could be stopped.[1]

Why did this unfamiliar, far-off land suddenly become so critical to United States foreign policy? From time immemorial, Korea had been a pawn in the unending power struggle between China and Japan. In the Second World War it was under steel-booted Japanese occupation. At the Cairo Conference of 1943, the United States, Great Britain, and China had agreed that, with victory over the Axis, Korea would become "free and independent." This was stimu- lated less by any sentimental attachment to the people of Korea than by the practical desirability of taking so potent a piece of Far Eastern military geography away from the Japanese. The Russians subscribed to this purpose as a part of the Yalta agreements by which they agreed to enter the war against Japan.

When the surrender came, in August 1945, there were tens of thousands of Japanese troops and civilian administrators in Korea. The Russians sent an occupation force of approximately a full divi- sion across the border from Manchuria; and elements of the United States 24th Army Corps, under Lieutenant General John R. Hodge, landed at the southern port of Pusan for the same purpose. To sim- plify the problems of disarming and repatriating the enemy and of running the civilian government during those first weeks, the two allies agreed that, purely as a matter of convenience, the Russians would take care of things north of the 38th parallel and the Ameri- cans to the south. This geographer's line was chosen simply because it cut the country approximately in two, not because of any political or economic considerations.

But what the Americans had regarded as demarcation was inter- preted by the Russians as partition. It soon became evident that they had no interest in a unified Korea. They embargoed traffic across the parallel, cut off electric power and the transfer of goods southward, and set up a provisional government modeled on Com- munist lines. In 1947 the United States put the issue before the UN, and the General Assembly established a special mission on the unifi- cation of Korea and on overseeing general elections there the next year. The Russians and their North Korean puppets refused to let the election commissioners cross the line into their territory, and so the election of 1948 was held only in the south. It resulted in the formation of the Republic of Korea on August 15 under the presi- dency of the aged and despotically inclined Syngman Rhee, no great favorite with Washington even then. The Communist answer was to announce, a few weeks later, the formation of the Democratic People's Republic of Korea, with Kim Il Sung, a Moscow-trained revolutionary, as Premier.

In 1949, Russia and the United States, in a rare act of common consent, withdrew their occupation forces from the peninsula, leaving behind training cadres for the native armies. The United Nations still dutifully carried "the problem of Korea" on its agenda, evidence of its commitment to a unified Korea. But for all practical purposes there were now two autonomous Koreas, mutually hostile, mutually suspicious, oriented toward opposite ends of the political axis, and each eager to be at the other's throat.

Korea was one of many postwar trouble spots on the world map, but, in the view of American planners, rather a minor one that could probably be safely ignored. The Joint Chiefs of Staff in 1947 had dismissed Korea as being of little military concern to this government in terms of its broad defensive strategy in the Pacific. Congress turned down President Truman's request for $60 million of economic aid to Korea in the 1950-51 budget. And on January 12, 1950, Secretary Acheson, in a speech to the National Press Club (it was to achieve a delayed fame of sorts), lumped Korea with "other areas in the Pacific [which] it must be clear that no person can guarantee against military attack."

This was a good deal less than the "invitation to the Communists to attack Korea," which Republican critics of the Secretary tried later to squeeze out of his words. But taken in conjunction with other indications of this government's apparent disinterest in Korea, it is not surprising that the Communists figured there was at least a gambler's chance that the United States would not fight to protect South Korea.

George F. Kennan has advanced another explanation for the Russians' willingness to make the Korean gamble. He has said:

They saw us at this time moving rapidly toward a Japanese peace treaty to which they would not be a party. They had been waiting ever since the surrender to see if we couldn't be induced to leave Japan with our forces and give them what would amount to a free hand in Korea.

When they saw it wasn't going to work out that way, they concluded: "If this is all we are going to get out of a Japanese settlement, we had better get our hands on Korea fast before the Americans let the Japanese back in there."[2]

It is Kennan's position, as well as that of several other experts, that initially the Communist thrust into South Korea was a joint

venture of the Russians and their North Korea puppets, and that the
Chinese Communists were not brought into the action until later.

Whatever motives were at work in this desperate game of chance,
the irrevocable first move was made at 4 A.M., Sunday, June 24,
1950, Korean time. Now it was Washington's turn. The policy of
containment had run into its first challenge by force of arms.

Seven Days in June

As President Truman flew eastward to Washington that Sunday
afternoon, the UN Security Council met in emergency session at its
headquarters at Lake Success, Long Island. By a stroke of historic
good fortune, the Russians were not present. They had boycotted
the Council since January, protesting the UN's refusal to seat Communist China. On this Sunday afternoon in June, the chair of Delegate Jacob Malik of the U.S.S.R. was conveniently empty. By this
failure to apply his almost certain veto, the Council voted 9 to 0 to
brand the North Korean aggression "a breach of the peace." It
called for an immediate end to hostilities and the withdrawal of the
invaders beyond the 38th parallel. This was a significant one-up for
the West.

The President was met at Washington's National Airport by Dean
Acheson, Defense Secretary Johnson, and Army Secretary Pace
when his plane landed at 7:15 that evening. They drove immediately to Blair House (the temporary White House residence),
where other top aides awaited them. Harry Truman went straight to
his bedroom telephone to inform Bess of his safe arrival, as he always did when they were apart. Then he went downstairs to begin
as momentous a conference on national strategy as he had ever
participated in.

Ranged informally about him for predinner cocktails in the handsome drawing room of the old mansion was the top brass of the
United States "high command": from the Department of State, Secretary Acheson, Under Secretary James P. Webb, Assistant Secretaries Rusk and Hickerson, and UN Ambassador-at-Large Jessup;
from the Department of Defense, Secretary Johnson; the service
secretaries for War (Pace), Navy (Francis P. Mathews), and Air
(Thomas K. Finletter); the Chairman of the Joint Chiefs of Staff,
General Bradley; the service chiefs for the Army (General J.
Lawton Collins), the Navy (Admiral Forrest Sherman), and the Air

Force (General Hoyt S. Vandenberg). A Communist bomb at 1628 Pennsylvania Avenue that evening would have wiped out in one crippling blast the whole top layer of this nation's military and diplomatic leadership.

These were the best experts on national security in the United States. In the mind of each was the realization that the nation faced a major crisis, perhaps as great a crisis as it had ever faced. Also in the mind of each was the realization that there was only one response the United States could make: "This shall not be allowed to happen." What this determination might bring in its train not one of them could say. But while they could propose, only the President could dispose. To him alone fell the responsibility for decision. And, characteristically, he met it head on.

The big mahogany dining table was cleared after dinner and the group went to work. First there were summaries of the latest information from Korea. There were hopeful signs that the Republic of Korea (ROK) Army might be able to contain the assault from the North. At least one main thrust through the mountains northeast of Seoul, at Chunchon, appeared for the moment to have been stalled. Acheson read a number of recommendations that had been made for action. These were discussed freely around the table.

In the end the President chose three of the recommendations:

1. MacArthur was to be instructed to send the planes and ships necessary to evacuate all American civilian personnel from Korea. His fighter planes were to protect these operations from interference, staying south of the 38th parallel, if possible, but going beyond if it became necessary.

2. MacArthur was to get as much ammunition and other supplies into the hands of the ROK Army as possible.

3. The 7th Fleet was to be called north from the Philippines into the Formosa Strait and instructed to prevent the spread of the conflict in that area.

These were first steps only, based on the assumption that the aggression would continue. In addition, the President ordered that fresh intelligence estimates be made of other tension points around the world where Soviet aggression might occur. The Korean adventure might be only a feint to cancel a stronger thrust elsewhere. He also demanded a military study of possible retaliation by this country against Soviet bases in the Far East should they actively intervene on behalf of the North Koreans.

Recollections of persons who attended this meeting are nearly unanimous in describing it as relaxed and wide open. The President gave everyone a chance to speak his mind, and apparently everyone did.

There was no question on the part of anyone that the only course for the United States was to take a firm stand to help Korea and to stick by it, whatever the cost. "If we are going to prevent a third world war," one of those present said, "we have to draw a line somewhere. We might as well draw it here and now."

The Navy and Air Force spokesmen said they thought the first show of American strength from the sea and air would cause the invaders to run for cover and give up. General Bradley and others were dubious. The enemy would have to be driven out on the ground, but the ROK Army should be able to do it if given enough supplies.

There was at this meeting, unhappily, a bleak unawareness both of the massive strength of the North Korean People's Army (NKPA) and of its determination to win. Only later were the Blair House conferees to learn how sketchy and inaccurate their Korean intelligence had been.

There was another gnawing realization on the minds of the policy makers at Blair House that night. This was the blunt fact that the United States did not have the military muscle to back up a "get tough" diplomacy anywhere in the world. In pruning the defense budget that year down to a wantonly inadequate $13.2 billion, Congress and the administration had cut away bone and sinew along with the fat.[*] The United States Army, in 1950, numbered 592,000 men, less than half what it had been at that other climactic moment of unpreparedness, Pearl Harbor Day. It was split up into ten understrength divisions armed principally with World War II weapons. The Eighth Army, on occupation duty in Japan (and the nearest to Korea), totaled about 80,000 men and consisted of four infantry divisions and a regimental combat team. The Navy had been cut almost as heavily as the Army, but the Air Force remained in fairly strong condition. Lieutenant General George Stratemeyer's Far Eastern Command was composed of nearly 1,200 aircraft of all types.

The ROK Army, which had been trained and equipped by the United States, consisted of eight infantry divisions with a total manpower of 65,000 men—a total that was to be ground down to

---

[*] Mr. Truman cannot escape responsibility for this. He was determined to achieve the first peacetime "economy budget" in ten years. But the public blame for "starving" the military fell on his hapless Defense Secretary, Louis Johnson.

less than 25,000 before the first week of fighting was over. It had been deliberately denied offensive weapons—tanks, heavy artillery, combat aircraft—to circumvent President Rhee's intemperate ambition to bring about unification with his northern neighbors by force. This cautionary strategy was to prove very nearly fatal in the opening weeks of the war. The ROK Army was brave and willing to fight, but it was outnumbered and hopelessly outgunned by the enemy— to an extent not then suspected by the Blair House conferees.

On Monday the President was at his office early. Associates in the White House recalled rarely having seen him in a grimmer, more determined mood. He gave his staff a concise rundown on the weekend's developments and the previous night's conference at Blair House. Walking over to the big globe in his office, he put his hand on Korea and said:

"This is the Greece of the Far East. If we are tough enough now, there won't have to be any next step."

At 11:30 he issued through his press secretary his first formal statement on the Korean crisis. It was carefully worded to avoid hysteria, but firm and forthright. It said:

The attack on Korea makes it plain that communism has passed beyond the use of subversion to conquer independent nations, and will now use armed invasion as well. . . .

Those responsible for this act of aggression must realize how seriously the government of the United States views such threats to the peace of the world. Willful disregard of the obligation to keep the peace cannot be tolerated by nations that support the United Nations Charter.

That afternoon the President received the Korean Ambassador, Dr. John Myun Chang, whom he reassured to the extent that he could. The Ambassador, shaking his head sadly, told reporters as he left the White House, "The hour is late."

On the far side of the world, meanwhile, consternation and panic were growing in Seoul, the South Korean capital lying less than 50 miles below the 38th parallel. ROK resistance had crumpled after a brief stand at Chunchon, and elsewhere along the front. Refugees and fleeing troops were pouring into the city. The Rhee government was planning to move its headquarters further south, to Taejon. Ambassador Muccio had begun the evacuation of American civilians under air cover provided from MacArthur's forces in Japan. Three Yak fighters of the NKPA had been shot down by American planes over Inchon, where they had attempted to strafe a Danish

freighter taking American refugees aboard. The Ambassador ra-
dioed his grave apprehensions to Washington. ROK infantry, without tanks or heavy artillery, he said, appeared to be helpless before
the NKPA drive, spearheaded by Russian-built T-34 tanks. Mac-
Arthur had advised the Joint Chiefs that, on the basis of reports
from his observers on the scene, the fall of Seoul was imminent.

That night President Truman again summoned his "war cabinet"
to an emergency meeting at Blair House. The reports from Korea
cast a far more ominous shadow than they had twenty-four hours
earlier. It was becoming apparent that the ROK forces needed more
substantial help than airdrops of ammunition and supplies. It was
decided that the Navy and the Air Force units under MacArthur's
command should give direct tactical support to the defenders, but
only south of the 38th parallel. This was a momentous decision, for
it committed this government to military as well as moral support of
the South Korean forces.*

In addition, new instructions went out to the 7th Fleet to prevent
any attack by the Chinese Communists on Formosa, and likewise to
thwart any schemes Chiang Kai-shek might have to put his Nationalists ashore on the mainland. Washington wanted no resumption of
the civil war in China at a moment like this.

Finally, Acheson was directed to prepare a message to the
Kremlin asking its intercession with the Korean Communists to respect the UN demand for a cease-fire. And UN Ambassador Warren
Austin was directed to seek a resolution supporting these stronger
moves from the Security Council.

* There was a king-sized flap in the State and Defense Departments over the
timing of a public announcement on this. Technically, this tactical support could be
given only under the auspices of the UN, but the matter could not be brought up
in the Security Council until the following day, Tuesday. But the urgency of the
situation required that MacArthur get his ships to sea and his planes in the air
without a moment's delay. The Joint Chiefs of Staff group went directly from
Blair House to the Pentagon that night to set up a "hot line" telecommunications
circuit to the General's headquarters in Tokyo to give him his instructions.

It was also urgent that MacArthur immediately let the government and the
people of South Korea know that help was on the way: their collapse, otherwise,
might be only a matter of hours. But if this vital information hit the news wires
before it got to the UN—as it almost certainly would—there would be hell to pay.
It would also make trouble if certain members of Congress learned about it for the
first time in their newspapers Tuesday morning.

The ingenious, but almost wholly imperfect, solution to this dilemma was that
MacArthur was to withhhold his announcement to the Tokyo press corps until
noon, Washington time, Tuesday, but to make an immediate announcement of it
by radio to the people of Korea—in Korean. What the Washington "brass" did not
comprehend was that most American correspondents in Japan had interpreters who
were monitoring the local radio around the clock. The story, accordingly, was carried
fully in late editions of morning newspapers here and in radio newscasts.

As the Blair House meeting broke up that night, Mr. Truman observed ruefully: "Everything I have done in the past five years has been to try to avoid making a decision such as I had to make tonight."

Tuesday morning President Truman summoned the congressional leaders of both parties to a conference at the White House. He also brought into this meeting his full Cabinet, the top Secretaries and Officers from the Department of Defense, and a similar group from the Department of State. More than forty persons sat around the long, coffin-shaped table in the Cabinet Room to hear the President report on the latest news from Korea and to give an account of his actions so far during the crisis. He read them the text of a formal statement summarizing these actions, which he planned to release at noon.

There were many questions from the legislators, most of them in the vein of whether the nation needed additional military strength and whether our actions were consonant with the UN Charter. Not one spoke except in commendation of what the President had done. When his message was read in the Senate and House later that day, both bodies cheered. The decision to act promptly and vigorously to check the Communist aggression in Korea, and to throw in the Navy and the Air Force without quibbling over diplomatic proprieties, drew an almost unanimous outpouring of praise for the President from the nation's press and from many capitals abroad.

At 10:45 that night, the UN Security Council, responding to the urging of the United States chief delegate, Warren Austin, adopted one of the strongest resolutions in its history up to that time—a call for armed intervention against an aggressor. It called on the member nations to "render such assistance to the Republic of Korea as may be necessary to repel the armed attack and to restore international peace and security to the area." The vote was 7 to 1, with Yugoslavia voting "No" and the Soviet Union again absent.

Wednesday passed without momentous new decisions having to be taken in Washington. The Senate unanimously adopted a bill passed by the House for a one-year extension of the military draft, and heard Senator Taft complain that President Truman had "usurped the power of Congress" by his war-making decisions on Korea. No one, however, paid the Ohioan much attention, for once. There was more interest in the news that Prime Minister Attlee had just told the House of Commons that all British warships in Japanese waters had been placed at the disposal of the American commander there for employment in behalf of the ROK.

But momentous things were happening in Korea that day. The Communist invasion had now smashed through virtually the last ROK defenses in the mountains and valleys along the 38th parallel, and two mighty columns of armor and foot soldiery had now converged on the northern outskirts of Seoul. Thousands of soldiers from the disrupted ROK units, plus thousands of tattered, terror-stricken peasants from the countryside, streamed into and through the city, clogging its streets and the bridges spanning the wide Han River on its southern outskirts.

There were other thousands of ROK troops—at least three divisions, loyal and well-trained—garrisoned in Seoul and capable of a substantial delaying action against the invaders. But they were virtually leaderless as the ROK Army staff headquarters succumbed to the prevailing confusion and hysteria. The handful of American officers in the Korean Military Assistance Group did their best to retrieve some sense of order out of the chaos, but without avail. By nightfall, with the thunder of Communist guns roaring in the northern reaches of the city, a milling, fighting, screaming mass of humanity choked the river bridges, seeking a way to freedom. The destruction of these bridges had been ordained by the ROK high command as a last-ditch deterrent to the invaders. At 2:15 on Thursday morning the bridges were engulfed in simultaneous dynamite blasts, sending hundreds of refugees still struggling across them to a fiery death. Most of the ROK troops in Seoul, with their equipment and transport, were trapped on the north bank. Seoul had fallen, and the army of South Korea had been all but destroyed.

MacArthur's and Muccio's reports of the Han River disaster reached Washington on Thursday. The President called the National Security Council together that afternoon to consider this alarming turn of events; also to hear directly from John Foster Dulles, who had just returned from the Far East.* He had been in

---

* A foretaste of the "MacArthur incident" which was to erupt later is seen in the following excerpt from the private diaries of a White House aide for the last week of June, 1950: "The President said we [several members of his staff] should have heard what John Foster Dulles had to say about MacArthur after his return from Tokyo. The President said Dulles was very strong in his comments; that when word of the outbreak came to Tokyo, MacArthur's people knew nothing about it. Dulles could get none of the staff to call MacArthur—they were afraid to disturb him—and Dulles finally had to do it himself. Dulles, the President indicated, would like to have MacArthur hauled back to the United States, but the President said he pointed out that MacArthur is involved politically in this country and that to call him back would create a tremendous reaction. Dulles agreed, the President said."

This diary was made available to the author on a promise of anonymity.

Seoul to address the National Assembly only three days before the invasion was launched. Dulles was dubious that the ROK Army alone could repel the invaders. He was supported by Defense Secretary Johnson and members of the Joint Chiefs.

Johnson also said it was becoming clear that restricting U.S. air cover and naval support to targets south of the 38th parallel was robbing the effort of its effectiveness. The long flight from bases in Japan gave the planes a too limited time over their targets, and the lack of good ground liaison made the location of targets difficult. The enemy's main supply depots and concentration points were north of the parallel, Johnson said, and unless these could be destroyed there was little prospect of checking his headlong progress down the peninsula. Acheson and Pace pointed out the hazards of carrying the fight into the enemy's territory, lest it offer a provocation for either Red China or Russia to jump in openly on the side of the North Koreans.

President Truman accepted parts of both viewpoints and had them put together in a new directive to General MacArthur. The General was authorized to send his planes north of the parallel, but to be scrupulously careful to hit military targets only. In addition, the General was ordered to bring enough American ground troops into Korea to set up a proper communications system for air control and to secure airfields and port facilities somewhere in the area of Pusan, then about 200 miles south of the combat area.

Word of this decision was received with relief at Far Eastern Command Headquarters in Tokyo. Within hours of its issuance, Major General Earl E. Partridge, Air Force Commander in the theater, received this terse directive from his chief: "Stratemeyer to Partridge: Take out North Korean airfields immediately. No Publicity. MacArthur approves."[3] A few hours later, thirty-three officers and men of the 507th Antiaircraft Artillery Battalion landed at Suwon airfield, 20 miles south of Seoul, and set up their M-55 machine guns. Hardly had they done this when a flight of four enemy Yak fighters swept across the field. One was shot down and the others fled.

After the National Security Council meeting in the Cabinet Room that Thursday afternoon, President Truman went to his Oval office and there held his first regular press conference since the onset of the Korean crisis. It was not notable save for one fact: The conflict got a label that was to prove politically troublesome to Mr. Truman for years to come. It was not his label, but he accepted it. Here, from the transcript of the press conference, is how the Korean war became known as a "police action"—a police action in which the United States was to suffer more than 100,000 casualties over the next three years.

Q. Mr. President, everybody is asking in this country, are we or are we not at war?

A. We are not at war.

Q. Mr. President, could you elaborate on that statement, "We are not at war," and could we use that in quotes?

A. Yes, I will allow you to use that in quotes. The Republic of Korea was set up with United Nations help. It was unlawfully attacked by a bunch of bandits which are neighbors, in North Korea. The United Nations held a meeting and asked the members to go to the relief of the Korean Republic, and the members of the United Nations are going to the relief of the Korean Republic to suppress a bandit raid on the Republic of Korea. That is all there is to it.

Q. Would it be correct to call it a police action under the United Nations?

A. Yes, that is exactly what it amounts to.

Sixteen nations, in time, were to make tangible contributions to this "police action," but the United States would bear 90 percent of the burden of helping the Republic of Korea defend itself.

While these events were going on in Washington, General Mac-Arthur was making his first on-the-spot inspection of the situation in Korea. His C-54, sentimentally named *Bataan*, was the first plane to land at Suwon airfield after the American antiaircraft detachment had taken over this landing field. He stepped out, casually resplendent as usual in his crushed military cap with the golden "spinach" on its visor, a black leather windbreaker over his open-throat khaki shirt, and the familiar oversized corncob pipe clamped in his teeth. He accepted a brief ceremonial welcome from President Rhee, and demanded to be driven at once toward the combat zone. He was taken all the way up to the Han River, where massed NKPA forces on the far bank were preparing to jump off on what they intended to be a swift, decisive sweep all the way to the Korea Strait.

Major General Charles A. Willoughby, MacArthur's chief of intelligence and his most reverent biographer, was present on this mission and has described its climax as follows:

Motoring forward under the constant air bombardment, he encountered all the dreadful backwash of a defeated and dispersed army. The

South Korean forces were in full flight. He reached the banks of the Han River just in time to be caught up in the last rearguard action to defend its bridges. Seoul was already in enemy hands, and he found himself once again the inheritor of a massive disaster, leader of yet another forlorn hope.

For full twenty minutes the General stood on a little mound just off the road, clogged with retreating, panting columns of disorganized troops interspersed with ambulances filled with groaning, broken men, the sky resonant with shrieking missiles of death, and everywhere the stench and misery and utter desolation of a stricken battlefield. His trained eye missed nothing—but in this brief interval his desperate plan was made. And desperate indeed it was! Completely outnumbered though he would be, he would bring his occupation forces from Japan and rely upon strategic maneuver to overcome the great odds against him.[4]

Shortly after 3 A.M. Friday, Washington time, teletype circuits from Tokyo began to chatter in the communications center at the Pentagon. MacArthur was reporting on his inspection of the Korean battlefront. The duty officer summoned General Collins, asleep in an anteroom in the Joint Chiefs of Staff quarters upstairs, who, in turn, put in calls that brought Dean Rusk and a handful of other officials speeding across the Potomac in the early dawn. A two-way circuit to Tokyo was set up so that the Far Eastern Commander and his superiors in Washington could "talk" back and forth via teletype.

The text of MacArthur's formal report was grim and explicitly urgent. The ROK forces, organized and equipped only for internal security duty, the General reported, had been hopelessly mauled by the heavily armed NKPA, and were in a state of shock and desperation. They were retreating in confusion; leadership was disintegrating; their supplies and equipment were falling to the enemy; and they had no visible prospect of recapturing the initiative.

General MacArthur declared:

The only assurance for holding the present line and the ability to regain later the lost ground is through the introduction of United States combat forces into the Korean battle area.

To continue to utilize the forces of our air and navy without an effective ground element cannot be decisive.

If authorized, it is my intention to immediately move a United States regimental combat team to the reinforcement of the vital area discussed and to provide for a possible build-up to two-division strength from the troops in Japan for an early counter-offensive.

Unless provision is made for the full utilization of the Army-Navy-Air team in this shattered area, our mission will at best be needlessly costly in life, money, and prestige. At worst, it might even be doomed to failure.[5]

General Collins told General MacArthur how concerned the President had been only the day before about the whole question of using ground troops and how this might draw retaliation in kind from either the Chinese or Russians. He also said that the President had wondered whether the existing order to carry air and naval strikes beyond the 38th parallel might not in some way be expanded to meet the need. In any event, Collins concluded, this was too big a request to be handled at the Joint Chiefs of Staff. It would have to be put up to the President in the morning.

To all of this MacArthur dissented vigorously. The North Korean strategy called for a dash all the way down the peninsula to Pusan before the Americans or anyone else could intervene. If that drive got rolling it would be impossible to reverse it. He urged Collins to get him an immediate decision. Minutes were what counted now.

It was 4:30 in the morning by General Collins' watch as he put through a call to his civilian chief, Secretary Pace. He filled the Secretary in on the crisis message from MacArthur and recommended that, in spite of the hour, the President be apprised of the emergency. Pace agreed, and at a few minutes before 5 A.M. he got President Truman on the White House phone—crisp-voiced and wide awake, already up and shaved.

The President heard Pace out in silence. Then, without hesitation, he granted the first of MacArthur's requests: the immediate dispatch of a regimental combat team by airlift from Japan to Korea. By 10 o'clock he had OK'd the two-division buildup that MacArthur had also requested. In addition, he authorized a naval blockade of North Korea as proposed by Admiral Sherman.

Now we were in, all the way. For the first time in history, a President, singlehandedly, had taken the nation into a shooting war. It had happened in one short, agonizing week—from Saturday, June 24, to Friday, June 30, 1950.

But what was historically more important, the United States had shown the world that it meant what it said about containing Communist aggression.

NSC-68

To understand the administration's almost instinctive response to the Communist aggression in Korea, as well as much of what followed, one has to know something about NSC–68, which is to say, Policy Paper Number 68 of the National Security Council. Few people outside a very select coterie in government have ever heard of it, much less seen it. But it is, according to Dean Acheson, "one of the great documents in our history," and its significance goes far beyond the Korean conflict.

The NSC was created under the National Defense Act of 1946 to provide a policy planning and advisory staff at the very pinnacle of government. It serves to focus at one spot, immediately under the President's hand and for his exclusive use, all that this government knows or can learn about conditions around the world affecting United States security, and the nation's capability for dealing with those conditions. Its purpose is not to grind out blueprints and directives but to evolve broad strategic concepts on which Presidential policies can be based. There might not have been a Pearl Harbor if FDR had had a National Security Council to guide him. There could hardly have been a NATO—or a Korean intervention—without it.

Late in January 1950, President Truman took the momentous step of authorizing a crash program to develop the hydrogen bomb, an infinitely more destructive weapon than the atomic bomb. As much as his decision to drop the first A-bomb over Hiroshima, this action confronted civilization with a potential choice between emancipation and extinction. And the odds on emancipation were not encouraging, considering such factors as Russia's recent mastery of nuclear energy, her growing might and continued belligerence toward the West, and the contrasting low state of defensive power in the free world. The total defense budget for the United States that year, for example, was a paltry $13 billion, which was little more than enough to maintain a standby Army, Navy, and Air Force thinly spread around the globe.

Mr. Truman had been driven to this penury in military spending by the persistent cry for "economy" welling up from Congress and much of the public as well. But on the same day that he authorized a long-shot exploration of the H-bomb, he put the NSC to work on a new comprehensive study of American defense and foreign policy in the light of world conditions as they then existed and as they might be expected to develop. The problem for which he sought an answer was not merely how many more soldiers, guns, and war planes we needed for our protection, but how to articulate and come to grips with one of the newest and most compelling political realities of the twentieth century: the inseparability of national security in its global aspect from the total web of government.

The study that was to become NSC–68 evolved through many weeks of labor by a handful of experts in the State and Defense Departments, the Central Intelligence Agency, the Atomic Energy Commission, and other branches of government. It was not a long paper, as such things go, but it was heavily documented with special studies and statistics. Its principal postulates and conclusions can be roughly summarized as follows:

Events since the end of World War II have created a new power relationship in the world which must be viewed not as a temporary distortion but as a long-range and fundamental realignment among nations. This has arisen out of two historical events: the Russian revolution and the growth of the Communist movement throughout the world; and the development of nuclear weapons with their capacity for unlimited destruction. The U.S. and the U.S.S.R. are the terminal poles of this new international axis.

Kremlin policy has three main objectives: (1) to preserve and to strengthen its position as the ideological and power center of the Communist world; (2) to extend and to consolidate that power by the acquisition of new satellites; and (3) to oppose and to weaken any competing system of power that threatens Communist world hegemony.

These objectives are inimical to American ideals, which are predicated on the concepts of freedom and human dignity. Our objectives in this context are set out nowhere better than in the Constitution: "to form a more perfect Union, establish Justice, insure domestic Tranquility, provide for the common defence, promote the general Welfare, and secure the Blessings of Liberty to ourselves and our Posterity."

It must be assumed that these concepts and objectives of American life will come under increasing attack. If they are to be protected, the nation must be determined, at whatever cost or sacrifice, to preserve at home and abroad those conditions of life in which these objectives can survive and prosper. We must seek to do this by peaceful means and with the cooperation of other like-minded peoples. But if peaceful means fail we must be willing and ready to fight.

Conceding the possibility of such a war, what are the relative capabilities of the U.S. and its probable allies, and the U.S.S.R. and its probable allies?

As a first consideration, Russia's progress in the development of atomic bombs probably means that an approximate stalemate in nuclear weapons will be reached by about 1954. The United States might extend its advantage for a few years longer if the hydrogen bomb should be perfected, but success in that effort is uncertain.

While the economic and productive capacity of the U.S.S.R. is markedly below that of the West, its potential for growth is great, and the Communist nations are striving more determinedly than the West to realize full potentials for growth.

In spite of these weaknesses, the Communist military capability for conventional, or nonatomic, warfare is now substantially superior to that of the West and is continuing to improve at a more rapid rate. This imbalance can be expected to continue for at least as long as it takes to achieve the economic rehabilitation of Western Europe and the full implementation of the NATO alliance.

Could the crisis between the two great powers be reduced through negotiation and particularly by mutual arms reduction? The prospects at present are poor, given the immutability of Soviet objectives and its advantage in military power. The West cannot abandon its efforts to negotiate, particularly to neutralize the threat of a nuclear holocaust,* but it must act in the realization that Stalin respects the reality of force a great deal more than he does the abstraction of peace.

Based on these premises, an indefinite period of tension and danger is foreseen for the United States and for the West—a period that should be defined less as a short-term crisis than as a permanent and fundamental alteration in the shape of international relations. To meet this new condition, four possible lines of action are open to the United States:

1. It can continue on its present course of reduced defense budgets and limited military capabilities, but without reducing its commitments to free-world security.

2. It can abandon these commitments, maintain its military capabilities at the present level, and withdraw behind the shield of a "fortress America."

3. It can attempt through "preventive war" a quick, violent but possibly more favorable redress in the world balance of power.

4. It can strike out on a bold and massive program of rebuilding the West's defensive potential to surpass that of the Soviet world, and of meeting each fresh challenge promptly and unequivocally. Such a program must have the United States at its political and material center with other free nations in variable orbits around it. The strength of such an alliance should be insurmountable as long as each of its members remains strong.

This fourth alternative is inescapably the preferred one. Its fulfillment calls for the United States to take the lead in a rapid and substantial

---

* It was August 1963 before the Nuclear Test Ban Treaty, the first meaningful international agreement in this field, was ratified by the United States, Great Britain, and the Soviet Union at a conference in Moscow.

buildup in the defensive power of the West, beginning "at the center" and radiating outward. This means virtual abandonment by the United States of trying to distinguish between national and global security. It also means the end of subordinating security needs to the traditional budgeting restrictions; of asking, "How much security can we afford?" In other words, security must henceforth become the dominant element in the national budget, and other elements must be accommodated to it.

The wealth potential of the country is such that as much as 20 percent of the gross national product can be devoted to security without causing national bankruptcy. This new concept of the security needs of the nation calls for annual appropriations of the order of $50 billion, or not much below the former wartime levels.[6]

President Truman initialed NSC–68 as "approved" in April, and it thereupon became official government policy. It was in the process of implementation when the crisis in Korea exploded.

NSC papers do not provide handy blueprints for action, and NSC–68 did not provide the President with a capsule formula for dealing with the Communist invasion of South Korea. What it did do was far more important: It provided what the diplomats like to call a "posture" from which it was possible for this government to react knowledgeably, confidently, and swiftly in a major crisis where delay and confusion almost certainly would be disastrous. It set up certain basic assumptions about the new world order and our role in it, and these assumptions served to indicate and to underpin the specific steps that had to be taken in Korea. Similarly, it provided a compelling rationale for perseverance in many other major aspects of our foreign policy, such as the Military Defense Assistance Program, which backed up the NATO alliance. And it is significant to note that, even as the nation focused its major energies on the fighting in Korea from 1950 to 1953, the arms buildup in Europe not only continued but was intensified.

What is perhaps most important to remember about NSC–68 is that it supplied the policy basis not only for what was *done* in Korea, but for much of what was *not done*. Paul Y. Hammond touches on this point succinctly in the following words:

Undoubtedly, much of what was done in the Korean buildup would have been done anyway. Yet the existence of NSC–68 at the outset of the war contributed a particular quality to that buildup.

From its beginning, and through its most frantic phases, *the Korean war remained only a part of the larger picture of the national strategy.* [Italics supplied.] For most people who knew anything about it, NSC–68 represented that larger picture.[7]

Paper Tiger with Claws

Six weeks of fighting—of slaughter and heartbreak—saw the American and South Korean forces chased into the Pusan perimeter, a 100- by 50-mile rectangle in the southeast corner of the peninsula. Heavily outnumbered and outgunned by the NKPA, the defenders, after the fall of Seoul, had been driven out of Chungju, across the Kum River, out of the provisional capital, Taejon, where the American 24th Division was nearly chewed to bits, through the steep passes of the Sobaek Mountains, and across the Naktong River. Here, at last, on the east bank of the Naktong, with their backs to the sea, the ROK and American forces were able to stabilize their lines in the first week of August and to hold the enemy at bay. Americans had fought on other and smaller beachheads in World War II—Anzio and Salerno, for example—but to many it looked as though Pusan might become the American Dunkirk.

Ground forces in Korea (United States and ROK) were under the command of Lieutenant General Walton H. Walker, the short-tempered and pugnacious commanding officer of the Eighth Army. As he pulled the gate shut on the Pusan perimeter on August 4, he had somewhere between 70,000 and 80,000 battered and weary frontline troops at his disposal: five ROK divisions, the 24th and 25th American Infantry Divisions, plus the 1st Cavalry and the 5th Regimental Combat Team, all of them severely understrength, and with no margins left over for reserves. The NKPA outnumbered Walker's forces by about two to one. While the North Koreans, initially at least, held an additional superiority in tanks and heavy artillery, the Americans had a near monopoly on air power.

But air power was not the decisive advantage it was cracked up to be, mainly because the Korean war was not the kind of war the Americans knew how to fight. American military doctrine, sharpened principally on the battlefields of Europe, was geared to "linear" strategy, where battlefronts and objectives were relatively well defined. It also relied heavily on wheels—motorized transport for everything from firepower to field rations. But the enemy in Korea knew or cared little about orthodox positional warfare. They fought in human waves who, when they met an obstacle, dissolved into guerrilla bands and flowed singly or in groups through the rice paddies and mountain trails to engulf their target from every direction. When the American planes shot up their supply columns on the open roads and trails, the North Koreans simply abandoned their trucks and disappeared into the brush, carrying their weapons and equipment by hand, each man a beast of burden as well as a fighter. Hard-muscled, uncomplaining under their harsh discipline, they could live for days on a pocketful of rice and cover incredible distances as stealthily as forest animals. American officers, in grudging admiration, compared them to the Indians of American frontier days. And because these tough, persistent little men seemed to be everywhere—invisible snipers by the hundreds picking men off as they went to the latrine or huddled together in machine-gun nests—they struck terror into the hearts of the green, bone-weary GI's. A graphic description of the agonies encountered by the American GI in Korea is given from firsthand experience by T. R. Fehrenbach in these words:

The hillsides of South Korea are steep; often slopes of 60 degrees are found on low ridges. Under the sullen sun, the ridges shimmered like furnaces, and there was almost no shade in the scrubby brush that covered them. And there is very little drinking water, outside the brownish stuff in the fecal paddies. . . .

When they left their trucks and moved up onto the hills and ridges, American soldiers, as one officer put it, "dropped like flies." Their legs, unused to hard pulls, gave out. The heat and the exertion gave them throbbing headaches. . . . Short of water, lacking water discipline, they drank from ditches and paddies, developed searing dysentery.

They sweated until their shirts and belts rotted, and their bellies turned shark-white. Salt tablets became such an item of priority that they had to be air-dropped on units, along with vital ammunition. . . . During these weeks [of July and August] exhaustion and heat knocked out more men than NKPA bullets.

American troops, physically unhardened for foot marches, were road-bound. They defended on roads, attacked on roads, retreated on roads. If their vehicles couldn't go, they did not go either. . . .

Every American fighting man, seeing the decimated, dirty, exhausted, weaponless 24th Division pushed back beyond Taejon could only say to himself: "There but for the grace of God go I."

For the 24th Division certainly was no weaker than the Army as a whole. The other divisions from Japan displayed the identical weaknesses as [they] were committed to action. None of them was equipped, trained, or mentally prepared for combat. For the first time in recent American history, American ground units had been committed during the initial days of a war; there had been no allies to hold the line while America prepared. . . .

The majority of the young men of the other divisions thrown into Korea were no more interested in being soldiers than the men of the 24th had been. They had enlisted for every reason known to man, except to fight. They had no real antagonism for the enemy . . . no understanding of their nation's position in the world. . . .

Soldiers fight from discipline and training, citizens from motivation and ideals. Lacking both, it is amazing that the American troops did even as well as they did."[8]

The Pusan perimeter, a 120-mile arc anchored on the Sea of Japan on the east and the Korea Strait on the south, gave the American forces a line they could defend according to the traditional methods of combat with which they were familiar. Though they were spread woefully thin and almost totally lacking in reserves, Walker's men and their ROK allies at last found some respite from the succession of defeats and retreats. Pusan was one of the best ports in Korea, with four large piers berthing up to forty ships simultaneously and with railroad sidings for the quick movement of cargoes. And now, during August, the supplies began to pour in, along with a trickle of reinforcements.

A New York *Times* correspondent wrote from the scene:

The outskirts of Pusan to a depth of 15 miles have become a vast arsenal and supply depot. Forty-five ton Pershing tanks with their 90-mm guns are arriving in quantity. So are the big 155-mm howitzers. There is plenty of oil, fuel, and motor transport. There are supplies for a winter campaign—tents, heaters, sleeping bags, and cold weather clothing.

During the early days of August, the Eighth Army was reinforced by the arrival from the States of the 2nd Infantry Division and the 1st Marine Brigade, the latter in particular heavily seasoned with battle-wise veterans of Guadalcanal and Okinawa. Two thousand British riflemen, the 27th Brigade, arrived from Hong Kong and went immediately into the line.

Meanwhile, President Truman, pressing partial mobilization through Congress, had authorized a call-up of Organized Reserves and some National Guard units. Draft quotas were being stepped up, as were recruiting drives in all three services, with the objective of adding 600,000 men in uniform in the shortest possible time. There was little resistance to these measures, for American pride had been shocked by the Korean debacle.

A budding American confidence was expressed by General Walker in mid-August when he told a reporter: "The battle is not finished, but I am pretty sure now we will hold the beachhead we need." This confidence was matched by a growing desperation on the part of the NKPA, whose whole strategy had been built on a furious, headlong sweep down the length of the Korean Peninsula, pushing the ROK enemy ahead of them and into the sea before effective aid from the outside could arrive. The NKPA had not planned on a stalemate, nor on maintaining long lines of supply from their Chinese Communist allies, 500 miles away in Manchuria. But now they were stalemated at the Naktong, and were being harassed ever more furiously at their rear and along their tenuous lines of communication by American air fighters and bombers spraying them with machine-gun bullets, explosives, and napalm.

In a desperate last-ditch effort to retrieve their strategy, they hurled themselves at one part of the line after another, sometimes in suicidal assault waves, sometimes in stealthy infiltrations under the cover of night. They drove the defenders' line inward along the northern edge of the perimeter, and took the port at Pohang. Late in August the NKPA made their most determined drive of the war up to that time in an effort to take Taegu, the temporary capital lying just within the perimeter 55 miles northwest of Pusan. They punched through the defenders' line opposite the city and put 10,000 of their best troops on the east bank of the Naktong and drove to within 13 miles of Taegu before General Walker's men could stop them. For two weeks the Battle of the Naktong Bulge raged indecisively, with the American 1st Cavalry (motorized) taking the brunt of the punishment on a 35-mile line directly in front of Taegu.

But the NKPA was losing some of its punch. Its supply lines, under relentless air attack, were running dry. It had suffered heavy casualties, and replacements were being conscripted at bayonet point from the untrained and unwilling South Korean peasantry. And the buildup in American tanks and artillery had robbed the invaders of their early advantage in firepower. By the end of the first week in September, the threat to Taegu had eased, and it was clear that the Americans and South Koreans would hold their vital beach-head.

Then, in the early morning of Friday, September 15, came one of the most daring and dazzling exploits of the entire war: The 1st Marine Division, which had sailed secretly from San Francisco two weeks earlier, stormed ashore at Inchon, 150 miles in the enemy's rear. They were backed up by 262 ships of Task Force 77, which laid down a terrific covering of fire and aerial bombardment. Simultaneously the Eighth Army opened a slashing offensive above Taegu to break out of its beachhead.

MacArthur's grand strategy, to cut the enemy's lines in two and to seal him off from his source of supply, was at work. General Walker told his weary but exultant veterans: "Our days of purgatory have ended and we will pass to the offensive."

In ten days Seoul had been retaken, and the infantry from the Pusan beachhead had driven along a narrow corridor to link up with the Marines' beachhead at Inchon. By the end of September, UN forces were in control of the whole Korean Peninsula south of the 38th parallel. The NKPA, fleeing northward, was as disorganized and shattered as the American and ROK forces had been two months earlier.

All America exulted over the brilliant success of the Inchon maneuver. The nation's faith in its virility was restored, and it now looked certain that our crusade for South Korean freedom had been vindicated. The President sent MacArthur a note of extravagant praise:

I know that I speak for the entire American people when I send you my warmest congratulations on the victory that has been achieved under your leadership in Korea. . . . My thanks and the thanks of the people of all free nations go out to your gallant forces. I salute you all, and say to all of you from all of us at home, "Well and nobly done."

Surely, now the enemy had been contained and the end was in sight.

CHAPTER 12

◇◇◇◇◇◇◇◇◇◇◇◇◇◇◇◇◇◇◇◇◇◇◇◇◇◇◇

The President and the General

A Meeting at the Summit

THERE WERE two fronts in the Korean war—a military one between the forces of the United Nations and the Communist aggressors, and a political one between the President of the United States and his most colorful and headstrong General, Douglas MacArthur, headman of a disappearing military aristocracy and Commander of all forces in the Far East. Neither conflict went its full course. In the long run, however, the advantage in both conflicts came down on the side of the angels: the free world showed its willingness to fight to stay free, and the institution of the United States Presidency gained new stature and dignity. It is with the second, or political, aspect of the war that this chapter is principally concerned.

Even on what appeared to be the eve of victory, Washington was still concerned lest the embers of the Korean war be fanned into new life and spreading violence. There was apprehension over what the Chinese might do if the fighting approached too close to the borders of Manchuria. And the Russians? Their city of Vladivostok lay only 40 miles beyond the eastern tip of Korea; they might well become alarmed, too. The Joint Chiefs of Staff (JCS) urged caution on their Far Eastern Commander. Harass the fleeing enemy on his home territory beyond the 38th parallel, they told him, but do nothing to invite intervention from his Chinese or Russian allies beyond the Yalu River. The JCS recommended, in fact, that he establish his base line on Pyongyang-Wonson, about 120 miles above Seoul, and leave any adventures beyond that point to the ROK forces exclusively.

Washington was not at all certain that MacArthur saw eye to eye with his civilian chiefs on just why the United States was fighting in Korea or what its ultimate objective was. A war to *contain* an aggressor rather than to *destroy* him; a war of *limited objectives* against a secondary enemy to avoid *unlimited war* against a primary enemy—these concepts, it was feared, simply were not in the proud and arrogant old soldier's book.*

Douglas MacArthur's vanity and his manifest ability as a soldier (he wore five stars on his shoulder boards) had long made him a sort of semiautonomous power within the governmental structure. From Bataan to Tokyo he had shown something of a regal proconsul's disdain for the authority of the central bureaucracy in Washington. This heady independence had lately been reinforced as a powerful group of Republican politicians in the States had vested him as the shining symbol of their opposition to President Truman. Douglas MacArthur—handsome, arrogant, supremely self-assured— had not set foot in the United States in fourteen years. He had

* The General addressed himself rather directly to this point in the following colloquy during the Senate investigation of his recall in May 1951:

SENATOR SALTONSTALL. Now on April 15, the Assistant Secretary of State, Dean Rusk, in a television broadcast, stated in part: "What we are trying to do is to maintain peace and security without a general war. We are saying to the aggressors, 'You will not be allowed to get away with your crime. You must stop it.' At the same time we are trying to prevent a general conflagration which would consume the very things we are now trying to defend."
I would appreciate it very much, with your knowledge of the Far East, if you would give me your opinion of that statement.
GENERAL MACARTHUR. That policy, as you have read it, seems to me to introduce a new concept into military operations—the concept of appeasement, the concept that when you use force, you can limit the force.
The concept that I have is that when you go into war, you have exhausted all other potentialities of bringing the disagreements to an end.
As I understand what you have read, that we would apply to the military situation in Korea certain military appeasements; that is, that we would not use our Air Force to the maximum extent, that we would not use our navy except along the border lines of Korea . . .
If that is the concept of a continued and indefinite campaign in Korea, with no definite purpose of stopping it until the enemy gets tired or you yield to his terms, I think that introduces into the military sphere a political control such as I have not known in my life or have ever studied.—"Military Situations in the Far East," Hearings of the Committees on Armed Services and Foreign Relations, U.S. Senate, May-June, 1951. Part I, pp. 39-40.

acquired a hero's image of Olympian proportions, and he would be the last man to question its validity. Nor did he suffer lightly those who questioned his wisdom about that part of the world he had staked out as his own, the Far East.

Washington's anxiety about MacArthur suffered a fresh twinge late in July when he went to Formosa to check on the Nationalists' ability to defend themselves against a possible Communist attack from the mainland. His warm praise of Chiang and his subtly expressed displeasure over the "leashing" of the Generalissimo by the 7th Fleet sent shudders through the policy levels of Washington. Chiang was regarded as a heavy liability, and his eagerness to have the United States underwrite his ambition to retake the mainland was viewed with all the sympathy of a hot time bomb. Washington wanted nothing so much at the time as to keep Chiang quiet and to keep quiet about Chiang.

Clearly, MacArthur needed to be put straight on what the United States was up to, not only in Korea, but in the world at large. On August 3 the President sent out Averell Harriman as his missionary to the Far Eastern Commander. Harriman was graciously received. He and the General conferred for more than eight hours in two days' time. He talked with many members of MacArthur's staff and made a quick inspection trip to Korea. Then he flew home, in a state of puzzled uneasiness.

In his report to the President, Harriman said that the General had expressed full approval of the decision to intervene in Korea, that he was convinced that he would ultimately be able to destroy the North Korean forces, and that he foresaw no likelihood that either Communist China or Russia would pitch in directly to help the NKPA. But MacArthur was not happy about Washington's attitude toward Chiang Kai-shek as a potential ally, and Harriman had gone to considerable lengths to try to elucidate this policy for the General —without much success, as he said in his report to the President:

"For reasons which are difficult to explain, I did not feel that we came to a full agreement on the way we believed things should be handled on Formosa and with the Generalissimo. He accepted the President's position and will act accordingly, but without full conviction. He has a strange idea that we should back anybody who will fight communism."[1]

The President was reassured, or so he said. He told a press conference after Harriman's return that he and General MacArthur saw "eye to eye" on Formosa, and, it was assumed, on other basic problems of foreign policy as well. His reassurance did not last two weeks.

On August 26 the news wires carried the text of a message MacArthur had addressed to the annual encampment of the Veterans of Foreign Wars, describing what was, in the view of the State Department, a new foreign policy for the whole of the Pacific. It delineated a proposed United States defense line stretching from Vladivostok to Singapore, which, properly protected with United States air, naval, and ground forces, would make the Pacific "a peaceful lake." He wound up by decrying as "appeasement" the "fallacious and threadbare argument" that to encourage the Chinese in Formosa would endanger our status in the rest of Asia. This was a poorly concealed slap at the administration's established policy of keeping Chiang under wraps.

President Truman was in "a cold anger" when he read this statement, according to one official who was summoned to an emergency conference at the White House the next morning. With his Secretaries of State and Defense and the members of the Joint Chiefs of Staff around him, the President asked each in turn, like a schoolmaster, if he had any advance knowledge of the MacArthur statement. Each replied that he had not. Then, turning to Secretary of Defense Louis Johnson he said:

"I want this message withdrawn, and I want you to send an order to MacArthur to withdraw it and tell him it is an order from me. Do you understand that?"

"Yes, sir," answered the Secretary.

The MacArthur statement was, of course, already in all the papers. The General was nevertheless obliged to "recall" it.

Mr. Truman records in his memoirs that he contemplated at this time relieving MacArthur of his Korean command and leaving him only the responsibility for the Japanese occupation. The hard feelings engendered by the VFW episode were, however, soon erased by the exciting happenings at Inchon and the victorious march of the UN forces back toward the 38th parallel. But when operations began to go north of the parallel, and when the first intelligence reports came in, early in October, of the massing of Chinese troops on the Manchurian border, the President's anxiety about his headstrong field commander again came to the surface. He decided he had better have a face-to-face talk with MacArthur. In later years he gave these reasons:

The first and simplest reason why I wanted to meet with General MacArthur was that we had never had any personal contacts at all, and I thought that he ought to know his Commander in Chief and that I ought to know the senior field commander in the Far East.

Events since June had shown me that MacArthur had lost some of his contacts with the country and its people in the many years of his absence. I had made efforts through Harriman and others to let him see the world-wide picture as we saw it in Washington, but I felt that we had had little success.

The Peiping reports of threatened intervention in Korea by the Chinese Communists were another reason for my desire to confer with General MacArthur. I wanted to get the benefit of his firsthand information and judgment.[2]

It is probably true, as some Republicans charged at the time, that Mr. Truman had a lesser and concealed motive—namely, that he wanted, for personal political reasons, to warm up his own image within the radiant MacArthurian nimbus. He was having political problems aplenty on the domestic front at the time, and the Democrats were in the midst of a tough congressional election campaign. Even in going two-thirds of the way around the world for a "summit" with his Far Eastern Commander (Truman would travel 4,700 ocean miles from San Francisco, MacArthur only 1,900 from Tokyo), the President could blamelessly redress the suspected distortion in public opinion about who was boss.

The historic meeting at Wake Island, a lonely dot of land in the far Pacific, occurred in the early daylight hours of Sunday, October 15. The President was accompanied by Dean Rusk, Averell Harriman, Chairman Omar Bradley of the Joint Chiefs of Staff, and a handful of aides and reporters. In MacArthur's party were his principal aide, Brigadier General Courtney Whitney, Admiral Arthur W. Radford, commander of the Pacific Fleet, and Ambassador Muccio.

Major General Chester V. Clifton (at the time of the Wake Island meeting he was a Colonel and the principal aide to General Bradley) recalls that there was some uneasiness in the President's party about the attitude MacArthur would display toward his Commander in Chief. To avoid any confusions in protocol, the pilot was instructed to make sure that MacArthur's plane was already on the ground before he brought the President's plane in for a landing. This he did, but as the latter taxied up the runway toward the operations building where the welcoming party was waiting, anxious eyes on board scanned the group in vain for MacArthur. Was the haughty General about to demean his chief by not walking out to greet him?

The engines stopped, a landing platform was wheeled out, and
the door of the plane was thrown open. Still no MacArthur.

Mr. Truman, General Clifton recalls, sat glued to his seat, his
mouth drawn in a tight, angry line. "I'm not going to walk out there
and be insulted," he said grimly.

There was a tense and paralyzing interval aboard the Presidential
plane when no one spoke or moved. Then they saw the door of the
operations building open, and the unmistakable figure of MacArthur
—the rakish cap, the dark sunglasses, the open-collar shirt, all made
familiar in hundreds of newspaper and magazine photographs—
came striding out to the foot of the landing platform.

"Not until that moment," General Clifton has said, "did President
Truman leave his seat. He just wasn't going out to be downgraded
by one of his Generals."[3]

The actual greeting between the two principals thereafter was
cordial enough, according to eyewitnesses, and they climbed into
the back seat of a dilapidated Chevrolet for the short drive to the
squat cinder-block building, headquarters for a Civil Aeronautics
outpost, where the conference was to be held.

Actually, there was little of great strategical importance that
came out of the Wake Island conference. Its principal interest lies in
the evidentiary grist it supplied six months later in the howling
controversy over the General's dismissal.

The actual conference was in two parts. First, the President and
MacArthur shut themselves in a small room alone for an hour's face-
to-face dialogue. Later, the entire group sat for another couple of
hours around a long conference table improvised by shoving five
smaller tables together. The tropic sun beat down on the building,
which was not air-conditioned, and the conferees sat in their shirt-
sleeves. There was no formal agenda. The President conducted the
meeting from penciled notes he had jotted on a tablet during the
last hour of his flight from Honolulu. Most of the discussion consisted of questions addressed to the General and his responses.
There was little time given to the details of the fighting in Korea, for
in everyone's mind that was virtually a closed book with the
promise of a happy ending. Most of the talk centered around plans
for Korea's postwar rehabilitation, the perfection of a Japanese
peace treaty, and the broad problems of the Pacific area. There were
also mutual congratulations.

MacArthur said he expected the fighting to be substantially over
by Thanksgiving. He planned to have the Eighth Army back in
Japan by Christmas and told General Bradley he probably would be

able to release the 2nd Division for reassignment to Europe in January.

He thought there was very little prospect of Chinese or Soviet intervention. If they had come in during the first couple of months, he said, their interference might have been decisive, but now it was too late for them to affect things. "We are no longer standing hat in hand," he said.

His intelligence showed, MacArthur said, about 300,000 Chinese troops in Manchuria, of whom not more than 135,000 were distributed along the Yalu River. Under the best of circumstances, he said, not more than 50,000 to 60,000 of these troops could be got across the river for offensive operations, since the Chinese had no air power to give them protection. (Even as the General spoke, and completely unknown to him and his G-2, 120,000 men of the Chinese Communist Fourth Field Army had already crossed the Yalu under cover of darkness and had secreted themselves in the barren wastes of the North Korean hills. Others, with their Russian-made tanks and artillery, were crossing nightly.)

The General said he favored moving all non-Korean troops out of Korea as soon as possible. The greatest calamity in Asia, he said, would be for the Korean people to turn against their defenders because of some friction between the UN and the Rhee government.

Asked what additional assistance he needed from Washington, MacArthur said: "No commander in the history of war has ever had more complete and adequate support from all agencies in Washington than I have."*

There is less certainty about what went on in the first half of the conference—the private confrontation between the President and the General. Did the Commander in Chief take his subordinate "to the woodshed," as he had done five years earlier with a balky Secretary of State, Jimmy Byrnes? No one knows for certain. In his memoirs, Mr. Truman says only that, during their private talk, it was MacArthur who brought up the subject of his statement about Formosa to the Veterans of Foreign Wars, adding:

* The minutes of this conference were put together a day later by General Bradley from a partial stenographic transcript and from notes which he and some other participants made. They were kept under a top secret classification until they were published in an exclusive dispatch by Anthony Leviero, White House correspondent for the New York *Times*, on April 21, 1951, a piece of journalistic enterprise which was to earn him a Pulitzer prize. The minutes were formally declassified a few weeks later during the course of the Senate investigation into General MacArthur's recall. The General claimed not to know of their existence, although a member of his staff had signed a receipt for a copy of the transcript at the Tokyo headquarters. However, he did not dispute the general accuracy of this report.

He [MacArthur] said he was sorry if it caused any embarrassment. I told him I considered the incident closed. He said he wanted me to understand that he was not in politics in any way—that he had allowed the politicians to make a "chump" (his word) of him in 1948 and that it would not happen again. . . . I told him something of our plans for strengthening Europe. . . . Our conversation was very friendly—I might say, much more so than I had expected.[4]

In the full conference that followed, the President told the group: "General MacArthur and I have talked fully about Formosa. There is no need to cover that subject again. The General and I are in full agreement."

Six months later, however, MacArthur told the Senate committee that the subject of Formosa never came up in the discussions at Wake Island.

At all events, the whole show at the mid-Pacific "summit" was over by midmorning. A bland, uninformative communiqué initialed by both Truman and MacArthur, as though they were the sovereigns of separate powers, was issued. The President told the reporters who had traveled with him: "I've never had a more satisfactory conference since I've been President." While the General, with what some thought to be graciousness touched with acerbity, for his part said: "All the comments will have to come from the publicity man for the President." Well before noon, the principals had taken off for their separate destinations, Truman for Honolulu and MacArthur for Tokyo.

"President Truman," Anthony Leviero said in the next morning's New York *Times*, "left Wake Island highly pleased with the results, like an insurance salesman who has at last signed up an important prospect, while the latter [MacArthur] appeared dubious over the extent of the coverage."

In truth, of course, not much of anything had been settled between these two strong and stubborn men.

Strategic Backfire

Even before the Wake Island meeting, an ominous storm warning had been run up in Peiping, which both the Far Eastern Commander and his superiors in Washington had failed to read correctly. The Chinese Foreign Minister, Chou En-lai, on October 1, called in the Indian Ambassador, Sardar Panikkar, and gravely told him that the Chinese People's Republic would enter the war on the side of the North Koreans if United Nations forces carried their new offensive beyond the 38th parallel into North Korean territory. There were no diplomatic ambiguities in Chou's language. He made himself unmistakably clear. Panikkar flashed the warning to New Delhi, and from there it went to all the capitals of the world, including Washington. A week later, Chou En-lai repeated his threat over the official government radio for all the world to hear.

But to General Willoughby, MacArthur's intelligence chief, the threat lacked substance. He characterized it as being "probably in a category of diplomatic blackmail."[5] He reasoned that with a final victory for the UN over the NKPA so palpably near, and the obvious ability of the Air Force to smash any sizable Chinese crossing of the Yalu, Chou could only be talking for propaganda purposes. MacArthur accepted Willoughby's interpretation. And, since he was the man on the scene and they were 16,000 miles away, the men in the Pentagon* and the State Department accepted it too. Chou En-lai's bluster could not disturb the euphoric confidence that prevailed at Wake.

On his return to Tokyo, MacArthur began to plan his great final offensive that would make good his promise to "have the boys home by Christmas." It was envisioned as a swift mopping up of the dispersed and disorganized elements of the NKPA, who had retreated into the central mountain ranges of North Korea and the plains of the Yalu Valley. It was predicated on the assumption that the Soviet Union had decided not to intervene and that the Chinese Communists would not dare to.

MacArthur's plan was for a giant pincer movement that would pin the enemy in a pocket against the Yalu barrier, where he would either have to surrender or flee into Manchuria. The Eighth Army, moving north from the vicinity of Pyongyang, would be the western arm of this pincer. The eastern arm was to be the X Corps, shifted by sea from Inchon around the peninsula to Wonsan, with the main elements of the ROK Army moving up the center and also lending support to the X Corps. There was an element of desperation and rashness in this plan about which military men will long argue, for MacArthur detached the X Corps from General Walker's overall command and placed it under GHQ, Tokyo. In

---

* General George C. Marshall had replaced Louis Johnson as Secretary of Defense in September 1950.

addition, he left these two halves of his army, still understrength and lacking adequate reserves, virtually cut off from each other by the treacherous and almost trackless mountain terrain of north central Korea. The few roads were little more than vague dirt trails winding through the steep hills and dark gorges of the north-south mountain ranges, with no lateral connections between them. It was impossible terrain for a motorized Western army, but very nearly ideal for Asiatic guerrillas. T. R. Fehrenbach writes:

What the UN did, it did in the light of the restricting terrain and in the view, in late October, that no real enemy opposed it. And above all else it was the terrain and a complete failure of intelligence that brought disaster. Marching northward, the UN trumpeted to the world its composition, its battle plans and even the hour of its execution.

Without effort the enemy knew everything there was to know about the UN forces. The UN, in turn, never knew the enemy existed—until it was much too late.[6]

By the end of October there were already more than a quarter million battle-hardened Chinese Communist soldiers spread out in invisible clusters in the paths of the oncoming "liberators." Unencumbered by heavy equipment and motor transport, the hordes of harshly disciplined and stout-legged peasant soldiers moved silently by night and disappeared by day into the mountain crags and hollows where they could watch, but never be seen by, the endless flights of American reconnaissance planes with their modern cameras.

MacArthur advised the Joint Chiefs on October 24 that he was moving out from the Pyongyang-Wonsan line on his final sweep to the north. A dozen spearheads of the Eighth Army and X Corps probed toward the Chongchen River, in the northwest, and the Changjin Reservoir in the northeast in the first development of the pincers plan. For the first week the UN forces met little opposition, but their advance was a crawl over the difficult terrain, with their supply lines steadily growing more tenuous. Here and there in patrol clashes, the UN forces picked up prisoners who were unmistakably Chinese, but it was improbable, in the view of GHQ, that these "volunteers" were present in sufficient numbers to affect the outcome.

Then, on November 1, a U.S. Cavalry battalion that had worked its way across the Chongchen suddenly found itself enveloped in murderous rifle and machine-gun fire and swarmed over by screaming Chinese soldiers from every direction. At almost the same time, an ROK division on their right and a Marine battalion with the X Corps far to the east were similarly engaged. The fighting waged furiously for four days, then ceased as suddenly as it had begun. The attackers simply dissolved into the hills. But the UN forces had suffered heavy losses and a severe psychological shock. There now was no question but that their attackers had been, not Chinese "volunteers," but professional Chinese soldiers in organized units.

On November 6, an alarmed MacArthur messaged the Joint Chiefs that men and matériel were pouring over all bridges of the Yalu from Manchuria in such numbers as to threaten the destruction of the forces under his command. He asked immediate authority to bomb these bridges and other installations in the "north area" supporting the enemy. The previous restrictions against bombing within five miles of the Yalu, he said, would have "disastrous effects" if not lifted immediately. He still was not convinced, he told the Chiefs, that this presaged a full-scale commitment by the Chinese Communists, but it did greatly enhance such a possibility. At his Tokyo headquarters that same day he issued a communiqué saying that his forces were now faced by a new and fresh army backed up with substantial supplies and reserves—"one of the most offensive acts of international lawlessness ever known in history."

Permission to bomb the Yalu bridges was promptly forthcoming from Washington, but it was coupled with a repeated reminder to avoid targets inside Manchuria and, in particular, the Yalu dam and power installations. "Because of the necessity of maintaining optimum position with United Nations policy and directives," MacArthur's instructions from the Joint Chiefs read, "and because it is vital in the national interest of the United States to localize the fighting in Korea, it is important that extreme care be taken to avoid violation of Manchurian territory and airspace."

After this first Chinese feint there was a long lull that lent credence to General Willoughby's contention that the Communists were engaged in diplomatic blackmail instead of serious warfare. The two halves of the UN army solidified their respective positions above the Chongchon River, on the western front, and the Changjin-Chosin Reservoir, on the east, roughly some 50 miles south of the Manchurian border. Some 200,000 UN and ROK troops were in the line or in reserve; supply lines had been strengthened; the Air Force roamed the skies at will, without seeing anything suspicious south of the Yalu River to bomb; and elements of the 7th Fleet stood offshore near Hungnam, in the Sea of Japan. With considerable fanfare, turkey was served for Thanksgiving dinner at even the forward UN troop positions, and the talk of "home by Christmas" revived.

On November 24, MacArthur flew to Korea and announced the immediate jump-off of a final offensive to end the war. His official communiqué on that day read:

The United Nations massive compression envelopment in North Korea against new Red Armies operating there is now approaching its decisive effort. Our air forces of all types have for the past three weeks, in a sustained attack of model coordination and effectiveness, successfully interdicted enemy lines of support from the north so that further reinforcement therefrom has been sharply curtailed. The eastern sector of our pincer . . . has now reached commanding enveloping position, cutting in two the northern reaches of the enemy's geographical potential. This morning, the western sector of the pincer moves forward in general assault in an effort to complete the compression and close the vise. If successful, this should for all practical purposes end the war. . . . [7]

More than 300,000 Chinese troops lay in wait for the UN advance. On the 25th they struck with devastating fury, first upon elements of the ROK II Corps in the central mountain ranges, near Tekchen, whom they virtually demolished, and then against the United States 24th Division at Unsan, on the west, driving it back across the Chongchon River. On the X Corps's east front, the 1st Marine Division in the hills near the Chosin Reservoir bore the brunt of this opening assault and by nightfall were hopelessly surrounded, 50 miles away from their base at Hungnam. The UN forces were not only caught by surprise but were outnumbered almost two to one by a tough, well-trained enemy thoroughly skilled in fluid guerrilla warfare—the only kind of warfare that can win in the climate and topography of northern Korea.

By the 28th, General Walker realized his Eighth Army had but two choices—annihilation or retreat—and he chose retreat. General Almond, on the western front, faced a similar dilemma, and he began pulling back toward his Hungnam beachhead. MacArthur was not exaggerating when he sent an urgent communiqué to the United Nations that day, saying, "We face an entirely new war." By the end of the first week in December, the main line of UN resistance had been pushed back to within 50 miles of the 38th parallel on the western and central fronts, while in the west the X Corps, with the 1st Marine Division still cut off in the area of the Chosin Reservoir, was pinned in a narrow pocket around Hungnam. On December 3, MacArthur told the Chiefs of Staff that his forces were severely depleted and near exhaustion and that he was attempting a withdrawal to the vicinity of Seoul. He said:

This small command is facing the entire Chinese Nation in an undeclared war. Unless some positive and immediate action is taken, hope for success cannot be justified, and steady attrition leading to final destruction can reasonably be contemplated. . . . The general evaluation of the situation here must be viewed on the basis of an entirely new war against an entirely new power of great military strength and under entirely new conditions. . . .

The strategic concept suitable for operations against the North Korean Army, which was so successful, is not susceptible to continued application against such a power. This calls for political decisions and strategic plans in implementation thereof adequate fully to meet the realities involved.[8]

What MacArthur was saying, of course, was "Unleash me. Let me send my bombers streaking into the privileged sanctuary of Manchuria to destroy the enemy's bases of supply. Give me the men, the guns, the ships—above all, give me free rein—to smash the enemy, whoever and wherever he may be!" His desperation was and is understandable. He was the first great commander to be handcuffed by a new military concept: a limited war for limited goals. He either would not or could not accept that limitation, but Washington did.

By mid-December the Eighth Army had pulled back to a line a few miles south of the 38th parallel, and main elements of the X Corps were being evacuated by sea from Hungnam. The American press, or most of it, depicted the events of the preceding three weeks as one of the great military disasters of all time—"the worst the United States ever suffered," according to *Time* magazine. Public opinion, at home and around the world, seemed to be numbed by this second melancholy demonstration of Western weakness and Asian might.

General MacArthur, in his public statements, went to the other extreme by minimizing his reversal and calling it "a tactical withdrawal" that had been accomplished "in a superior manner." His November offensive in the first place, he said, had been no more than a "reconnaissance in force" to make the enemy show his hand. But this explanation is hard to take in the light of his buoyant declaration on November 24 that his "massive compression envelopment against new Red armies operating in North Korea is now approaching its decisive effort. . . . *If successful, this effort should for all practical purposes end the war.*" (Italics supplied.)

In actuality, of course, this defeat of the UN forces was neither as devastating as some reports described it at the time, nor as trivial as the General tried to make it appear. Both the Eighth Army and the X Corps got out of their traps in relatively good shape, all things considered. But they had failed woefully in their objective. The Chinese Communists achieved a brilliant strategy of deception, and MacArthur was ingloriously routed because he underrated the enemy and did not know what they were up to.

These early weeks of December were a period of desperate reappraisal in Washington of the whole Korean involvement. President Truman met almost daily with his chief advisers from the State Department and the Pentagon, his so-called "war cabinet." The National Security Council was called into emergency session every two or three days. The telecom circuits to Tokyo were chattering around the clock. There was a constant stream of anxious messages to and from officials of the United Nations.

A glaring new truth had to be faced: This country's bold attempt to enforce a political settlement in Korea by arms had been frustrated, probably for good, by the intervention of the Chinese Communists. We were in a war we could not win and could not walk away from, but neither could we afford to lose it. The hard question for Mr. Truman was, "What do we do now?"

Washington was still gripped by the fear that the Soviets were using the North Korean aggression as a diversion for a thrust in some other part of the world, most likely Europe. The Joint Chiefs of Staff were unanimous in their judgment that we simply could not risk draining our defenses at home and in Europe to meet MacArthur's ambition for an all-out counteroffensive against the Chinese. They strongly suspected that a giant trap was being laid to lead us into the endless reaches of mainland China and a hopeless war of attrition against the four hundred million Chinese people.

Another factor with which Washington had to contend, but which MacArthur seemed to ignore, was the necessity of preserving the support of the United Nations. On the one hand, the UN provided the shield of political respectability that justified our military presence in Korea. On the other hand, the UN had become a prisoner of United States policy in Korea. MacArthur's thrust across the 38th parallel and on toward the Manchurian border sent chills of apprehension through the United Nations headquarters that this country might indeed, by intention or by accident, be about to commit the international body to a cataclysmic ideological war. The consensus of world opinion, which had supported the United States in its swift move against a simple act of aggression by the North Koreans, was now in danger of reversing itself.

Mr. Truman added immeasurably to this apprehension when, in a press conference on November 30, he implied both that the atomic bomb might be used against the Chinese and that the decision to use it would be up to the commander in the field, General MacArthur. It was one of those "shoot from the hip" answers to a question for which the President was not properly prepared. His press office quickly issued a clarifying statement. What the President meant, it said, was that "the use of any weapon is always implicit in the possession of that weapon," but the authority to use the A-bomb can, by law, be given only by the President, "and no such authorization has been given." But the President's reassurances were a long time catching up with the shock waves of his earlier words. The NATO allies, as well as the member states of the UN, were alarmed, and Prime Minister Attlee hurried over from London the next day for a face-to-face talk with President Truman.

No forward-moving strategy was possible in the face of the military set back and the policy confusion of the moment. On December 3, the Joint Chiefs told MacArthur, in effect, that since he could not *win* he should do his best to *hold.* "We consider that the preservation of your forces is now the primary consideration. Consolidation of forces into beachheads is concurred in." This would have to do until some way out of the hateful dilemma showed itself.

"The Buck Stops Here"

It was in the midst of this painful impasse that MacArthur returned to the political offensive against his superiors in Washington. He suddenly became highly accessible at his Tokyo headquarters for personal and cabled interviews with members of the press. In response to a long inquiry from the editors of *United States News and World Report* during the first week in December, he attributed his difficulties in Korea to "the extraordinary inhibitions . . . without precedent in military history" which denied him the opportunity to carry the war into the "privileged sanctuary" of the enemy. To Hugh Baillie, president of the United Press, he addressed a long and

subtly critical dissertation on the UN's strategic policy in the Far
East, saying that the existing situation "results largely from the acceptance of military odds without precedent in history—the odds of
permitting offensive action without defensive retaliation."*

These extraordinary comments from a field commander reached
the White House and the Pentagon by way of the public press. "I
should have fired MacArthur then and there," Mr. Truman said
later. And the only reason he didn't, he added, was that he did not
want it to appear that the General was being punished because of
the failure of his offensive. Instead, on December 6, Truman had the
Joint Chiefs of Staff send directly to MacArthur a new directive (ap-
plicable to all military officers overseas) instructing him that "no
speech, press release, or public statement" should henceforth be
issued in respect to foreign policy unless first cleared with the Department of State, or, in the case of military policy, with the Department of Defense.

"Every second lieutenant knows best what his platoon ought to
be given to do," the former artillery captain sitting in the White
House said later. "He thinks the higher-ups are just blind when they
don't see things his way. But General MacArthur—and rightly too—
would have court-martialed any second lieutenant who gave press
interviews to express his disagreement."

Four corollary developments during this tense December should
be noted at this point in order to keep the events in Korea in proper
perspective:

1. President Truman pressed Congress to increase defense appropriations to approximately $50 billion, stating that it was just as
urgent to build up the defenses of the NATO allies as it was to
block Communist aggression in the Far East. Six months earlier, the
level (exclusive of MDAP) had been on the order of $13.5 billion.

2. On December 15, he declared a national emergency which allowed for a rapid buildup in military manpower to a projected level
of about 3,500,000 (it stood at approximately 2,300,000 at the

---

* General MacArthur is said to have believed that he was victimized by a
Washington-based espionage plot that fed information on UN strategy to the enemy.
Specifically, according to his G-2 chief, General Willoughby, the Reds knew before
he did that their "privileged sanctuary" behind the Yalu would be respected. "That
the Red Chinese commander apparently knew such a decision would be forthcoming
while General MacArthur did not, represents one of the blackest pages ever recorded." (Willoughby, *MacArthur, 1941-1951*, p. 383.) This assertion seems rather
farfetched in the light of the many communications between the Far Eastern Commander and the JCS made public during the Senate hearings in 1951.

time), and the resumption of certain wartime controls. He made it plain, however, that his goal was something less than all-out mobilization. The papers described it as moving the country "into second speed, not high gear."

3. The UN General Assembly adopted a resolution designed to seek a cease-fire in the Korean conflict. The proposal was rejected by a Chinese Communist delegation especially invited to Lake Success to discuss it. But a cease-fire now became the dominant goal in UN policy in spite of the Chinese rejection.

4. Republicans in the House and Senate, by a substantial vote, asked the President to fire Dean Acheson as his Secretary of State because "he had lost the confidence of the country." This reflected the bitter partisanship that had developed not only over the frustrating course of events in Korea, but over the rising hysteria created by Senator Joseph McCarthy's hunt for Communists in the government. President Truman refused even to consider the Republican demand.

The gulf of misunderstanding—or of nonaccommodation— between MacArthur and his chiefs in Washington continued to widen. To the temperamental Far Eastern Commander it seemed that his genius as a soldier and a maker of history was being hampered by small-minded civilians half a world away from the scene of conflict, whose strategic vision was clouded by petty and irrelevant political considerations. His communications to them were heavy with grandiose language that carried subtle barbs of disdain. To President Truman, to Secretaries Acheson and Marshall, and even to MacArthur's old comrades in arms on the Joint Chiefs of Staff, it seemed that the hero of Bataan and Corregidor was arbitrarily refusing to countenance the prospect of a lesser glory for himself in Korea. He wanted to win in Korea, and win big, or get out. Sympathize as they might with his soldier's frustration at being stalemated by an enemy he held in such profound contempt, they were at the same time provoked and confused by his refusal to face the realities of the kind of war he was in. To some, at least, it appeared that his intransigence had a design—namely, to prepare an alibi against his inability to win a shining victory.

These mutual suspicions and clashing purposes reached a peak early in January 1951—a peak that brought a long step nearer the ultimate showdown between the General and his Commander-in-Chief.

On January 10, MacArthur told the Joint Chiefs that if his forces were to be pinned down in an indefinite defensive operation in Korea, he could no longer guarantee the security of Japan. He asked that he either be given substantial reinforcements or be authorized to pull out of Korea.

The Joint Chiefs replied in a long memorandum that they concurred in his estimate that the Communists, if they determined to do so, could force the United Nations to evacuate Korea. But no substantial reinforcements, they said, could be sent to the Far East for at least two months, when certain National Guard divisions would have completed their training. Meanwhile, it was essential to stave off evacuation as long as possible. The message continued:

> We are forced to the conclusion, based upon all the factors known to us . . . that it is infeasible under existing conditions, including sustained major effort by Communist China, to hold the position in Korea for a protracted period.
>
> It would be to our national interest, however, and also to the interest of the UN, before you issue firm instructions for initiation of evacuation of troops from Korea, to gain some further time for essential military and diplomatic consultations with UN countries participating in the Korean effort.
>
> It is important also . . . that maximum practicable punishment be inflicted on Communist aggressors and that Korea not be evacuated unless actually forced by military considerations. . . .
>
> You are now directed to defend [your line] in successive positions . . . subject to the continued threat to Japan, and to determine in advance our last favorable opportunity for an orderly evacuation.[9]

MacArthur's reaction to this was an attempt to instruct Washington in the realities of Far Eastern policy. In a long message, couched in phrases of urgency and impatience, he pointed out that Communist China was already in the war to the full extent of its capability. This, he said, was the clear and present danger, while the danger of Soviet aggression in Europe or elsewhere was tentative and remote. If Communist momentum could be checked decisively now in Korea, he argued, the likelihood of its eruption on another front would be greatly reduced.

To accomplish this, he proposed a four-pronged offensive: (1) a naval blockade of China; (2) destruction of Chinese military and industrial capacity by unrestricted air and naval bombardment; (3) the employment of 30,000 ground troops from Formosa, offered by Chiang Kai-shek to the UN command; and (4) removal of all restrictions on the Nationalist garrisons on Formosa to mount diversionary attacks against the China mainland.

What MacArthur was proposing, in effect, was a total reversal of the limited war policy of the Truman administration and the United Nations. He was asking for the right not only to make war against the Chinese People's Republic, which was linked in a mutual defense treaty with the Soviet Union, but to underwrite Chiang Kai-shek in a resumption of the Chinese civil war.

MacArthur's message created consternation in Washington. It was promptly put before a special meeting of the National Security Council (Secretary Acheson left a sickbed to attend it). Without delay, the General was told that his design for an expanded war was overruled.* But it was clear to the members of the NSC that new instructions, compellingly specific in terms, had to be sent out to the Far Eastern Commander before some headstrong action committed the nation beyond recall.

The result was a double-barreled communication issued from Washington on January 12. The first was a directive from the JCS that restated in more explicit terms what MacArthur had been told two weeks earlier: Hold out in Korea wherever you can for as long as you can, with the safety of your troops and the security of Japan

---

* One of the bitterest disputes in the whole Truman-MacArthur controversy revolved around this point. In his testimony before the Senate committee and elsewhere, the General gave the impression that the four-pronged offensive he advocated had initially been approved by the JCS but was mysteriously countermanded later. In a colloquy with Chairman Russell of the investigating committee ("Military Situation in the Far East," Hearings of the Committee on Armed Services and Foreign Relations, Part 1, pp. 13-14), the following exchange took place:

CHAIRMAN. Was that message, that document from which you just read, transmitted to you as part of your instructions?

MACARTHUR. No, sir. This was *the recommendation*, the study made by the Joint Chiefs of Staff which was submitted to the Secretary of Defense. A copy of it was furnished me. [Italics supplied.]

CHAIRMAN. But it was furnished to you as a recommendation to the Secretary of Defense, and you of course awaited a decision from that source before proceeding along . . .

MACARTHUR. A decision putting this into effect never arrived. . . .

CHAIRMAN. Did you get any instructions that it was not to be put into effect?

MACARTHUR. No, sir. . . .

CHAIRMAN. So, if that was a recommendation of the Joint Chiefs, *it encountered a veto somewhere along the line,* either from the Secretary of Defense or the President of the United States? [Italics supplied.]

MACARTHUR. I would assume so, Sir.

General Willoughby is more emphatic in his interpretation. In his book *Mac-Arthur, 1941-1951,* he states on page 416:

"He [MacArthur] recommended to Washington that he be permitted air bombardment in due course of military installations north of the Yalu . . . naval blockade

being the primary considerations; no offensive actions outside North Korea; evacuate only in the face of overwhelming military necessity. The second barrel of the communication was a long personal message from the President to explain again and to reemphasize the international political considerations that underlay the national policy regarding Korea.

To reinforce the importance of these two messages, two members of the Joint Chiefs, Generals Collins and Vandenberg, were dispatched to Tokyo on the same day, January 12, to give General MacArthur any additional clarification he might require.

The President's message to the Far Eastern Commander was so carefully phrased as to be almost deferential. It avoided any hint of criticism or reprimand but emphasized the value of the General's advice and the brilliance of his leadership. "We need your judgment," it said, "as to the maximum effort which could reasonably be expected from the United Nations forces under your command to support the resistance to aggression which we are trying rapidly to organize on a world-wide basis."

The President itemized three political goals which, it was hoped, might be reached by continuing the resistance in Korea: (1) to demonstrate that Communist aggression against free people would

---

of the China coast to cut off enemy supplies, and renewed his request for the utilization of Nationalist Chinese troops available in Formosa. These recommendations were *actually approved* by the Joint Chiefs of Staff, but somewhere between the offices of the Secretary of Defense, the Secretary of State, and President Truman, they were *pigeonholed*." [Italics supplied.]

Both versions are contrary to those of President Truman, Secretaries Marshall and Acheson, and the Chiefs of Staff. The four courses of offensive action alluded to by MacArthur, it was held, were among a total of sixteen possible actions which a JCS study committee said might be considered in the event of an all-out war against Communist China. As General Bradley told the Senate Committee (Hearings, Part 2, p. 736):

"I want to emphasize again that it was not a directive. It was a study. . . . When we send a directive to the Commander-in-Chief, Far East, we draw up a draft, take it to the Secretary of Defense who approves or disapproves it, and if it has political implications we discuss it with the Secretary of State, and then it is taken to the President who okays it or passes judgment on it. It is then sent out as a directive.

"This particular study never went through that routine. It was never intended as a prospective directive to be handled in that way. It was a study for consideration along with other things that were going on at the time."

General Bradley's recollections were backed up by the testimony of Secretary Marshall and others. It seems highly improbable that a man of MacArthur's sagacity and experience (he had once been Chief of Staff himself) could have innocently misread and misinterpreted so important a military document. But the myth that sinister forces in the White House or the State Department first granted and then withdrew permission for MacArthur to "win the war" flamed high across the land, searing the Truman administration with its heat. Some of the embers still smolder today.

not be tolerated; (2) to demonstrate that the UN was a viable and vigorous force that could not be brushed aside; and (3) to strengthen the will to resist of hard-pressed governments in Europe and the Middle East. His message continued as follows:

Our course of action at this time should be such as to consolidate the great majority of the United Nations. This majority is not merely part of the organization but is also the nations whom we would desperately need to count on in the event the Soviet Union moves against us.

Further, pending the build-up of our national strength, we must act with great prudence so far as extending the area of hostilities is concerned. Steps which in themselves might be fully justified and which might lend some assistance to the campaign in Korea would not be beneficial if they thereby involved Japan or Western Europe in large-scale hostilities.[10]

In sum, the President was telling his General, "I sympathize with your problem and admire the way you are handling it, but please remember that I have problems too, which are at least as great if not greater than yours." There was admirable restraint and magnanimity in the President's words, but his patience was running out.

Mr. Truman's patience was being worn thin not only by the regal intransigence of his Far Eastern Commander and the complexities of the Korean war, but by the steadily mounting pinpricks and body blows of domestic politics. A President is many men, and he must bear not just some but all of a nation's burden.

In mid-January, the Senate became embroiled in "the great debate" over the issue of sending troops to Europe under the NATO agreement. Should it be done at all? Former President Herbert Hoover said No, that we should wash our hands of Europe's chronic troublemaking and concentrate on our own "Fortress America." Should the President have exclusive authority to send troops, or only with the permission of Congress? Senator Robert Taft held out with biting eloquence for the congressional prerogative "to declare war." Isolationist and anti-Truman sentiment converged behind the Hoover-Taft thesis. The debacle of "Truman's war" in Korea was exhibited as a horrible example of the alternative. The controversy raged for three months before the President's hand was upheld by what, in the end, was a needless and meaningless Senate resolution expressing support of his policy.

The President ordered, during January, the reinstitution of limited wage and price controls as part of his mobilization program. He was immediately engaged in familiar combat with business on the one hand, and labor on the other. A massive railroad strike threatened but petered out before serious damage was done. A Senate committee reported widespread corruption in the Reconstruction Finance Corporation and demanded a cleanup. The President said the report was "asinine," and the hounds of righteousness were upon him. Alger Hiss went to prison, launching the bleak epoch of "McCarthyism." A Washington music critic said Margaret Truman was not a very good singer, and the President wrote him a letter threatening him with mayhem. Dr. George Gallup ran a popularity poll that showed the President trailing his archenemy, Senator Taft.

In what seems to have been a generous understatement, Anthony Leviero, White House correspondent for the New York *Times*, wrote on February 18: "President Truman's political prestige happens to be on one of those downcurves." But he went on more believably to observe:

It is likely, however, that he is less concerned about it than are other leaders of the Democratic Party.

There is no doubt that the multiplying vexations of his office have sharpened his temper and irritated him. Yet there is no question that his essential confidence and serenity remain intact.

The pace of combat in Korea began to slacken in mid-January, 1951, an uncertain prelude to the long period of stalemate that was to follow. General Walker had been killed in a jeep crash on December 23, and his place was taken by a soldier of equal skill but of calmer and more judicious temperament, Lieutenant General Matthew Ridgway, a hatchet-faced West Pointer who organized this country's first Airborne Division in World War II and jumped with his men onto the beaches of Sicily and Normandy. After a firsthand survey of the Korean battle area, he set about consolidating and strengthening his positions along a line roughly 50 miles south of the 38th parallel, but with Seoul still in enemy hands. He won from MacArthur the concession of incorporating the X Corps under his command along with the Eighth Army, thus ending one of the most troublesome inconsistencies with which his predecessor had had to cope.

All told, General Ridgway now had about 365,000 men under his command. Symbolically, at least, it was an international army, with combat and support elements (most of token size) representing fifteen nations in addition to the United States and the Republic of Korea. Opposing him, General Lin Piao commanded a force of approximately 485,000, with Chinese regulars outnumbering the reconstituted NKPA roughly two to one. The enemy's numerical advantage was partially offset by the length and exposure of his supply lines, stretching 200 miles and more to the Manchurian border. And the enemy's tactical advantage—the uncanny ability of his tough Asian battalions to dissolve suddenly into suicidal guerrilla fighters—was undercut as Ridgway rooted out the road-bound psychology of his troops and made them, too, fight on foot in the hills and rice paddies.

Late in January the UN forces launched a cautious, probing offensive all alone the line, with a strong armored spearhead aimed toward Seoul. The enemy was dug in securely and in depth, taking full advantage of the deep snows and murderous cold of the Korean winter. For weeks the two lines surged futilely against each other like conflicting sea currents, punching through for a gain of a few miles here, giving up a few bloody acres there. But little by little, almost mile by mile, Ridgway's men moved forward, never giving up quite as much today as they gained yesterday. By mid-March they had retaken Seoul—or rather its burned-out shell—and again that bewitched and mystical barrier, the 38th parallel, lay almost in reach just over the horizon.

But the idea that a clear-cut military victory could be won in Korea had all but evaporated in Washington. Within the UN, particularly among the NATO nations of Europe, clamorous demands were rising for an end to the conflict—any end—before its spreading flames should envelop them. The time was about as propitious as it was likely to be in the foreseeable future to try for a negotiated peace. The Communists had been persuaded that they could not win either, even if they might not be beaten.

A move toward negotiation would be certain to raise new cries of "appeasement" from the Republican ranks of Congress, but the President and his advisers were prepared to take this risk. Acheson, Marshall, Rusk, and the Joint Chiefs of Staff put their heads together and produced a carefully worded statement to be issued by the President. It set forth that, with the aggressors now cleared out of the Republic of Korea, the United Nations would be receptive to the idea of a cease-fire and peace negotiations. The draft of the statement was completed on March 20, and on the same day copies were sent for study to each of the fourteen UN allies. A copy was also sent by radio to MacArthur, with this coverage message from the Joint Chiefs of Staff:

State planning Presidential announcement shortly that, with clearing of bulk of South Korea of aggression, UN now prepared to discuss conditions of settlement in Korea. Strong UN feeling persists that further diplomatic effort toward settlement should be made before any advance with major forces north of the 38th parallel. . . . State has asked JCS what authority you should have to provide security for the UN forces and maintain contact with the enemy.[11]

The clear purport of this message was to tell the Far Eastern Commander that his Chief was preparing to negotiate a settlement of the conflict at the highest level of diplomacy, and to ask what he needed in order to preserve the military *status quo* while these negotiations were in progress. The General's immediate reply was to the point: He needed no additional authority over what he already had; he asked only that no additional restrictions be placed on him in the meantime.

But four days later, entirely on his own authority and with no warning to Washington, MacArthur made his own offer to negotiate with the enemy through a public statement couched in the florid prose and the tone of elegant disdain for which he had become noted. He pointed out that in spite of the "inhibitions and restrictions" under which the UN command labored, it had thoroughly frustrated the enemy's aggressive design. The enemy should be "painfully aware," moreover, that if the UN should decide "to depart from its tolerant effort to contain the war to the area of Korea," the whole of Red China would be "doomed to imminent military collapse."

Having thus threatened the Chinese with destruction of their homeland, MacArthur offered the enemy a way out:

Within the area of my authority as the military commander, however, it would be needless to say that I stand ready at any time to confer in the field with the commander in chief of the enemy forces . . . to find means whereby realization of the military objectives of the United Nations in Korea might be accomplished without further bloodshed.[12]

This was an extraordinary announcement for a field commander to make. It assayed, first, to reverse the basic strategy of the United Nations by threatening to carry the war to Red China. Second, it deliberately violated the JCS directive of December 6 that all but the most routine statements from the Far Eastern Commander should first be cleared with Washington. And finally and most grievously, it cut the ground from under his President and Commander in Chief in the midst of diplomatic maneuvers of the greatest urgency and complexity.*

Word of MacArthur's manifesto reached Washington via the news wires late on March 23 (24, Korean time). A rump meeting of half a dozen members of the "war cabinet"—Rusk, Lovett, Lucius Battle, and Alexis Johnson among them—convened at 11 o'clock that night in the living room of Secretary of State Dean Acheson's Georgetown home. They were angry, fed up, and ready for drastic action, whatever the cost. MacArthur had to go! Lovett urged Acheson to get the President on the telephone forthwith and put the recommendation up to him. But the Secretary refused to be rushed. He said they all had better sleep on it and then talk with the President the next day. The meeting broke up at 1 o'clock.

Harry Truman is an impulsive man, but in moments of great trial he has the inner strength to control his impulses. He did on this Saturday forenoon when Acheson and the others gathered about his desk to discuss the latest affront from Tokyo.

"MacArthur left me no choice," the President recalled later. "I could no longer tolerate his insubordination."

But as he so often did in moments of crisis, he thumbed back in his mind through the parallels of history, so familiar to him. He saw the melancholy face of Lincoln, almost a hundred years earlier, within these same White House walls, wrestling with the insubordination of *his* leading General, McClellan. He weighed, too, the encroachment upon the dignity and authority of the Presidential office of what he now judged to be the most demeaning challenge it had

---

* General MacArthur, in his appearance before the Senate investigating committee, professed dismay that his statement had been interpreted as exceeding his authority. In a colloquy with Senator Wayne Morse, he said: "The notice I put out was merely that which every commander at any time can put out; that he would confer with the opposing commander-in-chief in an endeavor to bring hostilities to an end. . . . I can't believe that [this] authority . . . would be the subject of criticism from any source in the world."

Asked if he had not been made aware of the President's plans to seek armistice negotiations, he said: "Yes, I received such a message. It had nothing to do with my statement whatever, though . . . There is nothing unusual or unorthodox or improper that I can possibly read into the statement that I made on March 24." (Hearings, Part 1, pp. 69-70.)

Secretary Marshall, in his appearance before the same group, had a different view of the matter. He said: "My understanding was that it created a very serious situation with our allies, along the line of their uncertainty as to just how we were proceeding; the President bringing something to their attention, and gauging their action to find agreement with him, and before that can be accomplished, the leader in the field comes forward with a proposition which terminates that endeavor of the Chief Executive to handle the matter. It created, I think specifically, a loss of confidence in the leadership of the Government." (Hearings, Part 1, pp. 483-86.)

faced since Lincoln's day. A President can be demeaned with impunity, Mr. Truman believes, but not the Presidency.

His mind was made up on this Saturday. He knew what he had to do, and he was going to do it. MacArthur would be stripped of his command. But he wanted time to calculate each step of what could prove to be the most momentous decision he would take as President—and probably the most costly in terms of his own stature and political welfare. Moreover, he wanted time for the National Security Council to assess both the military and political consequences of so drastic an upheaval in the United Nations Far Eastern Command. The dismissal of MacArthur had to be accomplished with the least possible backlash on the precarious *status quo* in world affairs.

It was while these delicate arrangements and deliberations were in process that the firing pin on this time bomb was pulled. The date was Thursday, April 5, 1951.

Shortly before noon that day, Joseph W. Martin, the rumpled, mumble-voiced minority leader of the House of Representatives, took the floor to read into the record a letter he had received from General MacArthur. Martin was one of the half dozen most powerful Republicans in the country, an only partially reconstructed isolationist and a rock-ribbed conservative who shared control of the GOP with such men as Robert Taft, Kenneth Wherry, Charley Halleck, and others of the Old Guard. Though personally friendly to Truman, he was one of the President's most effective and implacable political foes, especially as to foreign policy and the conduct of the Korean war.

Now he told the House that some weeks earlier he had written MacArthur asking his views about the administration's policy of refusing to make use of Chiang Kai-shek's Nationalist troops against the Chinese Reds. He had asked the General's views to be put either on or off the record. But the letter which he now held in his hand, Joe Martin said, carried no stipulation of confidentiality, and he felt, "I owe it to the American people to tell them the information I have from a great and reliable source."

Martin had quietly passed the word that he would drop a bombshell in the House that day, so he had a large and expectant audience as he rose to speak. He read the General's letter:

My views and recommendations with respect to the situation created by Red China's entry into war against us in Korea have been submitted to Washington in most complete detail. Generally those views are well known and generally understood, as they follow the conventional pattern of meeting force with maximum counterforce as we have never failed to do in the past. Your [Martin's] view with respect to the utilization of the Chinese forces on Formosa is in conflict with neither logic nor this tradition.

It seems strangely difficult for some to realize that here in Asia is where the Communist conspirators have elected to make their play for global conquest, and that we have joined the issue thus raised on the battlefield; that here we fight Europe's war with arms while the diplomats there still fight it with words; that if we lose this war to Communism in Asia the fall of Europe is inevitable; win it and Europe most probably would avoid war and yet preserve freedom.

As you point out, we must win. There is no substitute for victory.

The newspapers had been humming for several weeks with speculation on the prospect of another showdown between the President and his outspoken Far Eastern Commander. MacArthur's persistent disdain had put Truman in a bad light, and cartoonists and columnists were picturing him as cringing in helpless frustration before MacArthur's imperious scorn. Editorialists were demanding on the one hand that the President give MacArthur a free hand to wind up the war as he said he could do, or, on the other hand, to bring him home for a face-to-face dressing down. The Martin letter brought all such speculation to a new boil. A headline in the Washington *Post* said: MACARTHUR RECALL RULED OUT BY PRESIDENT, HILL HEARS. REPRIMAND IS STILL SEEN POSSIBLE.

A showdown now seemed inevitable between the Missouri politician in the White House and the regal General of the Army. But few in Washington or elsewhere were prepared for the brass-knuckled finality with which Mr. Truman marched at last into the fray.

Friday and Saturday, the President met several times with Acheson, Harriman, Marshall, Bradley, and others of the "war cabinet." The consensus was that MacArthur would have to be relieved of his command, not only in Korea but in the whole Far Eastern theater as well. The hazards of such a move were enormous. Secretary Marshall said he feared it would imperil the huge defense budget then pending in Congress. Secretary Acheson said it would plunge the President "into the biggest fight of your administration." The President said that the one assurance he needed was that there would be complete unanimity for what he was about to do, not only among those present but among the members of the Joint Chiefs as well. He asked each of them to search his conscience thoroughly over the weekend, and he asked General Bradley to put the matter squarely to the other Chiefs and report back to him Monday morning.

On Monday the same group gathered in the President's office at 9 o'clock. General Bradley reported that the Joint Chiefs were unanimous in their decision that MacArthur should be recalled and his whole command turned over to General Ridgway. The others present stated their agreement. The President said it had been his unaltered intention since March 24 that MacArthur would have to go, and that he was pleased that no reservations about it lingered in the minds of any of them. He then directed General Bradley to prepare the official orders for an orderly and dignified change of command, and he suggested that Army Secretary Frank Pace, Jr., who was then in Korea, be instructed to deliver these orders to General MacArthur in person.

On Tuesday, late in the afternoon, Bradley, Marshall, Acheson, and Harriman returned to the White House to go over, with the President, the text of the orders to MacArthur and the plans for their delivery. Mr. Truman signed the necessary papers and left at about 6 o'clock for Blair House and dinner. The others stayed on in the Cabinet room to complete the details of the instructions to Secretary Pace. At about 7 o'clock, Joe Short, the White House Press Secretary, burst into the room and breathlessly told them the Chicago *Tribune* "has got the whole story and is going to print it tomorrow morning."[*]

Here was a mess indeed! If the newspapers printed the story before MacArthur could officially be informed, or the key members of Congress and UN Ambassadors properly advised, this whole delicate operation would be turned into a shambles. Obviously, the timetable had to be speeded up to beat the presses with the news.

General Bradley hurried across the street to Blair House to tell the President about the new development. If MacArthur got the

---

[*] Walter Trohan, the veteran chief Washington correspondent for the *Tribune*, recalls this as one of the classic snafus of his career. "Our tip was sound, but both my managing editor and I went soft on it and we let it pass."

As Trohan recalls the incident, he had a call during the afternoon from his managing editor, William D. Maxwell, saying the paper had received a tip from a source in Tokyo that MacArthur was to be fired the next morning. This was believable in the light of all the recent speculation and the intensified air of secrecy and suspense around the White House over the weekend. Trohan went to Short's office for comment on the tip, and, as he had expected, the Press Secretary threw it down. "There's nothing to it," Short said. Trohan, unimpressed by this denial, started to write a hard prediction that MacArthur was to be fired, when he received another call from Maxwell. "Forget that MacArthur tip," Maxwell told him. "We've checked this source in Tokyo, and it turns out this fellow doesn't know what he's talking about." Reluctantly, because his newsman's hunch told him the story was solid, Trohan pulled the scoop of the year from his typewriter and threw it into the wastebasket.

news before he received his official orders, Bradley said, the General probably would try to beat the President to the punch by resigning.

"He's not going to be allowed to quit on me," Mr. Truman exploded. "He's going to be fired!"

He told Bradley to get the official notification to MacArthur in the shortest time possible, and to keep the White House informed hour by hour. General Bradley went directly to the Pentagon. He discarded the long explanatory message to Secretary Pace and wrote out in longhand a shorter one telling him to fly to Tokyo within the hour and advise MacArthur of his recall, and Ridgway of his elevation. Bradley took the message to the communications room himself and restlessly hovered for an hour over the teletype machine, awaiting Pace's acknowledgment. It did not come; the Secretary was in a plane with General Ridgway flying over the battle area.

Meanwhile, there was intense activity at the White House and in the State Department. Acheson got Chairman Tom Connally of the Senate Foreign Relations Committee out of bed to tell him what was impending. He alerted John Foster Dulles to take off for Tokyo the next morning in order to reassure the Japanese Government that their interests would not be adversely affected. He called Sir Oliver Franks, the British Ambassador, and other key diplomats and gave them the news. At the White House Harriman and others were preparing a statement for the President and pulling together certain documents which would be released simultaneously with the public announcement of MacArthur's recall.

At 11 o'clock that night a harassed Bradley telephoned the President that he was unable to get through to Secretary Pace and that, with the President's permission, he would now send the message directly to MacArthur telling him to turn over his full command immediately to Ridgway. Accordingly, shortly before midnight, Tuesday, April 10, these words in scrambled code flashed from the Pentagon in Washington to the Dai Ichi Building in Tokyo, Headquarters for the Far Eastern Command:

To General MacArthur from the President.

I deeply regret that it becomes my duty as President and Commander-in-Chief of the United States military forces to replace you as Supreme Commander, Allied Powers; Commander-in-Chief, United Nations Command; Commander-in-Chief, Far East; and Commanding General, U.S. Army, Far East.

You will turn over your commands, effective at once, to Lieutenant

General Matthew B. Ridgway. You are authorized to have issued such orders as are necessary to complete desired travel to such place as you select.

My reasons for your replacement will be made public concurrently with the delivery to you of the foregoing message.

The deed was done!

Shortly after midnight, Press Secretary Short telephoned the principal news offices in Washington, summoning reporters to an extraordinary 1:00 A.M. press conference. When they had assembled in bleary-eyed expectancy, he read to them a statement of the President of the United States: "With deep regret I have concluded that General of the Army Douglas MacArthur is unable to give his wholehearted support to the policies of the United States and of the United Nations. . . ." Short also handed out a packet of mimeographed documents containing the actual order of recall to General MacArthur, the December 6 directive, the President's message of January 12 to the General, and other directives and memorandums bearing on the conflict. Finally, he told the reporters the President would go on the air at 10:30 that night (Wednesday) to explain his action to the American people.

When he was faced with a tough decision, President Truman often remarked, "There's no passing the buck when you sit in this chair." One of the prized possessions among the varied gadgetry of his desk was a small hand-lettered sign which read, THE BUCK STOPS HERE.

Few political events in American history have created such an explosive public reaction as President Truman's dismissal of General MacArthur from his command. There was a minority of informed and thoughtful citizens who promptly approved the President's action as consistent with his Constitutional responsibility. But to a far greater majorty his action smacked of insolence, jealousy, vindictiveness, even sacrilege. Their outcry was shattering. Letters by the tens of thousands poured in upon the White House, congressional offices, newspapers, and radio stations in every part of the land. Individuals and groups bought advertising space to condemn the "outrage." Preachers thundered about it from their pulpits. Legion posts, service clubs, and PTA's passed angrily worded resolutions. Figures labeled "Truman" and "Acheson" were burned in effigy on college campuses and in town squares.

Congressional Republicans were hardly less inflamed. They held emergency caucuses in the House and Senate Wednesday morning to vent their wrath against the President. Later, on the Senate floor, William E. Jenner, of Indiana, roared: "I charge that this country today is in the hands of a secret inner coterie which is directed by agents of the Soviet Union. Our only choice is to impeach President Truman." House Minority Leader Joe Martin put through a telephone call to MacArthur's headquarters in Tokyo, inviting him to come immediately to Washington to address a joint session of Congress. The groundwork was laid for a joint investigation of the affair by the Foreign Relations and Armed Services Committees of the Senate. Some Democrats in Congress defended their President, but most, in those first torrid days of shock, stood mute in dismay and indecision.

At the United Nations and most foreign capitals, the decision was received with relief—relief that a spreading of the Korean war was now minimized, and relief that President Truman had reasserted his control over this nation's foreign policy. The London *Evening Standard* proclaimed the event in a jubilant banner headline: MAC IS SACKED.

Obviously, shock and anger were felt by MacArthur's loyal staff at the Far Eastern Command Headquarters in Tokyo, but things were a little different in Seoul. Murray Schumach, reporting for the New York *Times* from Eighth Army Headquarters, wrote: "The widespread feeling among officers of field rank is that the relationship between General Headquarters in Tokyo and the Eighth Army in Korea will become more pleasant. Despite denials in Tokyo, there have been many indications in Korea of friction between Ridgway's men and MacArthur's men."

In the controversy which still swirls about the firing of MacArthur, one question that for many minds has never been satisfactorily answered is, How truly unanimous were the Joint Chiefs in making their recommendation to the President? Were they pressured into it, perhaps, by their civilian bosses? They told the Senate investigators that they all agreed, "on purely military grounds," that the General should be relieved. But nowhere did they tell what those grounds were. The reason for their hesitancy is now apparent: They wanted to spare their haughty old comrade an additional humiliation.

The Chiefs reached their unanimous decision at a special meeting in the Pentagon on the Sunday afternoon following the April 7 conference at the White House. The minutes of this conference have never been disclosed to anyone outside the JCS structure. However, we now know from an observer what went on. The observer was Colonel (now Major General) Chester V. Clifton currently the military aide to President Johnson. As General Bradley's aide, it was his duty, a few weeks after the meeting (to which he had not been admitted), to prepare the detailed documentation on which General Bradley and the others based their testimony before the Senate committee that investigated the dismissal. As well as any man living today, General Clifton knows how this consensus on MacArthur was reached. He has told the writer in an interview:

There was no question about the Chiefs being in thorough agreement on this. They had become disenchanted with MacArthur a long way back—as far back as February or January in any event—and on military rather than on political grounds.

A part of their dissatisfaction was with some of his strategic and tactical decisions, such as splitting his forces in Korea and jumping off on his November offensive with inadequate field intelligence about the enemy. But these things were of lesser importance.

What really counted was that MacArthur had lost confidence in himself and was beginning to lose the confidence of his field officers and troops. There is nothing in the book that more seriously undermines a commander's effectiveness than this. When it happens, he's through.

This was happening to MacArthur. It was visible to the people sent out from Washington to consult him; it was visible in his behavior; and it was visible in the tone of his communications. From January on, his messages to Washington were dominated by petulance and ill-tempered complaints. It had become almost impossible to get firm estimates or positive commitments from him on anything. He emphasized what he could not do instead of what he could do.

It had also become pretty clear that he was jealous of Ridgway. Ridgway (in immediate command of the Eighth Army) had turned the war around, and in a steady, unspectacular way was pushing the enemy back across the parallel. He had managed to boost the morale of his men, and to give them some sense of their mission and some hope that they could get the job done. While MacArthur was licking his wounds in public, Ridgway was turning the Eighth Army into a first-class fighting force, and the men responded to this just the way you would expect them to do.

When Collins and Vandenberg were in Korea early in March, they talked about this very thing with Ridgway. They asked if it would help morale if MacArthur were separated from his command in Korea, but left in charge of things in Japan. But Ridgway recommended against it. He said he was getting things pretty well in hand in spite of MacArthur, and that a big shake-up at the top might set things back instead of helping.

It was against this background of a growing disenchantment with Mac-Arthur as a military commander—a commander who was losing his drive and his hold on his men—that the Joint Chiefs had to consider his recall. And when he committed the final error of insubordination to the Commander-in-Chief—and there's absolutely no question about that—they had no trouble at all deciding what had to be done.

MacArthur's return to the United States was marked by a pageantry and a wave of emotionalism that has rarely been equaled in this country. His plane, the *Bataan*, put down in San Francisco on Tuesday, April 17. He received a tumultuous greeting as he set foot on his native soil for the first time since 1937, and said: "The only politics I have is contained in the simple phrase known well by all of you: God bless America."

He reached Washington a few minutes after midnight Thursday morning. Twelve thousand hysterical well-wishers at National Airport broke through the police lines and made a shambles of the official welcome planned by Secretary Marshall, the Joint Chiefs of Staff, and virtually the entire Republican membership of Congress.

At 12:30 that day he made one of the most memorable orations ever heard in the Capitol, before a joint meeting of the House and Senate and a radio-television audience of untold millions. He was a stirring, romantic figure out of the pages of a Kipling or a Richard Harding Davis as he mounted the rostrum in the House of Representatives and with a benevolent smile waited for the two-minute ovation to subside. He was handsome, proud, resonant of voice, confident of manner, and yet humble in a magisterial sort of way as he thanked the Congress for giving him this last great honor "in the fading twilight of my life."

As he progressed, the tone of wistfulness gave way to harsh indictment of the administration's policy in the Far East, and to thinly veiled scorn for men who would not see that "There is no substitute for victory." Of those who claimed that American strength was inadequate to face the enemy on more than one front, he said: "I can think of no greater expression of defeatism. If a potential enemy can divide his strength on two fronts, it is for us to counter his effort. You cannot appease or otherwise surrender to communism in Asia without simultaneously undermining our efforts to halt its advance in Europe." The "new war," of which he said he had warned when the Red Chinese came in on the side of the North Koreans, called for "new decisions in the diplomatic sphere," but such decisions "have not been forthcoming."

Nearly every sentence he spoke was punctuated by applause.

There were tears in his eyes when, at last, he uttered his peroration:

Since I took the oath at West Point, the hopes and dreams [of youth] have all vanished. But I still remember the refrain of one of the most popular barracks ballads of that day, which proclaimed most proudly that old soldiers never die, they just fade away.

And like the old soldier of that ballad, I now close my military career and just fade away, an old soldier who tried to do his duty as God gave him the light to see that duty.

Good-bye.

This was Douglas MacArthur's finest hour, the zenith of his career as a master of dramaturgy, as a national hero, and as a symbol of a nation's wrath. Thereafter, everything was anticlimax.

The next day he made a triumphal entry into New York. His welcome was the greatest the city had ever staged—a four-hour parade down Broadway to City Hall; 7,500,000 persons cheering along the route; 780 tons of confetti and ticker tape showered upon him from office windows. He and Mrs. MacArthur and their 13-year-old son, Arthur, took up residence in a $130-a-day suite in the Waldorf Towers, where they had another aging hero, Herbert Hoover, as their neighbor.

The General's suite was besieged for days by a stream of callers, all of high estate. Many of them (such as Robert A. Taft) were Republican strategists seeking the ultimate obliteration of Harry Truman in the next year's election. MacArthur was a willing collaborator.

The Senate investigation of the General's dismissal was conducted in the high-ceilinged, marble-columned Caucus Room in the Senate Office Building. It began on May 3, with General MacArthur as the first witness (he was to spend 21 hours and 10 minutes on the stand in three days). It ran until June 25. Thirteen witnesses were questioned, including the Secretaries of State and Defense and the members of the Joint Chiefs of Staff. Reams of official and unofficial documents were inserted into the record. Scores of Senators who were not members of the Foreign Relations or Armed Services Committees crowded into the room during the first days of the session. The hearings were closed to the public and the press because of the highly classified nature of much of the testimony. But the transcripts of the session were fed out to reporters almost page by page, after being filtered through a group of military censors. Many newspapers carried from six to twenty columns of the verbatim testimony each day. The total wordage recorded during the seven weeks is estimated at more than two million. In spite of the censorship, the uncovering to enemy eyes of this nation's secret diplomatic and military strategy in Korea, and of its intelligence resources and weaknesses, must stand as a melancholy record of the sort of irresponsibility that avenging politicians have too often shown.

In spite of the efforts of the Chairman, Senator Richard B. Russell, of Georgia, the proceedings were about as partisan as conceivably possible. The Republican members of the panel, regarding Far Eastern policy as *terra franca* in the current political dialogue, were intent on establishing through MacArthur the bankruptcy of the Truman administration. They were led chiefly by Senator William F. Knowland, of California, acting as adjutant for Senator Taft, who was not a member of the committee. The Democrats, with somewhat less dedication and intensity (one could not risk being anti-MacArthur) tried to justify their President's position. One of the most effective in this respect, incidentally, was a freshman Senator from Texas, Lyndon Baines Johnson.

Throughout his testimony, MacArthur leveled his attack at the civilian policy makers. Of the Chiefs of Staff, he said (quite inaccurately) that there had never been any differences with them that he was aware of. His troubles came exclusively from those who made the "political decisions" that governed his operations as a military commander. "There is no policy," he protested bitterly at one point. "There is nothing, I tell you, no plan, no anything."

But as the hearings dragged relentlessly on, day after day and week after week, it became clear to all who were willing to see that MacArthur was not infallible; that in the heroic legend there was also a strong vein of arrogance and vanity and stubbornness. They could see too that Harry Truman had his side of the story; that the Constitution is greater than any war or any General; and that the President is, in the last resort, the defender and symbol of the Constitution.

The MacArthur hearings were one of the most lamentable and misguided exhibitions of the working of the democratic process this government has had to endure. But they provided a safety valve for letting off a dangerous excess of emotion in the body politic, which might have spent itself in some more damaging fashion. Senator

Jenner's demand for the impeachment of the President was never taken seriously. But another circumstance *was* serious! On the day MacArthur rode in triumph down Broadway under clouds of ticker tape, President Truman stood up in his box at Washington's Griffith Stadium to throw out the first baseball of the new season. A sullen thunder of boos rolled across the stands.

Many of Mr. Truman's admirers feel that his decision to relieve General MacArthur was the single most courageous act of his Presidency. I asked him once during an interview if he agreed.

"Courage didn't have anything to do with it," he snapped. "General MacArthur was insubordinate and I fired him. That's all there was to it."

A stalemate settled over the 38th parallel in 1951, and "Truman's war" dragged inconclusively into "Eisenhower's appeasement." The armistice, which the new President negotiated in 1953, is still in effect. It is a poor substitute for victory but a tolerable substitute for war.

CHAPTER 13

◇◇◇◇◇◇◇◇◇◇◇◇◇◇◇◇◇◇◇◇◇◇◇◇◇◇◇◇

Loyalty and Demagogues

Star Chamber

IN MARCH 1948, Dorothy Bailey, 41 years old and a graduate of the University of Minnesota and of Bryn Mawr, was branded as disloyal to the United States and fired from her job in the United States Employment Service, where she had worked for nearly fifteen years. She was dismissed on the basis of anonymous reports to the Civil Service Commission that she was, or had been, a member of the Communist Party and had "associated on numerous occasions with known Communist Party members." Her case was heard by the regional Loyalty Board for the District of Columbia, which questioned her not only about the formal accusations, but about her activities as president of her local of the United Public Workers of America. She was confronted with no evidence beyond a summary of the reports of the anonymous informants, nor did any witnesses appear against her. She denied the charges of Communist affiliation and produced a number of character witnesses in her own behalf. The regional Loyalty Board, nevertheless, confirmed her dismissal, and she appealed to the Loyalty Review Board, the ultimate tribunal in such cases.

When her case came before this board, Miss Bailey's counsel, Paul A. Porter, argued that the charges must have originated out of malicious gossip arising from an interunion power struggle in which his client had been involved. The board chairman, Seth Richardson, replied that "five or six of the reports came from informants certified to us by the Federal Bureau of Investigation as experienced and entirely reliable." He refused to identify them further, saying: "I haven't the slightest knowledge as to who they are or how active they have been in anything."

Further along in the inquiry, this colloquy occurred between members of the board and Miss Bailey and her counsel:

BOARD MEMBER: Then another one says it first came to the informant's attention about 1936, at which time [you were] a known member of the so-called "closed group" of the Communist Party operating in the District of Columbia.

MISS BAILEY: First of all, I didn't know, or don't know, that there is a "closed group." The terminology is unfamiliar to me. I can say under oath and with the strongest conviction that I was not then and have never been a member of the Communist Party.

BOARD MEMBER: Here is another that says you were a member of the Communist Party, and he bases his statement on his knowledge of your association with known Communists for the past seven or eight years. That is part of the evidence that was submitted to us.

MR. PORTER: It is part of the allegations. I don't think that can be considered evidence.

CHAIRMAN RICHARDSON: It is evidence.

MR. PORTER: We renew our request, although we recognize the futility of it, that some identification of this malicious gossip be given this respondent or her counsel.

CHAIRMAN RICHARDSON: Of course, that doesn't help us a bit. If this testimony is true, it is neither gossip or malicious. We are under the difficulty of not being able to disclose this.

MR. PORTER: Is it under oath?

CHAIRMAN RICHARDSON: I don't think so.

BOARD MEMBER: It is a person of known responsibility who has proffered information concerning Communist activity in the District of Columbia.

MISS BAILEY: You see, that point in it worries me, because if I am convicted here that will make this person who has made these charges considered a reliable witness; and they are not, because the charges are not true, and whatever is said here should not add to their reliability.[1]

Dorothy Bailey took her case to the Supreme Court, contending that she had been deprived of her good name and livelihood without due process of law. The verdict against her was sustained on April 30, 1951, in a tortured, inconclusive four-to-four *per curiam* opinion of the Court, which Mr. Justice Jackson bitterly described as, "justice turned bottom side up."

Dorothy Bailey was one of several hundred victims of one of the most brutal inquisitions in American history—the anti-Communist hysteria that gripped the nation in the decade following the Second World War. Such lapses from national sanity, such mass retreats from the Constitutional guarantees of freedom of thought and due processes of law, are not uncommon in the American past. From the time of the Alien and Sedition Acts of the early nineteenth century through the "Red hunt" of Wilson's Attorney General, A. Mitchell Palmer, after the First World War, we have occasionally descended into a semibarbarous fear reaction to unseen and largely imaginary evil spirits. To exorcise these devils, who threaten us not with spears and flame but with the conjuring of an alien philosophy, we have ourselves resorted to the weapons of witchcraft, including human sacrifice. Its most recent manifestation put a new word into the vocabulary—McCarthyism—a word that, for the generation of Americans who lived in the mid-1950's, does not need to be put in quotation marks or defined.

There was, indeed, a substantial morsel of fact for the Red scare of the forties and fifties to feed upon, just as there were, among the witches of Salem, epileptic fits that rendered them culpable in the eyes of the judges. From the days of the New Deal onward, there were in the government in Washington a few genuine Communists, more fellow travelers, and still more with liberal- to left-wing political convictions. Carl Marzani, Alger Hiss, Julian Wadleigh, Lee Pressman, and a score of others of their kind were not imaginary figures. Nor is there any doubt that the Soviet espionage apparatus was behind the activities of a Klaus Fuchs or a David Greenglass. But from the morsel of fact, an irrational wave of vigilantism was generated that swept over people like Dorothy Bailey, Philip Jessup, John Stewart Service, and hundreds of others whose only guilt was a point of view.

Alan Barth, in 1951, made this observation on the new meaning of loyalty:

"Loyalty" has become a cult, an obsession, in the United States. But even loyalty itself is now defined negatively. It is thought of not so much in terms of an affirmative faith in the great purposes for which the American nation was created, as in terms of stereotypes the mere questioning of which is deemed "disloyal." The whole post-war accent is on something called "un-Americanism"—a hyphenated synonym for unorthodoxy. "Loyalty" today consists in not being un-American. The term "Disloyalty" as it is commonly used today is nothing more or less than a circumlocution for treason.[2]

McCarthyism was an evil demagogy which corrupted the political life of the nation for a decade. It was sustained no less by the cynical men who were its manipulators than by the hypocritical men who could have destroyed it but did not. McCarthyism did not attain its full cancerous growth until well after President Truman's term had ended, but the disease began—and got out of hand—while he was in the White House.

Loyalty of Free Men

Communism, with its dream of world conquest, is unquestionably hostile to the security of the United States, but the measures taken to combat it have often posed as great a threat to freedom as communism itself. The loyalty program of 1947 is a case in point.

Radicalism in the United States has historically been of the home-grown variety, mounted usually by indigenous malcontents against felt defects in the existing political or social structure. With the organization of the American Communist Party in 1919, radicalism acquired a new and baffling dimension. It was nonmilitant in the sense that its weapons were ideological—propaganda, subversion, and (much later) espionage. Its physical weight has never been impressive: the high-water mark was registered in 1932, in the very trough of the Great Depression, when it mustered a Presidential vote of 103,000. But its effect and its power to threaten the established order lay in its largely unseen—and therefore more frightening—peripheral influence.

Communist goals are seldom labeled "Communist." They are labeled "peace," "justice," "democracy." Communism has found its supporters in this country not among the downtrodden masses—it never made any progress among Negroes, and only briefly among the ranks of union labor—but among intellectuals and idealists. The result is that it has often been difficult to distinguish between Communists and genuine reformers.

Communists themselves have encouraged this confusion. "Boring from within" is, in fact, a part of the Leninist strategy. Communist "fronts" and organized infiltration began to flourish during the Great Depression, feeding upon the distress and anxiety of a people groping through what seemed to many of them the rubble of a dying capitalism. The infiltration was intensified as the threat of war darkened the skies of Europe. It suited the Soviet purpose initially to neutralize the power of the United States in Hitler's war on France and Britain. But the American Communist "peace offensive" ended abruptly when Hitler turned on Moscow and Russia became an ally of the West. A by-product of this always distrustful alliance was a spreading and strengthening of Communist espionage in all capitals of the West, and in the United States particularly.

The Communist threat is part crime and part heresy, part substance and part shadow, and the line between is not always clear. But in the prevailing American view it is all abhorrent in varying degree. For this reason, communism has been the reigning hobgoblin in American political life for half a century, commanding the earnest attention of statesmen and philosophers on the one hand, and the morbid fascination of demagogues on the other.

Martin Dies, a bull-voiced, xenophobic Congressman from Texas, was among the first to exploit the rich political subsoil of systematic anticommunism. A Democrat who detested the New Deal, he charged that Communists and fellow travelers had saturated the government under Roosevelt. In 1938 he persuaded the House to set up a special committee on un-American activities, with himself as chairman, to hunt down and expose these nests of treachery. Over the next several years he staged a series of flamboyant public investigations; seized the membership lists of a number of such organizations as the League for Peace and Democracy; filched the roster of clients of the leftish Washington Cooperative Book Shop from the manager's parked automobile; and demanded wholesale purges of the "Communists, Socialists, and pinkos" whom he found on the payroll of TVA, the National Labor Relations Board, and some of the new war agencies.

The committee went into partial eclipse after Pearl Harbor, as the FBI and the military intelligence agencies moved in on the antisubversion front. But by that time the Dies Committee had become firmly entrenched as the principal sounding board in Congress and in the country for organized anticommunism.

Meanwhile the government itself was tightening up its wartime security precautions, not only against Nazi spies and saboteurs but against more subtle forms of subversion. The Roosevelt administration fostered legislation to deny government jobs to anyone owing allegiance "to any foreign prince, potentate, or government," and, in another instance, to anyone belonging to an organization advocating violent overthrow of the government. The Secretaries of War and Navy were given powers of summary dismissal of any employees suspected of disloyalty, and the FBI was authorized to make employee security checks for any agency requesting it. In February 1943, President Roosevelt set up an interdepartmental commission to recommend uniform standards for the screening of government employees and for getting rid of those considered undesirable. The commission produced a set of guidelines, but these were advisory only. Most agencies continued to deal with their employee security problems on an *ad hoc,* trial-and-error basis.

One signal contribution of the interdepartmental commission was to obtain from the Attorney General, Francis Biddle, a list of allegedly subversive organizations, membership in which might be considered as a basis for questioning an employee's loyalty. The list was compiled from information furnished by the FBI, which did not give the proscribed organizations an opportunity to argue their case. It covered a wide spectrum on the ideological left, from the Communist Party itself to the League for Peace and Democracy. (The German-American Bund and other pro-Nazi organizations were also included.) This was to be a bitter point of contention later on, for the Attorney General's list was to acquire, willy-nilly, almost the majesty of statutory law in the star-chamber proceedings of the loyalty courts. The list was to provide a cloak of often specious legitimacy for verdicts of guilt by association.

The wartime system for handling suspected disloyalty was haphazard at best, and it became even more chaotic under the changed conditions of the postwar period. Some agencies had fired suspected employees by the hundreds, often unjustly and without recourse to any form of appeal. Other departments lumbered through complicated quasi-judicial proceedings with hearings, witnesses, and testimony that sometimes got into the newspapers. In 1946, Bert Andrews, a Washington newsman, wrote a book titled *Washington Witch Hunt,* which gave some of the more shocking case histories of injustice. These disclosures brought cries of dismay and outrage from liberal quarters. But critics on the right read the same facts and figures and concluded that their worst fears about Communist infiltration of the government had been proved. They increased their clamor for wholesale purges of the disloyal, centering their fire particularly on the Department of State. Leading the cry was the Un-American Activities Committee, no less bellicose for the fact that the fire-eating Martin Dies had been retired to private life in Texas in 1944.

President Truman, still uncertain of himself, faced a hard dilemma in the tugging and hauling of these opposed forces as 1946 opened. Instinctively, he detected the partisan political overtones in the anti-Communist clamor, for it was antiliberal as well. It was also anti-Democratic and anti-Truman, because congressional elections were coming up that year, and the Republicans were driving to upset his control of Congress as a prelude to taking the White House in 1948.

The idea of scuttling the concept of civil rights in order to get at a few disloyal culprits was abhorrent to Truman. "I have never believed," he was to say later, "that this government could be subverted or overturned from within by Communists. The security agencies of the government are well able to deal quietly and effectively with any Communists who sneak into the government without invoking Gestapo methods."

But the President's instinct for restraint came up against some hard realities that gave him alarm.

In June 1945, FBI agents had raided the New York offices of an obscure and scholarly magazine, *Amerasia*, and seized hundreds of copies of government documents, many of them classified "top secret." The magazine and its editor, Philip Jaffe, were noted for their partiality to the Communist cause in China as opposed to the Kuomintang. Arrested along with Jaffe were two State Department employees, John Stewart Service and Emanuel Larsen, and a young lieutenant in Naval Intelligence, Andrew Roth. The news of Service's arrest was particularly shocking, since he was a mature member of the Foreign Service with many years of experience in the Far East.

The *Amerasia* case proved to be a dud when it was brought to trial later that year, although it was to have a long afterlife as a totem among the anti-Communist right. Service, Larsen, and Roth admitted giving copies of some of their routine reports and other papers to Jaffe, whom they respected as a reputable journalist, but all charges against them were dismissed. Jaffe was convicted on the relatively innocuous charge of unauthorized possession of government property and fined $2,500. Although the *Amerasia* case washed out as the great spy shocker it was at first thought to be, it was a

stern reminder to the President and other thoughtful people that
subversion and disloyalty in the government were, potentially, at
least, genuine dangers,

Several months later the President received confidential information on the unfolding in Canada of one of the most elaborate Communist espionage networks ever uncovered. Igor Gouzenko, a code
clerk in the Soviet Embassy at Ottawa, had gone to Canadian authorities with a garish but documented story of how scores of
persons, many of them in government, had been tricked or forced
into supplying secret information on defense and atomic operations
to Soviet agents. The United States and Canada shared many confidences of a military and political nature, and the investigation by
Canadian authorities clearly implied that the Canadian spy ring had
its counterpart in Washington.

In February 1946 the President received from FBI Chief J. Edgar
Hoover a report on espionage operations within the United States
Government just as shocking, if considerably less well documented,
as those in Canada. A tense, overwrought spinster named Elizabeth
Bentley and a moody senior editor of *Time* Magazine, Whittaker
Chambers, each claiming to be a refugee from the Communist espionage network, had spilled their stories to FBI agents in New
York—stories that were so incredible that the FBI at first refused to
countenance them.* Among scores of persons implicated in these
bizarre tales were Lauchlin Currie, formerly a top adviser to President Roosevelt; Alger Hiss, director of the Office of Political Affairs
in the Department of State; and Harry Dexter White, an Assistant
Secretary of the Treasury.

It has not been possible to reconstruct exactly what effect this
alarming report from the FBI had on the President. Some years
later, when he was under attack for his handling of the White case,
he first denied that he had ever seen the Hoover report. He later
hedged and said he had "fired" White after reading the report. This
doesn't hold water, either. The known facts are these:

The President had already sent to the Senate White's nomination
as United States Director of the International Monetary Fund when
the Hoover memorandum reached his desk in February 1946. He

---

* Miss Bentley first took her story to the FBI field division in New Haven, Conn.,
in August 1945. The agents thanked her politely but apparently were unimpressed.
It was not until two months later when, by prearrangement, she was observed accepting a $2,000 payment on a dark New York street from Anatol Gromov, an
official of the Soviet Embassy, that they began to take her seriously. This and
other details are recounted in Miss Bentley's autobiography, *Out of Bondage*.

immediately called in Secretary of the Treasury Fred Vinson and Attorney General Tom Clark to help him decide what to do.

They agreed that this picture of the double life of a highly placed government official was shocking. But key pieces were missing from the depiction of White as a traitor. There was no evidence that he had done any spying, that he had divulged any secrets, that he had passed any documents to a foreign agent—nothing, in fact, except that he often associated with certain people who, the FBI said without providing any proof, were members of a spy ring.

The decision in the President's office that day was that there was not enough hard evidence of White's duplicity to warrant the uproar and scandal of withdrawing his nomination and dismissing him from the government. To do this would be to blacken his reputation irreparably, even if he should ultimately be proved innocent. And, if he was guilty, his premature dismissal would blow the case against his fellow conspirators. Accordingly, it was decided to allow White's nomination to stand and to keep him under special FBI surveillance in his new post. Meantime, the FBI was to put every available man and resource at its command on a top priority assignment digging into Communist espionage in the United States.

White served at the International Monetary Fund until April 1947, when he resigned to enter private business. Among the trophies he took with him was a cordial letter from President Truman praising his service to the government and wishing him well for the future.

The following year, White was called before the Un-American Activities Committee to be grilled about his alleged Communist connections. Although some of the associates with whom he had been linked in the FBI report had taken the Fifth Amendment when they were questioned, White denied the allegations from top to bottom—just as he had done months earlier, he reminded the committee, before a grand jury that asked the same questions. Two days later, he died of a heart attack.

The Harry Dexter White case had a sensational revival in 1953. Herbert Brownell, Eisenhower's first Attorney General, echoing the "soft on communism" theme of the previous year's campaign, charged in a speech at Detroit and later before a congressional committee that "White was known to be a Communist spy by the very people [Truman, naturally] who appointed him to the most sensitive position he ever held in the government."

The proof of Harry White's treason, if any, died with him.

Brownell did not produce it, but neither have White's friends, for all their efforts, wholly dissipated the cloud of suspicion that shadows his memory.

As for President Truman, he was never convinced that White was a spy, in spite of the questionable company he kept. Had the President been more prudent than brave, he could have eased White out at almost any time in the spring or summer of 1946 and rid himself of a possible future embarrassment. But he liked to think that a man was innocent until proved guilty.

The time was fast coming when President Truman could no longer be certain that his instinct for tolerance would serve the national interest. The *Amerasia* case, the Canadian spy ring, the White case—all raised the chilling possibility, if not the fact, that Communist spies *had* infiltrated the government. Such an effort was clearly consistent with the spreading ambitions and open contempt that the Russian leaders were showing at international conference tables. Meanwhile, the existing machinery for screening potential spies out of the Federal bureaucracy was in general disrepute, and the President's critics in Congress and the press were accusing him of turning his back on the problem.

In the November elections of 1946, Republicans won control of Congress for the first time in eleven years. At the top of their list of campaign pledges was the promise to "clean the Communists and fellow travelers out of the government." Their solution was to define loyalty by statute and to provide criminal penalties for the disloyal —a sure prescription, in Mr. Truman's view, for a legalized witch-hunt. Obviously, if he did not grab the initiative in a hurry, it would pass irretrievably to Congress and probably into the hands of fanatics.

Late in November, after the election and while Congress was in recess, the President set up a Temporary Commission on Employee Loyalty, made up of ranking officials of the Federal departments and the Civil Service Commission. They were told to devise a new loyalty program that would apply uniformly throughout the government, protect the security interests of the nation, and zealously protect the personal dignity and the Constitutional rights of the individual employee. It was an overambitious goal, as it turned out. The Commission completed its labors in the late winter of 1947 and put a blueprint on the President's desk. The President adopted the recommendations virtually intact and on March 2 issued Executive

Order 9835, which set up the Federal Employee Loyalty Program. This was a milestone in the life of the United States—a wretched one that sanctioned government prying into the privacy of its citizens' minds and consciences. But it was an inevitable one in the context of the time in which it was reached.

"The program as I saw it operate had a lot of flaws in it," Mr. Truman admitted later. "It was by no means a perfect instrumentality. [But] it did give anyone who was accused as fair an opportunity to have his case adjudicated as was possible under the climate of opinion that then existed."

The loyalty program was vast in magnitude and complex in execution. It called for the FBI to make a "name check" on each of the more than 2,000,000 persons already on the Federal payroll, from letter carriers to Cabinet officers, and of the approximately 500,000 who would apply for jobs each year. Wherever any "derogatory information" about the loyalty of an individual was found, a "full field investigation" was to be conducted, which meant probing into his past life and associations as far back as high school and earlier years. The substance of these investigations was then transmitted to a loyalty board in the agency where the individual worked or sought a job. In the board's discretion, it could either throw out the charges or call the accused before it for a hearing. If the verdict of the board after such a hearing was adverse (job applicants were rarely accorded a hearing; they just weren't hired if any question had been raised about them), the employee could appeal the decision first to a regional loyalty board and finally to the Loyalty Review Board in Washington. This was the court of ultimate jurisdiction, and if it said that the employee had to go, that was the end.

The basic criterion for an adverse finding by the loyalty boards was the semantically vulnerable phrase, "reasonable grounds for belief" in the disloyalty of the accused.* Six categories of proscribed acts or behavior that could be used in reaching this judgment were set forth. Three of these related to such obvious crimes as treason and espionage; one to advocacy of violent overthrow of the government, already covered under the Hatch Act; one to breaches of official duty, such as disclosure of confidential information; and one (as

---

* In her definitive study of the loyalty program, Eleanor Bontecou observes: " 'Reasonable doubt' is a phrase of art which in other fields of the law has gradually acquired concrete meaning through case-by-case decisions. It is still undefined, however, in the loyalty program, where it is applied against instead of in favor of the accused person."—*The Federal Loyalty-Security Program* (Cornell Univ. Press, 1953), p. 70.

it turned out, overwhelmingly the most important) to membership
in or association with any of the organizations designated by the
Attorney General as subversive.

The procedures for a loyalty hearing, as set forth in the Executive
Order, required that "The charges shall be stated as specifically and
completely as, in the discretion of the employing department or
agency, *security considerations permit.*" (Italics supplied.) The procedures did not require that an accused person be confronted by
his accusers, nor did they entitle him to substantive proof of an
allegation against him. In actual practice, the loyalty boards adhered to the rule of the FBI that to disclose the identity of a "confidential informant" is destructive of its investigation techniques, and
so inimical to the national security.

Most loyalty hearings were therefore in the nature of star-
chamber proceedings such as Dorothy Bailey experienced, and were
shorn of the "due process" protection of the Sixth Amendment. The
first Chairman of the Loyalty Review Board, Seth B. Richardson, a
crusty New England Republican who was nearing his seventieth
birthday, rationalized this reversal of the normal concepts of American justice by falling back upon a plausible but obfuscating cliché:
"Public employment is a privilege, not a right." The Government
has a natural right, he argued, to discharge whom it will for any
reason it chooses, and it has no inherent obligation to provide hearings or to produce witnesses to justify its actions.

This line of reasoning seemed to put both the judge and the jury
on the side of the confidential informant. The full burden of proof
thus fell upon the accused. It was up to him to prove his innocence
of charges that were usually vague and unspecific, made by persons
whom he did not know, whom he could not confront, and whose
credibility he could not challenge. In the great majority of cases
reaching the loyalty boards, the indictment rested on guilt by association, rather than on overt acts. In a typical case reported by
Eleanor Bontecou, the formal charges against which a civilian employee of the Air Force was required to defend himself read in
part as follows:

The evidence indicates that:
(a) Your name appeared as one of the signers of an open letter . . .
of the National Federation for Constitutional Liberties dated 26 December 1941. The National Federation for Constitutional Liberties has been
cited by the Attorney General as Communist.
(b) Your name appeared in an article in the 21 March, 1946, edition of

the "New World" as a sponsor of a Seattle, Washington, mass meeting . . . sponsored by the National Committee to Win the Peace. The National Committee to Win the Peace has been cited by the Attorney General as Communist.

(c) Since 1939 you have been a close associate of ———, an individual who, evidence in our files indicates, has displayed an active, sympathetic interest in the principles and policies of the Communist Party.

(d) During your period of employment at the University of Washington you made statements to the effect that you believe "the House Un-American Activities Committee hearings in Washington, D.C., are more of a threat to civil liberties than is the Communist Party because they infringe upon free speech. . . ."

The foregoing information indicates that you have been and are a member, close affiliate, or sympathetic associate of the Communist Party. . . .[3]

As Miss Bontecou points out in her thoughtful study: "No matter what the purpose of the questions which are asked at the loyalty hearings, they appear to identify intellectual curiosity and reform with communism, to be directed toward the enforcement of conformity and to have little to do with the safety of the nation."

The loyalty program was an unloved changeling on every hand. To the security zealot in Congress it was a devious scheme by President Truman to thwart a genuine attack on subversion in the government. Agency heads were under almost constant harassment from congressional committees to explain and defend their conduct of loyalty investigations, and where zeal seemed to be lagging they were confronted with a threatened cut in their appropriations or other reprisals.

To most liberals and many legal experts the program was both fruitless and a betrayal of fundamental American concepts of justice and civil rights. One's loyalty, it was argued, could not be measured by legalistic yardsticks, and attempts to do so meant a probing into political beliefs and affiliations. A group of professors at Harvard Law School, headed by Zechariah Chafee and Erwin N. Griswold, denounced the program for its disregard of legal procedures and for its reliance for evidence upon the untested validity of the Attorney General's list. And John Lord O'Brien, writing in the *Harvard Law Review* in April 1948, condemned the novel and cruel concept of guilt by association.

"In practical effect," he wrote, "the result of a finding of such association [in the absence of an overt act] is analagous to that of a criminal conviction—loss of occupation, lasting disgrace and a continued impairment of his ability to earn a livelihood."

From late 1947, when it went into operation, through the end of the Truman administration in 1952, the loyalty program was a conspicuous feature of the political landscape.* It was under almost constant attack from both the right and the left, alternately denounced and defended in countless editorials, speeches, and congressional debates. Its own security system was regularly breached, and its supposedly secret interrogations and findings leaked freely to the outside world and to Capitol Hill in particular. It spread a pall of fear through the ranks of the Federal bureaucracy, from file clerks to bureau heads. For one never knew what his loyalty board "had" on him, or who among his colleagues might be an informer. Merely to have been questioned by a security officer was enough, in many instances, to put a person under suspicion and to have his neighbors shun him.

By mid-1952, slightly more than 4,000,000 persons, actual and prospective employees of the Federal Government, had undergone at least a routine loyalty check through the files of the FBI. Against how many some derogatory information was found is not known, but agency loyalty boards placed tentative charges against 9,077 and brought 2,961 to formal hearings. Of these, 378 were either dismissed from their jobs or denied employment—.002 percent of the total.

How grave a risk were these 378 to the national security? Chairman Richardson suggested the answer when he told a Senate Committee in 1950: "Not one single case or evidence directing toward a case of espionage has been disclosed in the record. Not one single syllable of evidence has been found by the FBI indicating that a particular case involves a question of espionage."

---

* It remained so, in fact, well into the second Eisenhower administration. The Republicans put more teeth in the program by broadening the definition of disloyalty and imposing harsher standards of punishment. Through two political campaigns— 1954 and 1956—Republican Party spokesmen played an avid "numbers game" with the monthly statistics of the Loyalty Review Board to demonstrate the GOP's prowess in cleaning out the Communists left behind by the Democrats. The totals were made to look impressive by lumping voluntary resignations with dismissals. When this bit of chicanery was exposed by the press, the "numbers game" fell into disuse. The loyalty program underwent a number of modifications during the 1950's. Its vestiges remain today in the administrative custody of the Civil Service Commission, where the emphasis is on "security" rather than "loyalty," a more realistic and defensible criterion.

Alger Hiss

Elizabeth Bentley and Whittaker Chambers told their stories of Communist espionage in public for the first time in the summer of 1948. Drab, middle-aged, hesitant of speech and manner, they were about as unglamorous a pair of secret agents as could be imagined, but the tale they told could not have been more melodramatic if their names had been Mata Hari and James Bond. Each, according to the testimony, had been a dedicated, card-carrying Communist in the 1930's. Each had become an active part of the Soviet espionage network, although the well-worn paths of the two between New York and Washington had seldom crossed. And each, in anguish of spirit and in fear of physical harm, had broken away from the party—Chambers in 1938, Miss Bentley in 1945. In time they told their separate stories to the FBI and to a Federal Grand Jury.

Miss Bentley appeared before the Senate Subcommittee on Expenditures in the Executive Departments on Saturday, July 31. The following Monday she was claimed by the House Un-American Activities Committee, and two days later she was followed there by Chambers. For the better part of three weeks, before massed reporters and photographers in a packed hearing room in the Old House Office Building they spelled one another spinning one of the eeriest cloak-and-dagger thrillers of modern times. The question of how much they said was fiction and how much was real is still debatable. They were both, understandably, overwrought and probably psychotic. But the net effect of their performances was to give an appearance of hard and ominous reality—names, dates, and places—to what had been largely a circumstantial and hard-to-believe supposition, that Communist agents *had* infiltrated the United States Government.

President Truman, caught up in the greatest political battle of his life for reelection, committed, during that first week, the memorable blunder of labeling the hearings "a red herring." Whatever truth there may have been in this unguarded assessment, its effect was to douse the flames with a pail of gasoline.

More than two years earlier, the Bentley-Chambers disclosures to the FBI in New York had set off a major countrywide investigation into Communist activities of all kinds. The President had ordered this in response to the disclosures about Harry Dexter White. When this investigation had been going for some eighteen months, the

Attorney General, in June 1947, impaneled a special blue-ribbon grand jury in New York to study the evidence that the FBI was assembling. Miss Bentley and Chambers were among more than a hundred witnesses questioned by the grand jury in airtight secrecy over a period of almost a year.

The first public acknowledgment that such a grand jury was sitting came late in June 1948, when indictments were handed up against twelve leaders of the Communist Party of America— virtually the entire party hierarchy, including William Z. Foster, Earl Browder's successor as leader and most recent Presidential candidate; Eugene Dennis, the general secretary; and Benjamin J. Davis and all members of the national board. They were charged under the Smith Act of 1940 with teaching and advocating the violent overthrow of the government. This was the first frontal attack on the legality of the Communist Party per se, and it was to have a long, tortuous journey through the legal labyrinths all the way to the Supreme Court before it could be sustained.

Word of the Bentley-Chambers testimony inevitably leaked to committee sources on Capitol Hill, and, in all probability, portions of the highly secret grand jury transcript as well. Questioning in the early phases of the congressional hearings by some of the committee members appeared to be framed in full knowledge of what the answers would be. Though the story unfolded in matter-of-fact terms, it had an air of Hollywood unreality about it.

Both Miss Bentley and Chambers, after joining the Communist Party in the middle years of the Great Depression, were drawn willingly into the espionage apparatus, they said. It was an ideological and philosophical commitment to help bring about a new social order, not necessarily to injure the United States. In due course, each of them came under the control of a Soviet contact—J. Peters, in the case of Chambers, and Jacob Golos originally in the case of Elizabeth Bentley. Golos was an agent of the Soviet intelligence agency, NKVD. Bentley and Chambers knew these agents only by code or cover names, and they were not permitted to know about others in the network beyond those with whom they had to work directly. Apparently, they had never heard of each other until they were brought together in 1945 by the FBI.

Because of their past familiarity with Washington, both had been assigned primarily to working with "cells" established there, as recruiters and as couriers who transmitted instructions or picked up contraband papers and microfilm from government files provided by the cell members. Both posed as journalists to give themselves a "cover identity." Their contacts with their sources were usually conducted in darkened doorways, obscure restaurants, and innocent-looking park benches. Apparently, neither one ever ran any risk of detection.

Chambers' operations occurred during the pre-World War II years. He had the dual function, he said, of maintaining an "elite corps" of Communists and sympathizers in high government posts and also an active spy ring which collected information, but the two groups frequently overlapped.

Among the dozen or more names that Chambers gave the House Un-American Activities Committee as members of the his Washington apparatus were the following: John Abt, then of the Agricultural Adjustment Administration; Lee Pressman, later to become general counsel of the Congress of Industrial Organizations; Victor Perlo, a minor official in the Treasury; Nathan Witt, of the National Labor Relations Board; and Alger Hiss.

Miss Bentley's activities spanned the war years. She described for the committee two somewhat amorphous spy rings in Washington that were her particular responsibility. The memberships and identities fluctuated and became confused during the progress of her testimony. One, she said, under the immediate direction of N. Gregory Silvermaster, an economist at the Treasury, included, among half a dozen others, Harry Dexter White, Lauchlin Currie, and William L. Ullman, a Major in the Air Force. In the basement of Ullman's house, she said, was a photographic laboratory where documents spirited out of the Treasury and other government departments were regularly transposed to microfilm, which she carried to Golos and later to Gromov in her handbag. The other ring she described was headed by Victor Perlo, by this time an official of the War Production Board; it included several officers from the Office of Strategic Services, a former secretary of columnist Walter Lippmann, and William Remington, at the time of her testimony a minor official in the Department of Commerce.

The Bentley-Chambers revelations created a sensation in Washington and dominated the headlines of the nation's press throughout most of August. The hearing room of the Un-American Activities Committee (it had virtually frozen out the Senate Committee) was daily besieged by throngs of spectators who stood in line for hours hoping to squeeze past the great mahogany doors for a first-hand glimpse of the drama. The proceedings were directed by the red-faced and short-tempered committee chairman, Republican Congressman J. Parnell Thomas of New Jersey (he was to be jailed a few months later for exacting salary kickbacks from his congressional staff) and by the committee's gaunt, poker-faced chief investigator, Robert E. Stripling. The atmosphere of the hearing room was chaotic, noisy, and vituperative as more than a score of the accused marched day after day across the witness stand. Some, like White, Hiss, and Remington heatedly denied any connection with or knowledge of the alleged spy rings. A few, like Abt and Pressman, acknowledged their Communist attachments but denied the espionage charges. The majority refused to answer any of the committee's questions, invoking the Fifth Amendment against self-incrimination.

But in spite of its highly charged melodrama, the spy hearing was beginning to run out of steam and also out of public interest by late August. One factor was public disgust with the crass, undignified conduct of the hearing itself. The proceedings had degenerated into a tawdry burlesque of a court trial. Another factor was that many of the accused had long since left the government, and the charges against them, mainly unsupported in the first place, now seemed empty. Most important of all, it was realized that all those called before the committee had also been questioned by the New York grand jury on the basis of the same accusations and evidence, and none had been charged with wrongdoings.* The public was beginning to suspect a hoax—and there the whole business might have rested if Alger Hiss had been content to leave well enough alone.

Alger Hiss was a tall, spare, intense man 44 years old, with crisp dark hair, sharp, intelligent eyes, and the confident bearing that so often accompanies a Harvard law degree. His fourteen-year career in the State Department had carried him very close to the top policy-making levels. He had accompanied President Roosevelt to the Yalta Conference in 1944 and had been a principal aide to Secretary of State Stettinius at the first United Nations conference at San Francisco in 1945. He qualified unquestionably as one of the "bright young men" of the late New Deal, and he and his wife, Priscilla,

* An assumption of innocence from this fact is not wholly valid. There is a three-year statute of limitations on violations of the espionage statute, and it is possible that the grand jury was deterred by this even if it had credible evidence that espionage had been committed. On the other hand, such a grand jury, where it lacks indictable evidence but believes that serious wrongdoing has occurred, may hand up a presentment calling the court's and the public's atttention to the facts but without a recommendation for prosecution. Whether the grand jury considered this alternative is, of course, not known.

were numbered among the adornments of the social-intellectual constellation of Georgetown, where they lived. He had left the government early in 1947 to become president of the Carnegie Foundation for International Peace in New York.

Whittaker Chambers' flat accusation on August 4 that Alger Hiss had been an accomplice of his in the Communist network left most of official Washington stunned with anger and disbelief. Hiss rejected the charge with unequivocal vigor. It was obvious that one man or the other was lying.

Chambers told the committee: "For a number of years, I, myself, served in the underground in Washington, D.C. I knew it at its top level, a group of seven or so men. A member of this group . . . was Alger Hiss."

Hiss told the committee two days later: "I am not and have never been a member of the Communist Party and have not followed the Communist Party line. . . . To the best of my knowledge I never heard of Whittaker Chambers until 1947, when two representatives of the FBI asked if I knew him. So far as I know, I have never laid eyes on him and I should like to have the opportunity to do so."

The committee questioned Chambers further in executive session to seek more proof of his familiarity with Hiss. He told them of his early intimacy with Hiss and the Hiss household; how he had stayed overnight on occasion at their Georgetown home; how the Hisses used to call one another "Hilly" and "Pross"; how they had owned a cocker spaniel; how in 1936 they had a dilapidated Ford which they gave Chambers for Communist Party use when they decided to buy a new car for themselves; how the family's frequent bird-watching expeditions along the banks of the Potomac had once been rewarded "to their great excitement" by seeing a prothonotary warbler. Such intimate details, the committee concluded, could come only from firsthand experience or an extraordinarily inventive imagination.

On August 17, two members of the committee, Richard M. Nixon of California and John McDowell of Pennsylvania, decided to give Hiss his wish to confront Chambers in person. The meeting was held in a suite in the Commodore Hotel in New York. It was a tense, angry session, in which Hiss finally identified his accuser as a man he had known many years before as George Crosley, an unsuccessful free-lance writer whom he had briefly befriended but whom he had dropped because Crosley was a "deadbeat."

"May I say for the record at this point," Hiss said to the two committeemen, "that I would like to invite Mr. Whittaker Chambers to make those same statements out of the presence of this committee without their being privileged for suit for libel?"

And then, turning to Chambers, he added: "I challenge you to do it, and I hope you will do it damn quickly."

That was the fatal blunder for Hiss. The Un-American Activities Committee by this time had virtually given up making a case out of the Bentley-Chambers exposé, including the charges against Hiss, and had sent its records to the Department of Justice for almost certain interment. But Hiss, by his impulsive challenge to Chambers, pushed his luck too far.

On Sunday, August 30, Whittaker Chambers appeared on "Meet the Press," a nationwide radio program. The first question put to him by a member of the panel, Edward T. Folliard of the Washington *Post*, was: "Are you willing to repeat your charge that Alger Hiss was a Communist?"

Chambers was fully prepared for this thorny hurdle, but facing it made him blanch and hesitate momentarily. Then, in a low but firm voice, he said: "Alger Hiss was a Communist and may still be one."

Hiss promptly brought suit for slander against Chambers, asking $75,000 damages. In mid-November his attorneys summoned Chambers for the taking of pretrial depositions in Baltimore. They asked what evidence he could produce to support his charge that Hiss was a part of the Communist underground. Chambers laid on the table a thick, faded manila envelope and took from it copies of sixty-five State Department cables and memorandums which he said Hiss had copied and turned over to him. They bore dates of 1937 and 1938 and carried such inscriptions as, "Paris: To the Secretary of State, Strictly Confidential . . . Signed Bullitt"; "Rome: To the Secretary of State . . . signed, Phillips"; "Vienna: To the Secretary of State . . . Signed, Messersmith," and so on. He also produced four handwritten notes, summaries of official cables, which he said were in the handwriting of Alger Hiss.*

---

* Hiss, in his trial and subsequently, did not deny the authenticity of these papers but maintained to the end that Chambers did not get them from him. In respect particularly to the handwritten notes, he has offered the following explanation:

"The volume of incoming cables was so heavy, often as many as a hundred in a day, that Mr. Sayre [Francis B. Sayre, Assistant Secretary and Hiss's superior at the time] did not have time to read them all in order to determine those of special interest to him. . . . For [this reason] I made hurried notes [of the contents of some] on small slips of paper. . . . These slips would remain attached in the piles of cables on my desk until I could make my report. When that had been completed, they would be disposed of. . . .

"It was four of these little notes to myself that Chambers produced in Baltimore on November 17, 1948, along with the typed pages. They could have come to him in a variety of ways [for instance, from messengers or charwomen]. . . . In

These documents were the first substantive evidence produced by either Chambers or Miss Bentley backing up their charges that espionage actually had been committed. Their disclosure in the deposition hearings threw Hiss's attorneys into consternation. But more significantly, they gave the grand jury (a continuation of the one that had previously studied the Bentley-Chambers charges), then sitting in New York, valuable fresh material on which to work. More significantly still, they led the Washington Bureau chief for the New York *Herald Tribune*, Bert Andrews, to put an obvious but so far unasked question to Chambers: "Are there any more documents where these came from?"

Chambers said, yes, there were, and agreed to lead Andrews and the committee investigators to them. Then followed the memorable visit to a garden patch behind the Chambers' Maryland farm home at 10:30 o'clock on the night of Thursday, December 2, and the production of the famous "pumpkin papers"—three rolls of undeveloped microfilm representing hundreds of government documents which Chambers had hidden in a hollowed-out pumpkin.

Government prosecutors were never to make a case on anything contained in the "pumpkin papers," but the very fact of their existence kept the question of Communists in the government a burning political issue for more than a decade. They made irrefutable Whittaker Chambers' confession of having been a Communist spy and lent credence, if not proof, to his accusations against others, including Hiss..

Alger Hiss was indicted by the grand jury on December 16, 1948, on two charges of perjury: denying before the jury that he had passed State Department papers to Chambers (the Baltimore papers, not the "pumpkin papers"); and denying that he had had contact with Chambers after 1937. He was not charged under the espionage or any related statute. His first trial in 1949 resulted in a hung jury. At his second trial, in January 1950, he was convicted and sentenced to five years in prison. His appeal went all the way to the Supreme Court, which in March 1951 refused to intervene. On March 22 he entered the Federal Penitentiary at Lewisburg, Pennsylvania, to begin serving his sentence.

---

the absence of specific knowledge on that score, the important point is that by their very nature they show they are not what Chambers pretended they were. . . .

"But he had to turn them into something else if he were to use them to support his new charges. So he said that I made the notes *for him* about documents which had passed under (my) eyes quickly and which (I) was unable to bring out. . . ." —(*In The Court of Public Opinion*, by Alger Hiss (New York: Alfred A. Knopf, 1957), pp. 259-60.)

The Alger Hiss case is an authentic and indestructible item of Americana, as dramatic and as endlessly mystifying as its French counterpart, the case of Captain Dreyfus. Millions of Americans have never been able to bring themselves to believe in his guilt, yet are unable to explain away the damaging evidence against him. To other millions, he was the consummate traitor, irrespective of the fact that he was found guilty only of perjury. Public opinion during the 1950's divided almost down the middle in this fashion, and neither side has won many converts from the other since.

There was nothing ambiguous, however, about the impact of the Hiss case on partisan politics of the late forties and early fifties. Little effort by the Republicans was needed to make Alger Hiss the symbol and living proof of their contention that the Truman administration was "soft on communism." The Hiss case was a scourge to Adlai Stevenson when he ran for President in 1952, and even today it still echoes occasionally from the hustings.

What Price Security?

Throughout his term of office, there was hardly any letup in President Truman's battle with Congress over who was to manage the nation's internal security—the executive or the legislative branch. This was not a sterile queston of legality and prerogative. It was a pragmatic question of workability first, and next, a philosophical question of finding a proper balance between the security needs of the government and the individual rights of its citizens. The President's surprising electoral victory of 1948 brought only a brief respite in this struggle. Another election lay ahead in 1950, and again in 1952, and Republicans were sure that there was no heavier bludgeon in their arsenal than the "soft on communism" issue. Harry Truman could see clearly what the political consequences for himself and the country would be if he lost this contest with Congress. Bigotry and vigilantism would ride roughshod across the land.

There were already signs aplenty of this as he began his new term in 1949. The legislatures of California and several other states had set up their carbon-copy Un-American Activities Committees to hunt down subversive influences in their own bailiwicks. Dozens of school boards and university regents began to demand loyalty oaths and security checks of their teachers and to fire those who resisted.

The American Legion and similar organizations in many communities set themselves up as censors of school texts, libraries, and public lecture platforms. Ku Klux Klan klaverns in the South and some parts of the Middle West shook the mothballs out of their long-disused robes to harass the "Communists, race-mixers, and atheists" whom they found in their midst.

In New York four enterprising ex-FBI agents, using the files of various congressional committees, published a book called *Red Channels*, in which they detailed the allegedly Communist connections of 150 writers, actors, directors, and others in the entertainment industry. One of the first victims of this commercialized blacklisting was the well-known actress Jean Muir, whose contract to star in a popular radio serial, "The Aldrich Family," was canceled by the National Broadcasting Company. NBC explained piously that it really didn't think Miss Muir was a Communist or even a fellow traveler, but her inclusion in *Red Channels* had made her "controversial," and that was bad for business. Scores of other actors, writers, professors, and figures in public life found themselves similarly stigmatized by *Red Channels* and its sudden spawn of imitators. Hollywood was particularly susceptible to this kind of intimidation.

This wave of bigotry was meanwhile being nourished by events in the real underworld of subversion. In March 1949, FBI agents in New York arrested Judith Coplon, a comely young woman employed in the Internal Security Division of the Department of Justice and charged her with delivering confidential information to a Soviet agent. During the summer of that year, the long-drawn-out trial of the twelve Communist Party leaders who had been indicted by the New York grand jury, produced a new climax of public anger over the tactics of obstruction and harassment used by the lawyers for the defense. Later, Klaus Fuchs, a British nuclear scientist who had worked at the top level of the atomic bomb project at Alamogordo was arrested in England, where he confessed to years of systematic espionage for the Russians. Two of his American accomplices, Harry Gold and David Greenglass, were picked up early in 1950 by the FBI in New York.

Meanwhile, investigators for the Senate Internal Security subcommittee had reopened the *Amerasia* case with dire hints that men high in the State Department would be implicated. Hiss was sent to prison at last, enormously enhancing the prestige and credibility of the House Un-American Activities Committee. And when, by the late summer of 1950, American soldiers in faraway Korea were actually being slaughtered by Communist bullets, some said that it was in retribution for the Truman administration's faithless betrayal of Chiang Kai-shek and the Nationalist Chinese.

"The greatest Kremlin asset in our history," Senator Taft told the Senate about this time, "has been the pro-Communist group in the State Department who promoted at every opportunity the Communist cause in China."

Events such as these stirred up a great wave of anti-Russian sentiment and raised questions of whether the United States, with its meticulous respect for the niceties of the law and of international relations, was able to defend itself against such a ruthless campaign of subversion. Public opinion polls and "letters to the editor" columns all over the country showed a rising state of alarm and of demands that the administration show more toughness in dealing with these enemies within the gates. Congress was eager to respond.

For years, various committees of the House and Senate had been searching for a legislative formula by which membership in the Communist Party could be made illegal. The more hotheaded sponsors envisioned mass trials at which Communist party members and fellow travelers would be herded off to jail by the thousands irrespective of their rights of free speech and assembly. But the Constitutional barriers were formidable. The Smith Act of 1940 had come close to outlawing the party by prohibiting membership in any organization that advocated violent overthrow of the government, but the Supreme Court had yet to fit the Communist Party–USA into that definition. That was what the current trial of the twelve party leaders was about.

Early in 1950, Chairman Pat McCarran of the Senate Judiciary Committee began to stir and blend a number of these legislative concoctions together, starting with the Mundt-Nixon bill, which had passed the House the year before by an easy margin. What McCarran came out with in the end was a well-nigh undecipherable bill, running to thirty-two printed pages, which, in essence, did *not* prohibit membership in the Communist Party but *did* require that all who belonged to it proclaim that fact by registering with the Attorney General—at which point they would automatically incriminate themselves in respect to the Smith Act. A Subversive Activities Control Board was called for to enforce these registration provisions. In addition, the bill denied employment to Communists and their "dupes" in defense facilities; prohibited the issuance of passports to them; called for the deportation of any alien who had ever been a Communist; and provided for the detention in wartime "of any person as to whom there is reason to believe he might engage in acts of espionage or sabotage." This meant Communists, obviously. It could also, presumably, mean anybody whom a McCarran (or an Un-American Activities Committee chairman) found to be, by the rule of guilt by association, a sympathizer or fellow traveler of the Communists. It was a dragnet such as any dictator might envy.

President Truman strongly opposed the bill. "It's just like the Alien and Sedition Act of 1798, and that didn't work either," he said. The McCarran bill, he argued, would fail in its main objective of stamping out communism by driving the Communists deeper underground, where it would be still more difficult to keep an eye on them. But even worse, he contended, was the fact that the bill was an unconstitutional invasion of the rights of freedom of speech and freedom of assembly, and any infringement of these precious rights would be more harmful to the country than anything the Communists could do. He had offered legislation of his own to stiffen the espionage statutes, in which, he argued, the real weakness and the remedy lay. But the President's proposal was brushed aside. Chairman McCarran committed it to a dusty pigeonhole of his Judiciary Committee, where it would not compete with his own bill.

After weeks of harsh debate, Congress passed the McCarran bill, on September 17, by lopsided margins of 354 to 20 in the House and 70 to 7 in the Senate. "Many who had criticized the bill in debate voted for it on final passage," the New York *Times* reported. "The feeling on Capitol Hill, apparently, is that it is too risky politically to vote against anti-Communist legislation in this election year."

But even while the debate was going on, the President was working on a veto message, one of the most urgent he was ever to issue. A memorandum prepared for him by his special counsel, Charles S. Murphy, discloses the pattern of the President's thinking. It read in part:

The signing of this bill would represent an action of moral appeasement on a matter of the highest principle. Since this legislation would not furnish an effective means for controlling Communism in this country . . . the next move would be to cry for still more repressive legislation.

Having once yielded on basic principles, the administration would find it difficult to make a stand when the next aggressive proposals came along . . . [it] would also greatly enlarge the field of activity of self-appointed loyalty censors, vigilantes and super patriots. . . .

Before we finish with this business we might well go through a period that would make the period of the alien and sedition laws look like one of moderation.[4]

The President was beset by conflicting advice on what to do about the McCarran bill, officially labeled the Internal Security Act of 1950, which now lay on his desk. Vice President Barkley and other Democratic legislative leaders urged him to sign. The political climate demanded it, they said, and a veto was certain to be overridden. They reminded him that the congressional elections were only a month and a half away. On the other hand, Dean Acheson and most members of the Cabinet argued for the veto on the ground that, though he could not prevent the bill from becoming law, he should at least sustain his moral position against it.

But there had never been any doubt in Truman's mind about what he would do. He would not only veto; he would put up a fight to have his veto upheld.

Congress was driving impatiently for adjournment that week in late September so that members could get home and begin their reelection campaigns. The security bill was the last item on their agenda. It reached the President's desk on Wednesday, September 20. He returned it at noon, Friday, with a hard-hitting and well-reasoned veto message that covered nine single-spaced legal pages.

He had also taken an unusual extra step. Each member of Congress found on his desk that morning a copy of the veto message along with a personal letter from the President. The President urged that the member, before casting his vote on the veto that day, read not only the full text of the McCarran bill but the President's reasons for refusing to sign it as well. As an old congressional hand himself, he was pretty sure that most members had only a vague notion of what was in the bill, and that if they took the trouble to find out they might be more receptive to his reasons for rejecting it.

The House totally ignored the President's request. Within an hour of its noon opening, and without debate, it voted to override the veto 286 to 48, which was far in excess of the two-thirds majority required. But the Senate, in its more deliberate fashion, delayed, and President Truman leaped to seize whatever advantage this might offer. He telephoned a high-spirited young first-termer, Hubert H. Humphrey (Majority Leader Scott Lucas was committed to vote to override), and asked him to muster what liberal forces he could to stave off a Senate vote until Saturday midnight. With adjournment set for that hour, such a filibuster just might succeed in sustaining the veto even if it couldn't be done with votes. In any event, Truman told Humphrey, a delay of twenty-four hours would give the press and radio time to alert the nation to what was involved in the conflict. Just possibly, this might build up a backfire at the grass roots.

It was a bold and desperate try, but it didn't work. Humphrey, with half a dozen liberal cohorts, including Paul Douglas of Illinois, Herbert Lehman of New York, and a roaring old maverick among Republicans, William Langer of North Dakota, held a resentful Senate in session through the night, spelling one another with hours of oratory. Langer collapsed from exhaustion shortly before daylight Saturday and was taken in an ambulance to a hospital. Humphrey and the others pushed doggedly on, but with diminishing hopes until midafternoon. After twenty-two hours of valiant futility, President Truman gave them permission to throw in the towel. At 4 o'clock the Senate voted 57 to 10 to override, and the Internal Security Act of 1950 became law.

It was a good fight, a typically Truman kind of to-hell-with-where-the-chips-may-fall fight. He had stood his ground against overwhelming odds for what he believed to be right. His enemies gloated over his defeat, but he won new respect with the more dispassionate editorial writers and columnists. And, just as he had prophesied, the McCarran Act did prove to be a legalistic and administrative monstrosity, destined to be fought over in the courts for more than a decade and adding little to the net security of the nation.

McCarthy

"It is one of the tragedies of our time," President Truman wrote after leaving the White House, "that the security program of the United States has been wickedly used by demagogues and sensational newspapers in an attempt to frighten and mislead the American people."

The one he principally had in mind was Senator Joseph R. McCarthy of Wisconsin, who, in the words of Richard H. Rovere, "was in many ways the most gifted demagogue ever bred on these shores. No bolder seditionist ever moved among us—nor any politician with a surer, swifter access to the dark places of the American mind."[5]

Joe McCarthy was a big, ambling, unkempt man who looked like a truck driver in a blue serge suit. He was "black Irish" with large, hairy hands; an omnipresent "five o'clock shadow" darkening his jowls; and coldly suspicious eyes under heavy black brows. There was menace in his bearing, like a fighter on the prowl, that was only partially dissipated by a quick, automatic grin and a crude, arm-around-the-shoulder sort of camaraderie. He apparently was a man who knew little of warmth, friendliness, and trust, and cared less. He had a paranoiac egotism—a bully's compulsive need to prove his toughness and to show his contempt for the conventions and amenities of softer men. He had few moral scruples and little sense of personal dignity or responsibility. He was a "rebel without a cause," for he had no crusader's goal, no vision for America, no plans even for himself beyond the sheer primitive satisfaction of being at the center of a brawl in which he was the only man with a club. Not even Joe McCarthy's most dedicated apologists have been able to endow his memory with any convincing attributes of nobility or compassion. He was simply a prodigiously effective mercenary.

Yet, for five years—from early 1950 through most of 1954—Joe McCarthy dominated the political life of this country as no demagogue had done before him. He scraped the raw nerve of the nation's anxiety and turned it into a neurosis. He spit in the eye of constituted authority, undermined public confidence in the government and its leaders, and tore at the nation's foreign policy with the indiscriminate ferocity of a bulldozer. He used lies, slander, and innuendo to smash his opponents and to build his own image of invincibility. He made cowards of all but a handful of his fellow Senators, and he kept two Presidents angrily and helplessly on the defensive in nearly everything they did.

It is lucky for the nation that Joe McCarthy was at heart a street fighter rather than a zealot. If he had had more guile and genius he might have wrecked the government.

Born poor on a farm in central Wisconsin, McCarthy came to the Senate in 1946 when he was 37 years old. He was an undistinguished and largely anonymous first-termer until he hoisted himself to sudden fame on the Communist issue in 1950. The choice of the issue was almost accidental. With a virtually blank record in the Senate, and facing reelection in two years, he was feeling about for any cause he could adopt that would enliven the interest of his constituents. A Catholic priest whom he met at dinner one night in January 1950 suggested to him that the conflict with communism was the overriding world problem of the day.

McCarthy's eyes suddenly brightened. "Why sure," he said, "the government is full of Communists. The thing to do is to hammer on them."*

The next day he told the speakers' bureau of the Republican National Committee that he was available for Lincoln's Birthday speaking assignments and that he would speak on communism. On the evening of February 9, he showed up for his first such engagement before the Republican Women's Club of Wheeling, West Virginia. An indifferent speaker who mumbled his words, he seemed nevertheless to have pleased his audience at the McLure Hotel that night with his homespun bluntness and his recitals of dark treason in high places. Actually, most of what he said was old hat. The stories of Alger Hiss, John Stewart Service, Julian Wadleigh, the familiar cast of characters from the loyalty investigations and the Bentley-Chambers testimony, had been hashed over in the papers and by other speakers for a couple of years. But McCarthy gave the story an extra fillip:

> The reason why we find ourselves in a position of impotency is not because our only powerful potential enemy has sent men to invade our shores, but rather because of the traitorous actions of those who have been treated so well by this nation. . . . This is glaringly true in the State Department. There the bright young men who were born with silver spoons in their mouths are the ones who have been most traitorous. . . .
>
> And ladies and gentlemen, while I cannot take the time to name all of the men in the State Department who have been named as active members of the Communist Party and members of a spy ring, I have here in my hand a list of 205—a list of names that were made known to the Secretary of State as being members of the Communist Party and who nevertheless are still working and shaping policy in the State Department.[6]

This statement simply was not true, and McCarthy knew it wasn't. In scrounging around for material for his speech, a staff man on the House Appropriations Committee gave the Senator a look at a confidential summary the committee had received in 1947 on 108 cases then under study by the State Department Loyalty Board. The individuals were designated by code numbers, not by name. McCarthy had no way of knowing what final disposition had been

---

* This encounter is described in some detail by Eric F. Goldman, in *The Crucial Decade* (Vintage Books, 1960).

made of any of them. In addition, he had come across a 1946 memorandum from Secretary of State Byrnes to Representative Adolph Sabath of Illinois to the effect that of 4,000 persons from OWI and elsewhere transferred to the Department at the end of the war, recommendations against permanent employment had been made in respect to 284, and that 79 actually had been separated.

It was from these dusty and inconclusive archives that McCarthy shaped his charge of "traitors" in the State Department. By what arithmetic he arrived first at 205, then 57, and at another time 81 "card-carrying Communists" in the State Department is not known. But by the time he had repeated his Wheeling speech on successive nights at Reno and Salt Lake City, where he fired off a telegram to President Truman demanding a housecleaning, "McCarthyism" had been launched.

Back in Washington ten days after his speeches in the West, McCarthy held the Senate in session until nearly midnight while he regaled it with the details of treachery of "81 known Communist agents in the State Department" whose identity he had managed to "dig out" but whose names he refused to divulge. One, he said, was "one of our foreign ministers," who had passed highly secret information to a Soviet agent in a European "listening post." Another, he said, was now working in the office of an Assistant Secretary of State; still another was a "high official" of the Voice of America; and another, denied a security clearance by the Department of State, was "now a speech writer in the White House." President Truman, he said, had become "a prisoner of a bunch of twisted intellectuals telling him only what they want him to know," and it was up to Congress to clean out the Communists for him.

This obscure freshman senator from Wisconsin was not saying much about disloyalty in the government that more seasoned Red baiters like William Jenner, Parnell Thomas, and Richard Nixon had not said before. But he managed better than they to evoke the dark specter of treason and to back up his charges, however ambiguously, with case histories. McCarthy's Republican colleagues welcomed him as a promising recruit to their "soft on communism" battery. The Democratic leadership decided to smother the new boy with kindness. Instead of deriding his charges, they would give him a special forum in which to prove them—or, as they confidently expected, to be shown up as a fake. Senate Majority Leader Scott Lucas proposed a full investigation of McCarthy's charges by the Foreign Relations Committee. He included in his resolution a Republican amendment that the committee be given the "right" to subpoena State Department loyalty files, which Lucas well knew they could not exercise without the President's permission. The Senate unanimously approved Lucas' resolution on February 23.

President Truman, asked the next day by reporters how he regarded the prospect of loyalty files being subpoenaed by a Senate committee, reminded them of a quip by President Andrew Jackson under somewhat similar circumstances: "The Chief Justice of the Supreme Court has made his decision. Now let's see him enforce it." Truman smiled his puckish smile and said, "That's your answer."

The Foreign Relations Subcommittee set up to hear McCarthy's charges was, in fact, a blue-ribbon panel. It was headed by Millard E. Tydings of Maryland, a tall, gray-haired patrician with an impeccable respect for the law and for the dignity of the Senate. Other Democratic members were the equally distinguished Theodore Francis Green of Rhode Island and Brian McMahon of Connecticut. The Republican members were Henry Cabot Lodge of Massachusetts and Bourke B. Hickenlooper of Iowa. Intellectually and politically, it was a "stacked" committee as far as McCarthy and his Red-hunting friends were concerned, for only the blunt-spoken and pragmatic Hickenlooper had any genuine sympathy for McCarthy's cause. But Joe McCarthy was to hack his committee into mincemeat and leave it writhing in frustration.

The scene of the hearings was that familiar arena where many another senatorial spectacle has been staged: the marble-walled, high-ceilinged Caucus Room of the Old Senate Office Building. When the opening session was called to order at 10 o'clock on Monday, March 8, the great chamber was packed with thrill-hungry spectators and crackling with suspense. The five members of the subcommittee were arranged along the wide, polished committee table, and behind them were banked a score of visiting Senators and staff members. A hundred reporters crowded shoulder to shoulder at long press tables on either side of the witness stand, and the whole scene was bathed in the harsh glare of klieg lights set up for the photographers and newsreel cameras. Just as the chairman was about to gavel the session to order, there was a mild commotion at the door as McCarthy shoved his way through the standees and moved toward the center of the stage. He was accompanied by a single aide and carried a bulging brown briefcase. He smiled a sly, enigmatic smile at reporters as he took a chair immediately behind the witness table and awaited the formality of being called.

That first day's session was to set the pattern of confusion, irrationality, contentiousness, and of maneuvering for tactical supremacy between McCarthy and Chairman Tydings that was to mark the whole four-month-long course of the hearing. The very first encounter, consuming almost an hour, found Tydings trying to extract from the witness a promise to advise the committee beforehand if the names of individuals charged with subversion were to be introduced in public testimony. He did not succeed. McCarthy revealed himself to be a master of the art of obfuscation; of the stubborn, long-winded circumlocution; of the reiterated and angrily defended non sequitur. Tydings, who was a verbal jouster of great repute in Maryland courtrooms and on the Senate floor, was often driven to sputtering exasperation by McCarthy's tenacious illogic and evasions. The Chairman had a stout ally in Senator McMahon, whose Irishness matched McCarthy's, but the gentle Senator Green was out of his element in this sort of combat. McCarthy got sporadic assistance from Hickenlooper and even from Lodge. By the sheer magnitude of his gall and persistence, Joe McCarthy soon had the whip hand in the proceedings and held on to it to the end.

His technique was to read off a series of damaging allegations about an individual and then, in effect, challenge the committee to scour the files of the FBI, the Civil Service Commission, or the loyalty boards to prove or disprove his charges. "This committee can very well determine where the truth lies," he said, "by saying, 'We shall get those files.' When you get those files, then you will know whether every word I have spoken here is true."

This was a shrewd device for shifting the burden of proof from the prosecutor onto the court, a tactic which McCarthy was to employ with great effect throughout his subsequent career. While such a tactic would not be countenanced in any courtroom, it could not be entirely ruled out under the fuzzy and elastic rules of procedure of a congressional committee. It was, accordingly, a perfect instrument for generating chaos, as was illustrated in one of the first cases McCarthy laid before the committee.

This involved a former New York City Municipal Judge, Dorothy Kenyon, who had been named by the Secretary of State in 1947 to the United Nations Commission on the Status of Women. McCarthy charged that for a decade and more she had been affiliated "with at least 28 Communist front organizations."

"I think it is important," McCarthy told the committee, "to know that the statement I shall make here today . . . is based on documented evidence, and these documents I will present to the committee as I go along."

The evidence he submitted consisted of letterheads, lists of signers of petitions and sponsors of meetings for a variety of causes, newspaper clippings, and unsupported allegations made before such groups as the House and the California Un-American Activities Committees, in which Miss Kenyon had been mentioned. One typical exchange between the witness and committee went as follows:

SEN. McCARTHY: For the guidance of the committee, I hand you herewith exhibit No. 2 (a printed letterhead), which fully documents Miss Kenyon's affiliation with the National Council of American-Soviet Friendship. On November 16, 1948, Miss Kenyon, as a member of the board of sponsors of this officially declared subversive organization, welcomed the Red Dean of Canterbury, Hewlett Johnson, at a rally in Madison Square Garden in the City of New York.

SEN. McMAHON: Just a minute, Senator. The National Council of American-Soviet Friendship had quite a vogue when we were co-belligerents back during the war days. I think there are a couple of Senators of the United States who are still members.

SEN. McCARTHY: The Senator is talking about war days. This document is dated late 1948. In this case, it was declared subversive by the House Un-American Activities Committee, the California Un-American Activities Committee, and the Attorney General.

SEN. TYDINGS: Senator McCarthy, I see some names here which I think it only fair ought to be associated with the evidence you have given. I see such names as Ernest Hemingway, Dr. Harold Urey . . . The Honorable Stanley Isaacs . . . [Tydings then read into the record the other fifty names on the letterhead, constituting almost a "Who's Who" of the intellectual elite of the country.]

SEN. McCARTHY: Mr. Chairman, I think as I give the documents showing the Communist Front organizations that this individual has belonged to, you will find a sizable number of names of some fine individuals. I think that it is possible that you, yourself, may be duped into joining or having your name used on some Communist Front organizations. The reason I submit the vast number is that it is impossible for any normal individual, of normal intelligence, to be so deceived that they can act as sponsors for 28 different Communist Front organizations. I personally would not be caught dead belonging to any one of them.

SEN. TYDINGS: That is an opinion, Senator. We would like to have the evidence and the facts.[7]

Day after day, as McCarthy spun out his tale of treachery, he supplemented his testimony before the committee with broad "leaks" to newsmen and speeches on the Senate floor. Most of those

he implicated were obscure, but a few names commanded top headlines, such as Philip C. Jessup, United States Ambassador-at-Large
specializing in Far Eastern affairs, and John Stewart Service. The
veteran Foreign Service officer already had been cleared by the
State Department Loyalty Board of charges identical to Mc-
Carthy's; they had first been made in 1946, by Ambassador Patrick
Hurley. Both Jessup and Service were recalled from missions overseas to go before the Tydings committee to refute McCarthy's
charges.

John E. Peurifoy, Deputy Under Secretary of State, angrily denounced the charges as "a shame and a disgrace" and said Mc-
Carthy had dredged up old allegations that were "dead, discredited
and disproven." McCarthy replied that this was "just another
effort by the State Department to cover up and confuse the issue."
President Truman, vacationing in Key West, branded McCarthy "a
liar" and said he was being abetted by Republicans who wanted a
campaign issue in the fall elections. The President made it known
that Jessup and Service had his full confidence.

McCarthy now began to take his case to the Senate floor, using
that forum to elaborate charges he had made before the committee
and to accuse the committee itself of conniving with the administration and Secretary of State Acheson in a monster cover-up. Acheson
became his primary target because, he said, the "Red Dean" used
his office to protect the Communists in his employ.

McCarthy used the press as assiduously as he used the Senate in
his campaign. He was always available to reporters; when they
didn't seek him out, he would seek them out, often summoning them
out of the press gallery with a meaningful wink and nod of the head.
He knew about deadlines and edition times, and how to blanket an
unfavorable story with one that served his purpose. He would throw
a heavy arm about a favorite reporter's shoulder while walking
down a Senate corridor, or would take him to his office for a drink
and give him a tip on the next "exposé." What many reporters suspected then was later proved to be true—namely, that McCarthy
had laid pipelines into State and other government departments.
Strategically placed malcontents in the bureaucracy were acting as
a secret intelligence network for McCarthy, feeding him material
from the security files and other confidential information. Any Capitol Hill reporter in need of copy on a dull day or an "informed
sources" to speculate on what was coming next on the loyalty front
could always count on Joe.

Late in March, in a speech well advertised in advance, McCarthy told the Senate that the "top Soviet espionage agent" in the State Department was Professor Owen Lattimore of Johns Hopkins University, a widely known expert on Far Eastern affairs. He was not only a member of the Communist Party, McCarthy said, but an active agent in the Russian espionage network and had contributed to the downfall of Chiang Kai-shek. Dean Acheson, he added, was the "voice and mind of Lattimore" in the State Department. So sure was he of his ground, McCarthy boasted, that he was willing to let his whole case against the State Department "stand or fall on the guilt of this one man."

Owen Lattimore, a thin, intense, scholarly man of 49, had spent many years in China and Mongolia, had written many books on the Far East, and had served briefly in the Second World War as a political adviser to Chiang Kai-shek. In this country, he had been a leading figure during the prewar years in the Institute for Pacific Relations, which was the channel through which his name entered the security pipeline and thus came into McCarthy's hands. Since the end of the war, he had been on the faculty at Johns Hopkins University in Baltimore. He had never worked for the State Department, but his standing there as an authority and occasional consultant had been high for many years. At the moment when McCarthy was condemning him, Lattimore was on a special mission to Afghanistan for the United Nations.

At the White House and the State Department, McCarthy's charges against Lattimore seemed so preposterous, and his boast that he would "stand or fall" on this one case so inviting, that Chairman Tydings was urged to force the Wisconsin Senator's hand. Lattimore was summoned back from Afghanistan, and McCarthy was invited to put his evidence before the committee. As usual, however, McCarthy taunted the committee by telling them the proof of his charges would be found in the files of the loyalty boards and the FBI. Tydings had a trump ready for that play. He had induced President Truman to relax his ban on opening loyalty files to the committee in this single instance at least.

On April 6, Lattimore appeared before the committee for a full day of questioning in one of the most dramatic sessions up to that time. He was a good witness in his own behalf—keen-witted, articulate, persuasive. He had never been a Communist nor been led by Communist doctrine, he said. Near the close of the proceedings, Chairman Tydings unobtrusively ignited the depth charge which he hoped would blow Joe McCarthy out of the water. With the solemnity of a judge delivering an opinion, he said:

Dr. Lattimore, your case has been designated the No. 1 case in the charges made by Senator McCarthy. You have been called, substantially if not accurately, the top Red spy agent in America. We have been told that if we had access to certain files that this would be shown.

As chairman of this committee, I owe it to you and to the country to tell you that four of the five members of this committee [the absentee was Hickenlooper], in the presence of Mr. J. Edgar Hoover, had a complete summary of your file made available to them. . . . At the conclusion of the reading of that summary, it was the universal opinion of all of the members of the committee present and all others in the room that there was nothing in that file to show that you were a Communist or had ever been a Communist, or that you were in any way connected with any espionage. . . . The FBI file puts you completely, up to this moment at least, in the clear.[8]

There was a burst of applause from the packed hearing room. Lattimore leaned back in his chair with a smile of triumph on his face. The members of the committee looked almost equally triumphant, and Brian McMahon walked around the end of the long table to shake the Professor's hand. But Joe McCarthy, who had left his guest seat at the table empty that day (had he been tipped to what was coming?) was not pleased. To a reporter who sought him out in his office, he said:

"Either Tydings hasn't seen the file, or he is lying. There is no other alternative."[*]

Joe McCarthy was not easily dismayed. Instead of his expressed willingness to "stand or fall" on the verdict in the Lattimore case, as he had promised to do, he stepped up his attacks. His almost daily speeches in the Senate and his impromptu press conferences were heavy with a new scorn and vindictiveness. The Senate seemed to regard him with a mixture of awe and repugnance. Few Democrats rose to challenge him, even when he impugned the President or the Secretary of State. To most Republicans he seemed a dubious sort of blessing. McCarthy was sharpening the best political weapon they

* Two prominent former leaders of the Communist Party later gave conflicting testimony about Lattimore. Louis Budenz said that he had been told in 1937, and that he believed, that the Professor was a party member. Earl Browder told the committee that he had never heard of Lattimore in connection with any party affairs. Senator Tydings' exoneration of Lattimore did not save him from further attacks by McCarthy nor from subsequent harassment by the Un-American Activities and the Internal Security Committees.

had—but at what cost to values of decency and responsibility that the party needed to maintain?

It was Republicans, not Democrats, who posed the first effective rebuke to McCarthy. Margaret Chase Smith, the trim, silver-haired ex-schoolteacher from Maine, and the only woman in the Senate, rose unannounced on the floor on the afternoon of June 1 to deliver an eloquent and memorable homily on the subject of political morality. Maggie Smith, always her own woman in the Senate, had never run with the pack as either a conservative or a liberal. It was, however, as the spokesman for a small band of liberals—Ives of New York, Tobey of New Hampshire, Aiken of Vermont, Morse of Oregon, among others—that she sternly lectured McCarthy that day in what became known as the Republican "Declaration of Conscience."

Mrs. Smith gave the Democratic administration its lumps for having created a bad situation in the first place, in which a climate of fear and frustration could flourish. But it was members of her own party, and McCarthy in particular (whom she did not need to identify by name), whom she reproached for recklessly exploiting the situation. In a level, controlled voice she said:

I speak as briefly as possible, because too much harm already has been done with irresponsible words of bitterness and selfish political opportunism.

The United States Senate has long enjoyed a worldwide reputation as the greatest deliberative body. But recently that deliberative character has too often been debased to the level of a forum of hate and character assassination sheltered by the shield of congressional immunity.

The extraordinary tone of Mrs. Smith's speech went flashing over the Senate grapevine, bringing reporters crowding into the press gallery and loitering members back to their desks from the corridors and cloakrooms. Many eyes were turned on McCarthy, seated only a few feet behind his accuser with an impassive scowl on his face. Mrs. Smith went on to say:

The American people are sick and tired of being afraid to speak their minds lest they be politically smeared as "Communists" or "Fascists." The American people are sick and tired of seeing innocent people smeared and guilty people whitewashed. . . .

The record of the present Democratic administration has provided us with sufficient campaign issues without the necessity of resorting to political smears. Yet to replace it with a Republican regime that lacks political integrity or intellectual honesty would be equally disastrous.

The nation sorely needs a Republican victory. But I don't want to see

the Republican Party ride to victory on the Four Horsemen of Calumny—
Fear, Ignorance, Bigotry, and Smear.

I don't want to see my party win that way. While it might be a fleeting
victory for the Republican Party, it would be a more lasting defeat for the
American people.

As Senator Smith took her seat, other Senators crowded around to
congratulate her and to shake her hand. McCarthy, his face white
and unsmiling, got up and walked out of the Chamber.

Maggie Smith's "Declaration of Conscience" was a milestone in
the campaign to curb McCarthy, but it was a lonely one. Beyond
her six Republican cosponsors and a handful of Democratic liberals,
such as Herbert Lehman and Hubert Humphrey, who occasionally
raised their voices in protest, there was no rising tide of indignation
or reproof in the Senate. Important Republican leaders like Taft of
Ohio and William Knowland of California either encouraged Mc-
Carthy openly or condoned his conduct by their silence. Among the
Democratic titans, such as Connally of Texas and Russell of Georgia, there was only an attitude of hands-off disdain. It was apparent
that McCarthy was a dangerous man to tangle with, and those with
enough stature to call him to account were not willing to risk their
prestige in any such encounter.

The Tydings committee closed its investigation late in June. It
had run for four months, heard 25 witnesses, taken almost 3,000,000
words of testimony, and was probably unmatched in Senate history
for acrimony. On July 20, the committee submitted its report to the
Senate—signed, inevitably, only by the three Democratic members,
and with separate views from each of the two Republicans. All
agreed, however, on the central fact that McCarthy had failed to
substantiate his charge of "81 card-carrying Communists in the
State Department." Indeed, not one Communist or suspected Communist was found. The majority report went on to castigate Mc-
Carthy in terms rarely used in the Senate about a member:

We are constrained to call the charges, and the methods used to give
them ostensible validity, what they truly are: a fraud and a hoax per-
petrated on the Senate of the United States and the American people.
They represent perhaps the most nefarious campaign of half-truths and
untruth in the history of this Republic . . . the totalitarian technique of the
"big lie" employed on a sustained basis.

In their separate conclusions, the two Republicans tried only half-
heartedly to defend McCarthy's performance, criticizing the Demo-

cratic majority instead, for a lack of thoroughness in exploring his charges.

The Senate fought through a long and bitter day over whether to accept the report, which would carry the implication, if not the fact, of a censure against McCarthy—unusual punishment in Senate terms. Tydings and McMahon carried the attack, and the defense force was led by William E. Jenner of Indiana and Kenneth Wherry of Nebraska, two stout McCarthy partisans. It was as wild and angry a scrimmage as has ever been seen on the Senate floor, and all the rules of decorum and courtesy were flouted. The effect was to obliterate objective judgment about the merits of the issue, which was whether McCarthy was to be chastised, and to put in its place the question of bedrock partisan loyalty. On the final showdown, 45 Democrats voted to accept the report and 37 Republicans voted against. There was not a defection on either side. Even Mrs. Smith and her coauthors of the "Declaration of Conscience" hewed straight to the Republican Party line.

Joe McCarthy had sat as a silent, faintly amused spectator throughout the fray. When it was over, he was ready with a press release. He said:

Today, Tydings tried to notify the Communists in the government that they are safe in their positions.

However, I want to assure them that they are not. [They] will be dug out one by one, regardless of how frantically Tydings screams for their protection.

The job will be a long and difficult one in view of the fact that all of the power of the administration is dedicated to the task of protecting the traitors, Communists, and fellow travelers in our government.

The Korean war, which had erupted at the height of the controversy over the Tydings report, deflected the march of McCarthyism only briefly. As President Truman struggled to contain a diplomatic crisis as fluid and explosive as any the nation had ever faced, McCarthy and his friends continued to hack away at public confidence in the administration. The aggression of the North Korean Communists, they said, was the bitter fruit of the United States policy of "sabotaging" Chiang Kai-shek and the Chinese Nationalists. By its definition of the defense perimeter in the Pacific, they charged, the Truman administration "gave a green light to the Communists to attack South Korea." Dean Acheson, said Senator Wherry, "has the blood of our boys in Korea on his hands." In the face of all this, it took unusual courage for Truman to veto the McCarran internal security act that September. The smashing margin by which the veto was overridden gave new impetus and arrogance to McCarthy's campaign.

These events cast a long and ominous shadow on the Democrats' prospects in the upcoming congressional elections. On the one hand, there was a war in progress, which normally brings a closing of ranks behind a President and his party. But on the other hand, this was an unpopular war with the voters, and it was made even more so by Republican charges that it was brought about by the administration's blunders. "Seldom, perhaps never, in American history," Arthur Krock wrote in the New York *Times*, "has a congressional election been scheduled in a similar atmosphere."

Joe McCarthy moved into this thicket of doubt and anxiety with the confident stealth of a wolf invading a sheepfold. While most members of Congress were pinned down in Washington because of the war crisis (an election recess was taken from September 27 to November 17), the Wisconsin Red-hunter was crisscrossing the nation as the most sought-after political speaker of the day. He flayed the Democrats for obstructing his holy war against Communists and branded Truman and Acheson as traitors. He went barn-burning in every state (except Ohio and Pennsylvania) where Republican candidates had a chance of unseating Democrats.

One state, however, proved more attractive to him than the others. This was Maryland, where Millard Tydings, veteran of almost thirty years in Congress, faced what seemed to be negligible Republican opposition from a politically obscure Baltimore lawyer, John Marshall Butler. McCarthy virtually took over the running and financing of Butler's campaign. He channeled money into it from his right-wing supporters and hired a Chicago publicity man, Jon M. Jonkel, to be its manager. Jonkel's most memorable feat in that endeavor (aside from paying a $5,000 fine for violation of the Federal Corrupt Practices Act) was the distribution four days before election of a tabloid called "From the Record." This purported to show Tydings' connection with a host of subversive organizations and contained a faked photograph of the Senator in amiable conversation with the one-time Communist chief, Earl Browder. The principal thrust of the campaign against Tydings was, of course, that he had whitewashed McCarthy's attempt to show up the disloyalty in the State Department.

McCarthy had his revenge on Tydings. The Marylander was

smothered under a plurality of more than 40,000 votes. But so gamey was the odor arising from the battle that the Senate refused at first to seat the victor, Butler, when the new Congress assembled in January. An election subcommittee, which spent two months investigating the campaign, condemned Butler and McCarthy equally for conduct bordering on fraud, but—in the immemorial way of the Senate with its own transgressors—that was the end of the matter. Butler ultimately was seated.

Another important McCarthy victim was Senate Majority Leader Scott Lucas of Illinois, who was defeated by a former Republican member of the House, Everett McKinley Dirksen. And in California, McCarthy's specialized talents were largely responsible for promoting Representative Richard M. Nixon to the Senate over the bid of Helen Gahagan Douglas, a liberal Democrat who was successfully bracketed by campaign propaganda with "pinks and fellow travelers."

The Republicans had won a solid victory, picking up five seats in the Senate and gaining twenty-eight seats in the House. It was a crushing setback for President Truman and the Democrats—and a tremendous enhancement of McCarthy's prestige. In its assessment of the election, the New York *Times* wrote that the overriding issue had been the Korean war and foreign policy, but added:

This mood appears to be heavily colored by "McCarthyism." Whether or not the voters actually believe Senator McCarthy's charges, many of them apparently do feel that something has gone wrong with the United States policy and that this may well be the fault of the principal architect of that policy, Secretary of State Dean Acheson.

The Republicans now had a crowd-rousing champion in Joe McCarthy such as they had not had since the days of Wendell Willkie, although the comparison in other respects was meager. The GOP had always been in short supply of hell-raisers, and now they had one who could not be silenced and who could command almost as much space in the newspapers as the President of the United States. McCarthy had at his beck a solid phalanx of right-wing fanatics, anti-Communists, and organized patrioteers in all parts of the country, some of whom were as noisy and vituperative as he. He was also getting powerful support from the Chicago *Tribune*, the Washington *Times-Herald*, most of the Hearst newspapers, and a handful of columnists and radio commentators. Money was coming to him from a variety of people, big and small, who wanted "to help in the fight against communism." Between 1949 and 1952, more than

$200,000 was deposited to his account and that of his administrative assistant, Ray Kiermas, at the Riggs National Bank in Washington.*

McCarthy was becoming, in fact, a political "third force." Many in the GOP feared him, many detested him, and most distrusted him. The majority, who could not bring themselves to an outright endorsement of him, consoled themselves with some such cynical rationalization as, "While I don't always approve of Joe's methods, he's doing a job that needs to be done." But in a coldly pragmatic sense he was the most lethal political weapon the Republicans had. They put him in the front rank of their assault force to take the White House in 1952.

President Truman and most Democratic leaders were stunned by the spreading reach of McCarthy's powers. There seemed to be no effective counterstrategy against him. In the spring of 1950, the President set up a special task force in the White House headed by Stephen J. Spingarn and Max Lowenthal to supply congressional Democrats and the press with instant rebuttals to every charge McCarthy made. Inevitably, the denials seldom caught up with the allegations. Even the most responsible newspapers found themselves trapped by the ancient rubrics of their craft into headlining whatever McCarthy said because it was "news," regardless of how specious, inaccurate, or self-serving they suspected the news of being. The President used his press conferences and occasional speeches to rebuke McCarthy, but he could not say in public what he so frankly said in private about "that s.o.b." When Truman, in a speech to the American Legion, denounced unnamed "scandal mongers and character assassins" in Congress, McCarthy demanded and got free time from the three radio networks to reply. Senate Democrats shrank from open encounters with him, and in the conservative wing of the party, among Southerners particularly, McCarthy was winning sycophants if not converts.

It was the Democratic Chairman of the Senate Judiciary Committee, implacable old Pat McCarran of Nevada, who derailed the one major counteroffensive against McCarthyism which President Truman mounted in 1951. This was a proposal to set up a high-level civilian commission (retired Admiral Chester W. Nimitz was proposed as its head) to restudy the whole loyalty program and the legislative domain of the Internal Security Act. The President rea-

* Report of the Senate Rules Committee on S. Res. 187 and 304, 1952. The committee raised the strong suspicion that little of this money ever found its way into McCarthy's anti-Communist campaign.

soned that some improvement in these fields was desperately needed, and that placing the problem in the hands of a prestigious White House commission would put it out of target range of McCarthy and his men. But the plan had to be abandoned when McCarran's committee, after months of delay, refused to waive technical conflict-of-interest barriers to Senate confirmation of the commission members. Under a strict interpretation of the conflict-of-interest statutes such as McCarran was prepared to impose, Admiral Nimitz and others who served with him would have had to divest themselves of all stock holdings and pension rights. This was more of a sacrifice for public service than they were willing to make or the President to ask.

One man alone in the Senate that year had the temerity to challenge Joe McCarthy head on. That was a freshman Democrat from Connecticut, William Benton, a sensitive, sober, politically naïve, former advertising executive. For this challenge, he paid with his political life.

In June 1951, McCarthy attained a new peak of vindictiveness when he accused General George C. Marshall, then Secretary of Defense, with being part of a "conspiracy so immense and an infamy so black as to dwarf any previous such venture in the history of man." In a rambling, largely incoherent 60,000-word speech, most of which he inserted into the *Congressional Record* unread, McCarthy professed to show that in all that the distinguished soldier-statesman had done in the Second World War and on his mission to China in 1946, he consciously played into the hands of this nation's enemies in the Kremlin.

This charge was so preposterous that even McCarthy's Republican backers feared he had taken leave of his senses. Most Democrats ignored the speech on the mistaken assumption that by this crowning act of irresponsibility McCarthy had at last done himself in. Benton made no such assumption. Innocent of the easy, ambivalent morality of the Senate, the don't-stick-your-neck-out doctrine of senatorial survival, he decided that if this reckless Goliath was to be slain he would have to be the David. He spent weeks combing over the record of the Tydings investigation and all the other McCarthy lore he could come by. On August 6 he rose on the Senate floor and offered a resolution calling for the expulsion of the Junior Senator from Wisconsin on ten charges of perjury, deceit, fraud, and lack of fitness for the office.

Since the convening of the first Congress, only twenty-one Senators have been expelled. Two-thirds of these cases occurred during the hate-scarred early months of the Civil War, and most of the rest as the immediate result of election frauds. To attempt to dislodge a sitting member on the grounds of misconduct while in office was very nearly unprecedented. It went against the grain of the "gentleman's club" spirit of the Senate. It was also fraught with all sorts of personal hazards when applied to a vindictive, crockery-smashing brawler like Joe McCarthy. There was just no telling who among his fellow club members he might swing on next.

The Senate shuddered with apprehension as it adopted the Benton resolution by a straight party-line vote. The Rules Committee, to which it was referred, drew back in horror from its dreaded responsibility. McCarthy said that Benton was a "mental midget" and a "megaphone for the Communists" and that he would ignore the whole business.

The Rules Committee's investigation of the Benton charges, which dragged on for sixteen months, was a dismal farce of ineptitude, evasion, and simple cowardice. The only public testimony it took was Benton's, in a single session. McCarthy refused to testify or to make any meaningful answer to the charges. In a letter to Chairman Guy M. Gillette early in the proceedings, he said:

Frankly, Guy, I have not and do not intend to even read, much less answer, Benton's smear attack. I am sure that you realize that the Benton type of material can be found in the *Daily Worker* almost any day of the week and will continue to flow from the mouths and pens of the camp-followers as long as I continue my attack against Communists in government.[9]

Communications between McCarthy and the committee were thereafter conducted by letter and telegram, most of which McCarthy ignored. More than a year after the investigation had opened, the committee posed six written questions to the Senator about various financial transactions, campaign practices, and activities in behalf of housing and sugar interests and the China lobby, which had turned up from a study of his record. McCarthy wrote back: "The answer to your six insulting questions is 'No.'"

The committee was armed with subpoena powers, but it dared not use them against the Senator or to extract testimony from his staff and associates. "It would have been an unfair position to place them in," the committee humbly explained. As its investigators began to comb through McCarthy's many bank and brokerage accounts, McCarthy accused the committee of "dishonesty" and of "picking the pockets of the taxpayers of tens of thousands of dollars" in an effort to smear him. He attacked Chairman Gillette with such ferocity, on and off the Senate floor, that the Iowa Senator resigned from the committee. McCarthy demanded and got full personnel files on the members of the committee staff, ostensibly to expose their Communist connections. Two resigned just before the September Wisconsin primary, in which McCarthy was a candidate, and they issued press releases "exposing" an anti-McCarthy plot by the Democratic members of the committee.

If the Benton resolution, which had been introduced on August 6, 1951, was to have any effect or even pertinency beyond that of a footnote of history, it had to be reported out and acted upon by the Senate before adjournment for the election campaign of 1952. But the Rules Committee was so paralyzed that it was not until six weeks after the election that it produced its report.

There is no other document in the Senate archives quite like it. Its introduction is a long lament over the frustrations and abuse it suffered at the hands of Senator McCarthy. Its main body is a series of labored disquisitions, each framed about a hypothetical question such as "whether funds supplied to Senator McCarthy to fight Communism were diverted to his own use," to which no direct answers are given. The rest of the document—341 out of 400 printed pages —consists of exhibits such as correspondence, bank and brokerage statements, and canceled checks. These exhibits resemble the parts of a picture puzzle from which a few key pieces are missing, but in which the design is clear—in this case, of McCarthy as the manipulator of large sums of money from uncertain sources through a confusing network of bank accounts, stock and commodity transactions, political campaigns, and other operations too opaque for close scrutiny.

From all this, the report reached this melancholy conclusion: "The committee itself is not making any recommendations in this matter. The record should speak for itself. The issue raised is one for the entire Senate."

William Benton was soundly defeated in his bid for reelection from Connecticut. Joe McCarthy won by a landslide in Wisconsin. But from here on, McCarthyism would be Dwight Eisenhower's cross to bear, not Harry Truman's.

CHAPTER 14

<><><><><><><><><><><><><><><><><><><><><>

1952

"Whatsoever Thy Hand Findeth . . ."

"**R**IGHT ON ALL THE BIG THINGS, wrong on all the little ones," was the way gruff, wise, hardheaded old Sam Rayburn characterized his friend in the White House. And how very true this assessment proved to be as Harry Truman's Presidency drew to a close. In spite of the fumbles of human frailty, the pettiness he often displayed, the impetuousness that often spoiled his aim, he impressed his image constructively and permanently on the history of his world. He enhanced this country's role of leadership abroad and advanced the welfare of the citizens at home. He left the American Presidency a stronger, more effective instrument for human governance than he found it.

"A President," said Woodrow Wilson, "is at liberty to be as great a man as he can." Harry Truman probably never thought of making a choice in the matter. He simply applied what talents he had according to the old Biblical prescription, "Whatsoever thy hand findeth to do, do it with all thy might." Martha Truman taught him that as a boy, and he practiced it all his life. It gave him the will to face up squarely to the toughest decisions and never to shirk a responsibility. It led him to respect such strength and wisdom as the Lord had given him and not to lament what the Lord had withheld. He was a great President,* not because he had brilliance—which he did not— but because he had courage.

---

* So subjective a judgment is bound to be disputed. But this view of Truman's stature is shared by many competent authorities. Professsor Clinton Rossiter, the

It is certainly true that no President had a greater respect and reverence for that high office than he did. He was awed not so much by its power as by its responsibility and symbolism. He often talked about this with friends and members of his staff, and the phrase "the representative of *all* the people," which he conceived the President to be, was no simple slogan but a deeply felt obligation laid upon him by Providence.

And yet, there was a strange dichotomy in his own relationship to the Presidency—a detachment between the man and the office. Franklin Delano Roosevelt identified himself wholly with the institution; to him, the President and the Presidency were a metaphysical unity, like the King and the Monarchy. This apotheosis never came to Harry Truman. He was like a man who has won the right to wear the robes of the high priest but has never entered into the mysteries of the temple. He always saw himself as Truman the President or as Truman the man, and they were separate entities. Because of this, he could sit at his White House desk and indulge freely in barnyard humor or threaten to beat up a music critic who had offended his daughter, without, as he saw it, demeaning the great office which he held. Many who underrated Truman because of his flippancy, his earthiness, and his bucolic and unsophisticated wit misjudged his devotion to and respect for the office he held.

Over and over in the latter years of his administration he said to his associates: "I mean to pass this office on to my successor unimpaired." Truman was a close student of history. He knew that the Presidency was the least static, the least confined in its dimensions, of any of the three coordinate arms of government. He believed that the powers not specifically denied to the President in the Constitution were meant to be used by him. He knew the record of each of his predecessors, and he knew that the nation's fortunes had advanced under the bold and strong Presidents—the Presidents who would take and use the vast arsenal of implied powers lying within their reach—and that those fortunes had stagnated or regressed under the cautious and the timid. His special heroes in the pantheon

---

country's leading scholar on the Presidency, wrote in 1956: "I am ready to hazard an opinion, to which I did not come easily or lightly, that Harry Truman will eventually win a place as President, if not as a hero, alongside Jefferson and Theodore Roosevelt." And Harvard historian Arthur M. Schlesinger published the result of a poll of seventy-five historians in 1962 in which Truman was ranked ninth among thirty-one occupants of the White House. Schlesinger put him in the category of "near great" rather than "great," but a number of those in the poll rated Truman among the top five.

of Presidents were Andrew Jackson, Lincoln, Wilson, and the two Roosevelts—activists all under whom the power and the dignity of the Presidency had grown.

The natural enemy of Presidential power is the Congress—the massed might of many parochial interests opposed to a single national interest. There is a chronic suspicion and jealousy between the President and the Congress that is only briefly alleviated by occasional "honeymoons." This is an inevitable by-product of the Constitutional concept of limited and coordinate powers. Instead of a decalogue of "thou shalts" and "thou shalt nots," the Constitution simply delineates areas of responsibility and leaves it to the occupants to maneuver and contend for possession of the marginal terrain. Is the President only the "agent of Congress," with no function but to "see that the laws be faithfully executed"? The Whigs and their successors down to the present day have so argued. Or is he the Chief Executive—the leader and the initiator—through whom the national purpose finds expression? All history testifies that this is what a President must be.

Harry Truman's greatest contribution to the Presidency was that he refused to let Presidential initiative be eroded by Congressional encroachment. It was a battle that engaged him almost constantly throughout his tenure, and at times it rose to heights of fury. He lost many skirmishes along the way, but the sum of his victories was to reaffirm, in a striking way and against heavy odds, what Jackson, Lincoln, and the two Roosevelts had asserted before him—namely, that in this government of divided powers the President is "first among equals."

His decision to intervene in Korea, for example, came close to preempting the right to declare war. A declaration of war is probably an anachronism in any event in this age of nuclear missiles and political aggression, but all Presidents are now armed with the Truman precedent to strike swiftly on their own, wherever and with whatever force is necessary, when they believe the national security demands it.

President Truman had full authority to dismiss General MacArthur. Though precedent and prudence dictated that he accede to the overpowering opposition of Congress by finding an easier solution, he did no such thing. He agreed on his own to take up Britain's burdens in Greece and Turkey, and then led Congress to back him up with the Marshall Plan. He repeatedly defied congressional demands for employee loyalty files, and he steadfastly ignored their clamor to get rid of Dean Acheson. These were affronts to the Presidential prerogative. He vetoed more bills (250) than any two-term President in history. He went more often over the head of Congress to appeal directly to the people. And he was the only President to base virtually an entire reelection campaign on the failures and deficiencies of Congress.

Truman was a man of Congress himself. He had spent ten years in the Senate before becoming Vice President. He venerated the Congress as an institution and loved it for its excitement, its companionship, and the sense of personal fulfillment it provided. But he also knew at first hand the frailties of Congress, its parochial shortsightedness, its tendency to yield to the whims and prejudices of a handful of strong men—and occasionally of demagogues. Congress, he knew, cannot govern, and it cannot lead. What it can do is to be a partner in governing with a strong Executive, and that was the relationship he insisted upon and fought for as President.

But it was not only in conflict with Congress that Truman brought new strength to the Presidency. He enhanced the prestige and effectiveness of the Office of the President with certain appurtenances, both statutory and administrative, that have become permanent parts of the Presidential machinery. The Atomic Energy Act of 1946 places this awesome force for good and evil under the ultimate jurisdiction of the President, where it cannot be tampered with by politicians, exploiters, or trigger-happy soldiers. The Employment Act of 1946 created the Council of Economic Advisers, which gave the President a tool (such as had never existed before) with which to measure the vital heartbeat of the national economy. The unification of the Armed Forces swept away innumerable barriers to effective control by the President of the nation's defense. Along with this innovation came another, the National Security Council (established in 1947) and its sibling, the Central Intelligence Agency, to bring together in one place for the President's use the best information and the best advice available to the government on the state of the world as it affects the security of the United States.

The establishment of the Hoover Commission of 1947-49 put a new lever in the President's hands to simplify the problem of reorganizing the executive branch and thinning out the bureaucratic deadwood. Mr. Truman elevated the stature of the Bureau of the Budget by giving it responsibilities as the "office manager" for the whole executive bureaucracy, with the authority to impose modern management and accounting procedures. He instituted the plan of holding regular budget briefings for reporters each January, so that they could better explain the mysteries of the Federal budget (a document about the size of the Washington telephone directory) to the public. He created the first systematic table of organization for the White House staff and enlarged its personnel from Roosevelt's peak of 600 to more than 1,200. After the election of 1952 he did what no retiring President before him had done: He asked his successor to meet with him at once so that they could plan together an orderly transfer of the business of the Presidency two months later.

There are many yardsticks for measuring the greatness of a President. One of the most relevant is, "Did he actively use the potentialities of his position to advance the national interest?"

In Truman's case the answer is an emphatic Yes. Once having emerged from the humbling shadow of FDR, he became a creative and aggressive President, pushing the nation steadily toward new goals of national welfare and international security. His gains on the domestic front, in the end, were modest, but in the area of foreign policy they were monumental. His was the Era of the Cold War. His two terms in office were overshadowed at all times by a kind of danger no other President had ever had to face: the grinding rebalancing of world power between two hostile and incompatible forces, each capable of utterly destroying the other. Truman met that danger with bold, imaginative, and durable countermeasures. The Truman Doctrine, the European Recovery Program, NATO, the Berlin airlift, the Korean intervention—these are landmarks of historical proportions along the road of national maturity. They have profoundly and permanently affected the destiny of the American people and of the world.

In April 1945, people were asking in fear and honest perplexity, "Who the hell is Harry Truman?" Death and the caprice of politics had suddenly made this plain, undistinguished little man from Missouri their President. And he, sharing their dismay, had said to a group of reporters, "If you fellows know how to pray, pray for me now."

In April 1952, at his 300th press conference as President, he said to some of those same reporters:

My reason for not running again is based on the fact that I don't think any man—I don't care how good he is—is indispensable in this job. The Presidency itself is a continuing office, the greatest office in the history of the world, and that office ought to be continuing as far as individuals are concerned.

And another thing. When a man has been in this very responsible position for eight years, which I will practically have been by next January 20th, he has, or should have by that time, made all the contributions he can to the welfare of the nation. He has either done it well or not well.

I have tried my best to give the nation everything I have in me. There are a great many people—I suppose a million in this country—who could have done the job better than I did it. But I had the job and I had to do it.

I always quote an epitaph which is in the cemetery at Tombstone, Arizona. It says: "Here lies Jack Williams. He done his damnedest." I think that is the greatest epitaph a man can have—when he gives everything that is in him to the job he has before him. That is all that you can ask of him and that is what I have tried to do.

"My People Are All Honorable—All of Them Are"

In the light of his performance, why did President Truman lose the confidence of the country in the closing months of his term?

That he did can hardly be questioned. From 1951 onward, his administration was on the defensive, its forward thrust halted not only by enemy action but by faintheartedness and defections among his own Democratic troops. His popularity rating on a national public opinion poll in the spring of 1952 reached an all-time low of 26 percent. Public wariness with the "police action" in Korea, with the relentless tensions of the cold war, and with the seemingly endless conflict between labor and management, was evident on every hand. The country was prosperous, profits were rising, and jobs were abundant, but political discontent rumbled across the land. The Republican campaign slogan—"Time for a Change"—touched more than a political nerve end. It touched, for millions of people, a deeply felt, if imperfectly understood, need of which Truman was somehow the cause and symbol. Even his hand-picked successor, Adlai Stevenson, shunned him as a campaign liability.

Why? There were several reasons. In perspective, two stand out.

One was that Harry Truman did not have the capacity—the magnetism, charm, charisma, or whatever that ineluctable quality is—for strong personal leadership. He was liked, he was admired, he evoked steadfast loyalty in many, but he could not inspire. People gave him their hands but not their hearts. He could make them laugh, but he could not make them cry. He was a plain man with honesty and guts ("Give-'em-hell-Harry"), but you couldn't picture him in gleaming armor astride a white horse. The public is a fickle lover at best, and in Truman's case that love was never more than skin deep. When the jealous tongue-waggers got busy on him, there was not much reserve to hold the romance together.

The other, and more palapable, reason was that President Truman was deficient as an administrator. He could always see "the big picture" and he could organize and digest a staggering mass of detail, but he was never certain about what was going on outside his range of vision. His faith in the people around him was instinctive and deep. To a reporter who once raised a question about an aide's honesty, the President said angrily: "My people are all honorable—all of them are." While he might question their judgment, he never questioned their sincerity or their honesty. When he gave an assignment to a Cabinet officer or a White House aide, he did not peer over their shoulders to see how they were doing. He assumed the competence of those he trusted, and paid back their loyalty with a fiercer loyalty of his own. He publicly branded a newspaper columnist an "s.o.b." because of attacks on his military aide, General Harry Vaughan. But he was never known to "chew out" a faltering subordinate in the presence of others.

"Wrongdoers have no house with me," he said defiantly. But his house had already fallen into disarray, partly because of wrongdoers but chiefly because of the appearance of wrongdoing. It was "the mess in Washington" that, more than any other single factor, caused President Truman's image to fade as his term drew to a close.

"That image," as Arthur Krock wrote in the New York Times in December 1951, "is beginning to take on the lineaments of Presidents Grant and Harding 'betrayed' by their friends. When history offers to posterity the complete portrait of Mr. Truman, this resemblance may have vanished. But for the moment it is there."

The resemblance has diminished greatly with the years. There were no scandals in the Truman administration remotely approaching those of Teapot Dome. The "mess in Washington" was exaggerated during the 1952 campaign far beyond its actual proportions. But there was more than there should have been—enough in any event to give credibility at the time to Krock's troubled assessment.

Truman may himself have contributed unwittingly to creating the

climate in which a handful of cheats, frauds, and simple four-flush-
ers in the government managed to spray the tint of corruption across
his second administration. One of Truman's closest associates while
he was President (this associate must remain anonymous here; the
account that follows is the verbatim text of a portion of a taped
interview he gave the present writer) offers this analysis of the onset
of that climate:

Something happened between Truman's first and second terms that is
hard to pin down. There was a change of atmosphere around the White
House, a subtle change in the relationship between the President and
those of us who worked closely with him. During the first term, we were
all playing it pretty much by ear—sensing what had to be done and
getting on with it. There wasn't much pressure from the outside, from the
lobbies and the special interest pleaders or the big politicians. They
looked on him as just a sort of caretaker President, and they didn't expect
him to run for a full term. He seemed for a time to reflect that sort of
attitude too.

And then came the 1948 election, and—my God!—how cocky he was
after that. He had shown the world that he could come up off the floor
and knock the champ right out of the ring. Now he was all bustle and
decisiveness and full of big plans, and to hell with the details. This was
going to be *his* administration, and he was going to put the Fair Deal
right up there in history in letters as big as the New Deal. It was quite an
experience, I can tell you.

But now the outside pressures began to close in on him and on us. Here
was a fellow who was going to be President in his own right for four
whole years. The people who wanted things now knew they had to deal
with him or not deal at all. So now they began to scheme and to ponder
and to sort of feel around to see what was the best way of getting to him.
Who were the friends or advisers or politicians who could get his ear?
And that was where fellows like Harry Vaughan and poor Matt Connelly
and the Democratic National Committee began to take on a new importance. People thought they had influence, so they were after them all the
time, in and out of the White House and everywhere else.

There was nothing sinister about this you could put your finger on. But
it was a new mood and a new climate, and in a way Mr. Truman was a
captive of it, although I'm sure he was never aware of it.

The "mess in Washington" began to come to light in 1949, with
the President's good friend and military aide, General Vaughan, in
the center focus.

In August of that year a special Senate investigating subcommittee began to look into the activities of the five-percenters who were clustered like leaches around the Defense Department, the War Assets Administration, the Reconstruction Finance Corporation, and other sources of government largesse. The five-percenters in Washington are a ubiquitous and hardy breed whose lineage goes back to the founding of the Republic and whose progeny continue to flourish in the Capital to this day. They are the "influence peddlers," shrewd and often unscrupulous ex-politicians, ex-government officials, or just ordinary confidence men who offer, for a fee, to help businessmen get contracts, legislative favors, or whatever their hearts desire out of the vast and forbidding cornucopia of government. Their pitch is that they "know the ropes" in Washington, have "drag" in the important departments and bureaus, and can bypass all the tedious bureaucratic channels by getting a sympathetic hearing directly with the man at the top. It is a lucrative racket for many, generally within the law but usually beyond the pale of propriety. Not even the most virtuous administrations have been able to stamp it out.

The Senate investigators uncovered a crowded nest of these predators, some of them sleazy, fly-by-night operators, others rolling in $100,000-a-year retainers and glittering prestige. One of the latter was Colonel James V. Hunt, late of the Army and Quartermaster Corps, whose elegant suite of offices was adorned with autographed portraits of just about every figure of prominence in the government, including President Truman and most of the Cabinet.

The central figure in the inquiry turned out to be the President's bluff and hearty poker-playing pal, Harry Vaughan. He was the accessible and accommodating "man at the top" whom Colonel Hunt and several others like him relied upon. Vaughan's White House office was open to them; they could reach him on the telephone while an awestruck client sat by their desks. And he could be persuaded to "drop in for a drink" or to grace an intimate cocktail party. From time to time he would throw his considerable weight into some project in which they were interested, by making a phone call or writing a letter to a procurement official at the Pentagon, the commissioner of a regulatory agency, or the Passport Office of the State Department.

While wartime restrictions were still in effect, Vaughan produced a passport plus a "to whom it may concern" note of introduction on White House stationery for one of his friends to go to France and Italy to buy essential oils for a perfume manufacturer. He helped another to get an allocation of scarce structural steel to build a racetrack in California, and another to get supplies of scarce commercial sugar. Evidence before the Senate subcommittee showed that he had poked his nose into the fields of public housing and surplus property disposal, into Federal trade regulations, and even into the Department of Agriculture, where the legitimate interests of the military aide to the President would seem to be minimal.

There was no evidence of direct payoffs in these transactions, but Vaughan seems to have been the recipient of a number of generous campaign contributions to the Democratic Party, and, of course, he got a free Deepfreeze from one of Colonel Hunt's grateful clients. That Deepfreeze, immortalized by scores of cartoonists and furnishing a text for yards of newspaper columns and hours of political oratory, came to symbolize "the mess in Washington." President Truman angrily defended his military aide against charges of wrongdoing, but the repercussions of the five-percenter investigation continued to boil up for many months.

Meanwhile, early in 1950, the tangled affairs of the Reconstruction Finance Corporation (RFC) were coming under the critical scrutiny of another Senate investigating committee, in which another of President Truman's principal aides, Donald Dawson, was to get his fingers burned. The story was to be a repetition, on a grander scale, of the five-percenter inquiry.

The RFC was invented by Herbert Hoover early in the depression to lend money to business enterprises that faced collapse because they could not qualify for commercial bank credit. During the war, the RFC was diverted chiefly to financing new or expanding suppliers of critical defense needs, such as railroads, synthetic rubber manufacturers, steel mills, and the like. In the postwar period, after the initial pains of reconversion had been weathered, there was a diminishing need for such free and easy government credit as RFC provided. But it was kept in business as a hedge against a possible recession.

In fact, it flourished mightily in the late forties, extending its benevolence not only to faltering railroads and established businesses, but to a variety of speculative enterprises such as oil-drilling operations, prefabricated-housing manufacture, and resort hotels in such underprivileged backwaters as Miami and Las Vegas. From time to time some of the more exotic of these transactions, or a spectacular collapse of an RFC-backed venture, would make the headlines, and tales would spread about irregularities, favoritism, and political pressures at work in the agency. In February 1950, the Senate Banking and Currency Committee decided to have a look and turned the job over to one of its sober and scholarly junior members, Senator J. William Fulbright of Arkansas.

Fulbright's subcommittee spent a painstaking and largely unpublicized year combing through the incredibly complex affairs of the RFC. Its report, issued in February 1951, blasted the RFC for mismanagement and for yielding to political influence in the making of loans. It cited Donald Dawson, special assistant to the President for personnel affairs, as a potent wielder of influence, and said that the Democratic National Committee had undertaken to offer its own recommendations on making loans to entrepreneurs. An office diary of RFC Director Walter Dunham was put into the record. It showed scores of telephone calls (during a fifteen-month period in 1949-50) received at his office from Dawson and other members of the influence ring that Dawson headed.

When President Truman blazed back that the report was "asinine," Chairman Fulbright said, "All right, we will put on a series of public hearings with sworn testimony to show that the committee is not talking through its hat."

The public disclosures that followed fully justified the committee's indictment. Scores of witnesses took their places before the reporters and cameras in the Senate Caucus Room to piece together a bizarre tapestry of high finance and dubious ethics in the RFC; of tottering corporations being propped up with government loans so that their backers could cash in and get out; of multimillion-dollar loans made on flimsy or fraudulently inflated collateral; and of borrowers once rejected becoming suddenly acceptable when they came with the proper political credentials.

Dawson was disclosed by one witness after another as "the man to see" when favors were needed at the RFC. He knew the agency and its five-man board intimately, having been chief of personnel there when the President picked him for the White House assignment. From his new eminence, the counsel he gave to the RFC carried almost the weight of command.

A Dawson protégé was E. Merle Young, a gifted young man who rose in less than ten years from the rank of messenger to chief RFC examiner—a job in which he supplemented his government salary with large "retainers" from companies with loan applications pending before the agency. Young's wife had worked on Capitol Hill as a secretary for Senator Truman, and now worked for him at the White House. With the advantage of having inside knowledge and excellent contacts, Young set himself up in business as a free-lance "expediter" of RFC loans. Later on, a grand jury indicted him, his brother, and several associates for perjury in connection with their testimony before the Fulbright committee.

Another good friend of Young and Dawson was William M. Boyle, Jr., who was named chairman of the Democratic National Committee in mid-1949. These three men were all Missourians, and testimony showed that they shared a tidy working relationship with top officials at RFC in deciding which questionable borrowers should be favored and which should not. One of these was the American Lithofold Company of St. Louis, which had twice been denied a $500,000 refinancing loan. But on the next try, after it had paid Boyle an $8,000 retainer in 1949 (he was then the unsalaried vice chairman of the Democratic Committee), the application was swiftly approved. In spite of the uproar over this disclosure, Boyle continued to hang onto his chairmanship, stoutly defended by President Truman. He resigned "for reasons of health" three months later.

Dawson, like Harry Vaughan, remained in the good graces of the President.

One day in December 1951, a beefy Chicago lawyer, with a Miami suntan and the apprehensive manner of a reform school truant, eased his perspiring figure into the witness chair of an investigating committee on Capitol Hill. He identified himself as Abraham Teitelbaum and said that, among other things, he had been one of the defense attorneys for the late Al Capone. He told the committee that he was in trouble with the Bureau of Internal Revenue and had very nearly fallen into a trap laid for him by some highly placed blackmailers. It was the blackmailers the committee was interested in, and Teitelbaum was willing to oblige.

He said that a little over a year ago he had mentioned his tax difficulties to an acquaintance in Miami by the name of Frank Nathan. Nathan talked as if he knew a lot about such matters and introduced Teitelbaum to an even more knowledgeable friend, Burt Naster. Nathan and Naster painted a pretty grave picture of Teitelbaum's predicament; he probably would have to pay a huge fine and penalty and serve time in jail as well.

There was, however, a way out of his dilemma, his acquaintances told him, if he was willing to pay the price. There was a "clique of high officials" in Washington who fixed important cases like his, they said, which included such people as Theron Lamar Caudle, the Assistant Attorney General in charge of the Tax Division; Charles Oliphant, General Counsel for the Bureau of Internal Revenue; Joseph Nunan, former Commissioner of Internal Revenue; and Jess Larson, chief of the General Services Administration.

Nathan and Naster told Teitelbaum they would see what they could do for him. A few days later, Teitelbaum said, they told him "the clique" had agreed to take care of his tax problems for $500,-ooo. They intimated very strongly that if he didn't go along with the deal his predicament with the government would get a lot worse than it already was. Teitelbaum testified that he was badly shaken by all this and that he accused Nathan of trying to frame him. Nathan's reply, he said, was: "Well, what would you expect me to do? Wouldn't you as a lawyer put anybody in trouble if you could make half a million dollars? How can I go back to my friends and offer them less than $500,000?"

The forum for Abe Teitelbaum's troubled confession was a special House Ways and Means Subcommittee headed by Representative Cecil King, Democrat of California. It had been set up six months earlier, while the din of the Senate's RFC exposé was filling the air, to investigate widespread reports of irregularities in the government's tax collection agency. Teitelbaum's account of the attempted shakedown was never fully substantiated before the King committee. But there was enough substance in it, when laid alongside other evidence produced at the hearings, to shake the tax service from top to bottom and to send Caudle and a number of other officials to prison.*

The Bureau of Internal Revenue (it was to be reorganized later as the Internal Revenue Service) is an arm of the Treasury. It was originally set up with sixty-four regional offices blanketing the country, each under the direction of a Collector of Internal Revenue. Suspected tax frauds discovered by the Collector were referred to the office of the BIR Counsel in Washington, and, if prosecution seemed warranted, that official turned the case over to the Tax Division of the Department of Justice for trial. All the top officials in this

* Caudle, along with Matthew H. Connelly, who had been President Truman's appointments secretary, was convicted in 1956 of a conspiracy to fix the tax case of a St. Louis businessman, Irving Sachs. Both served brief prison terms. Connelly received a full Presidential pardon on November 22, 1962, and Caudle on August 18, 1965. Altogether, nine persons who served in the Truman administration between 1950 and 1952 faced criminal actions growing out of the tax scandals.

sub-bureaucracy, from the Commissioner down to the Deputy Collectors, were political appointees. It was one of the most fruitful fields of patronage available to an administration in power. The Collectors, whose jobs were particularly choice as a means of rewarding local party strong men, were in a unique position to reward their friends and to punish their enemies. It had been that way since the tax service was created.

As early as the summer of 1950, Treasury Secretary John Snyder had had his own quiet investigation under way trying to get at the truth of persistent rumors of bribery and other irregularities in certain of the Collectors' offices. Boston and New York were particularly troublesome. In California, the State Crime Commission charged that a link existed between the underworld and Collector James G. Smyth in San Francisco. Secretary Snyder had himself asked for the resignation of Collector James P. Finnegan of St. Louis, but Finnegan's political moorings were so secure that he could not be budged until April 1951, when a grand jury looked into his affairs. He resigned then and was subsequently indicted for attempting to conceal $103,000 of taxable income on his own tax returns.

Now, as the King committee began to probe behind the scenes too, tax officials began dropping like leaves from an autumn tree. Dennis Delaney, Collector at Boston, resigned in June and was indicted for accepting bribes to "fix" tax delinquencies. Internal Revenue Commissioner George J. Schoenman, once a White House aide to President Truman, resigned suddenly in July "for reasons of health." In September, Secretary Snyder suspended Collector Smyth in San Francisco and eight of his associates. Smyth was indicted for fraud in fixing tax claims. In October, Joseph P. Marcelle, Collector for Brooklyn, was fired for an unexplained delinquency of $32,000 in his own returns, and one of his assistants, Mordecai Miller, was dropped for refusing to explain the sources of his outside income to the King committee.

The President sacked Assistant Attorney General Caudle even before Abe Teitelbaum told his story to the King committee. A self-depicted "po' boy fum No'th C'lina" who feigned an incredible naïveté, Caudle protested to the committee in October that he never dreamed there was anything wrong in being friends with defendants in tax cases pending before his division, or in accepting gifts, loans, and free vacations from them. When he was recalled to the stand after Teitelbaum had testified, he admitted that he had had many conversations with Frank Nathan, had visited in his Miami home, and was aware of Nathan's shady record as a "Washington fixer" who had once been prosecuted for a Federal offense. But he swore piously that he had never talked to Nathan or anyone else about Mr. Teitelbaum's tax problems. Charles Oliphant, the BIR General Counsel, followed Caudle to the stand to enter a similar denial for himself to the Teitelbaum and other allegations, but the next day, on December 4, he turned in his resignation.

The tax scandals were by far the most odorous ingredient of "the mess in Washington." They showed an unmistakable pattern of dishonesty, shady dealings, and political favoritism in a branch of the government toward which the average citizen has an innate suspicion to begin with. Altogether, sixty-six persons in the Bureau of Internal Revenue and the Justice Department were to be purged by the end of 1952, and nine ultimately were to go to jail for their misdeeds. But as bad as the tax scandals were, they were being pumped up by the Republicans to look a good deal worse, as the New York *Times*—not a conspicuous fan of Mr. Truman at the time —was quick to note. In an editorial during December 1951, it said:

> Mr. Truman has made himself vulnerable by not acting voluntarily and sooner. . . . [But] not all Mr. Truman's critics are filled with an unadulterated zeal for righteousness. Some of them, as is perfectly natural, are primarily concerned with winning next year's national elections. . . . What we suffer from is a deterioration of ethical standards. This might have taken place if the Republicans had been in power and the Democrats in opposition. Neither party is chemically pure.

President Truman had gone to Key West before Thanksgiving, but he cut short his vacation and returned to Washington early in December. He was furious over the disclosures by the King committee and over Caudle and Oliphant in particular. He told friends that he had been "sold down the river" by people whom he trusted. He had already put through Congress a bill to reorganize the RFC, and was working on another to overhaul the Revenue Service and to put the Collectors and most other top officials under civil service. In addition, he had determined to create a special White House Commission to study the question of corruption in government. Such a commission, he reasoned, should not only identify the weak spots in the bureaucracy and propose ways of strengthening them but also take some of the political heat out of the issue before the 1952 campaign got under way.

His first choice to head the commission was Judge Thomas F.

Murphy of the Federal District Court in New York City. Murphy was a big, imperturbable man with a massive black mustache, who commanded wide respect. As a United States attorney he had prosecuted Alger Hiss, and earlier he had conducted a reorganization of the New York City police department. Murphy gave the President every indication that he would accept the assignment, and then, just before Christmas, backed out. He gave no reason for his sudden change of heart (some sources said he became convinced that the project was a political man-trap), and his withdrawal was a humiliating setback for the President.

In January 1952 Mr. Truman announced that the cleanup job would be turned over to Attorney General J. Howard McGrath (he had succeeded Tom Clark the year before) and the Justice Department. To many this looked like setting Democrats to investigate Democrats, for McGrath was a former chairman of the Democratic National Committee, and the department he now headed bore some scratches and bruises of its own from the tax scandals. Even the liberal Americans for Democratic Action (ADA) joined the Republicans in denouncing this as an attempted whitewash. The Democrat controlled House Judiciary Committee reacted by voting to investigate Mr. McGrath and the Justice Department.

The President's next choice to head the corruption probe was Newbold Morris, a liberal Republican lawyer who had once been president of the New York City Council, and whose passion for civic uplift was fortified by an indomitable cheerfulness and optimism. His cachet of appointment from the President early in February must have contained some ambiguities, for while Attorney General McGrath thought Morris would be working for him, Morris thought he was a free agent answerable only to the President.

With disarming insouciance, Morris dropped one lighted match after another into this flammable bureaucratic tinder. On his first Sunday in Washington he told the radio audience of "Meet the Press" that an investigation of the Justice Department was near the top of his agenda. He declined McGrath's proffer of desk space in the Justice Department and established headquarters in an office building downtown and began to assemble his own staff. He asked for independent subpoena powers, which Congress refused to grant. In two months he had antagonized just about everybody in sight, including most of his fellow Republicans on Capitol Hill, who preferred corruption to a cleanup, at least until after the election. Finally, Mr. Morris found himself also entangled in the fringes of the corruption issue. He was called before a Senate committee to explain the involvement of his New York law firm in an allegedly illegal resale of surplus government oil tankers to a foreign government. He did not help his case when he told the investigating Senators that they had "diseased minds" and were bent on "character destruction."

As the opening gambit in his corruption probe, Morris prepared a long questionnaire that he planned to have filled out by all Federal employees, from Cabinet Secretaries down, listing their assets and sources of income. When word of this got out late in March, it sent a new wave of bureaucratic indignation rolling against the anti-vice crusader. Even the President felt that the questionnaire was an improper invasion of individual rights and privacy. He quarreled publicly with McGarth for his laxity in overseeing the corruption inquiry and for letting Morris get out of hand, but he hesitated to cripple further Morris' effort by ordering the questionnaire withdrawn.

A few days later, boiling mad, McGrath told a congressional committee that he would not fill out such a questionnaire himself and that he would forbid its distribution to the personnel of his department. When he got back to his office that afternoon, he dictated a terse note to Morris advising him, "Your appointment is hereby terminated." When the President heard of this for the first time from the news-ticker, he picked up the telephone and told McGrath *he* was fired too—instanter.

With this farcical denouement the administration's tardy and ill-conceived scheme to do its own housecleaning blew up. It had been a miserable performance from start to finish, almost a burlesque of executive management, and the net result was to underline "the mess in Washington" as a good deal more than a gloating Republican catchphrase. The five-percenters, the influence peddlers, and the tax fixers had been put to flight—temporarily at least—but it was Congress that had flushed them out and wielded the whip. The President on his own had followed up by drastically reorganizing the RFC and the tax service and by the abortive enlistment of Mr. Morris with his mop and pail. But in the minds of most of the public these gestures looked as futile as locking the barn door after the horses are gone. And there, by golly, was old Harry Vaughan, a little bit subdued but still sporting the gold braid and the chest full of medals of Military Aide to the President.

But now it was April, and the draft had been turned up in the political furnaces. It was too late for the Democrats to do much about the taunts about "the mess in Washington" except to endure them.

Right on all the big things, wrong on all the little ones. James Reston probably had this epigram in mind when he wrote in the New York *Times* on April 6, 1952:

The events of this week are typical of one important and unfortunate aspect of the entire administration of Harry S. Truman.

From beginning to end the great projects of his administration—the noble efforts to bind up the wounds of the great war, the attempts to build a new security system throughout the world, the defense against Communist aggression in Korea and elsewhere—have all been obscured by petty political bickering or by acrimonious and sometimes even squalid personal squabbles . . .

This is the way it has been from the beginning of his Presidential tour of duty, seven years ago this month. . . .

Nevertheless, the historians will probably deal more kindly with Mr. Truman than his contemporaries. Though the recent incidents have given his administration some of the aspects of a sinking ship, the man from Missouri is not through yet.

The Reluctant Heir

About 11:15 one evening late in January 1952, the telephone rang in the home of a prominent Washington newspaper correspondent. The voice on the other end of the line was highly agitated, but it had the unmistakably clipped accent and elegant tone of the Governor of Illinois, an old friend.

"This is Adlai," the voice said, "and I've just had the most incredible experience. Would you mind terribly coming down to the hotel for a little talk?"

The correspondent dressed and called a cab. He directed the driver to the Roger Smith Hotel, an undistinguished hostelry on upper Pennsylvania Avenue, a few blocks from the White House favored by tourists. He knocked on the door of the room to which he had been directed and was confronted by the plump, shirtsleeved figure of Adlai Ewing Stevenson, his long expressive face and intelligent blue eyes aglow with a sort of incredulous ebullience.

"I've just come from the White House," he said, "and the President wants me to save the world from Dwight Eisenhower."

The visitor was not a man easily dismayed, but he boggled slightly at this disclosure.

"He wants me to be the Democratic candidate against Eisenhower," Stevenson continued. "The President is almost certain Ike will get the Republican nomination. He has a pretty high regard for the General personally, but he thinks he will become the captive of Taft and possibly sell out Truman's foreign policy."

Stevenson went on to say that he had received a call from a White House emissary at the Governor's mansion in Springfield two days earlier, saying the President would like to talk with him whenever he came to Washington. He vaguely suspected what the purpose of the conference would be, but there had been no inkling of it in the summons. So he had showed up at the White House after dinner that night not fully prepared for what was to unfold.

The President, Stevenson told his friend, discoursed at some length on the history and accomplishments of his administration and how it had extended and solidified the liberal and international objectives of the New Deal. But there were many things in the area of foreign policy, the President said, that still needed urgently to be carried forward. There could be no interruption or letup in the perfecting of the NATO alliance, in the rebuilding of the free world under the Economic Cooperation Administration and Point Four, in pursuing the difficult goals the administration had set for itself in Korea. General Eisenhower, the President said, was in full sympathy with these policies; as NATO Commander, in fact, he was helping to carry them out. But Ike had now let himself be talked into going after the Republican nomination, and in all probability would get it. While his intentions were good, he was totally inexperienced in politics and, Mr. Truman believed, would never be able to make himself master of the Republican household. Thus foreign policy, to say nothing of the domestic program of the Fair Deal, would fall under the baleful influence of such men as Bob Taft in the Senate and John Taber in the House.

It was therefore essential, as any sensible man could see, the President went on, that a Democratic administration be continued in the White House for at least four more years.

There was no doubt in his mind, Mr. Truman had said, that he could be elected for another term if he chose to run. But he had decided not to do that both for personal reasons and for reasons of principle: He simply believed that the two-term tradition was a sound one. As President, he could dictate the Democratic choice of a candidate to succeed him, and could also, in all probability assure his victory in the election. He would like Stevenson to be that candidate.

Stevenson told his visitor in the hotel room that while he was flattered beyond measure by the President's invitation, he had withheld his assent. He was not at all sure, he said, that he wanted to be President in any event. He had already invested a good part of his life in public service; he was enjoying his career as Governor of Illinois; and he was pretty well committed to running for a second term there. He also had a family problem to consider.

Even more important, the Governor philosophized, he was far from certain that it was desirable for the Democrats to win another four-year lease on the White House. They had had unbroken tenure for twenty years already, and there were indisputable signs that softness and decadence were beginning to take their toll of the party. Maybe giving the Republicans a turn under a decent fellow like Eisenhower would be a good thing all around.

"Sure," the reporter said, "there's truth in everything you say, as there always is. But when the President puts the arm on you this way, there's nothing for you to do but to go along. Isn't that right?"

There was an explosive cackle of Stevenson laughter.

"You mean to say that the fate of civilization depends on my beating Ike Eisenhower? Oh, come off it!"

"Maybe not the fate of civilizaton," his friend said soberly, "but the fate of the Democratic Party sure as hell may."

Mr. Truman's decision not to seek reelection was made in the early part of 1950. He wrote a memorandum about it to himself at that time and put it away in his desk. It reads in part:

I am not a candidate for nomination by the Democratic convention.

My first election to public office took place in November, 1922. I served two years in the armed forces in World War I, ten years in the Senate, two months and 20 days as Vice President and President of the Senate. I have been in public office well over 30 years, having been President of the United States almost two complete terms.

In my opinion eight years as President is enough and sometimes too much for any man to serve in that capacity.

. . . I know I could be elected again and break the old [two-term] precedent as it was broken by FDR. It should not be done. That precedent should continue, not by a Constitutional amendment [the Twenty-second, then pending before the states and later ratified], but by custom based on the honor of the man in the office.*

In the fall of 1951 Mr. Truman disclosed his intentions in confidence to a few of his closest aides. Some, at least, were relieved, for they felt that his political luck had run out and they did not want to see him exposed to defeat and disappointment, but they did not tell him so. (In his memoirs Mr. Truman writes: "The staff responded with deep emotion and expressions of protest and disappointment.")

The President's first—and, at that time, only—choice for a successor was his greatly admired friend, Fred M. Vinson, whom he had appointed Chief Justice in 1946. He invited Vinson down to Key West in the fall of 1951 and told the Chief Justice that he would like to back him for the nomination. After long deliberation, Vinson turned down the offer and said that he preferred to remain on the Court. This dismayed and disappointed the President, and he began to look elsewhere for a candidate. It was David Lloyd, one of the President's administrative assistants, who first proposed consideration of Adlai Stevenson, with whom he had served in Washington during the war. The President knew Stevenson only slightly, but he was impressed by Lloyd's advocacy. He asked Lloyd to invite the Illinois Governor to Washington for the late January conference.

That conference, incidentally, ended on an awkward note of confusion. Mr. Truman was left with the impression that Stevenson was receptive to the proposition and required only a week or so of meditation and family consultation to affirm his consent. Stevenson, on the other hand, although he had not irrevocably rejected the offer, thought that he had made his reservations sufficiently clear so that the President would continue to search for a more amenable prospect. It was not until early March, with Truman's irritation at the Governor's long silence mounting daily, that Stevenson realized he had committed a gaffe and moved to retrieve it. He came to Washington and told the President that he felt his commitment to a second term at Springfield precluded his seeking the Presidential nomination.

The President was more irritated than ever. He could not understand a politician who would turn down such an opportunity to go for the top prize. While he had an instinctive distrust of men of such elegant intellectualism as Stevenson possessed (Dean Acheson, Bob Lovett, and a few others excepted), he nevertheless had become

* Truman *Memoirs*, vol. 2, p. 488.

greatly impressed with the talents of the man who in 1948 had rolled up the biggest plurality of any governor in Illinois history. Now Stevenson had plunged him into a real dilemma.

Meanwhile, the Republican pot was boiling furiously. Senator Taft had announced his candidacy as early as October 1951, and had been stumping the country at a fast pace ever since. On Sunday, January 6, 1952, Senator Henry Cabot Lodge, who four months earlier had been designated chairman of a "Draft Eisenhower" campaign, announced that success had crowned his efforts: Ike had agreed to let his name go into the first-in-the-nation preferential primary in New Hampshire. From his NATO headquarters at Rocquencourt, outside Paris, the day after the Lodge announcement, a broadly smiling Ike modestly conceded that if enough of his friends insisted upon it, he would have no recourse but to accept a call to "duty that would transcend my present responsibility."

The news created a sensation and set the Presidential campaign of 1952 roaring into high gear. But the only flags flying were Republican flags. The Democratic banner hung limply on its pole, sodden with "corruption," "Communists in government," and a dismal stalemate in Korea. The party needed desperately a new face and a new war cry to set its banner waving again.

With Stevenson's withdrawal, there was no new face—not, at least, one acceptable to the head of the party.

Estes Kefauver, who had been tramping the hustings in his coonskin cap like a medicine man and rousing the hopes of the rustics? The President had been irked immeasurably at Kefauver's Senate crime investigation a year earlier, which had put some Democratic mayors in hot water. As an old pro, Truman distrusted political reformers. He wanted no part of Kefauver.

Senator Dick Russell, the Georgia strong man? The President admired Russell as a Senator, but the Southern conservatives and all the old Dixiecrat crowd were massed behind Russell, and the Northern liberals would never accept him.

Averell Harriman, the devoted, slow-spoken man-of-all-work? A good man, but he had no strong political base, had never been in a campaign. It would be hard to build him up as a serious candidate.

Alben Barkley, his amiable Vice President, whom everybody loved? Too old at 72.

That Stevenson . . . ! What was eating the fellow?

Well, the time was coming to fish or cut bait. Briefly, Truman toyed with the idea of reversing his earlier decision and going for another term himself. One night, late in March, he invited a few of his close advisers, including the new Democratic Chairman, Frank E. McKinney, to a small dinner at Blair House. He sounded them out, tentatively, on the proposition of his being a candidate to succeed himself. But his guests, as tactfully as they could, said no. The President said "the Boss"—Mrs. Truman—was against the idea too, and he guessed that made it unanimous. He gave each of those around the dinner table a newly minted silver dollar to show there were no hard feelings from their verdict.

A week later—Saturday, March 29—at the Jackson Day Dinner in the District of Columbia National Guard Armory, the President made his decision official. At the end of a long, teasingly misleading "give 'em hell" speech, he said: "I shall not be a candidate for re-election. I have served my country long, and I think efficiently and honorably. I do not feel that it is my duty to spend another four years in the White House."

To say that the Democratic race was now wide open would be an understatement. The nomination was going begging, and everyone knew it. The only apparent beneficiary was Kefauver, who kept plodding steadily from one courthouse rally to another, shaking hands by the thousands, winning delegates almost by default in a primary here and a state convention there. He was to walk into the convention late in July with a bag of 248½ delegate votes as compared to 191 for his nearest rival, Russell. But the patient, tireless Tennessean was never to win the accolade that counted most: endorsement by the Democratic big wheels and party bosses. The convention, it was beginning to seem, would be a battle royal among second-besters.

Faced with this intolerable prospect, party leaders in many parts of the country began to turn the heat on the reluctant Stevenson. More and more, he seemed to be the only man—the indispensable man—who could avert disaster for the party. The party leaders made pilgrimages to see him in person at his office in Springfield; they inundated him with letters, telegrams, long-distance telephone calls; they attacked obliquely, through his friends and political associates. He became literally a man under siege, fighting desperately to defend his privilege to be left alone.

At last a crack appeared in his battlements. At the annual Governors' Conference in June, which is a natural magnet for the nation's top political writers and commentators, Stevenson was cornered into issuing a formal statement on his intentions about the

candidacy. He did not avail himself, as he might have, of the curt
and irrevocable Sherman negative. Instead, he employed the ambiguous, open-ended locution of the hopeful noncandidate. He said
that in the "unlikely event" a draft should develop for him at the
convention, "I will decide what to do at that time in the light of
conditions then existing."

Was he or wasn't he a candidate?

The Republican convention opened on Monday, July 7, in the
vast Chicago Amphitheater, hard by the stockyards. In five days of
acrimony and tactical maneuver, the hardened troops of a bewildered Ike Eisenhower smashed at last through the defenses of the
bitterly resisting Taftites. The ultimate victory was almost an anticlimax. The real bloodletting had come in the first four days in the
battle over the seating of delegates. When the first roll call of the
states was completed on Friday, Eisenhower had 595 votes—nine
short of a winning majority—and Taft had 500. Before a second
ballot could be called, Minnesota's delegates threw their 19 Stassen
votes to Ike, and it was over. A few hours later, Richard M. Nixon
was named the Vice Presidential candidate by acclamation.

(For the first time, virtually an entire nation was able to be a
ringside spectator at a national political convention. Through the
new magic of television, an estimated 70,000,000 persons witnessed
the unfolding drama at Chicago. This new method of communication was to become a profound influence on future conventions.)

The Democrats moved onto the same Chicago stage two weeks
later. What their script lacked in quality was more than compen-
sated for in suspense and slapstick confusion. The 1,200 delegates
and their supporting troops and camp followers converged on Chicago on Monday, July 21, facing an almost certain deadlock between Kefauver, Russell, and Harriman. The only apparent tie-
breaker was either Truman or Stevenson, and each was maintaining
his firm intention to reject the role. A week before, the President had
given Barkley his rather tepid blessing to seek the nomination. But
the crestfallen Vice President tossed in the towel on the opening day
of the convention after leaders of the labor bloc told him they could
not support him because of his age.

Truman was again a free agent to cast his support where he
chose. But the outlook for a choice was not good. He had given up
on Stevenson, and all the other contestants were distinctly second-
best. He told reporters who pressed him for his choice to "watch

how Tom Garvin votes. That will be my choice." Thomas J. Garvin, of Kansas City, was Mr. Truman's alternate on the Missouri delegation and would sit in for him, since the President planned to remain in Washington until the final day of the convention.

The Donnybrook that was the Democratic convention of 1952 has rarely been matched in all the annals of partisan politics. It resulted in the first genuine draft of a major Presidential candidate in 72 years, a circumstance which can arise only when all the disciplines of party organization fall to the ground. Against a background of strife over convention rules, a civil-rights platform, and a loyalty oath binding the delegates to support the party's nominee, the partisans of Kefauver, Russell, and Harriman launched repeated guerrilla forays against one another, and then alternately banded and disbanded to attack a common but largely amorphous foe—the Stevenson brigade.

On the Sunday preceding the Monday opening of the convention, the Illinois delegation caucused in a private dining room of the Morrison Hotel in Chicago. As chairman of the delegation, Governor Stevenson pleaded earnestly with his fellow delegates neither to place his name in nomination nor to support such an action by any other delegation. There could be no question that he was desperately serious in his request. But one delegate after another rose to insist that the Democratic Party faced a disastrous deadlock if he did not run and that he had an obligation both to the party and to the country to step into this breach. The assurances he had pleaded for were not given. While no final commitments were made one way or the other, it was obvious that Stevenson's name would go before the convention regardless of his wishes.

The press had been excluded from the meeting. But the room had been "bugged" by an enterprising radio correspondent, and a group of other reporters, clustered behind a plastic room divider behind the speaker's table, overheard the entire proceedings. Even before the caucus broke up, news wires across the country were crackling with speculations "on the highest and most unimpeachable authority" that Adlai Stevenson's name would be put in nomination and that he would not block it.

One of the most determined bands of Stevenson backers was led by Senator Francis J. Myers, of Pennsylvania. When the news of Stevenson's virtual capitulation before the Illinois caucus began to filter through the jammed lobbies and smoke-filled rooms of the convention hotels on Sunday afternoon, Myers and his cohorts were swamped with eager recruits scrambling for a place on the band-wagon. Myers decided for strategic reasons to delay raising the flag of his "draft Stevenson" campaign until after the Governor had delivered his welcoming address to the convention on Monday. But that the flag would go up was now widely expected, and when Stevenson walked out onto the high pulpit of the convention hall a little after noon that day, he was met with a bedlam of shouts and handclapping.

The first three days of the convention were a noisy, confused mélange of strategies and counterstrategies, of deals and counterdeals, of coalitions hastily put together in smoke-filled rooms and hastily coming unstuck in telephone booths. The common enemy was the amorphous Stevenson force, still without an acknowledged candidate but an almost certainly available one. The Kefauver and Harriman troops joined briefly together in a "stop Stevenson" compact, then fell apart over the question of how tough a loyalty pledge to exact from the Southern delegations. The Russell forces sought to tie their banner to the tail of the Stevenson kite to choke off Kefauver and Harriman. A variety of favorite sons peddled their votes like auctioneers looking for the highest bidder.

Thursday was the payoff day, the day for nominating speeches. That morning a harassed, bleary-eyed Stevenson—he had been up virtually all night in endless harangues with his supporters—telephoned President Truman at the White House. He said he had finally agreed to let his name go before the convention, and he hoped that the President, at this late hour, would not object.

"Well, I blew up," Mr. Truman said later about this episode. "I talked to him in language I think he had never heard before. I told him that for months I had been trying to get him to be the candidate. Now, at the last possible moment, he had changed his mind. But he was at that time the best prospect we had, and I said I would support him."

The nominating speech for Stevenson that night by Indiana's Governor Henry F. Schricker set off the noisiest and most spontaneous demonstration of the convention. It is probable that a first-ballot sweep was missed only because of the premidnight intervention of the Chicago Fire Marshall; he insisted on clearing the convention hall because of the hazard of fire from the ankle-deep litter of paper and other debris on the floor.

With the balloting put over until Friday, the Kefauver and Russell forces had a chance to regroup and strengthen their lines. With

616 votes needed to nominate, the Tennessean was comfortably in the lead on the first ballot that day with 340 votes to 273 for Stevenson, 268 for Russell, 123½ for Harriman, and the others scattered. On the second ballot Kefauver still held the lead with 362½, but his gain was less than Stevenson's, who now had 324½, and Russell's at 296. Harriman had slipped to 121 and apparently was out of the running.

While the second roll call was in progress late in the afternoon, President Truman's plane landed at Midway Airport. When the convention took a recess for dinner, the President went to the Saddle and Sirloin Club, close by the convention hall, for dinner with a group that included Paul Fitzpatrick, New York Democratic state chairman and the leader of the Harriman contingent. Over steaks and good bourbon whiskey they sealed the fate of the 1952 convention. When the night session was gaveled to order, Fitzpatrick went to the rostrum and read a letter from Harriman saying that he was pulling out of the contest and asking his supporters to cast their votes for Adlai Stevenson.

Now the bandwagon was rolling on a downhill grade, and state after state switched votes and hopped aboard as it came by. At the final tally Stevenson had amassed 613 votes, three short of a winning majority. Out of the shadows of the high rostrum the bulking, solemn figure of Estes Kefauver now emerged into the glare and the bedlam. Asking "Mista Chai'man" for recognition, he proclaimed his withdrawal from the race. The Utah chairman leaped to his feet, announced the switch of his Kefauver delegates to Stevenson—4½ votes—and the battle was over.

At 1:30 Saturday morning, the President and the nominee walked arm in arm down the long floodlit runway to the rostrum. The bone-weary delegates and the spectators called up their last reserves of energy to send up a deafening roar of welcome. Mr. Truman, grinning broadly and exhibiting an exuberance he almost certainly did not feel, introduced Stevenson by saying, "You have nominated a winner, and I am going to take off my coat and do everything I can to help him win." Stevenson managed a wan smile and looked ill at ease, but he picked up confidence as he swung into his acceptance speech—a speech he had written hastily but from the heart. The suddenly sobered convention heard him say:

Sacrifice, patience, understanding and implacable purpose may be our lot for years to come. Let's face it. Let's talk sense to the American people. Let's tell them the truth: that there are no gains without pains;

that this is the eve of great decisions, not easy decisions like resistance when you are attacked, but a long, costly, patient struggle against the great enemies of men—war and poverty and tyranny.

An hour later, in a hall half emptied by sheer exhaustion, Senator John Sparkman of Alabama was proclaimed the Vice Presidential candidate by acclamation. The Democratic campaign of 1952, born in confusion and uncertainty, was on its confused and uncertain way.

The Last Round

As a candidate, Adlai Stevenson confirmed Harry Truman's worst fears about eggheads as politicians. Stevenson's erudite philosophizing; his cautious, introspective, often tedious, rationalizations; his altruistic insistence on facing issues squarely instead of obliquely; his elegant, sophisticated wit, which went skimming over the heads of most of his hearers instead of socking them in the belly—these traits of the new breed of politician left the old graduate of the Pendergast school cold and apprehensive. Truman was a political pragmatist, or, as he preferred to put it, a political realist. In his book, an election campaign was not an educational process but a struggle for power. It was a fight in which there are no second-bests. And in order to survive one uses whatever weapons come to hand. In particular, he believed that no candidate for President could be elected who did not embrace wholeheartedly the record that his party had made in that office. Adlai Stevenson, Mr. Truman felt, seemed to be falling into this self-defeating heresy.

Their never cordial relations were further exacerbated in the weeks immediately following the convention. First, Stevenson removed Frank McKinney, a Truman protégé, as national chairman and put in his place a long-time friend of his own, Chicago lawyer Stephen A. Mitchell. Mitchell was an intense, conscientious, and, as it turned out, highly competent man for the job. But his political experience had been limited to the liberal-reformist movement centering on the University of Chicago, which had brought such unlikely figures as Stevenson and U.S. Senator Paul H. Douglas into the political limelight.

Next, Stevenson let it be known that his campaign headquarters would be in Springfield, not in Washington, nor, in defiance of another old tradition, in New York. He staffed it not with horny-handed veterans of previous Democratic wars, but with such relative amateurs as Wilson Wyatt, one-time mayor of Louisville, who was named campaign manager; Clayton Fritchey, a New Orleans newspaper man; Hyman Raskin and William M. Blair, members of his own Chicago law firm; and a large sprinkling of gray-haired New Dealers and gray-flanneled young Ivy Leaguers. In short order, the offices of the Democratic National Committee in Washington's Mayflower Hotel became no more than an outpost of the Springfield headquarters. Inevitably, the President felt cut off and isolated from a campaign in which he believed he should have at least equal billing with the star.

In simple truth, of course, Stevenson *was* attempting the impossible and badly conceived task of dissociating his campaign from the Truman administration. He could no more do so than he could dissociate himself from the Democratic Party, for the Democratic Party *was* the Truman administration, and the sordid mishaps were as much a part of the picture as the brilliant achievements.

In August Stevenson paid a visit to the President in the White House in the hope of working out a *modus vivendi* by which the President would remain in the background until the last couple of weeks of the campaign, while Stevenson created a public image and program of his own. The conference was held in the Cabinet room with the President and key members of his staff lined up on one side of the vast coffin-shaped table and, on the other side, Stevenson and picked members of "the Springfield crowd"—like representatives of sovereign powers at a treaty conference. It was stiff, painfully uncomfortable, and largely inconclusive. One does not bluntly ask a President to stand aside in a major campaign of his own party, and Stevenson's circuitous hints either did not get through or were ignored if they did. At all events, it was absurd to think that a man of Harry Truman's temperament and political instinct would accept the role of a silent and dignified *éminence grise* in a campaign in which his record as President would be at stake.*

Mr. Truman's reflections on this point are bitter. In his *Memoirs* he said:

* On a later occasion, Stevenson sent Chairman Mitchell to suggest to the President that it would be a great help in the campaign if Dean Acheson, the main secondary target of the Republicans, could be persuaded to announce his intention to resign as Secretary of State as soon as the election was over. The President firmly rejected the proposal. How the word of this got to Acheson is not clear, but it did, and his attitude toward Stevenson ever after was one of frigid formality.

Stevenson's attitude toward the President he hoped to succeed was a mystery to me. Whether this was due to the urging of his advisers or to bad information or perhaps to the contagion other good citizens were suffering as a result of reading the anti-Democratic press, I do not know.

When it seemed to me almost too late, Stevenson asked me to get into the campaign, which I did as soon as I could, and I gave it all I had.

This last assertion is at variance with the recollection of Steve Mitchell, who told the present writer: "We didn't have to ask Mr. Truman to get into the campaign. He was raring to go from the start, and he opened up with a Labor Day speech in Milwaukee and whistlestopped all the way back to Washington. He was in the thick of it from then on. The only direct request that I recall we made of him was to appear at a big rally in Harlem, which came toward the end of the campaign. He did, and he put on a great show."*

The campaign of 1952 will stand in the history books for many years as one of the most intensive and one of the bitterest on record. It started out on a relatively high plane. Neither Stevenson nor Eisenhower was, by nature, a vindictive man. Stevenson traveled mainly by air, talking principally to large city audiences, giving them polished dissertations, often sparkling with wit, on the great issues of inflation, foreign policy, labor legislation, and the like. Eisenhower took to the trains, spinning an incongruous but enchanting web of glamour and folksiness from the rear platform, but stumbling incoherently over the big issues in his major speeches. Neither man, in the first few weeks of September, struck any notable sparks of public enthusiasm.

Then a series of events happened that changed the tone of things. The Scripps-Howard newspapers, which had been among Eisenhower's earliest and most enthusiastic backers, gave him an editorial tongue-lashing, saying he was "running like a dry creek," and urging him to start slugging. Next, he had a well-publicized meeting at his home in New York's Morningside Heights with his defeated rival for the nomination, Bob Taft. The Senator extracted certain concessions from the candidate in exchange for his support, one of which was that Eisenhower launch a full-scale attack on the foreign as well as the domestic policies of the Truman administration. And finally the "Nixon fund" hit the front pages of the nation's press with the force of dynamite, giving the Democrats—briefly, as it turned out—

* Mr. Truman's recollection is contained in his *Memoirs*, vol 2, p. 498. Mr. Mitchell's view was expressed in a personal letter to the author.

a wide-open opportunity for attacks on Nixon's integrity. They moved in with zest.

Goaded by these developments, the Eisenhower handlers got their man into a fighting mood. He stumped through the South and Middle West early in October calling for a "moral crusade" to "clean up the mess in Washington," and to "drive the crooks and the Communists from their seats of power." He said the Truman administration had "blundered into the Korean war" and had not the wit "either to win it or to end it." On a memorable foray into Wisconsin with Senator Joe McCarthy at his side, he crossed out, in the typed text of his speech, a brief tribute to his old chief, General George Marshall, whom McCarthy a few months earlier had branded as a traitor. But the undoctored text was already in the hands of the reporters, and the omission of the Marshall reference made more news than the rest of the candidate's speech. It also sent Harry Truman into a white blaze of fury.

Stevenson reacted to this new tempo of the Republican attack somewhat hesitantly. It was not until Nixon, some days later, accused him of being "soft on communism" because of a deposition he had given in the first trial of Alger Hiss, that Stevenson was really stung to anger and retaliation.

But Truman's short fuse had ignited instantly on Eisenhower's affront to Marshall, and he lashed out at him with all the righteous wrath of his being. The President had just set out on a two-week whistlestop tour that would take him all the way to the Pacific Northwest and back through the midcontinent states. In every speech and in every one of scores of back platform appearances, he reserved a part of his time to attack the intelligence and the honesty of Dwight Eisenhower.

"President Truman," Anthony Leviero of the New York *Times* reported from the Presidential train on the West Coast, "has engaged General Eisenhower in an epic political conflict, and before the November 4th finale, one of them is going to get hurt.

"If Harry Truman is successful he will have helped Governor Stevenson to defeat the Republican nominee. If he loses, the President will have aided General Eisenhower and damaged his own place in history. Mr. Truman is working in dead earnest to elect Governor Stevenson, but he is also seeking vindication of himself and his Fair Deal."

Arthur Krock, writing in the same newspaper a few weeks later, described the President's effort as "a protracted assault on the personal integrity of General Eisenhower that is without parallel for a man in Mr. Truman's position."

Truman's contagious wrath had an immediate stimulative effect on the Democratic campaign. It was transmitted to the Stevenson entourage, and the once reluctant candidate began to show a new zest and appetite for the battle. Some of the awkward restraint fell from his manner. He loosened up, and his cultured, high-pitched voice came over the loudspeakers with a new ring of urgency and zeal. He slashed at Eisenhower for "betraying" a foreign policy he had helped to construct; for being a "captive" of Taft isolationism; for duplicity and cowardice in joining forces with the McCarthy bigots; and for ignorance on the social and economic problems of the nation.

His quips, which used to be met with chuckles, now drew gales of belly laughter from his audiences. He ridiculed the General for "the surrender of Morningside Heights." Referring to the McCarthy incident, he said: "My opponent is worried about my funnybone, but I'm worried about his backbone."

Bigger and noisier crowds turned out for the Stevenson and Truman parties as the candidate and the President crisscrossed the nation in the hectic closing weeks of the campaign. There was a new touch of exuberance and spontaneity—in a farmer's lusty yell, "Give 'em hell, Adlai!" or in the spectacle of an exultant Truman whanging out "The Black Hawk Waltz" on a piano in the public square of New Britain, Connecticut. A dizzying sense of confidence began to dawn among the sweated hirelings and reporters on the campaign trains. They began to believe that maybe General Ike was not an invincible St. George after all. Even the public opinion pollsters, remembering how they had been scorched in 1948, began to hedge on their predictions of a Republican landslide.

But a landslide it was—a historic, peculiarly personal, Eisenhower landslide. When the votes were counted late on the night of Tuesday, November 4, the General had rolled up 55 percent of the popular vote—33,020,000 to 26,584,000—and had won the electoral votes of all but nine states. But the party whose banner he bore was left virtually awash in his triumphant wake. Never had a party won the White House by such a smashing margin and failed so dismally in the congressional contests. The Republicans gained only one seat in the Senate, for an all-but-invisible 48 to 47 majority, and 22 seats in the House for a margin of 12.

Stevenson had lost, even while rolling up the biggest total of any defeated candidate in history. But had Truman lost also? Was Eisenhower's victory a repudiation of the Fair Deal and all it stood for?

It was not. Eisenhower offered no fundamental alternatives to the Fair Deal program, either during his campaign or during his administration. He proposed neither to turn the country back nor to change substantially the compass bearings of its forward momentum. The nation voted only for a new face—the face of a simple, virtuous, warmhearted folk hero whose promise was not to lead but to go along.

The Truman administration (and, of course, Stevenson's candidacy) was vulnerable in the end not because of what it had done or not done for the country, but because of its style. Familiarity had made clichés of its slogans and bred apathy for its goals. Its trumpets no longer sounded a parade; rather, they sounded a forced march. And the splatterings of "The 3 C's: Crime, Corruption, Communism" clung unscrubbed to its features like the pigeon stains on a park monument. The genial, incorruptible Ike with his comfortable, uncluttered wisdom of the small-town philosopher and his incontestable soldier's halo, was the perfect, and inevitable, antidote for a nation jaded by a decade of conflict and challenge. When he said, late in the campaign, "I will go to Korea," he had it made.

Inauguration Day—Tuesday, January 20, 1953—was bright and bracing in Washington. The city was aglow with that euphoric madness which always seizes it on such occasions each four years— a projection on a huge scale of the excitement that used to grip small-town America when the circus came to town. Pennsylvania Avenue, from the White House to the Capitol, was decked with flags and bunting, and acres of bleachers along each side of the parade route had begun to fill up with blanketed spectators by the breakfast hour. For weeks, every hotel and boardinghouse room in the city and its environs had been reserved and exorbitantly paid for in advance. The vanguard of the 50,000 out-of-town visitors had begun to pour in on Sunday, filling the hotel lobbies (and the restaurants and bars along Connecticut Avenue and other downtown streets) with a milling, noisy throng. This was to be the biggest, costliest, and splashiest inaugural in history up to that time, a triumphant homecoming from twenty years of exile for the GOP—or, more accurately, a raising of the siege on the shrine of Capitalism by long-disfranchised Capitalists.

For the Eisenhower victory in November had instantly been interpreted as a victory for Free Enterprise, and now the Day of Deliverance had come. At the stroke of noon a Businessman's Administration would grasp the controls of government from the hands of the New Deal and Fair Deal do-gooders and theorists, who, of course, had very nearly run it into the ground, and some of whom, God knows, might have been getting their orders from Moscow.

It was a day of joyful retribution. But it was a day of poignancy, too. There had been losers as well as winners, and not only a Presidency but an era was coming to an end.

The President-elect had declined the invitation of the President for luncheon at the White House on Inauguration Day. Also, when he arrived at the White House shortly before noon to be escorted to the Capitol ceremonies by the out-going President, he ignored the tradition of entering the White House to be received by the President. Instead, the two chief celebrants of this ritual rode in glum, almost unbroken silence along the mile-long route in an open-top car, separately acknowledging with smiles and waves of the hand the cheers of the spectators. Their only conversational exchange, according to Mr. Truman, arose from a tart observation by General Eisenhower that he had stayed away from the 1948 inaugural to avoid drawing attention away from the President. To which Mr. Truman replied with equal tartness:

"You were not here in 1948 because I did not send for you. But if I had sent for you, you would have come."

As he walked from the rotunda out onto the flag-draped inaugural stand built over the north steps of the Capitol, Harry Truman received for the last time the Marine Band's stirring salute, "Hail to the Chief." He and Mrs. Truman and Margaret took their seats in the front row as the oath was administered to the new President by Chief Justice Vinson. From immediately behind them, General Marshall reached over to shake Mr. Truman's hand and to plant a kiss on Margaret's cheek. Mr. Truman later recalled:

I tried to listen attentively to Eisenhower's inaugural address, but I was preoccupied with many thoughts.

My principal concern on turning over the Presidency was how our foreign affairs would be conducted by the new administration to guard the peace of the world. How would it deal with the Communist challenge to the free world? How would it get along with our allies? I had some misgivings as to where the new administration might take us.

But the responsibility was no longer mine. When President Eisenhower finished his inaugural address, Mrs. Truman, Margaret, and I left the crowded scene at the Capitol.*

The Trumans had packed their belongings and cleared them out of the White House days before, and now there remained only a last farewell with a few friends before boarding the train to go back home to Independence. Their White House limousine was waiting for them at the edge of the crowd in the Capitol plaza, and they departed with only a single police motorcycle escort, headed via back streets for the home of Dean Acheson in Georgetown. In the meditative silence of that recessional, Margaret leaned over to her father and said, "Hi, *Mister* Truman!" The drawn face looked puzzled for a moment and then burst into laughter. For thirty years he had worn a title of some sort—Judge, Senator, Mr. Vice President, Mr. President—and now he was just plain Mr. Truman, and the idea amused him.

As the car swung into stately P Street, a crowd of more than 500 persons massed before the steps of the Achesons' lovely eighteenth-century home set up a cheer. Their reception was totally unexpected, for the Acheson party had not been publicized, and in any event might have been expected to be overlooked even by the curious in the light of the major festivities downtown. But these were neighbors and friends and loyal government workers, and Mr. Truman was touched.

Inside, all the Truman Cabinet members and a handful of other officials and their wives were assembled for a farewell luncheon for the ex-First Family. It was an afternoon of gaiety and warm sentimentality; of reminiscences and anecdotes and confessions; of acid or hilarious gossip about the new crowd taking over downtown; and of mutual reassurances about how well the old crowd had done, after all. As train time approached, Mr. Truman made a little speech that betokened, in a simple, throat-catching sort of way, the gratitude of a plain and unpretentious man for the strength these friends had given him to face great obstacles. A toast was drunk and some tears were shed.

When the party at the Achesons adjourned to take the Trumans to the train, the last floats and bands of the inaugural parade were still passing under the street lights of lower Pennsylvania Avenue. At Union Station, the great Concourse was jammed with more than 5,000 people who had prevailed over mountainous traffic jams to bid the Trumans good-bye. Shouting and cheering and waving home-

* Harry S. Truman, *Mr. Citizen* (Bernard Geis Associates, 1960), p. 16.

made placards with "So long, Harry" and similar sentiments, they poured through the gates and onto the loading platform as a police cordon wedged the Trumans aboard. Their car was the famous old "Ferdinand Magellan," veteran of thousands of miles of political campaigning, from whose back platform Harry Truman had introduced "whistlestopping" into the American vernacular.

Now he stepped again out onto that familiar enclosure, his tie slightly awry, his face smudged with lipstick, but his manner as bouncy and exuberant as if this were the beginning, not the end, of a campaign. He addressed the crowd:

May I say to you that I appreciate this more than any meeting I have ever attended as President or Vice President or Senator. This is the greatest demonstration that any man could have, because I'm just Mr. Truman, private citizen, now.

This is the first time you have ever sent me home in a blaze of glory. I can't adequately express my appreciation for what you are doing. I'll never forget it if I live to be a hundred.

He paused momentarily, leaned forward to chop the air with that familiar, awkward gesture that had become a Truman trademark, and added: *"And that's just what I expect to do!"*

The train lurched tentatively and then began slowly to pull away. A roar went up from the crowd, a roar that dissolved, raggedly at first but in thunderous unison after the first few bars, into "Auld Lang Syne."

Epilogue

ERIC SEVAREID: *An Unknown Side of Truman*

Reprinted with permission from the Washington *Evening Star*, February 4, 1964.

Public Scolding of Student Reveals Sensitivity of Former President

The devoted students of Sherlock Holmes are as divisive as they are numerous, but they must surely agree that there was a certain respect as well as affection implicit in Holmes' exclamation, "Good old Watson, you are the one fixed point in a changing age!"

This must be the sentiment of many Americans, at least those of middle age or more, as they see the news films of Harry Truman striding out on his morning walk, each foot firmly planted, each crisp pronouncement—on Panama, Lyndon Johnson, Barry Goldwater—delivered with the finality of a man who has no regrets, who relishes his enemies as much as his friends, and who enjoys the final freedom: contentment with life and no fear of death.

It is a good and inspiring thing to witness, this evening of a life that was full to the brim and never seriously

marred. A man's character is his fate, said the ancient Greeks. Chance, in good part, took Harry Truman to the presidency, but it was his character that kept him there and determined his historical fate: He is, without any doubt, destined to live in the books as one of the strongest and most decisive of the American Presidents.

It was Dean Acheson, Mr. Truman's Secretary of State, who said once, in musing about the presidency: "If a President will make decisions, you're in luck. That is the essential quality. And if he has a high batting average in the correctness of his decisions, then you're in clover."

About this quality of Truman's there was never any doubt from the beginning, in the minds of those of us who covered his presidency all the way through. His simplicity, his honesty and his self-discipline were so obvious as to be non-arguable, however much we disagreed about some of his actions and appointments. We were aware of his sensitivity about the institution of the presidency—"This is the most honorable office a man can hold," he used to say—and aware of his relative lack of sensitivity to criticism of himself. What we were not aware of, at least not I, was his sensitivity about the feelings of other people.

This has been a sadly belated discovery of recent days for this reporter. It was made during private and therefore, privileged conversations, but I think he will not mind if I extract the small portion of the talk that illustrates my theme. The talk had wandered back a dozen years or so, and an aide remarked that Mr. Truman should have fired so and so. The man who had occupied the most powerful office in the world immediately said, "No, no. That would not have been right. There were other ways to do it. What you don't understand is the power of a President to hurt."

An American President has the power to build, to set fateful events in motion, to destroy an enemy civilization, to win or lose a vast personal following. But the power of a President to hurt the feelings of another human being—this, I think, had scarcely occurred to me, and still less had it occurred to me that a President in office would have the time and the need to be aware of this particular power among so many others.

Mr. Truman went on to observe that a word, a harsh glance, a peremptory motion by a President of the United States could so injure another man's pride that it would remain a scar in his emotional system all his life.

He recalled a painful episode during one of the lectures he loves to make to student audiences about the story and the art of governing America. A college boy stood up to ask the former President what he thought of the State's Governor, whom he described as "our local yokel." Mr. Truman told the boy he should be ashamed of himself for his lack of respect toward the high office of Governor. The boy turned pale and sat down. Later, Mr. Truman made it a point to seek out the shaken, apologetic lad and to reassure him. He did much more. He had the boy's dean send him frequent reports on the lad's progress in school and followed his later career with the interest of a friend. What this interest by a former President must have done for the boy's pride and self-respect may be imagined.

The simple point here is that Mr. Truman had instantly realized how a public scolding by a former President could mark and mar the boy's inner life and his standing in the community.

I feel gratified to have heard this story. It has given me an insight to the responsibilities of a President that I did not have, and it has immeasurably added to my own residue of memories about the man from Missouri. He is nearly 80 now. He may live to be a 100—his is strong stock—but this, I know, is the specific memory that will return to me when his time does come.

◇◇◇◇◇◇◇◇◇◇◇◇◇◇◇◇◇◇◇◇◇◇◇◇◇◇◇

Notes on Sources

In the research for this book I have followed three broad avenues of inquiry.

The first was to establish a chronology and topical guide to the Truman Presidency so that I would know what I wanted to write about and what I wanted to ignore. As the basic source for this I chose the bound volumes of the New York *Times* Sunday "News of the Week in Review" for the years from 1945 through 1952, which are preserved in the library of the *Times* Washington Bureau. From these I constructed a running summary of the highlights of national and international affairs as they bore on Mr. Truman's performance. As I narrowed down the situations and events that I wished to include in my narrative, I pursued each of them in detail through the catalogued clipping files of the *Times* morgue and through the back files of other newspapers and periodicals in the Library of Congress.

Next, as I blocked out each chapter, I combed the libraries for authoritative writings on the subjects relevant to that chapter: books, articles, and official documents that would provide both additional facts and critical evaluation and insight. In most cases I found the supply overwhelming, so I chose a manageable few and trusted to luck that I had made the right selections.

Finally, over a period of several months I conducted interviews with more than twenty-five persons who had been closely connected, in either an official or an unofficial capacity, with the major developments of the Truman administration. I took the longer interviews down on a tape recorder and later had them transcribed. In others, I relied on handwritten notes. Most important of all, a number of these sources had quite extensive files of correspondence, memoranda, reports, and diaries—some of it the offbeat or unpublishable or "inside" type of information that is invaluable to the reporter or historian. These files were generously made available to me. In most cases of this kind, obviously, I am obliged to treat the information confidentially and to preserve the anonymity of the source. (This is an advantage which the reporter enjoys over the historian.)

A Word About Presidential Libraries

Before I agreed to undertake this project I discussed it informally with Mr. Truman during one of his visits to Washington late in 1961. Throughout his tenure in the White House I had enjoyed an amicable if not intimate professional relationship with him. On the occasion of my talk with him in 1961 he expressed his pleasure at my interest in doing the book and told me: "Come out to the Library. Everything I did as President is there, and you are welcome to all of it."

I went to the Harry S. Truman Memorial Library at Independence, Missouri, in the spring of 1962, prepared to stay a month or two. In less than two weeks I was disillusioned and on my way back home. The bulk of its claimed "five million papers on the Presidency" turned out to be largely routine public correspondence, printed reports, and documents available almost anywhere in the government, mimeographed speeches and statements issued through the White House Press Secretary, and Mr. Truman's office files while he was a Senator. When I asked for the working papers and other documents relating to such major policy matters as the Marshall Plan, NATO, the veto of the Taft-Hartley Act, and the loyalty investigations, I was told with evident embarrassment by the Library's director: "Well, you see, they are in Mr. Truman's wing of the Library. He regards those as his personal papers and we have never been permitted to examine or catalogue them."

A few days later I brought this matter up with Mr. Truman himself. He confirmed, rather testily in the end, what the librarian had told me: There were certain classes of papers that were "his" and he didn't plan to relinquish them "until I'm good and ready." This incident put something of a chill on our subsequent relationship. When I wrote him about a year later seeking clarification on certain points about the dismissal of General MacArthur, he replied as follows:

May 17, 1963

Dear Mr. Phillips:

In reply to your letter, I don't think I can in all fairness and propriety lend myself to any suggestions or contributions to your forthcoming book. There are some contractual obligations as well.

Sincerely yours,
Harry S. Truman

At the time Mr. Truman was under contract to Screen Gems, Inc., of New York, for a thirteen-week television series on his Presidential career— a series that ran during 1964 under the title "Conflict." It was a good program.

The only point I want to make about this now is that I think Presidential libraries, whether they are at Hyde Park, N.Y., Independence, Mo., or Johnson City, Tex., are not a good thing. They are sentimental mausoleums in which valuable historical materials are buried beyond the convenient reach of most of the people who need access to them. They should be in a central repository such as the National Archives in Washington, D.C.

In the notes that follow I would like to make several things clear.

First, I have not attempted an exhaustive bibliography on the Truman Presidency. Anyone who is interested can thumb for himself through the several drawers on the subject to be found in any large library. The sources cited are, in every case, those that I have consulted directly.

Second, I have given page references only where it has seemed necessary for historical accuracy or to accommodate the inquisitive reader who may want to pursue a point farther than what the text presents. I have omitted all citations of extracts from speeches and public statements by the President and other prominent figures which were widely carried in the press at the time they were made.

Finally, in the interest of an uncluttered text I have omitted all citations of the routine facts and day-to-day happenings out of which this narrative is woven. In almost every case they are gleaned from widely published accounts in the leading newspapers and periodicals of the time.

The two volumes of *Memoirs* by Harry S. Truman (Vol. I, *Years of Decision,* and Vol. II, *Years of Trial and Hope,* Doubleday & Co., 1955 and 1956) are referred to so frequently throughout the text that, for brevity, they are cited hereafter as Truman *Memoirs* with the appropriate volume number and page.

Epigraph

President John F. Kennedy, *Look* magazine, January 16, 1962.

Chapter 2

In the preparation of this chapter I found much useful material in the Truman Memorial Library, Independence, Missouri. I have also consulted the back files of the Kansas City *Star* and the St. Louis *Post-Dispatch* in the Library of Congress, and Alfred Steinberg's *The Man from Missouri* (Putnam, 1962).

1. Truman *Memoirs*, vol. 1, pp. 115-16.

2. Jonathan Daniels, *The Man of Independence* (Lippincott, 1950), p. 95. This is a highly literate, informative, and sympathetic narrative particularly valuable for its account of Mr. Truman's young manhood and his earliest years as President.

3. Truman *Memoirs*, vol. 1, p. 137.

4. William M. Reddig, *Tom's Town: Kansas City and the Pendergast Legend* (Lippincott, 1947), p. 265. A one-time reporter on the Kansas City *Star*, Mr. Reddig has written an authoritative and exciting history of the Pendergast machine.

5. The original of this note is in the Truman Library.

6. William Hillman, *Mr. President* (Farrar, Straus & Young, 1952), p. 189.

7. Truman *Memoirs*, vol. 1, p. 167.

8. These and many other details of this episode are recounted in Chapter 13 of Mr. Byrnes' memoir, *All in One Lifetime* (Harper, 1958).

9. Interview with the writer, September 1965.

10. Daniels, *op. cit,* p. 234.

Chapter 3

1. William L. Laurence, *Dawn Over Zero* (Knopf, 1947), p. 216. Also of interest is his *Men and Atoms* (Simon & Schuster, 1952).

2. Truman *Memoirs*, vol. 2, p. 421.

3. *Ibid,* p. 53.

4. Henry L. Stimson, *On Active Service in War and Peace* (Harper, 1948).

5. Herbert Feis, *Japan Subdued* (Princeton Univ. Press, 1961). I have

drawn heavily on both the Stimson and Feis works in the preparation of this chapter.

6. Stimson, *op. cit.*, p. 617.

7. Truman *Memoirs*, vol. 2, p. 420.

8. Stimson, *op. cit.*, p. 630.

9. *U.S. News & World Report*, issue of August 15, 1960, p. 65. This is in an article titled "Was A-Bomb on Japan a Mistake?" based on interviews fifteen years after the event with five men who had an important hand in the decision.

10. Reprinted in the New York *Times*, April 15, 1945.

11. Jonathan Daniels, *The Man of Independence* (Lippincott, 1950), p. 261.

12. Truman *Memoirs*, vol. 2, p. 314.

13. These figures were published in the New York *Times* of August 12, 1945, and tend to be lower than many subsequent calculations. There never has been a "final" accounting of the war's cost in terms of lives, money, and property.

14. Herbert Feis, *Churchill, Roosevelt and Stalin* (Princeton Univ. Press, 1957), p. 597.

15. Winston S. Churchill, *Triumph and Tragedy* (Houghton Mifflin, 1953), p. 455.

Chapter 4

In the preparation of this chapter I am particularly indebted to Averell Harriman, who sat for a long taped interview one evening and was generous with his time and counsel on several other occasions. I am also grateful to Paul H. Nitze for an interview, and to Benjamin V. Cohen, who read the chapter in manuscript and gave me much valuable advice.

In addition to the specific citations below I have consulted the following: Herbert Feis, *Between War and Peace* (Princeton Univ. Press, 1960); James F. Byrnes, *Speaking Frankly* (Harper, 1947); John Lukacs, *A History of the Cold War* (Doubleday, 1961); Robert E. Sherwood, *Roosevelt and Hopkins* (Harper, 1948), and certain unclassified papers relating to the Yalta and Potsdam conferences in the Historical Section of the Department of State.

1. Interview with the writer.

2. Jonathan Daniels, *The Man of Independence* (Lippincott, 1950), p. 265.

3. Winston S. Churchill, *Triumph and Tragedy* (Houghton Mifflin, 1953), p. 497.

4. Truman *Memoirs*, vol. 1, p. 340.

5. Churchill, *op. cit.*, p. 630.

6. *Ibid.*, p. 502.

7. Truman *Memoirs*, vol. 1, pp. 218 and 298.

8. Dwight D. Eisenhower, *Crusade in Europe* (Doubleday, 1948), p. 489.

9. Truman *Memoirs*, vol. 1, pp. 411-12.

Chapter 5

Contemporary press accounts have provided the principal source material for this chapter. This has been supplemented by interviews with a number of former officials of the Truman administration and by access to the personal files of some of them. Those who have been most helpful in this respect are Clark M. Clifford, Paul A. Porter (who read this chapter in manuscript and offered a number of valuable criticisms), Oscar L. Chapman, and Leon H. Keyserling. I also received help from the staff of the United Mine Workers *Journal* in the section relating to John L. Lewis. In addition to the sources specifically cited below I have consulted *Inflation in the United States 1940-1954,* by Lester V. Chandler (Harper, 1952) and a number of special studies by *Editorial Research Reports,* of Washington.

1. *Statistical Abstract of the United States: 1958* (U.S. Bureau of the Census, Washington, D.C.).

2. Truman *Memoirs*, vol. 1, p. 495.

3. This text is in the possession of a former government official who made it available to the writer.

4. Public correspondence on inflation. Truman Memorial Library, Independence, Missouri. Other documents in this collection also proved useful.

Chapter 6

I have been greatly assisted in the preparation of this chapter by Clark M. Clifford, who made his very extensive files available to me and who also read the chapter in manuscript. In addition to the sources specifically cited below, I found much useful information and insight in the following: Robert S. Allen and William V. Shannon, *The Truman Merry-Go-Round* (Vanguard, 1950); Merriman Smith, *Thank You Mr. President* (Harper, 1946); Jonathan Daniels, *Man of Independence* (Lippincott, 1950); Jules Abels, *The Truman Scandals* (Regnery, 1956).

1. I am indebted for this anecdote to Mrs. Beth Short, widow of Joseph H. Short, who was White House Press Secretary from 1950 to 1952.

2. Margaret Truman, *Souvenir* (McGraw-Hill, 1956), p. 95.

3. William Hillman, *Mr. President* (Farrar, Straus & Young, 1952), p. 143.

4. Interview with the writer.

5. Interview with the writer.

6. Interview with the writer.

7. Interview with the writer.

8. James F. Byrnes, *Speaking Frankly* (Harper, 1947), p. 240

9. Truman *Memoirs,* vol. 1, p. 560.

10. Interview with the writer.

11. Interview with the writer.

Chapter 7

During 1952 and 1953 a group of former officials of the Truman administration, met together privately at various intervals to conduct a candid and thoughtful postmortem on the principal events and policies of that period in which they had had a hand. Their purpose was to make a permanent historical record, while the facts were still fresh, of their firsthand knowledge and assessment of these happenings. These many long colloquies, which were informal and relaxed but systematically organized, were recorded on tape, and a limited number of typescripts were made. These are held privately by the participants, and as far as I am aware none has ever been made public. However, a member of the group did generously agree to make his file available to me on the understanding that the material would be used principally as background and that its source would remain confidential. I have, naturally, respected this injunction. Where it is necessary in this and succeeding chapters to indicate this material as the basis for some statement or observation, I have cited it simply as *Colloquy* and regret that I cannot be more explicit. My gratitude to this unnamed donor is boundless.

As helpful as this material was, however, it hardly exceeded in value a number of personal interviews I had with some of these same, and other, members of the Truman official family. In this connection I am particularly indebted to Dean G. Acheson, who read this chapter in manuscript and registered some pertinent dissents, and to Paul H. Nitze, Averell Harriman, Paul A. Porter, and Clark M. Clifford, all of whom were closely identified with the events covered here.

In addition to the specific citations mentioned below I have also consulted the following published works: James F. Byrnes, *Speaking*

Frankly (Harper, 1947); Morton A. Kaplan *et al., United States Foreign Policy, 1945-1955* (Brookings Institution, 1956); Edwin M. Borchard, "Intervention: The Truman Doctrine and the Marshall Plan," in the *American Journal of International Law*, vol. 41, 1947; Charles Burton Marshall, *The Limits of Foreign Policy* (Holt, 1954); *Foreign Policy for a Postwar European Recovery Program*, Hearings before the Foreign Affairs Committee, U.S. House of Representatives, 80th Cong., 1st sess., 1947. The Historical Division of the Department of State was most helpful in providing certain unclassified documents and summaries.

1. This incident and much of what follows is covered in fascinating and authoritative detail by Joseph M. Jones in *Fifteen Weeks* (Viking, 1955).

2. *Colloquy.*

3. In *Documents on American Foreign Relations* (Princeton Univ. Press), vol. 8, p. 863.

4. Truman *Memoirs*, vol. 2, p. 97.

5. *Ibid.*, p. 101.

6. *Colloquy.*

7. Text supplied by Historical Division, Department of State.

8. *Colloquy.*

9. Text supplied by Historical Division, Department of State.

10. Truman *Memoirs*, vol. 2, p. 119.

11. *Colloquy.*

12. From "General Report," Committee on European Economic Cooperation, vol. 1, 1947 (Department of State).

13. From *American Foreign Assistance* (Brookings Institution, 1955).

Chapters 8 and 9

These chapters are based largely on contemporary press reports of the New York *Times*, New York *Herald Tribune*, the Washington *Post*, and the weekly magazines *Time* and *Newsweek*, reinforced by my own experience as a reporter covering politics in Washington and the field throughout this period. I have also had the generous assistance of Clark M. Clifford, who made his files on the campaign and its antecedents available to me, and of Oscar L. Chapman, David Lloyd, and several other former members of the Truman administration and the Democratic National Committee. Arthur Krock of the *Times* and Edward T. Folliard of the *Post* supplied me with a number of interesting facts and anecdotes. Among the published works I have consulted the most useful by far were *Inside the Democratic Party*, by Jack Redding (Bobbs-Merrill, 1958), and *Out of the Jaws of Victory*, by Jules Abels (Holt, 1959), which are reasonably credible "inside" accounts of what went on in the Truman and Dewey camps, respectively. In addition I found much valuable information in the following: Karl M. Schmidt, *Henry A. Wallace: Quixotic Crusade, 1948* (Syracuse Univ. Press, 1960); V. O. Key, Jr., *Southern Politics* (Knopf, 1950), and *The Voter Decides*, by the Survey Research Center (University of Michigan, 1954).

Chapter 10

The literature on the foreign policy of the Truman administration is staggering in its magnitude and baffling in its diversity of viewpoint. My procedure in the construction of this chapter was to start with a framework of what happened day by day as reported in the press, and then to develop from other sources the background—the "who, how, and why" —of what seemed to me the most pertinent events to include in this narrative. The choice of both sources and events will seem inadequate to many, I am sure, but it was an exercise of judgment for which I offer no apologies.

Among the background sources the most valuable by far were the transcribed *Colloquies* described in the Notes for Chapter 7. In addition I have had the benefit of personal interviews with such key figures in the formulation of the Truman foreign policy as Dean G. Acheson, Averell Harriman, Paul H. Nitze, and Clark M. Clifford. I have not asked any of these to review or criticize the manuscript of this chapter, so the responsibility for the views and conclusions expressed is mine, not theirs. I have noted my debt to George F. Kennan in this chapter in a footnote to the section titled "Containment."

The most useful published works in the field, in my view, are those of that able and lucid historian Professor Herbert Feis, and in this chapter particularly I relied heavily on his *The China Tangle* (Princeton Univ. Press, 1953). In addition to those specifically cited below, I have also consulted the following: John Foster Dulles, *War or Peace* (Macmillan, 1950); H. Bradford Westerfield, *Foreign Policy and Party Politics* (Yale Univ. Press, 1955); John Lukacs, *History of the Cold War* (Doubleday, 1961); Eric F. Goldman, *The Crucial Decade* (Knopf, 1956); *A Decade of American Foreign Policy*, Senate Document 123, 81st Cong., 2nd sess., 1950.

1. Department of State *Bulletin*, Nov. 4, 1945, p. 711.

2. Walter Millis, ed., *The Forrestal Diaries* (Viking, 1951), p. 134.

3. The full text of the treaty occurs in the *United Nations Treaty Series*, vol. 54, No. 541, p. 244.

4. Interview with the writer.

5. Truman *Memoirs*, vol. 2, p. 63.

6. *American Policy Toward China*, statement of Secrtary of State Acheson before the Joint Armed Services and Foreign Affairs Committees, U.S. Senate, June 4, 1951, State Department Publication No. 4255.

7. *China White Paper*, State Department Publication No. 3573, 1949, p. 132.

8. William Reitzel *et al.*, *United States Foreign Policy 1945-1955* (Brookings Institution, 1956), p. 181.

9. Truman *Memoirs*, vol. 2, p. 82.

10. *Ibid.*, pp. 82-83.

11. *China White Paper*, pp. 763-64.

12. *Military Situation in the Far East*, Joint Committee on Armed Services and Foreign Relations, U.S. Senate, 82nd Cong., 1951, p. 1856.

13. Arthur Vandenberg, Jr., *The Private Papers of Senator Vandenberg* (Houghton Mifflin, 1952), pp. 526-27.

Chapter 11

In addition to the sources specifically cited below I have also consulted the following: Robert Leckie, *The War in Korea 1950-1953* (Random House, 1963); William Reitzel *et al.*, *United States Foreign Policy 1945-1955* (Brookings Institution, 1956); Arthur Vandenberg, Jr., *The Private Papers of Senator Vandenberg* (Houghton Mifflin, 1952); *United States in World Affairs*, annual volumes for 1950 and 1951, by the Committee on Foreign Relations (Harper); *A Historical Summary of United States–Korean Relations*, State Department Publication No. 7446, Nov. 1962; *Military Situation in the Far East*, Joint Senate Committees on Armed Services and Foreign Relations, 82nd Cong. 1951.

1. Truman *Memoirs*, vol. 2, p. 332.

2. *Colloquy* (see Notes for Chapter 7).

3. T. R. Fehrenbach, *This Kind of War* (Macmillan, 1963), p. 83. This is a big, comprehensive and exciting narrative of the Korean war on which I have drawn heavily.

4. Charles A Willoughby and John Chamberlain, *MacArthur, 1941-1951* (McGraw-Hill, 1954), p. 356.

5. Fehrenbach, *op. cit.*, p. 89.

6. This account is based in large part on *NSC–68: Prologue to Rearmament*, a study by Paul Y. Hammond and the Institute for War and Peace Studies (Columbia University, 1962).

7. *Ibid.*

8. Fehrenbach, *op. cit.*, pp. 148 and 154-55.

Chapter 12

In the preparation of this chapter I have relied principally on the exhaustive hearings into General MacArthur's dismissal, *Military Situation in the Far East,* conducted during May and June, 1951, by the Joint Senate Committees on Armed Services and Foreign Relations, 82nd Cong., cited below as Hearings.

In addition to the specific citations below I have also consulted the following: a privately recorded colloquy by various former officials of the Truman administration (see Notes for Chapter 7); Courtney Whitney, *MacArthur: His Rendezvous with Destiny* (Knopf, 1956); Frazier Hunt, *The Untold Story of MacArthur* (Devin-Adair, 1954); John W. Spannier, *The Truman-MacArthur Controversy and the Korean War* (Harvard Univ. Press, 1959); Arthur H. Schlesinger, Jr., and Richard Rovere, *The General and the President* (Farrar, Straus & Young, 1951); Robert E. Osgood, *Limited War* (Univ. of Chicago Press, 1957).

1. Truman *Memoirs,* vol. 2, p. 351
2. *Ibid.,* pp. 362-63.
3. Interview with the writer.
4. Truman *Memoirs,* vol. 2, p. 365.
5. T. R. Fehrenbach, *This Kind of War* (Macmillan, 1963), p. 282.
6. *Ibid.,* p. 286.
7. Hearings, p. 3491.
8. Fehrenbach, *op. cit.,* p. 379.
9. Robert Leckie, *The War in Korea, 1950-1953* (Random House, 1963), p. 245.
10. Hearings, p. 503.
11. *Ibid.,* p. 1022.
12. Fehrenbach, *op. cit.,* p. 413.

Chapter 13

In addition to the specific citations below I have also consulted the following: Bert Andrews, *Washington Witch Hunt* (Random House, 1948); Francis Biddle, *The Fear of Freedom* (Doubleday, 1952); Elizabeth Bentley, *Out of Bondage* (Devin-Adair, 1951); Whittaker Chambers, *Witness* (Random House, 1952); Benjamin Ginzburg, *Rededication to Freedom* (Simon & Schuster, 1959); Alger Hiss, *In the Court of Public Opinion* (Knopf, 1957); *Report of the Special Committee on the Federal Loyalty-Security Program of the Association of the Bar of New York City* (Dodd, Mead, 1956); *Communist Espionage in the United States Gov-*

ernment, Hearings of the Committee on Un-American Activities, House of Representatives, 80th Cong., 2nd sess. 1948. I have also received great assistance through interviews with, and in some instances access to the personal files of, the following: Clark M. Clifford, Steven J. Spingarn, David Lloyd, and Adrian S. Fisher, all of whom were associated, either through the White House or the Department of State, with the events covered in this chapter, and also with George A. Eddy, of Alexandria, Va., who has made an extensive study of the operation of the loyalty-security program.

1. Alan Barth, *Loyalty of Free Men* (Viking, 1951), p. 111.

2. *Ibid.,* p. 7.

3. Eleanor Bontecou, *The Federal Loyalty-Security Program* (Cornell Univ. Press, 1953), p. 107. This is the most authoritative study of the subject I have encountered.

4. From the file on internal security, Truman Memorial Library, Independence, Mo.

5. Richard H. Rovere, *Senator Joe McCarthy* (Meridian, 1960), p. 3.

6. *State Department Employee Loyalty Investigation,* Hearings before a subcommittee of the Senate Committee on Foreign Relations, 81st Cong., 2nd sess., 1950, p. 1760.

7. *Ibid.,* p. 20.

8. *Ibid.,* p. 484.

9. *Investigations of Senators Joseph R. McCarthy and William Benton,* Pursuant to S. Res. 187 and S. Res. 304, Report of the Senate Committee on Rules and Administration, 1952 (committee print), p. 3. Public distribution of this document was severely limited. It was privately reproduced by the Beacon Press, Boston, in May 1953, in cooperation with Americans for Democratic Action. It is such a copy that I have used here.

Chapter 14

The principal sources for this chapter are contemporary news accounts and my own experiences and observations as a reporter. I have been greatly assisted by the recollections of many others who were either participants in or close observers of the events covered here, among them Arthur Krock and James Reston of the New York *Times;* Edward T. Folliard of the Washington *Post;* Merriman Smith of United Press International; and Clark M. Clifford, Charles S. Murphy, Leon H. Keyserling, David Lloyd, and Paul A. Porter, all of whom were closely connected with either the White House or Democratic Party affairs during the period covered. I am particularly indebted to Stephen A. Mitchell, former Chairman of the Democratic National Committee, for two very long, handwritten letters sent from Turkey in March 1965, where he was on a mission for the UN, providing me with a unique insight into the 1952 campaign and some of the key personalities involved. Eric Sevareid very kindly gave permission for the use of his column of February 4, 1964, which I have incorporated as an epilogue.

INDEX